JONES & BARTLETT LEARNING INFORMATION SYSTEMS SECURITY & ASSURANCE SERIES

System Forensics, Investigation, and Response

CHUCK EASTTOM

SECOND EDITION

JONES & BARTLETT
LEARNING

World Headquarters
Jones & Bartlett Learning
5 Wall Street
Burlington, MA 01803
978-443-5000
info@jblearning.com
www.jblearning.com

Jones & Bartlett Learning books and products are available through most bookstores and online booksellers. To contact Jones & Bartlett Learning directly, call 800-832-0034, fax 978-443-8000, or visit our website, www.jblearning.com.

Substantial discounts on bulk quantities of Jones & Bartlett Learning publications are available to corporations, professional associations, and other qualified organizations. For details and specific discount information, contact the special sales department at Jones & Bartlett Learning via the above contact information or send an email to specialsales@jblearning.com.

Production Credits

Chief Executive Officer: Ty Field
President: James Homer
Chief Product Officer: Eduardo Moura
SVP, Curriculum Solutions: Christopher Will
Director of Sales, Curriculum Solutions: Randi Roger
Senior Marketing Manager: Andrea DeFronzo
Associate Marketing Manager: Kelly Thompson
VP, Design and Production: Anne Spencer
VP, Manufacturing and Inventory Control: Therese Connell
Manufacturing and Inventory Control Supervisor: Amy Bacus
Editorial Management: High Stakes Writing, LLC,
   President: Lawrence J. Goodrich

Senior Editor, HSW: Ruth Walker
Copy Editor, HSW: Karen Annett
Associate Program Manager: Rainna Erikson
Production Manager: Susan Schultz
Composition: Gamut+Hue, LLC
Cover Design: Kristin E. Parker
Director of Photo Research and Permissions: Amy Wrynn
Photo Research Coordinator: Joseph Veiga
Cover Image: © HunThomas/ShutterStock, Inc.
Chapter Opener Image: © Rodolfo Clix/Dreamstime.com
Printing and Binding: Edwards Brothers Malloy
Cover Printing: Edwards Brothers Malloy

ISBN: 978-1-284-03105-8

Library of Congress Cataloging-in-Publication Data
Not available at time of printing.

6048

Printed in the United States of America
17 16   10 9 8 7 6 5 4

Contents

Preface   xv

PART ONE   The System Forensics Landscape   1

CHAPTER 1   Introduction to Forensics   2

What Is Computer Forensics?   3
  Using Scientific Knowledge   4
  Collecting   5
  Analyzing   5
  Presenting   5

Understanding the Field of Digital Forensics   7
  What Is Digital Evidence?   8
  Scope-Related Challenges to System Forensics   9
  Types of Digital System Forensics Analysis   12
  General Guidelines   13

Knowledge Needed for Computer Forensics Analysis   13
  Hardware   14
  Software   16
  Networks   19
  Addresses   19
  Obscured Information and Anti-Forensics   24

The Daubert Standard   25

U.S. Laws Affecting Digital Forensics   26
  The Federal Privacy Act of 1974   26
  The Privacy Protection Act of 1980   26
  The Communications Assistance to Law Enforcement Act of 1994   26
  The Electronic Communications Privacy Act of 1986   26
  The Computer Security Act of 1987   27
  The Foreign Intelligence Surveillance Act of 1978   27
  The Child Protection and Sexual Predator Punishment Act of 1998   27
  The Children's Online Privacy Protection Act of 1988   27
  The Communications Decency Act of 1996   27
  The Telecommunications Act of 1996   27
  The Wireless Communications and Public Safety Act of 1999   27

The USA Patriot Act   28
The Sarbanes-Oxley Act of 2002   28
Warrants   28

Federal Guidelines   29

The FBI   29
The Secret Service   29
The Regional Computer Forensics Laboratory Program   30

CHAPTER SUMMARY   **31**

KEY CONCEPTS AND TERMS   **31**

CHAPTER 1 ASSESSMENT   **32**

CHAPTER 2   **Overview of Computer Crime**   **33**

How Computer Crime Affects Forensics   34

Identity Theft   35

Phishing   36
Spyware   37
Discarded Information   39
How Does This Crime Affect Forensics?   39

Hacking   39

SQL Injection   40
Ophcrack   41
Tricking Tech Support   43
Hacking in General   44

Cyberstalking and Harassment   44

Real Cyberstalking Cases   45

Fraud   47

Investment Offers   47
Data Piracy   48

Non-Access Computer Crimes   49

Denial of Service   49
Viruses   51
Logic Bombs   52

Cyberterrorism   53

How Does This Crime Affect Forensics?   54

CHAPTER SUMMARY   **54**

KEY CONCEPTS AND TERMS   **54**

CHAPTER 2 ASSESSMENT   **55**

CHAPTER 3 **Forensic Methods and Labs** **56**

Forensic Methodologies 57
   Handle Original Data as Little as Possible 57
   Comply with the Rules of Evidence 57
   Avoid Exceeding Your Knowledge 58
   Create an Analysis Plan 59
   Technical Information Collection Considerations 60

Formal Forensic Approaches 61
   DoD Forensic Standards 61
   The DFRWS Framework 61
   An Event-Based Digital Forensics Investigation Framework 62

Documentation of Methodologies and Findings 62
   Disk Structure 62
   File Slack Searching 63

Evidence-Handling Tasks 63
   Evidence-Gathering Measures 63
   Expert Reports 64

How to Set Up a Forensic Lab 65
   Equipment 65
   Security 65
   American Society of Crime Laboratory Directors 66

Common Forensic Software Programs 67
   EnCase 67
   Forensic Toolkit 69
   Helix 71
   BackTrack 71
   AnaDisk Disk Analysis Tool 72
   CopyQM Plus Disk Duplication Software 72
   The Sleuth Kit 72
   Disk Investigator 73

Forensic Certifications 73
   EnCase Certified Examiner Certification 74
   AccessData Certified Examiner 75
   EC Council Certified Hacking Forensic Investigator 75
   High Tech Crime Network Certifications 75
   Global Information Assurance Certification Certifications 75

CHAPTER SUMMARY 76

KEY CONCEPTS AND TERMS 76

CHAPTER 3 ASSESSMENT 77

PART TWO Technical Overview: System Forensics Tools, Techniques, and Methods   79

CHAPTER 4 **Collecting, Seizing, and Protecting Evidence**   **80**

Proper Procedure   81
  Shutting Down the Computer   81
  Transporting the Computer System to a Secure Location   84
  Preparing the System   84
  Documenting the Hardware Configuration of the System   85
  Mathematically Authenticating Data on All Storage Devices   86

Handling Evidence   87
  Collecting Data   87
  Documenting Filenames, Dates, and Times   88
  Identifying File, Program, and Storage Anomalies   88
  Evidence-Gathering Measures   88

Storage Formats   91
  Magnetic Media   92
  Solid-State Drives   92
  Digital Audio Tape Drives   93
  Digital Linear Tape and Super DLT   93
  Optical Media   94
  Using USB Drives   94
  File Formats   94

Forensic Imaging   95
  Imaging with EnCase   96
  Imaging with FTK   99

RAID Acquisitions   100

CHAPTER SUMMARY   101

KEY CONCEPTS AND TERMS   101

CHAPTER 4 ASSESSMENT   102

CHAPTER 5 **Understanding Techniques for Hiding and Scrambling Information**   **103**

Steganography   104
  Historical Steganography   106
  Steganophony   106
  Video Steganography   106
  Steganalysis   106
  Invisible Secrets   107
  MP3Stego   110
  Additional Resources   111

Encryption   111
   The History of Encryption   112
   Modern Cryptography   116
   Breaking Encryption   125

CHAPTER SUMMARY   128

KEY CONCEPTS AND TERMS   128

CHAPTER 5 ASSESSMENT   129

CHAPTER 6   **Recovering Data   130**

Undeleting Data   131
   Windows   131
   Linux   138
   Macintosh   141

Recovering Information from Damaged Media   142
   Physical Damage Recovery Techniques   143
   Recovering Data After Logical Damage   144

CHAPTER SUMMARY   146

KEY CONCEPTS AND TERMS   146

CHAPTER 6 ASSESSMENT   146

CHAPTER 7   **E-mail Forensics   147**

How E-mail Works   148
   E-mail Protocols   149
   Faking E-mail   150

E-mail Headers   151
   Getting Headers in Outlook 2010   153
   Getting Headers from Yahoo! E-mail   154
   Getting Headers from Gmail   154
   Other E-mail Clients   156
   E-mail Files   157
   Paraben's E-mail Examiner   158
   ReadPST   160

Tracing E-mail   160

E-mail Server Forensics   161

E-mail and the Law   161
   The Fourth Amendment to the U.S. Constitution   161
   The Electronic Communications Privacy Act   161
   The CAN-SPAM Act   162
   18 U.S.C. 2252B   163
   The Communication Assistance to Law Enforcement Act   163
   The Foreign Intelligence Surveillance Act   164
   The USA Patriot Act   164

CHAPTER SUMMARY   165

KEY CONCEPTS AND TERMS   165

CHAPTER 7 ASSESSMENT   165

CHAPTER 8   Windows Forensics   166

Windows Details   167

    Windows History   167
    64 Bit   168
    The Boot Process   169
    Important Files   170

Volatile Data   170

    Tools   172

Windows Swap File   176

Windows Logs   177

Windows Directories   178

    UserAssist   179
    Unallocated/Slack Space   180
    Alternate Data Streams   180

Index.dat   180

The Registry   181

    USB Information   183
    Wireless Networks   183
    Associated Drives   183
    Tracking Word Documents in the Registry   184
    Malware in the Registry   184

CHAPTER SUMMARY   185

KEY CONCEPTS AND TERMS   185

CHAPTER 8 ASSESSMENT   185

CHAPTER 9   Linux Forensics   186

Linux Basics   187

    Linux History   187
    Linux Shells   188
    Graphical User Interface   190
    Linux Boot Process   192
    Linux Distributions   194

Linux File Systems   194

    Ext   194
    The Reiser File System   195
    The Berkeley Fast File System   195

Linux Logs   195

    The /var/log/faillog Log   195
    The /var/log/kern.log Log   195
    The /var/log/lpr.log Log   196
    The /var/log/mail.* Log   196
    The /var/log/mysql.* Log   196
    The /var/log/apache2/* Log   196
    The /var/log/lighttpd/* Log   197
    The /var/log/apport.log Log   197
    Other Logs   197
    Viewing Logs   197

Linux Directories   197

    The /root Directory   197
    The /bin Directory   198
    The /sbin Directory   198
    The /etc Directory   198
    The /etc/inittab Directory   198
    The /dev Directory   199
    The /mnt Directory   199
    The /boot Directory   199
    The /usr Directory   199
    The /var Directory   199
    The /var/spool Directory   200
    The /proc Directory   200

Shell Commands for Forensics   200

    The dmesg Command   201
    The fsck Command   201
    The grep Command   202
    The history Command   202
    The mount Command   202
    The ps Command   203
    The pstree Command   203
    The pgrep Command   204
    The top Command   204
    The kill Command   204
    The file Command   204
    The su Command   204
    The who Command   205
    The finger Method   205
    The dd Command   205
    The ls Command   205

Can You Undelete in Linux?   205

    Manual Method   206

CHAPTER SUMMARY   207

KEY CONCEPTS AND TERMS   207

CHAPTER 9 ASSESSMENT   208

CHAPTER 10 **Macintosh Forensics**   **209**

Mac Basics   210

Mac History   210
Mac File Systems   212
Partition Types   214

Macintosh Logs   215

The /var/log/ Log   215
The /var/spool/cups Folder   215
The /Library/Receipts Folder   215
The /Users/<user>/.bash_history Log   215
The var/vm Folder   215
The /Users/ Directory   216
The /Users/<user>/Library/Preferences/ Folder   216

Directories   216

The /Volumes Directory   216
The /Users Directory   216
The /Applications Directory   216
The /Network Directory   216
The /etc Directory   216
The /Library/Preferences/SystemConfiguration/dom.apple.preferences.plist File   216

Macintosh Forensic Techniques   217

Target Disk Mode   217
Searching Virtual Memory   218
Shell Commands   218

Can You Undelete in Mac?   219

CHAPTER SUMMARY   220

KEY CONCEPTS AND TERMS   220

CHAPTER 10 ASSESSMENT   220

CHAPTER 11 **Mobile Forensics**   **221**

Cellular Device Concepts   222

Terms   222
Networks   223
Operating Systems   224
The BlackBerry   226

What Evidence You Can Get from a Cell Phone   226

Types of Information   227

Seizing Evidence from a Mobile Device   228
   The iPhone   229
   BlackBerry   231

CHAPTER SUMMARY   232

KEY CONCEPTS AND TERMS   232

CHAPTER 11 ASSESSMENT   232

CHAPTER 12 Performing Network Analysis   233

Network Packet Analysis   234
   Network Packets   234
   Network Attacks   239
   Network Traffic Analysis Tools   240

Network Traffic Analysis   246
   Using Log Files as Evidence   246
   Wireless   247

Router Forensics   248
   Router Basics   248
   Types of Router Attacks   250
   Getting Evidence from the Router   250

Firewall Forensics   252
   Firewall Basics   252
   Collecting Data   252

CHAPTER SUMMARY   254

KEY CONCEPTS AND TERMS   254

CHAPTER 12 ASSESSMENT   254

PART THREE Incident Response and Resources   255

CHAPTER 13 Incident and Intrusion Response   256

Disaster Recovery   257
   Incident Response Plan   257
   Incident Response   260

Preserving Evidence   261

Adding Forensics to Incident Response   263
   Forensic Resources   263
   Forensics and Policy   263

CHAPTER SUMMARY   265

KEY CONCEPTS AND TERMS   265

CHAPTER 13 ASSESSMENT   265

CHAPTER 14   **Trends and Future Directions   266**

Technical Trends   267

What Impact Does This Have on Forensics?   268
Software as a Service   269
The Cloud   269
What Impact Does Cloud Computing Have on Forensics?   272
New Devices   272

Legal and Procedural Trends   273

Changes in the Law   274
Private Labs   274
International Issues   275
Techniques   275

CHAPTER SUMMARY   276
KEY CONCEPTS AND TERMS   276
CHAPTER 14 ASSESSMENT   276

CHAPTER 15   **System Forensics Resources   277**

Tools to Use   278

ASR Data Acquisition & Analysis   278
AccessData Forensic Toolkit   279
ComputerCOP   279
Digital Detective   279
Digital Intelligence   279
Disk Investigator   280
EnCase   280
The Sleuth Kit   281
X-Ways Software Technology AG   281
Other Tools   282

Resources   283

International Association of Computer Investigative Specialists   284
EnCase Certified Examiner Certification   284
AccessData Certified Examiner   284
Certified Hacking Forensic Investigator   284
SANS Institute   285
Web Sites   285
Journals   286
Conferences   287

Laws   288

The USA Patriot Act   288
The Electronic Communications Privacy Act of 1986   288
The Communications Assistance to Law Enforcement Act of 1996   289
The Health Insurance Portability and Accountability Act of 1996   289

CHAPTER SUMMARY   290
KEY CONCEPTS AND TERMS   290
CHAPTER 15 ASSESSMENT   290

APPENDIX A **Answer Key**   291

APPENDIX B **Standard Acronyms**   293

Glossary of Key Terms   295

References   301

Index   303

Preface

Purpose of This Book

This book is part of the Information Systems Security & Assurance Series from Jones & Bartlett Learning (*www.jblearning.com*). Designed for courses and curriculums in IT Security, Cybersecurity, Information Assurance, and Information Systems Security, this series features a comprehensive, consistent treatment of the most current thinking and trends in this critical subject area. These titles deliver fundamental information-security principles packed with real-world applications and examples. Authored by Certified Information Systems Security Professionals (CISSPs), they deliver comprehensive information on all aspects of information security. Reviewed word for word by leading technical experts in the field, these books are not just current, but forward-thinking—putting you in the position to solve the cybersecurity challenges not just of today, but of tomorrow, as well.

Computer crimes call for forensics specialists—people who know how to find and follow the evidence. This book begins by examining the fundamentals of system forensics: what forensics is, an overview of computer crime, the challenges of system forensics, and forensics methods and labs. The second part of this book addresses the tools, techniques, and methods used to perform computer forensics and investigation. These include collecting evidence, investigating information-hiding, recovering data, and scrutinizing e-mail. It also discusses how to perform forensics in the Windows, Linux, and Macintosh operating systems; on mobile devices; and on networks. Finally, the third part explores incident and intrusion response, emerging technologies and future directions of this field, and additional system forensics resources.

Learning Features

The writing style of this book is practical and conversational. Each chapter begins with a statement of learning objectives. Step-by-step examples of information security concepts and procedures are presented throughout the text. Illustrations are used both to clarify the material and to vary the presentation. The text is sprinkled with Notes, Tips, FYIs, Warnings, and sidebars to alert the reader to additional helpful information related to the subject under discussion. Chapter Assessments appear at the end of each chapter, with solutions provided in the back of the book.

Chapter summaries are included in the text to provide a rapid review or preview of the material and to help students understand the relative importance of the concepts presented.

Audience

The material is suitable for undergraduate or graduate computer science majors or information science majors, students at a two-year technical college or community college who have a basic technical background, or readers who have a basic understanding of IT security and want to expand their knowledge.

This book is dedicated to all the forensic analysts who work diligently to extract the evidence necessary to find the truth in criminal and civil cases.

About the Author

CHUCK EASTTOM is an internationally renowned computer security expert and trainer. He has been in the IT industry for more than 18 years and has been training for more than 10. He has conducted training for the Stanford Medical Schools Web Development Team and the Secret Service Electronic Crimes Task Force. He also has a master's degree in education as well as a master's of business administration (specializing in applied computer science) and has been named to both Who's Who in Education and Who's Who in Science and Technology. He holds more than 28 industry certifications, including CISSP, ISSAP, CEH, and MCT. In addition to his many certifications, he is a Microsoft Certified Trainer and an EC-Council certified instructor.

Chuck has been a speaker at the Harvard Computer Society, Columbia University ACM Chapter, TakeDownCon, and Hacker Halted.

## PART ONE

The System Forensics Landscape

CHAPTER 1 **Introduction to Forensics** 2

CHAPTER 2 **Overview of Computer Crime** 33

CHAPTER 3 **Forensic Methods and Labs** 56

Introduction to Forensics

THIS CHAPTER INTRODUCES YOU to the field of computer forensics. That means covering some legal issues, the basic concepts of the forensic process, and a review of the basic computer and networking knowledge you will need.

Chapter 1 Topics

This chapter covers the following topics and concepts:

- What computer forensics is
- What you need to know about the field of digital forensics
- What you need to know for computer forensics analysis
- What the Daubert standard is
- What the relevant laws are
- What the federal guidelines are

Chapter 1 Goals

When you complete this chapter, you will be able to:

- Understand the basic concepts of forensics
- Maintain the chain of custody
- Understand basic hardware and networking knowledge needed for forensics
- Know the basic laws related to computer forensics

What Is Computer Forensics?

Before you can answer the question, "What is computer forensics?" you should address the question, "What is forensics?" *The American Heritage Dictionary* defines *forensics* as "the use of science and technology to investigate and establish facts in criminal or civil courts of law."

Essentially, forensics is the use of science to process evidence so you can establish the facts of a case. The individual case being examined could be criminal or civil, but the process is the same. The evidence has to be examined and processed in a consistent scientific manner. This is to ensure that the evidence is not accidentally altered and that appropriate conclusions are derived from that evidence.

You have probably seen some crime drama wherein forensic techniques were a part of the investigative process. In such dramas, a bullet is found and forensics is used to determine the gun that fired the bullet. Or perhaps a drop of blood is found and forensics is used to match the DNA to a suspect. These are all valid aspects of forensics. However, our modern world is full of electronic devices with the capacity to store data. The extraction of that data in a consistent scientific manner is the subject of **computer forensics**.

The Computer Emergency Response Team (CERT) defines computer forensics in this manner:

> Forensics is the process of using scientific knowledge for collecting, analyzing, and presenting evidence to the courts.... Forensics deals primarily with the recovery and analysis of latent evidence. Latent evidence can take many forms, from finger-prints left on a window to DNA evidence recovered from bloodstains to the files on a hard drive.

According to the Web site Computer Forensics World:

> Generally, computer forensics is considered to be the use of analytical and investi-gative techniques to identify, collect, examine and preserve evidence/information which is magnetically stored or encoded.

The objective in computer forensics is to recover, analyze, and present computer-based material in such a way that it can be used as evidence in a court of law. In computer forensics, as in any other branch of forensic science, the emphasis must be on the integrity and security of evidence. A forensic specialist must adhere to stringent guide-lines and avoid taking shortcuts.

Any device that can store data is potentially the subject of computer forensics. Obviously, that includes devices such as network servers, personal computers, and laptops. However, computer forensics also encompasses devices such as smartphones, routers, tablets, printers, and global positioning system (GPS) devices. Remember that *any* device that can store data is a potential subject of computer forensics.

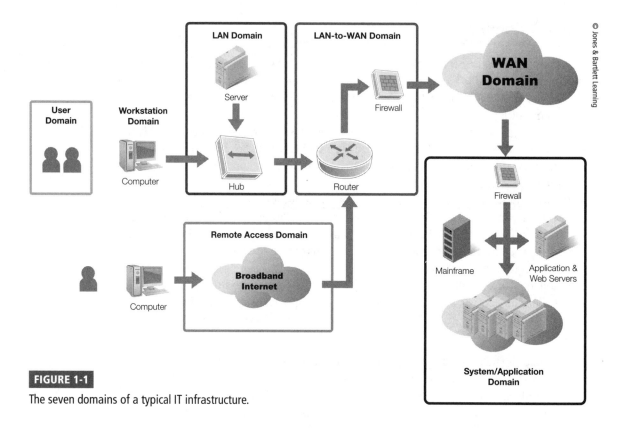

FIGURE 1-1

The seven domains of a typical IT infrastructure.

Although the subject of computer forensics, as well as the tools and techniques used, is significantly different from traditional forensics—like DNA analysis and bullet examination—the goal is the same: to obtain evidence that can be used in some legal proceeding. Computer forensics applies to all the domains of a typical IT infrastructure, from the User Domain and Remote Access Domain to the Wide Area Network (WAN) Domain and Internet Domain (see Figure 1-1).

Consider some elements of the preceding definitions. In particular, let's look at this sentence: "Forensics is the process of using scientific knowledge for collecting, analyzing, and presenting evidence to the courts." Each portion of this is critical, and the following sections of this chapter examine each one individually.

Using Scientific Knowledge

First and foremost, computer forensics is a science. This is not a process based on your "gut feelings" or personal whim. It is important to understand and apply scientific knowledge. That also means you must have scientific knowledge of the field. Computer forensics begins with a thorough understanding of computer hardware. Then you need to understand the operating system running on that device; even smartphones and routers have operating systems. You must also understand at least the basics of computer networks.

If you attempt to master forensics without this basic knowledge, you are not likely to be successful. Now if you find yourself starting in on a course and are not sure if you have the requisite knowledge, don't panic. First, you simply need a basic knowledge of computers and computer networks. If you have taken a couple of basic computer courses at a college or perhaps the CompTIA A+ certification, you have the baseline knowledge. Also, you will get a review of some basic concepts in this chapter.

However, the more you know about computers and networks, the better you will be at computer forensics. Even though some technical details change quickly, such as the capacity and materials of hard disks, other details change very slowly, if at all, such as the various file systems, the role of volatile and non-volatile memory, and the fact that criminals take advantage of the advancements in computer and digital technology to improve their lives as much as the businessman, student, or homeowner. A great deal of information is stored in computers. Keep learning what is there, where it is stored, and how that information may be used by computer user and computer criminal alike.

Collecting

Before you can do any forensic analysis or examination, you have to collect the evidence. There are very specific procedures for properly collecting evidence. You will be introduced to some general guidelines later in this chapter. The important thing to realize for now is that how you collect the evidence determines if that evidence is admissible in a court.

Analyzing

This is the fun part. Once you have collected the data, what does it mean? The real difference between a mediocre investigator and a star investigator is the analysis. The data is there, but do you know what it means? This is also related to your level of scientific knowledge. If you don't know enough, you may not see the significance of the data you have.

You also have to be able to solve puzzles. That is, in essence, what any forensic investigation is. It is solving a complex puzzle—putting together the data you have and finding out what sort of picture is revealed. You might try to approach a forensic investigation like Sherlock Holmes. Look at every detail. What does it mean? Before you jump to a conclusion, how much evidence do you have to support that conclusion? Are there alternatives and, in fact, better explanations for the data?

Presenting

You have finished your investigation, done your analysis, and obeyed all the rules and guidelines, but now what? You will have to present that evidence in one form or another. The two most basic forms are the expert report and expert testimony. In either case, it will be your job to interpret the arcane and seemingly impenetrable technical information using plain English that paints an accurate picture for the court. You must not use jargon and technobabble. Your clear use of language, and potentially graphics and demonstrations, if needed, may be the difference between a big win and a lost case. So you should take a quick look at each of these.

The Expert Report

An **expert report** is a formal document that lists what tests you conducted, what you found, and your conclusions. It also includes your **curriculum vitae (CV)**, which is like a résumé, only much more thorough and specific to your work experience as a forensic investigator. Specific rules will vary from court to court, but as a general rule, if you don't put it in your report, you cannot testify about it at trial. So you need to make very certain that your report is thorough. Put in every single test you used, every single thing you found, and your conclusions. Expert reports tend to be rather long.

> **⚠ WARNING**
>
> Court procedures vary from jurisdiction to jurisdiction, but in most cases an expert cannot directly testify about anything not in his or her expert report. That is why it is critical to be thorough and to put into the report anything you feel might be pertinent to the case. In your work as an expert witness, you will often find additional items in an investigation—items that are peripheral to the main case. If you put those in your report, however, you will be able to testify about them at trial.

It is also important to back up your conclusions. As a general rule, it's good to have at least two to three references for every conclusion. In other words, in addition to your own opinion, you want to have a few reputable references that either agree with that conclusion or provide support for how you came to that conclusion. This way, it is not just your expert opinion, but it is supported by other reputable sources. Make sure you use reputable sources. For example, CERT, the Federal Bureau of Investigation (FBI), the Secret Service, and the Cornell University Law School are all very reputable sources.

The reason for this is that in every legal case there are two sides. The opposing side will have an attorney and perhaps its own expert. The opposing attorney will want to pick apart every opinion and conclusion you have. If there is an opposing expert, he or she will be looking for alternative interpretations of the data or flaws in your method. You have to make sure you have fully supported your conclusions.

Expert Testimony

As a forensic specialist, you will testify as an expert witness; that is, on the basis of scientific or technical knowledge you have that is relevant to a case, rather than on the basis of direct personal experience. Your testimony will be referred to as **expert testimony**, and there are two scenarios in which you give it. The first is a deposition and the second is a trial. A *deposition*—testimony taken from a witness or party to a case before a trial—is less formal, and is typically held in an attorney's office. The other side's lawyer gets to ask you questions. In fact, the lawyer can even ask some questions that would probably be disallowed by a trial judge. But do remember, this is still sworn testimony, and lying under oath is a felony.

During a deposition, the opposing counsel has a few goals. The first goal is to find out as much as possible about your position, methods, conclusions, and even your side's legal strategy. It is important to answer honestly but as briefly as possible. Don't volunteer information unasked. That simply allows the other side to be better prepared for trial. The second thing a lawyer is looking for during a deposition is to get you to commit to a position you may not be able to defend later. So follow a few rules:

- If you don't fully understand the question, say so. Ask for clarification before you answer.
- If you really don't know, say so. Do not ever guess.
- If you are not 100 percent certain of an answer, say so. Say "to the best of my current recollection" or something to that effect.

The other way you may testify is at trial. The first thing you absolutely must understand is that the first time you testify, you will be nervous. You'll begin to wonder if you are properly prepared. Are your conclusions correct? Did you miss anything? Don't worry; each time you do this, it gets easier. Next, remember that the opposing counsel, by definition, disagrees with you, and wants to trip you up. It might be helpful to remind yourself, "The opposing counsel's default position is that I am both incompetent and a liar." So don't be too upset if he or she is trying to make you look bad. It is not personal.

The secret to deposition and trial testimony is simple: Be prepared. Not only should you make certain your forensic process is done correctly and well documented, including liberal use of charts, diagrams, and other graphics, but you should also prepare before you testify. Go over your report and your notes again. Often, your attorney will prep you, particularly if you have never testified before. Try to look objectively at your own report to see if there is anything the opposing counsel might use against you. Are there alternative ways to interpret the evidence? If so, why did you reject them?

The most important things on the stand are to keep calm and tell the truth. Obviously, any lie, even a very minor one that is not directly related to your investigation, would be devastating. But becoming agitated or angry on the stand can also undermine your credibility.

Understanding the Field of Digital Forensics

This field is changing very rapidly. First and foremost, standards are emerging. This means there are clearly defined ways of properly doing forensics. When computer forensics first began, most investigations were conducted according to the whim of the investigator rather than through a standardized methodology. But as the field has matured, it has also standardized. Today, there are clear, codified methods for conducting a forensic examination.

Another change is in who is doing forensics. At one time, all forensics, including computer forensics, was the exclusive domain of law enforcement. That is no longer the case. Today, the following entities are also involved in and actively using computer forensics:

- **The military**—The military uses digital forensics to gather intelligence information from computers captured during military actions.
- **Government agencies**—Government agencies use digital forensics to investigate crimes involving computers. These agencies include the Federal Bureau of Investigation (FBI), the U.S. Postal Inspection Service, the Federal Trade Commission, the U.S. Food and Drug Administration, and the U.S. Secret Service. They also include the U.S. Department of Justice's National Institute of Justice (NIJ), the National Institute of Standards and Technology (NIST) Office of Law Enforcement Standards (OLES), the Department of Homeland Security, and foreign government agencies, among others.

- **Law firms**—Law firms need experienced system forensics professionals to conduct investigations and testify as expert witnesses. For example, civil cases can use records found on computer systems that bear on cases involving fraud, divorce, discrimination, and harassment.
- **Criminal prosecutors**—Criminal prosecutors use digital evidence when working with incriminating documents. They try to link these documents to crimes such as drug trafficking, embezzlement, financial fraud, homicide, and child pornography.
- **Academia**—Academia is involved with forensic research and education. For example, many universities offer degrees in digital forensics and online criminal justice.
- **Data recovery firms**—Data recovery firms use digital forensics techniques to recover data after hardware or software failures and when data has been lost.
- **Corporations**—Corporations use digital forensics to assist in employee termination and prosecution. For example, corporations sometimes need to gather information concerning theft of intellectual property or trade secrets, fraud, embezzlement, sexual harassment, and network and computer intrusions. They also need to find evidence of unauthorized use of equipment, such as computers, fax machines, answering machines, personal digital assistants (PDAs), and mobile phones.
- **Insurance companies**—Insurance companies use digital evidence of possible fraud in accident, arson, and workers' compensation cases.
- **Individuals**—Individuals sometimes hire forensic specialists in support of possible claims. These cases may include, for example, wrongful termination, sexual harassment, or age discrimination.

What Is Digital Evidence?

Information includes raw numbers, pictures, and other "stuff" that may or may not have relevance to a particular event or incident under investigation. **Digital evidence** is information that has been processed and assembled so that it is relevant to an investigation and supports a specific finding or determination.

Investigators must carefully show an unbroken chain of custody to demonstrate that evidence has been protected from tampering. The **chain of custody** is the continuity of control of evidence that makes it possible to account for all that has happened to evidence between its original collection and its appearance in court, preferably unaltered. If forensic specialists can't demonstrate that they have maintained the chain of custody, then the court may consider all their conclusions invalid.

Courts deal with four types of evidence:

- **Real**—**Real evidence** is a physical object that someone can touch, hold, or directly observe. Examples of real evidence are a laptop with a suspect's fingerprints on the keyboard, a hard drive, a universal serial bus (USB) drive, or a handwritten note.
- **Documentary**—**Documentary evidence** is data stored as written matter, on paper or in electronic files. Documentary evidence includes memory-resident data and computer files. Examples are e-mail messages, logs, databases, photographs, and telephone call-detail records. Investigators must authenticate documentary evidence.

- **Testimonial**—**Testimonial evidence** is information that forensic specialists use to support or interpret real or documentary evidence. For example, they may employ testimonial evidence to demonstrate that the fingerprints found on a keyboard are those of a specific individual. Or system access controls might show that a particular user stored specific photographs on a desktop.

- **Demonstrative**—**Demonstrative evidence** is information that helps explain other evidence. An example is a chart that explains a technical concept to the judge and jury. Forensic specialists must often provide testimony to support the conclusions of their analyses. For example, a member of an incident response team might be required to testify that he or she identified the computer program that deleted customer records at a specified date and time. In such a case, the testimony must show how the investigator reached his or her conclusion. The testimony must also show that the specialist protected the information used from tampering in making the determination. That is, the testimony must show that the forensic investigator maintained the chain of custody. It must also show that the testifier based his or her conclusion on a reasonable, although not necessarily absolute, interpretation of the information. Further, the forensic specialist must present his or her testimony in a manner that avoids use of technical jargon and complex technical discussions and should use pictures, charts, and other graphics when helpful. Judges, juries, and lawyers aren't all technical experts. Therefore, a forensic specialist should translate technology into understandable descriptions. Pictures often communicate better than just numbers and words, so a forensic specialist may want to create charts and graphs.

Scope-Related Challenges to System Forensics

The scope of a forensic effort often presents not just an analytical challenge but a psychological challenge as well. Information systems collect and retain large volumes of data.

They store this data in a dizzying array of applications, formats, and hardware components. In completing an analysis, forensic specialists face variations in the following:

- The volume of data to be analyzed
- The complexity of the computer system
- The size and character of the crime scene, which might involve a network that crosses U.S. and foreign jurisdictions
- The size of the caseload and resource limitations

Forensic specialists must be prepared to quickly complete an analysis regardless of these factors. The following sections discuss these factors in more detail.

Large Volumes of Data

Digital forensics is useful in identifying and documenting evidence. It is a disciplined approach that looks at the entire physical media, such as a hard disk drive, for all information representations. A system forensics specialist has access to all the information contained on a device—not just what the end user sees. A forensic analyst examines *metadata*, which is data about information, such as disk partition structures and file tables. Who authored a file and when it was revised or updated are also important pieces of information for a forensic analyst to document. An analyst also examines the often-critical unused areas of the media where information might be hidden. Examining all areas of potential data storage and examining all potential data representations generates extremely large volumes of information. A forensic specialist must analyze, store, and control all this information for the full duration of the investigation and analysis.

The total amount of information that is potentially relevant to a case offers a challenge to forensic analysts. Most hard drives now contain in excess of 1 million file items. It is, in fact, common for a single desktop to have 1 billion bytes, or terabytes, of storage. When working with such large volumes, a forensic specialist must do the following:

- Ensure that his or her equipment is capable of manipulating large volumes of information quickly.

- Provide for duplicate storage so that the original media and its resident information are preserved and protected against tampering and other corruption.

- Create backups early and often to avoid losing actual information and its associated metadata.

- Document everything that is done in an investigation and maintain the chain of custody.

In addition to all these tasks, a forensic specialist must work within the forensic budget. Manipulating and controlling large volumes of information is expensive. An investigator should show how budget cost items contribute to the analysis and to maintaining the chain of custody. Resource limitations increase the potential for analysis error and may compromise the analysis. For example, a forensic analyst may need to explain how the addition of data custodians or additional hard drives can multiply costs.

System Complexity

Modern computer systems can be extremely complex. They use multiple file formats, including Adobe Portable Document Format (PDF) files, Microsoft Word (DOC and DOCX) documents, Microsoft Excel spreadsheets (XLS), video files (AVI, MOV, etc.), and image files (JPEG, GIF, BMP, TIFF, etc.), to name just a few. This does not even take into account formats of information "in motion" such as Voice over IP (VoIP), instant messaging protocols, or real-time video broadcast or two-way conferences. These systems connect to and share data with other systems that may be located anywhere in the world. In addition, the law may protect specific items and not others. No single forensic software application can deal with all the complexity.

Forensic specialists must use a set of software and hardware tools and supporting manual procedures. Further, a forensic specialist must build a case to support his or her interpretation of the "story" told by the information being analyzed. The specialist, therefore, must have an understanding of all digital information and its associated technology. The specialist should also be able to show corroboration that meets the traditional legal evidence tests. Specific tests of legal evidence can vary from venue to venue and from jurisdiction to jurisdiction—or both. There are a few basic tests that apply everywhere, but the chain of custody and the Daubert standard, both of which are discussed in this chapter, are nearly universal.

Individual pieces of information may have more than one possible interpretation. To reach a conclusion and turn raw information into supportable, actionable evidence, a forensic specialist must identify and analyze corroborating information. In other words, it is often the case that a single piece of information is not conclusive. It often takes the examination and correlation of multiple individual pieces of information to reach a conclusion. It is also a common practice for a forensic investigator to use more than one tool to conduct a test. For example, if you utilize one particular tool to recover deleted files, it can be a good idea to use yet another tool to conduct the same test. If two different tools yield the same result, this is compelling evidence that the information gathered is accurate and reliable. However, if the results differ, the forensic analyst has another situation to deal with.

Distributed Crime Scenes

Because networks are geographically dispersed, crime scenes may also be geographically dispersed. This creates practical as well as jurisdictional problems. Think about how difficult it is for a U.S. investigator to get evidence out of computers in China, for instance. Criminals take advantage of jurisdictional differences. A criminal may sell fake merchandise via the Internet from a foreign country to Americans in several states. The criminal may then route his or her Internet access, and the associated electronic payments, through several other countries before they reach their final destination.

Digital crime scenes can, and increasingly do, span the globe. Depending on the type of system connectivity and the controls in place, a forensic specialist may have to deal with information stored throughout the world and often in languages other than English. This could involve thousands of devices and network logs. Networks and centralized storage also present challenges because items of interest may not be stored on the target computer.

Gathering evidence from such a geographically far-flung digital crime scene requires the cooperation of local, state, and tribal governments, sometimes multiple national governments, and international agencies in tracking down the criminals and bringing them to justice. If all the governments and agencies do not cooperate with one another, the investigation may fail.

Growing Caseload and Limited Resources

The number of forensic specialists today is too small to analyze every cybercrime. Regardless of the state of the economy, digital forensics specialists can be assured of two things: Their caseload will grow, and their resources will, relative to caseload, become more limited.

The digital forensics analysis workload is growing and will continue to grow as computers are used more and in different ways in the commission of crimes. Driving this growth is the increasing use of technology in all aspects of modern life, not just in support of business objectives. Criminals utilize technology not only to conduct crimes, but also, in some cases, to hide the evidence. Forensic tools can also be used by criminals to eradicate evidence as easily as they can be used by investigators to locate, analyze, and catalog evidence.

Types of Digital System Forensics Analysis

Today, digital system forensics includes a number of specialties. The following are some examples:

- **Disk forensics**—The process of acquiring and analyzing information stored on physical storage media, such as computer hard drives, smartphones, GPS systems, and removable media. **Disk forensics** includes both the recovery of hidden and deleted information and the process of identifying who created a file or message.

- **E-mail forensics**—The study of the source and content of e-mail as evidence. **E-mail forensics** includes the process of identifying the sender, recipient, date, time, and origination location of an e-mail message. You can use e-mail forensics to identify harassment, discrimination, or unauthorized activities. There is also a body of laws that deal with retention and storage of e-mails that are specific to certain fields, such as financial and medical.

- **Network forensics**—The process of examining network traffic, including transaction logs and real-time monitoring using sniffers and tracing, is known as **network forensics**.

- **Internet forensics**—The process of piecing together where and when a user has been on the Internet. For example, you can use **Internet forensics** to determine whether inappropriate Internet content access and downloading were accidental.

- **Software forensics**—The process of examining malicious computer code is known as **software forensics**, also known as malware forensics.

- **Live system forensics**—The process of searching memory in real time, typically for working with compromised hosts or to identify system abuse, is **live system forensics**. Each of these types of forensic analysis requires specialized skills and training.

- **Cell-phone forensics**—The process of searching the contents of cell phones is called **cell-phone forensics**. A few years ago, this was just not a big issue, but with the ubiquitous nature of cell phones today, cell-phone forensics is a very important topic. A cell phone can be a treasure trove of evidence. Modern cell phones are essentially computers with processors, memory, even hard drives and operating systems, and they operate on networks. Phone forensics also includes VoIP and traditional phones and may overlap the Foreign Intelligence Surveillance Act of 1978 (FISA), the USA Patriot Act, and the Communications Assistance to Law Enforcement Act (CALEA) in the United States.

General Guidelines

Later in this chapter, you will read about specific federal guidelines, but you should keep a few general principles in mind when doing any forensic work, as discussed in the following sections.

Chain of Custody

This is the most important principle in any forensic effort, digital or nondigital. The chain of physical custody must be maintained. From the time the evidence is first seized by a law enforcement officer or civilian investigator until the moment it is shown in court, the whereabouts and custody of the evidence, and how it was handled and stored and by whom, must be able to be shown at all times. Failure to maintain proper chain of custody can lead to evidence being excluded from trial.

Don't Touch the Suspect Drive

One very important principle is to touch the system as little as possible. It is possible to make changes to the system in the process of examining it, which is very undesirable. Obviously, you have to interact with the system to investigate it. The answer is to make a forensic copy and work with that copy. You can make a forensic copy with most major forensic tools such as AccessData's Forensic Toolkit or Guidance Software's EnCase. There is also open source software that allows copying of original source information. To be specific, make a copy and analyze the copy.

Document Trail

The next issue is documentation. The rule is that you document everything. Who was present when the device was seized? What was connected to the device or showing on the screen when you seized it? What specific tools and techniques did you use? Who had access to the evidence from the time of seizure until the time of trial? All of this must be documented. And when in doubt, err on the side of overdocumentation.

Secure the Evidence

It is absolutely critical to the integrity of your investigation as well as to maintaining the chain of custody that you secure the evidence. It is common to have the forensic lab be a locked room with access given only to those who must enter. Then, evidence is usually secured in a safe, with access given out only on a need-to-know basis. You have to take every reasonable precaution to ensure that no one can tamper with the evidence.

Knowledge Needed for Computer Forensics Analysis

To conduct computer forensics, a certain background body of knowledge is required, just as with traditional forensics. For example, you cannot examine DNA without some basic education in blood and genetics. This applies to computer forensics as well. You must have an understanding of the systems you are examining in order to successfully examine them.

This chapter assumes that you have a basic understanding of computer hardware, software, and operating systems. This section briefly discusses the highlights of these areas that you need to know, however. If you find you are lacking in one or more areas, you should take some time to brush up on these topics before continuing.

Hardware

In general, the good digital forensics examiners begin with a working knowledge of the hardware for the devices they want to examine. For PCs and laptops, this includes knowledge equivalent to the CompTIA A+ certification or a basic PC hardware course. If you are doing phone or router forensics, you need a similar level of knowledge of the hardware on those devices.

For PCs, this means a strong understanding of hard drives, memory, motherboards, and expansion cards. What exactly is a "strong understanding"? Think about random access memory (RAM). You are probably aware that RAM is **volatile memory** and it stores the programs and data you currently have open, but only for as long as the computer has power supplied to it. However, that level of knowledge is inadequate for forensics. A forensic examiner needs to go much deeper and understand the various types of RAM, how they work, the type of information that is contained in each, and how the computer uses them.

Random Access Memory

RAM can be examined in multiple ways. One way is to look at the method whereby information is written to and read from the RAM. These are presented in sequential order from older to newer technologies:

- **Extended data out dynamic random access memory (EDO DRAM)**—Single-cycle EDO has the ability to carry out a complete memory transaction in one clock cycle. Otherwise, each sequential RAM access within the same page takes two clock cycles instead of three, once the page has been selected.

- **Burst EDO (BEDO) DRAM**—An evolution of the EDO, burst EDO DRAM can process four memory addresses in one burst.

- **Asynchronous dynamic random access memory (ADRAM)**—ADRAM is not synchronized to the CPU clock.

- **Synchronous dynamic random access memory (SDRAM)**—SDRAM is a replacement for EDO.

- **Double data rate (DDR) SDRAM**—DDR SDRAM was a later development of SDRAM. DDR2 and DDR3 are now available.

SDRAM and, more specifically, DDR2 and DDR3, are the most common forms of RAM found in PCs and laptops.

Another way to look at RAM, one that is particularly important from a forensic point of view, is to consider the volatility of the data stored. Volatility refers to how easily the data can be changed, either intentionally or unintentionally:

- **Random access memory (RAM)**—This is what most people think of when they say *memory*. It is easy to write to and read from. This is very volatile. As soon as power is discontinued, the data is gone.
- **Read-only memory (ROM)**—As the name suggests, this is not at all volatile; it cannot be changed. This is usually used for instructions embedded in chips and controls how the computer, option cards, peripherals, and other devices operate.
- **Programmable read-only memory (PROM)**—PROM can be programmed only once. Data is not lost when power is removed.
- **Erasable programmable read-only memory (EPROM)**—Data is not lost when power is removed. Again, this is a technique for storing instructions on chips.
- **Electronically erasable programmable read-only memory (EEPROM)**—This is how the instructions in your computer's BIOS are stored.

Hard Drives

A forensic specialist must also understand the following storage devices:

- **Small Computer System Interface (SCSI)**—This has been around for many years, and is particularly popular in high-end servers. This standard is actually fairly old, as it was established in 1986. SCSI devices must have a terminator at the end of the chain of devices to work and are limited to 16 chained devices.
- **Integrated Drive Electronics (IDE)**—This is an older standard but one that was commonly used on PCs for many years. It is obvious you are dealing with an IDE or EIDE drive if you encounter a 40-pin connector on the drive.
- **Enhanced Integrated Drive Electronics (EIDE)**—This is an extension/enhancement of IDE.
- **Parallel Advanced Technology Attachment (PATA)**—Parallel ATA is an enhancement of IDE. It uses either a 40-pin (like IDE) or 80-pin connector.
- **Serial Advanced Technology Attachment (SATA)**—This is what you are most likely to find today. These devices are commonly found in workstations and many servers. The internals of the hard drive are very similar to IDE and EIDE; it is the connectivity to the computer's motherboard that is different. Also, unlike IDE or EIDE drives, this type of drive has no jumpers to set the drive.
- **Serial SCSI**—This is an enhancement of SCSI. It supports up to 65,537 devices and does not require termination.

- **Solid-state drives**—These are becoming more common, so it's worthwhile to discuss them in a bit more detail. Solid-state drives (SSDs) use microchips that retain data in non-volatile memory chips and contain no moving parts. As of 2010, most SSDs use NAND-based flash memory, which retains memory even without power. NAND stands for "negated AND gate." Solid-state drives do not benefit from defragmentation. Any defragmentation process adds additional writes on the NAND flash, which already has a limited cycle life. High-performance flash-based SSDs generally require one-half to one-third the power of hard disk drives (HDDs); high-performance DRAM SSDs generally require as much power as HDDs and consume power when the rest of the system is shut down.

All of these, except for solid state, refer to how the hard drive connects to the motherboard and transfers data, and do not define how information is stored on the disk. For all but solid state, the following hard drive facts apply.

HDDs record data by magnetizing ferromagnetic material directionally, to represent either a 0 or a 1 binary digit. The magnetic data is stored on platters; the platters are organized on a spindle with a read/write head reading and writing data to and from the platters. The data is organized as follows:

- A *sector* is the basic unit of data storage on a hard disk, which is usually 512 bytes.
- A cluster is a logical grouping of sectors. Clusters can be 1 to 128 sectors in size. That means 512 bytes up to 64 KB. The minimum size a file can use is one cluster. If the file is less than the size of a cluster, the remaining space is simply unused.
- Sectors are in turn organized by tracks.

That is a basic description of most hard drives (with the exception of solid-state drives). Forensic examiners should know the following terms, which are used with all hard drives:

- **Drive geometry**—This term refers to the functional dimensions of a drive in terms of the number of heads, cylinders, and sectors per track.
- **Slack space**—This is the space between the end of a file and the end of the cluster, assuming the file does not occupy the entire cluster. This is space that can be used to hide data.
- **Low-level format**—This creates a structure of sectors, tracks, and clusters.
- **High-level format**—This is the process of setting up an empty file system on the disk and installing a boot sector. This is sometimes referred to as a quick format.

Software

Once you have a basic understanding of hardware, the next step is to learn about the software, and this begins with the operating system. It is imperative that you have a strong working knowledge of the operating system running on the device you want to examine.

Windows

There's a lot to know about Windows, but for now, here's a basic overview of how it works. The heart of Windows is the Windows Registry. The Windows Registry is essentially a repository of all settings, software, and parameters for Windows. If new software is installed, the Registry is updated to indicate the new software. If the background color of the desktop is changed, the Registry is updated to indicate the new color. From this Registry, you can get all kinds of information, including the password for wireless networks and the serial numbers for all USB devices that have been connected to that computer. This is really the most important part of Windows from both a technical-support and a forensic point of view.

Windows also has other interesting places to look for forensic evidence. There are certain folders and files—the index.dat file, for instance—that are great places to find evidence. Even browser cookies and history can be useful. Given that Windows is such a common operating system, it is advisable to be very familiar with Windows.

Linux

Linux is particularly interesting from a forensic point of view. Even though it is not as widely used as Windows, it is a favorite in the security and forensics community. You will find that a lot of free forensic tools come with Linux. In fact, one specific Linux distribution called BackTrack has an extensive collection of forensic, security, and hacking tools.

Linux is a UNIX clone, developed originally by Linus Torvalds. There are now well over 100 different distributions, or variations, of Linux. However, all have some commonalities. In the Linux world, work done from the command line, called the shell in Linux, is far more important than it is in Windows.

Macintosh

For many years, Apple Macintosh was a complete operating system. However, beginning with OS X, the Macintosh system has been based on FreeBSD, a UNIX clone very similar to Linux. The graphical user interface is just that, an interface. The underlying operating system is a UNIX-like system.

This means that many forensic techniques you can use on Linux can also be used on Macintosh, from the shell prompt.

Files and File Systems

Computers store discrete sets of related information in files. Any document, spreadsheet, picture, video, or even program is a file. It is a very easy thing to change the extension of a file so that it looks like some other type of file. However, that will not change the file structure itself. There are tools that allow viewing of the actual file structure and the file header. This is very important from a forensic perspective. The file header gives you an accurate understanding of the file, regardless of whether the extension has been changed. A few basic facts about files are as follows:

- File headers start at the first byte of a file.
- In graphics file formats, the header might give information about an image's size, resolution, number of colors, and the like.

- The Executable and Linkable Format (ELF, formerly called Extensible Linking Format) is a common standard file format for executables, object code, and shared libraries for UNIX-based systems.

- Portable Executable (PE) is used in Windows for executables and dynamic-link libraries (DLLs). PE files are derived from the earlier Common Object File Format (COFF) found on VAX/VMS, a common operating system for mainframe computers.

- Area density is the data per area of disk.

- Windows Office files have a globally unique identifier (GUID) to identify them.

Files are organized on the computer based on the file system. There are many file systems, but they can be divided into two categories. Journaling is basically the process whereby the file system keeps a record of what file transactions take place so that in the event of a hard drive crash, the files can be recovered. Journaling file systems are fault tolerant because the file system logs all changes to files, directories, or file structures. The log in which changes are recorded is referred to as the file systems journal—thus the term *journaling* file systems.

There are actually two types of journaling: physical and logical. With physical journaling, the system logs a copy of every block that is about to be written to the storage device, before it is written. The log also includes a checksum of those blocks, to make sure there is no error in writing the block. With logical journaling, only changes to file metadata are stored in the journal.

Here are some specific file systems:

- **File Allocation Table (FAT)**—This is an older system, which was popular with Microsoft operating systems for many years. FAT was first implemented in Microsoft Standalone Disk BASIC. FAT stores file locations by sector in a file called the file allocation table. This table contains information about which clusters are being used by which particular files and which clusters are free to be used. The various extensions of FAT, such as FAT16 and FAT32, differ in the number of bits available for filenames.

- **New Technology File System (NTFS)**—Microsoft eventually introduced a new file system to replace FAT. This file system is called New Technology File System (NTFS). This is the file system used by Windows NT 4, 2000, XP, Vista, 7, Server 2003, and Server 2008. One major improvement of NTFS over FAT was the increased volume sizes NTFS could support. The maximum NTFS volume size is $2^{64}-1$ clusters.

- **Extended file system**—This was the first file system created specifically for Linux. There have been many versions of EXT; the current version is 4. The EXT4 file system can support volumes with sizes up to 1 exabyte (10^{18} bytes, or 1 billion gigabytes) and files with sizes up to 16 terabytes. This is a huge file and volume size, and no current hard drives come even close to that volume size. For an administrator, one of the most exciting features of EXT4 is that it is backward compatible with EXT2 and EXT3, making it possible to mount drives that use those earlier versions of EXT.

- **ReiserFS**—This is a popular journaling file system, used primarily with Linux. ReiserFS was the first file system to be included with the standard Linux kernel, and first appeared in kernel version 2.4.1. Unlike some file systems, ReiserFS supported journaling from its inception, whereas EXT did not support journaling until version 3. ReiserFS is open source and was invented by Hans Reiser.

- **The Berkeley Fast File System**—This is also known as the UNIX file system. As its names suggest, it was developed at the University of California specifically for UNIX. Like many file systems, Berkeley uses a bitmap to track free clusters, indicating which clusters are available and which are not. Like EXT, Berkeley includes the FSCK utility. This is only one of many similarities between Berkeley and EXT. In fact, some sources consider EXT to just be a variant of the Berkeley Fast File System.

Networks

Digital forensics, like all branches of cybersecurity, breaks information into two types. There is information at rest and information in motion. Information at rest includes anything that is stored inside the computer, including in the file system or memory. Information in motion is information being transmitted between endpoints and includes the protocols and other information needed for transmission. The transmission of information across networks and the network components used is a vast, quickly changing field. The modern forensic investigator, however, should be very familiar with the components and how they work as well as the protocols and their operation if information in motion is to be considered as a part of the investigator's skill set. The modern forensic analyst who will consider information in motion must also be very familiar with the concepts and operation of both the seven-layer Open Systems Interconnection (OSI) Reference Model and the five-layer Internet Engineering Task Force (IETF) model. If you lack this knowledge, you must acquire it before proceeding any further.

Addresses

The digital forensics analyst must be aware of the way that computer information is addressed and the proper vocabulary for discussing the different types of addresses and units of information transfer. It is also important for the digital forensics analyst to understand that not all addresses are a part of every communication. If they are present, the addresses are part of a hierarchy and are placed, one within the other, like envelopes.

Physical Ports

Physical ports are physical. You can touch them. Even a wireless physical port can be touched, although you must open the computer or other device to find the antenna first. The physical ports operate at OSI Layer 1, the Physical Layer. The units of information transfer are 1 and 0 bits grouped into fixed-length units called Layer 1 frames.

MAC Addresses

In addition to the Physical Layer's units of information transfer, information being transmitted may be grouped into Layer 2 frames for transmission. Layer 1 frames are fixed in length, whereas Layer 2 frames are variable. Layer 2 frames have a header, a body, also known as a payload, and a trailer. The numeric address information contained in Layer 2 frames is the Media Access Control (MAC) address. The most common Layer 2 protocol is Ethernet, though there are many more.

A MAC address is supposed to be unique, is supposed to be tied to one and only one physical port, and is not supposed to be duplicated or reused for any reason. This just is not so. Duplication of MAC addresses can occur due to bad quality control or can be done intentionally for a variety of malicious reasons. The keen forensic investigator will never be fooled by duplicate MAC addresses.

IP Addresses

In addition to the Physical Layer's fixed-length Layer 1 frames, which use physical port addresses to carry the variable-length Layer 2 frame to its destination, are the contents, or payload, of the Layer 2 frame, which is the Layer 3 packet. The Layer 3 packet is variable in length and contains a header and payload. The most common protocol used at Layer 3 is IP; therefore, the entire transmission unit containing all of this information is usually called an IP packet.

Logical Port Numbers

Inside the fixed-length unit called a Layer 1 frame, sent to its destination by use of a physical address, is a variable-length unit called a Layer 2 frame, addressed with a MAC address and used to deliver a Layer 3 packet. This is addressed by the Layer 3 protocol, usually IP. Inside of the IP packet's payload is another unit that is either formatted by the rules of the Transmission Control Protocol (TCP) or the User Datagram Protocol (UDP). If the information is formatted per TCP rules, the unit is called a segment; if the information is formatted per the rules of UDP, it is called a datagram. In either case, the protocol uses one of three types of port numbers. It is not good that there are Layer 1 fixed-length frames and Layer 2 variable-length frames. It is equally bad that there are Layer 1 physical port numbers and Layer 5 logical port numbers. But there are. To keep things straight, it is best to talk about physical port numbers for Layer 1 and software port numbers for Layer 5.

Socket Numbers

Socket number is another important term. It is used by software programmers as well as by computer technicians and digital forensics specialists. A socket number is the concatenation of the IP address and the TCP or UDP port number and should be unique to a connection at a single moment in time. Lacking a uniform resource locator (URL), which is discussed next, a socket number can be typed directly into a browser. For instance, if you want to contact the server located at IP address 54.32.57.67 and communicate directly with its public Web service on well-known port number 80, you would type 54.32.57.67:80 directly into the Web browser.

Uniform Resource Locators

As the Internet grew and the number of servers and their IP addresses grew, the Domain Name System (DNS) was created to allow Internet users to type a name instead of an IP address. This level of simplification is great, but it introduces a number of potential forensic issues. Issues range from changing the mapping of Web site name to IP address permanently or temporarily and many different forms of this that can be used to redirect browsers incorrectly and befuddle forensic efforts.

Addressing Review

In a complete, end-to-end Internet communication, it is most common that user information, such as e-mail text, would be formatted as specified by the e-mail protocol. A URL would then be used to find the actual IP address of the recipient. The message would be formatted per the TCP protocol and sent with the proper TCP port number set to the IP addresses. The IP packet containing all of this would be put into a special envelope built per the protocol rules of Ethernet, which would make its way onto the actual wire, or go across the wireless or optical connection on its way through the cloud to its destination. At the destination, the process would be done in reverse and the e-mail, or at least a part of it, would have gotten through to its destination.

Basic Network Utilities

You can execute some basic network utilities from a command prompt (Windows) or from a shell (UNIX/Linux). This text's discussion executes the commands and discusses them from the Windows command-prompt perspective; however, it must be stressed that these utilities are available in all operating systems. This section covers the `ipconfig`, `ping`, and `tracert` utilities.

Working with `ipconfig`. The first thing you need to do is to get information about your own system. To accomplish this fact-finding mission, you need to get to a command prompt. In Windows XP, you do this by going to the Start menu and then selecting All Programs > Accessories > Command Prompt. For other versions of Windows, the process is identical, except the first option is called simply Programs rather than All Programs. Now you can type in `ipconfig`. You could input the same command in UNIX or Linux by typing in `ifconfig` from the shell. After typing in `ipconfig`—`ifconfig` in Linux—you should see something similar to what is shown in Figure 1-2.

This command gives you some information about your connection to a network or to the Internet. Most important, you find out your own IP address. The command also has the IP address for your default gateway, which is your connection to the outside world. Running the `ipconfig` command is a first step in determining your system's network configuration.

You can see that this option gives you much more information. For example, `ipconfig/all` gives the name of your computer, when your computer obtained its IP address, and more.

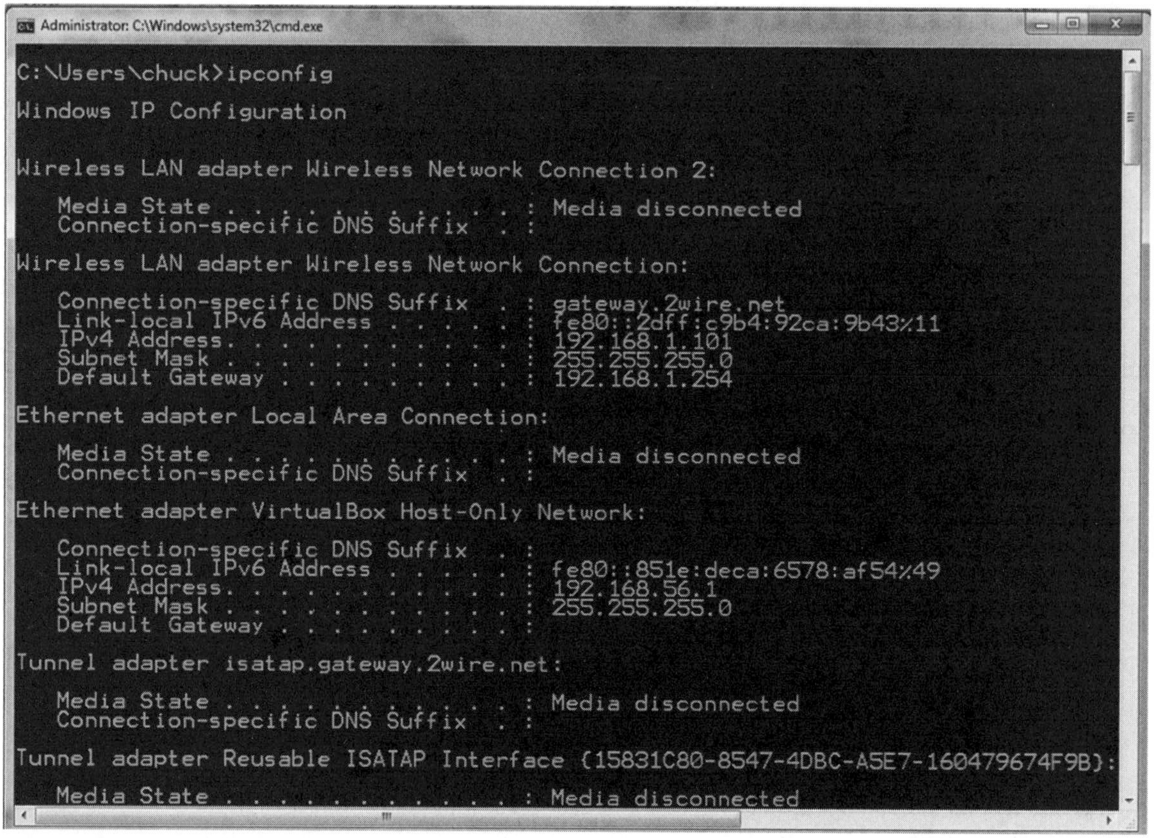

FIGURE 1-2

ipconfig.

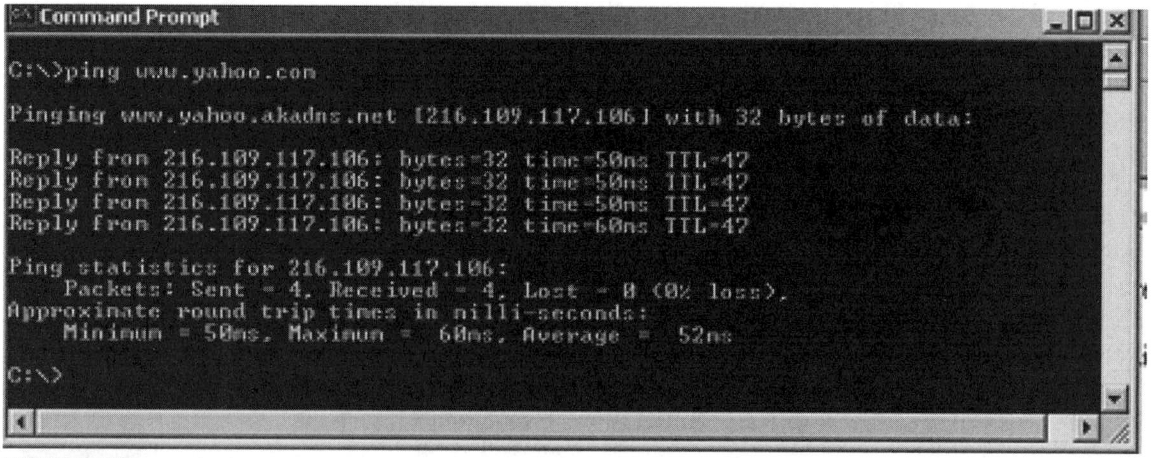

FIGURE 1-3

ping.

Using ping. Another commonly used command is ping, which is used to send a test packet, or echo packet, to a machine to find out if the machine is reachable and how long the packet takes to reach the machine. This useful diagnostic tool can be employed in elementary hacking techniques. The command is shown in Figure 1-3.

You can see in Figure 1-3 that a 32-byte echo packet was sent to the destination and returned. The TTL item means *time to live*. That time unit is how many intermediary steps, or hops, the packet should take to the destination before giving up. Remember that the Internet is a vast conglomerate of interconnected networks. Your packet probably won't go straight to its destination. It will have to take several hops to get there. As with ipconfig, you can type in ping -? to find out various ways you can refine your ping.

Working with tracert. The final command this section examines is the tracert command. While tracert can be useful for some live network troubleshooting, the information reported by tracert is not useful or trustworthy for forensic examination. This same command can be executed in Linux or UNIX, but there it is called "traceroute" rather than "tracert." You can see this command in Figure 1-4.

This section is just a brief overview of the hardware, software, and networking knowledge you should have in order to study forensics. If you find you are lacking in one or more areas, do some review in those areas before you proceed.

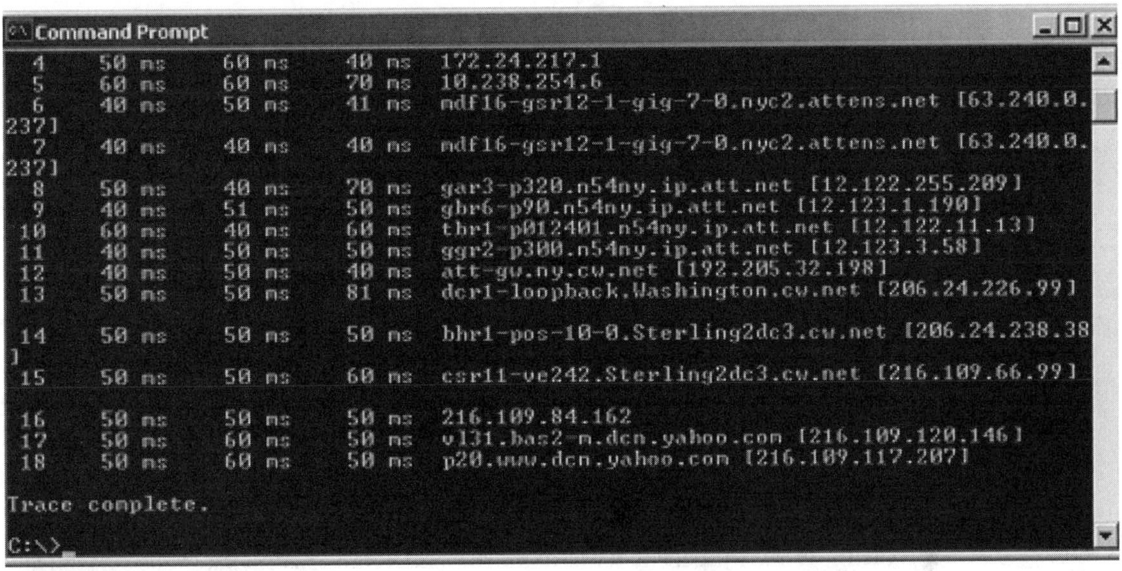

Used with permission from Microsoft

FIGURE 1-4

tracert.

Obscured Information and Anti-Forensics

Two more challenges in obtaining digital evidence are obscured information and anti-forensics.

Obscured Information

Information can be obscured in a number of ways. *Obscured information* may be scrambled by encryption, hidden using steganographic software, compressed, or in a proprietary format. Sometimes, cybercriminals obscure information to deter forensic examination. More often, companies use certain manipulation and storage techniques to protect business-sensitive information. Regardless of the reason for obscured data, collecting and analyzing it is difficult.

Data that has been obscured through encryption, steganography, compression, or proprietary formats can sometimes be converted with some serious detective work and the right tools. Forensic specialists often must do quite a bit of work to decrypt encrypted information. In many cases, the investigator cannot decrypt information unless the data owner provides the encryption key and algorithm. When digital evidence has been encrypted and is in use on a live system, an investigator might have to collect evidence through a live extraction process.

Anti-Forensics

Every investigation is unique. Investigations are not necessarily friendly activities. Forensic specialists may have to conduct the investigation with or without the cooperation of the information owner. And the information owner may or may not be the target of the investigation. Investigations with uncooperative information owners are difficult.

Attackers may use techniques to intentionally conceal their identities, locations, and behavior. For example, perpetrators may conceal their identities by using networked connections at a library, an Internet café, or another public computer kiosk. Or they may use encryption or anonymous services to protect themselves. The actions that perpetrators take to conceal their locations, activities, or identities are generally termed **anti-forensics**.

Cybercriminals are becoming better at covering their tracks as their awareness of digital forensics capabilities increases. The following are examples of anti-forensics techniques:

- **Data destruction**—Methods for disposing of data vary. They can be as simple as wiping the memory buffers used by a program. Or they can be as complex as repeatedly overwriting a cluster of data with patterns of 1s and 0s. Digital evidence can be destroyed easily. For example, starting a computer updates timestamps and modifies files. Attaching a hard disk or USB stick modifies file system timestamps. Powering off a machine destroys volatile memory. Suspects may delete files and folders and defrag their hard drives in an attempt to overwrite evidence.

- **Data hiding**—Suspects often store data where an investigator is unlikely to find it. They may hide data, for example, in reserved disk sectors or as logical partitions within a defined, public partition. Or they may simply change filenames and extensions.

- **Data transformation**—Suspects may process information in a way that disguises its meaning. For example, they may use encryption to scramble a message based on an algorithm. Or they may use steganography to hide a message inside a larger message.

- **Data contraception**—Suspects often store data where a forensic specialist can't analyze it. For example, they may prevent data from being written to disk by storing it in memory. To do so, they use memory-resident rootkits.

- **Data fabrication**—Suspects often overwhelm forensic analysts with false positives and false leads. For example, they may alter as many files as possible to make it difficult to use a checksum process to identify changed files.

- **File system alteration**—Suspects often corrupt data structures and files that organize data, such as a Windows NT File System (NTFS) volume.

The Daubert Standard

One legal principle that is key to forensics and is all too often overlooked in forensic books is the Daubert standard. The Cornell University Law School defines the **Daubert standard** as follows:

> Standard used by a trial judge to make a preliminary assessment of whether an expert's scientific testimony is based on reasoning or methodology that is scientifically valid and can properly be applied to the facts at issue. Under this standard, the factors that may be considered in determining whether the methodology is valid are: (1) whether the theory or technique in question can be and has been tested; (2) whether it has been subjected to peer review and publication; (3) its known or potential error rate; (4) the existence and maintenance of standards controlling its operation; and (5) whether it has attracted widespread acceptance within a relevant scientific community.

What this means, in layman's terms, is that any scientific evidence presented in a trial has to have been reviewed and tested by the relevant scientific community. For a computer forensics investigator, that means that any tools, techniques, or processes you utilize in your investigation should be ones that are widely accepted in the computer forensics community. You cannot simply make up new tests or procedures.

This, naturally, brings up the question, how do new techniques become widely accepted? Let's suppose you have developed a new tool that extracts forensic information from the Windows Registry. A first step might be to provide a copy of that tool to a few professors of forensics, allowing them to experiment with it. You might also publish an article describing it. After it has been tested by the forensic community and articles about it have been read (and possibly rebutted), then your tool would be usable in real forensic investigations.

It is important to remember the Daubert standard because it will affect your forensic approach. It also reminds us of an even more basic concept: The evidence you collect is important only if it is admissible in court. So you have to pay attention to the techniques and tools you use and maintain the chain of custody.

U.S. Laws Affecting Digital Forensics

There are many laws that affect digital forensics investigation. For example, some jurisdictions have passed laws that require the investigator to be either a law enforcement officer or a licensed private investigator to extract the evidence. Of course, that does not prevent a forensic investigator from working with information someone else extracted or extracting evidence if the information owner gave his or her permission. It is important to be aware of the legal requirements in the jurisdiction in which you work.

The Federal Privacy Act of 1974

The Privacy Act of 1974 establishes a code of information-handling practices that governs the collection, maintenance, use, and dissemination of information about individuals that is maintained in systems of records by U.S. federal agencies. A system of records is a group of records under the control of an agency from which information is retrieved by the name of the individual or by some identifier assigned to the individual.

The Privacy Protection Act of 1980

The Privacy Protection Act (PPA) of 1980 protects journalists from being required to turn over to law enforcement any work product and documentary materials, including sources, before it is disseminated to the public. Journalists who most need the protection of the PPA are those who are working on stories that are highly controversial or about criminal acts because the information gathered may also be useful to law enforcement.

The Communications Assistance to Law Enforcement Act of 1994

The Communications Assistance to Law Enforcement Act of 1994 is a federal wiretap law for traditional wired telephony. It was expanded to include wireless, voice over packet, and other forms of electronic communications, including signaling traffic and metadata.

The Electronic Communications Privacy Act of 1986

The Electronic Communications Privacy Act of 1986 governs the privacy and disclosure, access, and interception of content and traffic data related to electronic communications.

The Computer Security Act of 1987

The Computer Security Act of 1987 was passed to improve the security and privacy of sensitive information in federal computer systems. The law requires the establishment of minimum acceptable security practices, creation of computer security plans, and training of system users or owners of facilities that house sensitive information.

The Foreign Intelligence Surveillance Act of 1978

The Foreign Intelligence Surveillance Act of 1978 (FISA) is a law that allows for collection of "foreign intelligence information" between foreign powers and agents of foreign powers using physical and electronic surveillance. A warrant is issued by the FISA court for actions under FISA.

The Child Protection and Sexual Predator Punishment Act of 1998

The Child Protection and Sexual Predator Punishment Act of 1998 requires service providers that become aware of the storage or transmission of child pornography to report it to law enforcement.

The Children's Online Privacy Protection Act of 1998

The Children's Online Privacy Protection Act of 1998 (COPPA) protects children 13 years of age and under from the collection and use of their personal information by Web sites. It is noteworthy that COPPA replaces the Child Online Protection Act of 1988 (COPA), which was determined to be unconstitutional.

The Communications Decency Act of 1996

The Communications Decency Act of 1996 was designed to protect persons 18 years of age and under from downloading or viewing material considered indecent. This act has been subject to court cases that subsequently changed some definitions and penalties.

The Telecommunications Act of 1996

The Telecommunications Act of 1996 includes many provisions relative to the privacy and disclosure of information in motion through and across telephony and computer networks.

The Wireless Communications and Public Safety Act of 1999

The Wireless Communications and Public Safety Act of 1999 allows for collection and use of "empty" communications, which means nonverbal and nontext communications, such as GPS information.

The USA Patriot Act

The USA Patriot Act is the primary law under which a wide variety of Internet and communications information content and metadata is currently collected. Provisions exist within the Patriot Act to protect the identity and privacy of U.S. citizens.

The Sarbanes-Oxley Act of 2002

The Sarbanes-Oxley Act of 2002 contains many provisions about recordkeeping and destruction of electronic records relating to the management and operation of publicly held companies.

Warrants

According to the Supreme Court, a "seizure of property occurs when there is some meaningful interference with an individual's possessory interests in that property" (*United States v. Jacobsen*, 466 U.S. 109, 113 [1984]). The Court also characterized the interception of intangible communications as a seizure, in the case of *Berger v. New York* (388 U.S. 41, 59–60 [1967]). Now that means that law enforcement need not take property in order for it to be considered seizure. Merely interfering with an individual's access to his or her own property constitutes seizure. *Berger v. New York* extends that to communications. If law enforcement's conduct does not violate a person's "reasonable expectation of privacy," then formally it does not constitute a Fourth Amendment "search" and no warrant is required. There have been many cases where the issue of reasonable expectation of privacy has been argued. To use an example that is quite clear, if you save a message in an electronic diary, you clearly have a reasonable expectation of privacy; however, if you post such a message on a public bulletin board, you can have no expectation of privacy. In less clear cases, a general rule is that courts have held that law enforcement officers are prohibited from accessing and viewing information stored in a computer if it would be prohibited from opening a closed container and examining its contents in the same situation.

In computer crime cases, two consent issues arise particularly often. First, when does a search exceed the scope of consent? For example, when a person agrees to the search of a location, such as his or her apartment, does that consent authorize the retrieval of information stored in computers at the location? Second, who is the proper party to consent to a search? Can roommates, friends, and parents legally grant consent to a search of another person's computer files? These are all very critical questions that must be considered when searching a computer. In general, courts have held that only the actual owner of a property can grant consent. For example, a parent of a minor child can grant consent to search the child's living quarters and computers. However, a roommate who shares rent can grant consent to search only living quarters and computers co-owned by both parties. A roommate cannot grant consent to search the private property of the other person.

Federal Guidelines

If you are setting up a forensic lab, or if you are new to forensics, a good place to start is the federal guidelines. Two agencies in particular—the FBI and the Secret Service—are particularly important.

The FBI

If an incident occurs, the FBI recommends that the first responder preserve the state of the computer at the time of the incident by making a backup copy of any logs, any damaged or altered files, and any other files modified, viewed, or left by the intruder. This last part is critical. Hackers frequently use various tools and may leave traces of their presence. Furthermore, the FBI advises that if the incident is in progress, you should activate any auditing or recording software you might have available. Collect as much data about the incident as you can. In other words, this might be a case where you do not take the machine offline, but rather analyze the attack in progress.

The FBI computer forensics guidelines stress the importance of securing any evidence. They further stress that computer evidence can come in many forms. Here are a few common forms:

- Hard drives
- System logs
- Portable storage, such as USB drives and external drives
- Router logs
- E-mails
- Chat room logs
- Cell phones
- SIM cards for cell phones
- Logs from security devices, such as firewalls and intrusion detection systems
- Databases and database logs

What you secure will be dependent upon the nature of the cybercrime. For example, in the case of child predators, online stalkers, or online fraud, e-mail may be very important, but router logs may be irrelevant. The FBI also stresses that you should work with a copy of the hard drive, not the original.

The FBI has a cybercrimes Web page, which is a very useful resource for learning more about trends in cybercrime and in computer forensics.

The Secret Service

The United States Secret Service is the premier federal agency tasked with combating cybercrime. It has a Web site devoted to computer forensics that includes forensic courses. These courses are usually for law enforcement personnel.

The Secret Service also has released a guide for first responders to computer crime. The agency has listed its "golden rules" to begin the investigation. They are as follows:

- Officer safety: Secure the scene and make it safe.
- If you reasonably believe that the computer is involved in the crime you are investigating, take immediate steps to preserve the evidence.
- Determine whether you have a legal basis to seize the computer, such as plain view, search warrant, or consent.
- Do not access any computer files. If the computer is off, leave it off.
- If it is on, do not start searching through the computer. Instead, properly shut down the computer and prepare it for transport as evidence.
- If you reasonably believe that the computer is destroying evidence, immediately shut down the computer by pulling the power cord from the back of the computer.
- If a camera is available, and the computer is on, take pictures of the computer screen. If the computer is off, take pictures of the computer, the location of the computer, and any electronic media attached.
- Determine whether special legal or privacy considerations apply, such as those for doctors, attorneys, clergy, psychiatrists, newspapers, or publishers.

These are all important first steps to both preserving the chain of custody and ensuring the integrity of the investigation from the very first step.

The Regional Computer Forensics Laboratory Program

The Regional Computer Forensics Laboratory (RCFL) Program is a national network of forensic laboratories and training centers. The FBI provides startup and operational funding, training, staff, and equipment to the program. State, local, and other federal law enforcement agencies assign personnel to staff RCFL facilities.

Each of the 16 RCFLs examines digital evidence in support of criminal and national security investigations. The RCFL Program provides law enforcement at all levels with digital forensics expertise. It works with a wide variety of investigations, including terrorism, child pornography, fraud, and homicide.

The RCFL Program conducts digital forensics training. In 2008, for example, the program trained nearly 5,000 law enforcement personnel in system forensics tools and techniques. For more information, see *http://www.rcfl.gov*.

CHAPTER SUMMARY

This chapter explored the basics of computer forensics. You have learned general principles, such as working only with a copy of the drive you're investigating and maintaining the chain of custody. The chapter also examined the types of digital forensics done as well as the laws regarding digital forensics. You should be familiar with the Daubert standard, warrants, federal forensic guidelines, and the general forensic procedure.

KEY CONCEPTS AND TERMS

Anti-forensics	Digital evidence	Live system forensics
Cell-phone forensics	Disk forensics	Network forensics
Chain of custody	Documentary evidence	Real evidence
Computer forensics	E-mail forensics	Software forensics
Curriculum vitae (CV)	Expert report	Testimonial evidence
Daubert standard	Expert testimony	Volatile memory
Demonstrative evidence	Internet forensics	

CHAPTER 1 ASSESSMENT

1. In a computer forensics investigation, _____ describes the route that evidence takes from the time you find it until the case is closed or goes to court.

A. Rules of evidence
B. Law of probability
C. Chain of custody
D. Policy of separation

2. If the computer is turned on when you arrive, what does the Secret Service recommend you do?

A. Begin your investigation immediately.
B. Shut down according to recommended Secret Service procedure.
C. Transport the computer with power on.
D. Unplug the machine immediately.

3. Why should you note all cable connections for a computer you want to seize as evidence?

A. To know what outside connections existed
B. In case other devices were connected
C. To know what peripheral devices existed
D. To know what hardware existed

4. What is the essence of the Daubert standard?

A. That only experts can testify at trial
B. That an expert must affirm that a tool or technique is valid
C. That only tools or techniques that have been accepted by the scientific community are admissible at trial
D. That the chain of custody must be preserved

5. When cataloging digital evidence, the primary goal is to do what?

A. Make bitstream images of all hard drives.
B. Preserve evidence integrity.
C. Keep evidence from being removed from the scene.
D. Keep the computer from being turned off.

6. Which of the following are important to the investigator regarding logging?

A. The logging methods
B. Log retention
C. Location of stored logs
D. All of the above

7. Your roommate can give consent to search your computer.

A. True
B. False

8. Evidence need not be locked if it is at a police station.

A. True
B. False

Overview of Computer Crime

BEFORE DELVING INTO COMPUTER FORENSICS, it is important for you to understand the types of computer crimes that are likely to lead to forensic investigations. This chapter is not meant to be an exhaustive catalog of every computer crime that can be perpetrated, but rather a discussion of the most common computer crimes.

Chapter 2 Topics

This chapter covers the following topics and concepts:

- How computer crime affects forensics
- What the details of identity theft are
- What hacking is
- What the truth about cyberstalking and harassment is
- What you need to know about fraud on the Internet
- What the details about non-access computer crimes are
- What you need to know about the new frontier of cyberterrorism

Chapter 2 Goals

When you complete this chapter, you will be able to:

- Describe common computer crimes
- Understand varying forensic approaches to different crimes
- Apply the appropriate forensic strategy based on the specific crime

How Computer Crime Affects Forensics

Many small businesses and even large organizations do not properly protect their sensitive data. In this way, they leave the door open to cybercriminals. Many crimes today involve the use of computers and networks. A computer or another device can play one of three roles in a computer crime:

- It can be the target of the crime.
- It can be the instrument of the crime.
- It can be an evidence repository that stores valuable information about the crime.

In some cases, a computer can have multiple roles. It can be the instrument of a crime and also serve as a file cabinet that stores critical evidence. For example, an attacker may use a computer as a tool to break into another computer and steal files. The attacker may then store the stolen files on the computer used to perpetrate the theft. When investigating a case, it is important that the investigator know what roles a computer played in the crime and then tailor the investigative process to those roles.

Applying information about how a computer was used in a crime also helps when searching a system for evidence. If a computer was used to hack into a network password file, the investigator should look for password-cracking software and password files. If a computer was the target of a crime, such as an intrusion, the investigator should check audit logs and look for unfamiliar programs. Knowing how a computer was used in a crime helps narrow down the evidence collection process. Hard drives today are generally very large. Therefore, checking and analyzing every piece of data a computer and associated media contain can take a long time. Often, law enforcement officials need information quickly. Having a general idea of what to look for on a suspect computer speeds the evidence collection process.

Computers can be involved in a variety of types of crimes, including white-collar crimes, violent crimes such as murder and terrorism, counterintelligence, economic espionage, counterfeiting, child pornography, and drug dealing, among others.

The Internet has made targets much more accessible, and the risks involved for criminals are much lower than with traditional crimes. From the comfort of home or some other remote site, a cybercriminal can hack into a bank and transfer millions of dollars to a fictitious account. In essence, the criminal can rob the bank without the threat of being physically harmed while trying to escape.

Cybercrime can also involve modification of a traditional crime by using the Internet in some way. It can be as simple as the online illegal sale of prescription drugs or as sophisticated as cyberstalking. Pedophiles use the Internet to exchange child pornography and pose as children to lure victims into real-life kidnappings. Laws governing fraud apply with equal force, regardless of whether the activity is online or offline.

In the arena of computer forensics, the nature of the crime can have a significant effect on the forensic process. Certain crimes are more likely than others to yield certain types of forensic evidence. For example, identity theft is likely to leave e-mail evidence via phishing e-mails, but hacking into a system and stealing data probably does not leave any e-mail evidence. On the other hand, hacking into the system probably does leave evidence in the firewall and intrusion detection system logs, whereas phishing e-mails may not.

In order to select the appropriate forensic tests, the investigator must understand the types of computer crimes and how the crime affects the forensic process.

Most computer security books categorize computer attacks based on the nature of the attack. For example, such books look at denial of service attacks, malware, hacking into Web pages, and so forth. However, for our purposes, this chapter categorizes computer attacks based on the type of crime being done, regardless of how it was performed. As you proceed through this chapter, you will see that this makes more sense for forensic examinations. This chapter examines the following categories:

- Identity theft
- Hacking systems for data
- Cyberstalking/harassment
- Internet fraud
- Non-access computer crimes
- Cyberterrorism

These are rather broad categories that encompass a great many activities. But the categories work well for investigating criminal behavior.

Identity Theft

Identity theft is a growing problem. It is any use of another person's identity. Now that might seem like a pretty broad definition, but it is accurate. Most often, criminals commit identity theft in order to perpetrate some financial fraud. For example, a criminal might use the victim's information to obtain a credit card. Then, the victim is left with the bill. The U.S. Department of Justice defines identity theft and identity fraud as:

> ... terms used to refer to all types of crime in which someone wrongfully obtains and uses another person's personal data in some way that involves fraud or deception, typically for economic gain.

Notice that this definition states that it is *typically for economic gain*. Therefore, even unsuccessful identity theft is still a crime. The simple act of wrongfully obtaining another person's personal data is the crime, with or without stealing any money. However, a criminal might steal someone's identity for other reasons as well. For example, here is a real-world case. Some details have been changed to preserve confidentiality, but the essentials of the story are all true.

This crime occurred in a state that used Social Security numbers for driver's license numbers. No state does this anymore, for good reason. In this case, an individual worked at a local office of the Department of Motor Vehicles. When someone came in to renew a license, he or she surrendered the old license. The criminal in this case took some old licenses that he thought resembled him. He then put his picture on them and used one of them if he was pulled over for a traffic ticket. This caused the ticket to be issued to the individual who owned the license, along with a ticket for having an expired license. Eventually, however, an investigation tied the tickets to his car and license plate number.

This story illustrates one way in which criminals can accomplish identity theft— by getting official documents with someone else's information on them. It also shows an alternative reason for identity theft, one that does not involve bank accounts or credit. This is certainly not the most common example of identity theft, but it is one possible example. Criminals also use the following common methods to perpetrate identity theft:

- Phishing
- Spyware
- Discarded information

The following sections briefly examine each of these.

Phishing

Phishing is an attempt to trick a victim into giving up personal information. It is usually done by e-mailing the victim and claiming to be from some organization a victim would trust, like his or her bank or credit card company. In one of its simplest forms, a perpe-trator sends out an e-mail to a large number of people. It claims to be from some bank— for the purposes of this example, consider a fictitious bank called Trustworthy Bank. The e-mail claims that there is some issue with the recipient's account and states the recipient needs to click a link in the e-mail to address the problem. However, the link actually takes the recipient to a fake Web site that simply looks like the real Web site. When the victim types in his or her username and password, this fake system displays some message like "logon temporarily unavailable" or "error, please try later." What the perpetrator has done is tricked the victim into giving the criminal the victim's logon and password for his or her bank account.

Clearly, in any mass e-mail scenario, many recipients aren't customers of the financial institution being faked. And those recipients will likely just delete the e-mail. Even many of those who are customers of the spoofed financial institution won't fall for the scam. They will delete the e-mail, too. But, in this case, it is a numbers game for the criminal. If he or she sends out enough of these e-mails, it is certain that someone will fall for it. So the trick is to send out as many e-mails as possible, and know that only a small percentage will respond.

Phishing is generally a process of reaching out to as many people as possible, hoping enough people respond. In general, about as many people fall for scam e-mails as respond to other, legitimate, unsolicited bulk e-mail, or spam. A good fictitious e-mail gets a 1–3 percent response rate, according to the Federal Bureau of Investigation (FBI). An identity thief—if he or she uses the target organization's format, spells everything correctly, and uses logos and artwork that look legitimate—can count on a response of 10,000 to 30,000 clickthroughs per million e-mails sent.

Recent years have seen the growth of more targeted attacks. The first such targeted attack is called spear phishing. With spear phishing, the criminal targets a specific group. For example, the criminal may want to get information about the network of a specific bank, so he or she targets e-mails to the IT staff at that bank. The e-mails are a bit more specific, and thus more likely to look legitimate to the recipients.

Similar to spear phishing is whaling. This is phishing with a specific, high-value target in mind. For example, the attacker may target the CIO of a bank. First, the attacker performs a Web search on that CIO and learns as much about him or her as possible. LinkedIn, Facebook, and other social media can be very helpful in this regard. Then, the attacker sends an e-mail targeted to that specific individual. This makes it much more likely the e-mail will appear legitimate and the victim will respond.

One scenario is to research the target, the CIO, in this case, and find out his or her hobbies. For example, if the CIO is an avid fisherman, the attacker might send him or her an e-mail offering a free subscription to a fishing magazine if he or she fills out a survey. The survey is generic, but requires the target to select a password. This is important because most people reuse passwords. Whatever password the CIO selects, it is likely he or she used that same password elsewhere as well. Even if it is not used as his or her network logon password, it could be a password to a Hotmail, Gmail, LinkedIn, or Facebook account. This gives the attacker an inroad into that person's electronic life. From there, it is a matter of time before the attacker is able to secure the victim's network credentials. Information learned in phishing can also be used in social engineering or other highly targeted attacks such as advanced persistent threat attacks, which are ongoing attacks that make repeated and concerted attempts at phishing. It is usually for a specific, high-value target that several related phishing e-mails are sent.

Spyware

Spyware is any software that can monitor your activity on a computer. It may involve taking screenshots or perhaps logging keystrokes. It can even be as simple as a cookie that simply records a few brief facts about your visit to a Web site. For example, when you visit Amazon.com, the site remembers what you were last searching for. This is accomplished via cookies. Now some people might object to Web site cookies being labeled as spyware. And it should be pointed out that cookies have many legitimate uses. However, it is up to whoever programmed the Web site to decide what information is stored in a Web site cookie and how it will be used. This means that, at least technically speaking, cookies could be considered spyware.

It has been claimed that 80 percent of all computers connected to the Internet have spyware. Whether the number is really that high is hard to determine. However, it is a fact that spyware is quite prevalent. One reason is that the software itself is perfectly legal. It may surprise you to learn that spyware is perfectly legal, if used correctly. There are two situations that allow a person to monitor another person's computer usage. The first is parents monitoring minor children. If a child is under the age of 18, it is perfectly legal for the parents to monitor their child's computer activity. In fact, some experts would go so far as to say it is neglectful *not* to monitor a young child on the Internet. Another legal application of computer monitoring is in the workplace. Numerous court cases have upheld an employer's right to monitor computer and Internet usage on company-owned equipment.

Because there are legal applications of "spying" on a person's computer usage, a number of spyware products are easily and cheaply available. Just a few are listed here:

- **Power Spy**—This product can be found at *http://ematrixsoft.com/monitor-children-monitor-kids.php*.

- **Verity**—This product can be found at *http://www.nchsoftware.com/childmonitoring/index.html*.

- **ICU**—This product can be found at *http://www.softpedia.com/get/Security/Security-Related/ICU-Child-Monitoring-Software.shtml*.

- **WorkTime**—This product can be found at *http://www.nestersoft.com/worktime/corporate/employee_monitoring.shtml*.

The only issue for a criminal who wants to misuse this software is how to get it on the target system. In some cases, it is done via a Trojan horse. The victims are tricked into downloading the spyware onto their machines. In other cases, the spyware can be distributed like a virus, infecting various machines. It is also possible to manually put spyware on a machine. This is usually done when the spyware is being placed due to a warrant for a law enforcement agency to monitor a target system, or when a private citizen is legally placing spyware on a system.

Of course, spyware can also be placed on the target's machine by tricking the user into opening an attachment. You may get several e-mails every week that try to lure you into opening some attachment. These have either a virus, spyware, or Trojan horse. You can see one example of such an e-mail in Figure 2-1.

FIGURE 2-1

E-mail attachment.

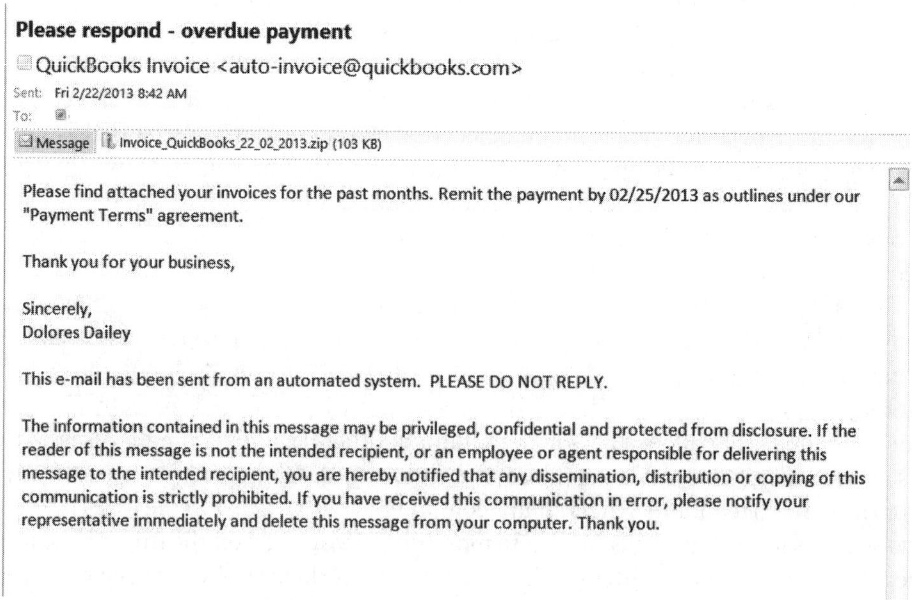

Please respond - overdue payment

QuickBooks Invoice <auto-invoice@quickbooks.com>

Sent: Fri 2/22/2013 8:42 AM

To:

Message | Invoice_QuickBooks_22_02_2013.zip (103 KB)

Please find attached your invoices for the past months. Remit the payment by 02/25/2013 as outlines under our "Payment Terms" agreement.

Thank you for your business,

Sincerely,
Dolores Dailey

This e-mail has been sent from an automated system. PLEASE DO NOT REPLY.

The information contained in this message may be privileged, confidential and protected from disclosure. If the reader of this message is not the intended recipient, or an employee or agent responsible for delivering this message to the intended recipient, you are hereby notified that any dissemination, distribution or copying of this communication is strictly prohibited. If you have received this communication in error, please notify your representative immediately and delete this message from your computer. Thank you.

The e-mail entices the user into clicking on the attachment and downloading it. At that point, some sort of malware is installed on the user's machine.

However, after the software is installed on the victim's computer, it then begins to gather information about that person's Internet and computer activities. For criminals, the most interesting information is usually financial data, bank logons, and so forth.

Discarded Information

Another method that allows a hacker to gather information about a person's identity is discarded information. Any documents that are thrown out without first being shredded could potentially aid an identity thief. This usually doesn't leave much forensic evidence, but it does indicate that the perpetrator is local in order to access the victim's trash, a practice commonly known as dumpster diving.

How Does This Crime Affect Forensics?

If the crime being investigated is identity theft, then the first thing the investigator should be looking for is spyware on the victim's machine. It is very likely that somewhere on the victim's machine is some type of spyware. If spyware exists, the investigator must start searching for where the spyware is sending its data. Yes, spyware collects data on the user's computer and Internet activities, but ultimately that data must be communicated to the criminal. It could be something as simple as a periodic e-mail with an attachment. Or it could be a stream of packets to a server the criminal has access to. Whatever the specific communication mechanism, there absolutely must be some way to get the information from the victim's computer to the attacker—and that will leave some forensic trace.

Another issue the investigator should explore is that of phishing e-mails. It is important to check the e-mail history for the victim's computer as well as the Web history. If a phishing Web site was involved, it is important to gather information about that site.

Hacking

Hacking is a generic term that has different meanings to different people. In the hacking community, it means to experiment with a system, learning its flaws, in order to better understand the system or to fix the flaws. In common speech, it means breaking into a system. This section uses the latter definition. It is certainly possible to break into a system remotely. Attackers can use a number of techniques to do this. The following sections discuss a few of these techniques.

⚠ WARNING

It is important to remember the limits of monitoring employees and minor children. You can monitor employee activities, but only on company systems. Further, the day a child turns 18, he or she is legally an adult and cannot be monitored. It is illegal for you to monitor other adults—even relatives living in your home.

▶ TIP

This is why paper must always be shredded or burned. A criminal could use any documents found in the trash to derive information that helps him or her perpetrate a crime, such as identity theft.

2

Overview of Computer Crime

SQL Injection

SQL injection may be the most common Web attack. It is based on inserting SQL commands into text boxes, often the username and password text fields on the logon screen. To understand how SQL injection works, you have to first understand the basics of how a logon screen is programmed. According to the most recent Verizon Terremark Data Breach Investigations Report, SQL injection was once one of the most common type of Web attack, but has fallen off in recent years thanks to better Web site coding practices. Still, it is remarkable how many sites remain susceptible.

A logon screen requires the user to enter a username and password, and these then have to be validated. Most likely they are validated by checking a database that has a table of users to see if the password matches that user. All modern databases "speak" Structured Query Language (SQL). If the programmer who created the logon is not careful, the Web page may be susceptible to SQL injection. Here is how that attack works. SQL looks a lot like English. For example, to check a username and password, you might want to query the database and see if there is any entry in the users table that matches the username and password that was entered. If there is, then you have a match. The SQL statements in the programming code for the Web site have to use quotation marks to separate the SQL code from the programming code. A typical SQL statement might look something like this:

```
SELECT * FROM tblUsers WHERE USERNAME = '" + txtUsername.Text +'
AND PASSWORD = '" + txtPassword.Text +"' .
```

If you enter username `'thisuser'` and the password `'letmein'`, this code produces the SQL command:

```
SELECT * FROM tblUsers WHERE USERNAME = 'thisuser' AND PASSWORD
 = 'letmein'
```

This is fairly easy to understand even for nonprogrammers. Plus, it is effective. If there is a match in the database, that means the username and password match. If no records are returned from the database, that means there was no match, and this is not a valid logon.

SQL injection is basically about subverting this process. The idea is to create a statement that will always be true. For example, you enter in `'' or '1' = '1'` into the username and password boxes. This causes the program to create this query:

```
SELECT * FROM tblUsers WHERE USERNAME = '' or '1' = '1' AND PASSWORD
 = '' or '1' = '1'.
```

So you are telling the database and application to return all records where username and password are blank or if $1 = 1$. The fact is that 1 always equals 1, so this works. Now if the programmer wrote the logon properly—to ignore or not allow the extra characters— this does not work. But in all too many cases, it does work. And then the intruder has logged on to your Web application and can do whatever any authorized user can do.

SQL injection can be a lot more sophisticated than this section demonstrates. This chapter looks at the simplest implementation of SQL injection. Many other methods are available, including related attacks such as cross-site scripting, in which script—often JavaScript—is put into input boxes so it will be executed on the target Web site.

The example just described is the simplest version of SQL injection. There are more advanced SQL injection techniques. In fact, SQL injection is limited only by your own knowledge of SQL. Obviously, SQL injection attacks can be very sophisticated, involving a complex array of SQL statements, or they can be as simple as the example just discussed.

There are even tools that make the process of executing this attack—or testing your Web site to see if it is vulnerable to this attack—even easier. A few are listed here:

- Several tools at Database Security at *http://www.databasesecurity.com/sqlinjection-tools.htm*
- Sqlmap at *http://sqlmap.org/*
- SQL Ninja at *http://sqlninja.sourceforge.net/*

How Does This Crime Affect Forensics?

Regardless of the sophistication of the SQL injection attack, or the lack thereof, such attacks leave specific forensic evidence. The first place you should look is in the firewall logs. There should be some indication of where the connection came from. Second, search your database logs; some relational database engines log transactions, when they occurred, and what they were. This can be invaluable in your investigation.

Ophcrack

Probably one of the most basic tools for physically accessing a Windows machine is Ophcrack. Ophcrack can be downloaded from *http://ophcrack.sourceforge.net/*. It is a tool to crack the local passwords on Windows systems. It is usually pretty effective. In fact, if an attacker can sit at a Windows machine on your network with an Ophcrack compact disc (CD) for 10 minutes or less, chances are that the attacker is going to get the local passwords. This is a significant problem on corporate networks that meet the following criteria:

- It is usually possible to find an unoccupied desk.
- If physical security is lax, an outsider can get in the building, often as a cleaning or maintenance person or temporary employee.
- Focus is on domain accounts, not local. There is a good chance that the local accounts for one Windows machine are the same throughout. The systems are usually just imaged from a base system.

How does Ophcrack work? First, let's discuss how Windows passwords work. When you choose your local Windows passwords, the password you choose is hashed and stored in the SAM file, which is found in the Windows\System32\ directory. The hash of the password is not the password itself, but it is created from the password using a hashing algorithm that makes two identical hashes for different passwords very unlikely.

To make this work, all you have to do is put the CD into the system and reboot. During the boot-up process, press F12 for a boot menu, then choose Boot from CD. Note that in Figure 2-2, the passwords that Ophcrack found are blocked out. There's a lot to know about hashes and cryptography, but for now you just need to know that a hash is one-way; you don't "unhash" something. When you log on to Windows, the system hashes whatever you type in, and compares it with whatever hash is in the SAM file. If there is an exact match, then you are given access.

In 1980, Martin Hellman described a method to find the value that was hashed. It is really rather simple. He took all the one-character key combinations from a keyboard, put them in one column, and then put the hash of each character in the second column.

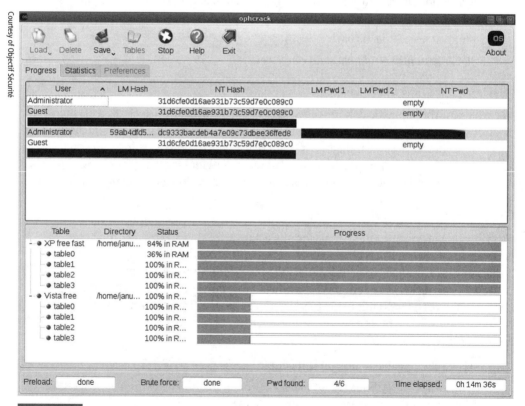

FIGURE 2-2

Ophcrack.

Note: This screenshot was taken from a live machine, so all nonstandard user accounts and all passwords were redacted.

Then he made another table and put all the two-character keyboard combinations in one column, and their hashes in the second column. Then he did the same for three-character combinations, four-character combinations, and so on. So now, you have all the possible hashes of all the possible keyboard combinations. All you have to do is search for the hash that is in the SAM file, and the column matching it will have the password. This is called a **rainbow table** because it contains every conceivable combination of keyboard characters under the rainbow and their associated hashed versions. These tables get huge very fast, so most are no more than 8 to 10 characters in length, which works for most passwords.

The problem is getting the SAM file to start with. When Windows boots up, long before you even get the logon screen, the system locks the SAM file—preventing you from copying or editing it. Well, that is where Ophcrack comes in. It boots to a Linux Live CD and then scans its rainbow table searching for matches. It displays all the passwords it finds in an easy-to-use graphical user interface.

Once the attacker has a valid logon account, particularly an administrator account, he or she can log on to that computer. This doesn't let the attacker join the domain, but he or she now has a foothold in your network. You can see this in Figure 2-2.

How Does This Crime Affect Forensics?

There may or may not be much in the logs for this crime. If the target system is a Windows Server 2003, 2008, or 2012 machine, then the rebooting of the machine will show in the log. If you see a reboot followed by a successful logon with an account like Administrator, it is an indication that a tool like Ophcrack might have been used. Another issue to examine is physical security. If a physical intrusion is suspected, then traditional forensic methods, such as examining security cameras and even fingerprints, become important. Of course, having an account logged on at a time when the actual user who is assigned that account is not present is also a clear sign that a breach of some kind has occurred.

Tricking Tech Support

The following is a simple trick, and one that is a follow-up to using Ophcrack to break local accounts. After the attacker has gained access to a local account, he or she will really want to get domain admin privileges. The command `net user` can help do this. First, the attacker writes the following two-line script:

```
net user /domain /add localaccountname password
net group /domain "Domain Admins" /add localaccount
```

The attacker then saves that script in the All Users startup folder. The next step is to get a domain admin to log on to this machine. If that happens, the script runs—in the background and not visible—and your local account is now a domain admin. But how do you get a domain administrator to log on? Well, it just so happens that in many organizations, the tech support personnel are in the domain admin group. So the attacker merely needs to do something to render the machine not fully operational. When a tech support person logs on to fix that problem, the script is run.

How Does This Crime Affect Forensics?

Searching the system for any unrecognized scripts, particularly in any startup folders, is a good first step if you suspect a physical breach. Of course, the usage of the compromised account also yields clues. If the network admin account shows as having been used at a time when the network administrator was away, this suggests the account has been compromised. And, as with Ophcrack, physical security is an issue in this crime; therefore, investigating physical breaches of the premises is important.

Hacking in General

Entire books have been written on hacking techniques, and entire certification courses, such as the EC Council Certified Ethical Hacker, focus on such skills. The purpose here is to introduce you to some techniques that an attacker might use. To go into all the common hacking techniques attackers use is beyond the scope of this text. However, this section illustrates an important point: Computer crime investigators should have a strong working knowledge of hacking techniques. Your forensic investigations will be drastically improved if you have an understanding of the techniques that attackers use.

Cyberstalking and Harassment

Cyberstalking, cyberbullying, and online harassment are getting increasing attention in the media. As society becomes ever more wired, conduct online becomes more important. With many people using social media to interact with others, dating sites to find that special someone, and online discussion boards to talk, inappropriate behavior online becomes more noticeable. Some would say that bad behavior is becoming more common online. People feel more comfortable ranting at a faceless name on a screen than at a real person. But where does rudeness cross the line into stalking or harassment? Surely not every rude word on the Internet constitutes a crime.

Cyberstalking or harassment is using electronic communications to harass or threaten another person. The U.S. Department of Justice puts it this way:

> Although there is no universally accepted definition of cyber stalking, the term is used in this report to refer to the use of the Internet, e-mail, or other electronic communications devices to stalk another person. Stalking generally involves harassing or threatening behavior that an individual engages in repeatedly, such as following a person, appearing at a person's home or place of business, making harassing phone calls, leaving written messages or objects, or vandalizing a person's property. Most stalking laws require that the perpetrator make a credible threat of violence against the victim; others include threats against the victim's immediate family; and still others require only that the alleged stalker's course of conduct constitute an implied threat. While some conduct involving annoying or menacing behavior might fall short of illegal stalking, such behavior may be a prelude to stalking and violence and should be treated seriously.

Now even after reading this description, you may still not know where the line between bad behavior and criminal behavior lies. Here are three criteria for law enforcement officers to bear in mind when considering cyberstalking and harassment cases. All three aren't necessarily essential to create a case of cyberstalking or harassment, but all three must be considered:

- **Is it possible?**—If a person makes a threat, is that threat credible? To illustrate this question, consider two extremes. In the first scenario, you are playing a game online and another player, who lives in a different country, tells you he is so mad at you he is going to punch you in the nose. Given that you are probably not even using your real name, and this person is thousands of miles away, this is not a credible threat. On the other extreme, consider a scenario in which you receive an e-mail threatening to kill you, but attached to the e-mail is a recent photo of you leaving the front door of your home. That is clearly alarming and indicates the sender has the means and intent to commit harm.

- **How frequent?**—Notice that the U.S. Department of Justice uses the term "repeatedly." People get angry and say things they later regret. Someone saying something rude and even violent, one time, is not necessarily stalking. Reasonable people calm down and regret the harsh words they said, and then they don't repeat them. Repeated behavior is a pattern, not a mistake.

- **How serious?**—Again, reasonable people can lose their temper and say things they don't mean. Many people have at some point uttered the words "I could kill ..." But they don't act on them. However, reasonable people do make vague statements in anger that they later regret and are embarrassed about. Specific and serious threats are more disconcerting. Someone saying, "I could just kill him" may be cause for concern, or may just be blowing off steam. Someone who makes such a statement and then goes on to detail just how he would go about killing the person, indicates he has put thought into this, and should be taken seriously as a threat.

Again, not all of these need to be present in order to constitute cyberstalking or harassment. However, all three need to be considered. Clearly, some people do make false reports to the police. Other people overreact to benign comments. On the other hand, cyberstalking can lead to real-world violent crimes.

Real Cyberstalking Cases

The following six cases should give you a good overview of cyberstalking. Examining the facts in these cases might help you to get an idea of what legally constitutes cyberstalking.

1. Seventy-year-old Joseph Medico met a 16-year-old girl at church. The girl was at the church volunteering, helping to prepare donations for homeless shelters. Mr. Medico followed the girl to her car and tried to talk her into going to dinner with him, and then back to his home. When she spurned his advances, he began calling and texting her several times a day.

When she realized he was not going to stop, she called the police. Mr. Medico was arrested and charged with stalking. This case illustrates how easy it is for an unstable person to become obsessed with the victim. It also demonstrates the proper way to handle this sort of situation. This is definitely a case to report to the police. An adult who is making overtures like this to a minor is a matter of grave concern.

2. In the first successful prosecution under California's cyberstalking law, prosecutors in the Los Angeles District Attorney's Office prosecuted a 50-year-old former security guard who used the Internet to solicit the rape of a woman who rejected his advances. The defendant terrorized his 28-year-old victim by impersonating her in various Internet chat rooms and on online bulletin boards, where he posted, along with her telephone number and address, messages that she fantasized about being raped. On at least six occasions, sometimes in the middle of the night, men knocked on the woman's door saying they wanted to rape her. The former security guard pled guilty in April 1999 to one count of stalking and three counts of solicitation of sexual assault.

3. A local prosecutor's office in Massachusetts charged a man who, using anonymous remailers, allegedly engaged in a systematic pattern of harassment of a coworker, which culminated in an attempt to extort sexual favors from the victim under threat of disclosing past sexual activities to the victim's new husband. (A *remailer* is an anonymous server that resends e-mails so they cannot be traced back to the original sender.)

4. An honors graduate from the University of San Diego terrorized five female university students over the Internet for more than a year. The victims received hundreds of violent and threatening e-mails, sometimes receiving four or five messages a day. The graduate student, who entered a guilty plea and faced up to six years in prison, told police he committed the crimes because he thought the women were laughing at him and causing others to ridicule him. In fact, the victims had never met him.

5. In England, Jason Smith continually harassed college student Alexandra Scarlett. He sent her as many as 30 messages a day threatening to slash her face, sexually assault her mother, or shoot her father. He was convicted and given a 12-month suspended sentence and a restraining order. However, within a week of this conviction, he used social networking sites to track down Ms. Scarlett and continue the campaign of harassment. Media in Britain have dubbed Mr. Smith "England's Most Obsessive Stalker." This case is also an example of stalking in response to unrequited romantic feelings. Mr. Smith had met Ms. Scarlett at a nightclub. She had given him her phone number. He then became convinced that they were in love and that they must be together. This led him to extreme jealousy, and eventually to the obsessive stalking.

6. Robert James Murphy was the first person charged under U.S. federal law for cyberstalking. He was accused of violating Title 47 of U.S. Code 223, which prohibits the use of telecommunications to annoy, abuse, threaten, or harass anyone. Mr. Murphy was accused of sending sexually explicit messages and photographs to his ex-girlfriend. This activity continued for a period of years. Mr. Murphy was charged and eventually pled guilty to two counts of cyberstalking.

How Does This Crime Affect Forensics?

Cyberstalking and harassment is an interesting computer crime in that the computer is simply incidental. The intent of the crime is to target the human victim; the computer is just a vehicle. Fortunately, stalkers are often not the most technically savvy computer criminals. In stalking cases, you should begin with tracing e-mails and text messages. In many cases, they come directly from the perpetrator with little or no attempt to obfuscate the crime. Of course, if a suspect is arrested, any electronic devices in his or her possession should be examined for evidence. Stalking, by definition, indicates obsessive behavior. This means there is likely to be some evidence retained by the criminal.

Fraud

Fraud is a broad category of crime that can encompass many different activities. Essentially, any attempt to gain financial reward through deception is fraud. Two major subclasses of fraud are as follows:

* Investment offers
* Data piracy

The following sections briefly examine these classes of computer fraud.

Investment Offers

Investment offers are neither new nor necessarily illegal. In fact, cold-calling is a legitimate sales technique when selling stocks. However, the process can be used to artificially and fraudulently inflate the value of a target stock. The most common version of this is called the "pump and dump." In this scheme, the perpetrators buy significant amounts of stock in a company that is relatively cheap, often penny stocks. Then, they fuel false rumors that the company is on the verge of some large contract or other business deal that would increase its value significantly. This artificially drives up the price of the stock. Once the rumors have raised the stock as high as the criminals think it will go, they dump their stock at an inflated price, thus making substantial profits. Eventually, once it is clear the rumors were not true, the stock's value will drop again. The people who purchased the stock at an inflated price, but were not in on the scam and did not know to sell their stock before its value plummeted, lose significant amounts of money.

The growth of the Internet did not create these scams—the Internet simply made them easier to perpetrate. For example, with the pump and dump, the Internet allows the perpetrator to create fake blogs, bulletin board postings, and e-mails, all claiming the target stock is likely to rise in value. The key to Internet-based fraud of this kind is, instead of cold-calling via the phone, to send an enticing e-mail to as many recipients as possible. Of course, the perpetrator realizes that most people will not respond to the e-mail, but if even a tiny percentage do, and the perpetrator sends out a million e-mails, he or she can still pull in a significant amount of money.

One of the more common Internet schemes involves sending out an e-mail that suggests that you can make a large sum of money with a very minimal investment. It may be a processing fee you must submit in order to receive some lottery winnings, or perhaps legal fees in order to receive some inheritance. Perhaps the most famous of these schemes has been the Nigerian fraud. In this scenario, an e-mail is sent to a large number of random e-mail addresses. Each e-mail contains a message purporting to be from a relative of some deceased Nigerian doctor or government official, always of significant social standing. (It's more likely to convince victims that the arrangement is legitimate if it seems to involve people of good social standing.) The offer goes like this: A person has a sum of money he or she wants to transfer out of his country, and he or she cannot use normal channels. He or she wants to use your bank account to "park" the funds temporarily. If you allow the person access to your account, you will receive a hefty fee. If you do agree to this arrangement, you will receive, via normal mail, a variety of very official-looking documents—enough to convince most casual observers that the arrangement is legitimate. You will then be asked to advance some money to cover items such as taxes and wire fees. Should you actually send any money, however, you will lose it, and you will never hear from these individuals again. The U.S. FBI has issued a bulletin detailing this particular fraud scheme. Further FBI Internet crime information is available at *http://www.fbi.gov/scams-safety/fraud/internet_fraud*.

How Does This Crime Affect Forensics?

The key in this sort of crime is to begin by tracing the communications. If it is a fake blog that is endorsing some investment, then someone had to register the domain for that blog. If there are e-mails involved, they had to come from somewhere. Of course, the more sophisticated the attacker, the less evidence there will be. Another way to seek evidence outside computer forensics is to follow the money. Someone is reaping financial rewards from the scheme.

Data Piracy

Intellectual property is a very real commodity. Large companies spend millions of dollars on filing patents and defending their patents and copyrights. The Internet makes distribution of illegally copied materials, or data piracy, very easy. You are probably quite familiar with illegal music downloads; however, that is only one aspect of intellectual property theft.

Illegal copies of software can be found on the Internet. There are Web sites that have such copies or the activation codes for software. These sites are colloquially referred to as warez (pronounced like wares) sites. As a consumer, the best advice to follow is "If it seems too good to be true, it is probably not true." In other words, if a Web site boasts of a $400 software package for $89, that is probably illegally copied software.

How Does This Crime Affect Forensics?

The investigation of this sort of crime involves trying to trace the owners of the Web site that is distributing the intellectual property. This involves finding out who registered the domain and performing a Whois search on that domain. If the perpetrator is clever, he or she will hide behind several identities. However, the starting point is to track the Web site distributing the intellectual property.

> ▶ **NOTE**
>
> Data piracy is frequently addressed via civil court rather than criminal. It is often a better option for the victim to sue the perpetrator rather than press criminal charges. This is one reason forensics is no longer just a law enforcement activity. There are myriad civilian reasons to utilize forensics.

Non-Access Computer Crimes

Non-access computer crimes are crimes that do not involve an attempt to actually access the target. For example, a virus or logic bomb does not require the attacker to attempt to hack into the target network. And denial of service attacks are designed to render the target unreachable by legitimate users, not to provide the attacker access to the site.

Denial of Service

A **denial of service (DoS) attack** is an attempt to prevent legitimate users from being able to access a given computer resource. The most common target is a Web site. Although there are a number of methods for executing this type of attack, they all come down to the simple fact that every technology can handle only a finite load. If you overload the capacity of a given technology, it ceases to function properly. A Web site, if you flood it with fake connections, becomes overloaded and unable to respond to legitimate connection attempts. This is a classic example of a denial of service attack. Although these attacks may not directly compromise data or seek to steal personal information, they can certainly cause serious economic damages. Imagine the cost incurred if a denial of service attack were to take eBay offline for a period of time!

Denial of service attacks are the cyber equivalent of vandalism. Rather than seek to break into the target system, the perpetrator simply wants to render the target system unusable. These attacks require minimal skill. For example, consider one of the most basic DoS attacks, called a SYN flood. This simple attack takes advantage of how connections to Web sites are established. So, first, let's take a look at how that works.

The client machine sends a Transmission Control Protocol (TCP) packet to the server with a synchronize flag turned on—it is a single bit that is turned to a 1. Because this is synchronizing, or starting the connection, it is called a SYN flag.

FIGURE 2-3

Low Orbit Ion Cannon.

The server sets aside enough resources to handle the connection and sends back a TCP packet with two flags turned on: the acknowledgment flag (ACK) and the synchronize (SYN) flag. Essentially, this is acknowledging the request to synchronize. The client is supposed to respond with a single ACK flag to allow communications to begin. This is called the **three-way handshake**.

In the SYN flood attack, the attacker keeps sending SYN packets but never responds to the SYN/ACK packets it receives from the server. Eventually, the server has opened up a number of connections for a client that never fully connects and can no longer respond to legitimate users.

In addition to various DoS attack types, there are tools that can be used to create a denial of service attack. One of the most easy to use is the Low Orbit Ion Cannon, shown in Figure 2-3.

This tool is freely available on the Internet and terribly easy to use. The prevalence of such easy-to-use tools is one reason why denial of service attacks are so common.

The Tribal Flood Network (TFN) is probably the most widely used distributed denial of service tool. There is a newer version of it called TFN2K. The new version sends decoy information to make tracing more difficult. Both the original and new version work by configuring the software to attack a particular target, and then getting the target on a specific machine. Usually, the attacker seeks to infect several machines with the TFN program in order to form a Tribal Flood Network. This variation is called a **distributed denial of service (DDoS) attack**.

You can get more details about TFN and TFN2K at these Web sites:

- Washington University at *http://staff.washington.edu/dittrich/misc/tfn.analysis.txt*
- Packetstorm Security at *http://packetstormsecurity.com/distributed/ TFN2k_Analysis-1.3.txt*
- The Computer Emergency Response Team (CERT) at *http://www.cert.org/advisories/ CA-1999-17.html*

Trin00 is another popular DoS tool. It was originally available only for UNIX but is now available for Windows as well. It is an alternative to TFN. One common technique attackers use is to send the Trin00 client to machines via a Trojan horse. Then, the infected machines can all be used to launch a coordinated attack on the target system.

Another type of DoS attack that has become more prevalent in recent years is the telephony denial of service (TDoS) attack. A TDoS attack is possible, and certainly has been documented, with traditional telephone systems by using an automatic dialer to tie up target phone lines. TDoS is flourishing, however, with the wide availability of Voice over IP tools that make automated TDoS attacks against traditional and IP-based VoIP very easy to carry out. The way that a TDoS attack works is that a call center or business receives so many inbound calls that the equipment and staff are overwhelmed and unable to do business. A call to a supervisor or manager demands a certain amount of money be sent or a certain eradication service be purchased to stop the attacks.

How Does This Crime Affect Forensics?

When investigating denial of service attacks launched from a single machine, the obvious task is to trace the packets coming from that machine. It is common for attackers to spoof some other IP address, but not as common for them to spoof a MAC address, which is related to the underlying hardware. If the attacker is not savvy enough to spoof the MAC address, then each packet contains evidence of the actual machine that it was launched from.

In distributed denial of service attacks, the packets come from a multitude of machines. Usually, the owners of these machines are unaware that their machines are being used in this way. However, that does not mean the investigation is at a dead end. You can still trace back the packets and get a group of infected machines. You can then seek out commonalities on those machines. Did they all download the same free game from the Internet or frequent the same Web site? Anything that all infected machines have in common is a candidate for where the machines got the software that launched the distributed denial of service attack.

Viruses

Viruses are a major problem in modern computer systems. A **virus** is any software that self-replicates, like a human or animal virus. It is common for viruses to also wreak havoc on infected machines, but the self-replication is the defining characteristic of a virus. Before discussing the forensics of viruses, it is a good idea to consider some recent viruses:

- **FakeAV86**—This is a fake antivirus. It purports to be a free antivirus scanner, but is really itself a virus. This virus first appeared in July 2012. It affected Windows systems ranging from Windows 95 to Windows 7 and Windows Server 2003. This is not the only fake antivirus to have been found, but it is a widespread one.

- **Flame**—No modern discussion of viruses would be complete without a discussion of Flame, a virus that targeted Windows operating systems. The first item that makes this virus notable is that it was specifically designed for espionage. It was first discovered in May 2012 at several locations, including Iranian government sites. Flame is spyware that can monitor network traffic and take screenshots of the infected system. This malware stores data in a local database that is heavily encrypted. Flame is also able to change its behavior based on the specific antivirus running on the target machine. This indicates that this malware is highly sophisticated. Also of note is that Flame is signed with a fraudulent Microsoft certificate. This means that Windows systems would trust the software.

These two viruses give you some idea of the impact a virus can have on an organization's network. Viruses range from terribly annoying, like FakeAV, to sophisticated mechanisms for espionage, like Flame.

How Does This Crime Affect Forensics?

Viruses are remarkably easy to locate, but difficult to trace back to the creator. The first step is to document the particulars of the virus—for example, its behavior, the file characteristics, and so on. Then, you must see if there is some commonality among infected computers. For example, if all infected computers visited the same Web site, then it is likely that the Web site itself is infected. In addition, numerous sources of information about known viruses are available on the Internet from software publishers and virus researchers, which is very useful in doing forensic research.

It is a slow and tedious process, but it is possible to track down the creator of a virus.

Logic Bombs

A **logic bomb** is malware that is designed to do harm to the system when some logical condition is reached. Often it is triggered based on a specific date and time. It is certainly possible to distribute a logic bomb via a Trojan horse, but this sort of attack is often perpetrated by employees. The following two cases illustrate this fact:

- In June 1992, Michael Lauffenburger, an employee of defense contractor General Dynamics, was arrested for inserting a logic bomb that would delete vital rocket project data. Another employee of General Dynamics found the bomb before it was triggered. Lauffenburger was charged with computer tampering and attempted fraud and faced potential fines of $500,000 and jail time, but was actually fined only $5,000.

- In June 2006, Roger Duronio, a system administrator for the Swiss bank UBS, was charged with using a logic bomb to damage the company's computer network. His plan was to drive the company stock down due to damage from the logic bomb; thus, he was charged with securities fraud. Duronio was later convicted and sentenced to 8 years and 1 month in prison, as well as $3.1 million in restitution to UBS.

How Does This Crime Affect Forensics?

Logic bombs that are created by disgruntled employees are actually reasonably straightforward to investigate. First, the nature of the logic bomb gives some indication of the creator. It has to be someone with access to the system and with a programming background. Then, traditional issues such as motive are also helpful in investigating a logic bomb. If the logic bomb is distributed randomly via a Trojan horse, then investigating it follows the same parameters as investigating a virus.

Cyberterrorism

You cannot discuss cybercrime without having some discussion of cyberterrorism. Just a few years ago, the idea of cyberterrorism seemed completely hypothetical, perhaps even a bit sensationalist. Now, however, cyberterrorism is seen by many to surpass terrorism as a threat. There are definite reasons to take it seriously:

- In 2008 and 2009, there were several reports of attacks that were traced back to North Korea or China. Given that both nations are totalitarian regimes with very strict control on their populace, it is difficult to believe that the governments of those countries were not at least aware of those attacks.

- In December of 2009, hackers broke into computer systems and stole secret defense plans of the United States and South Korea. The information stolen included a summary of plans for military operations by South Korean and U.S. troops in case of war with North Korea, though the attacks were traced back to a Chinese IP address.

- In March 2013, a cadre of the United States' top intelligence officials told Congress that cyberattacks led the numerous national security threats the United States faces. It is the first time since the September 11, 2001, terrorist attacks that anything other than an extremist physical threat has been the top concern in the Intelligence Community Worldwide Threat Assessment, which is presented annually to the Senate Select Committee on Intelligence. James Clapper, director of national intelligence, told the panel that cyber and financial threats were being added "to the list of weapons being used against us." They help define a new "soft" kind of war.

These cases clearly illustrate that cyberterrorism and cyberespionage are real threats that need to be examined and dealt with.

A critical topic in cyberterrorism is the subject of the China Eagle Union. This group consists of several thousand Chinese hackers whose stated goal is to infiltrate Western computer systems. There are a number of Web resources regarding this group:

- *http://www.thedarkvisitor.com/2007/10/china-eagle-union/*
- *https://news.hitb.org/node/6164*
- *http://archives.cnn.com/2001/WORLD/asiapcf/east/04/27/china.hackers/index.html*

Members and leaders of the group insist that not only does the Chinese government have no involvement in their activities, but that they are breaking Chinese law and are in constant danger of arrest and imprisonment. However, most analysts believe this group is working with the full knowledge and support of the Chinese government. Throughout the first quarter of 2013, accusations of cyberattacks were leveled by both the United States and Chinese governments.

 NOTE

Even at the time of this writing, the news was filled with more stories of the United States and China accusing each other of cyberespionage and warfare. It is clear that there is now a significant cyber component to any international conflict. This makes computer security an issue of national security.

How Does This Crime Affect Forensics?

Because cyberterrorism and cyberespionage use the same techniques as any other cybercrime, the actual technical portions of the investigation are the same. If it is a virus or denial of service attack, you investigate it as you would any virus or denial of service attack. However, the difference lies in the jurisdiction for the crime itself. Issues of cyberterrorism and cyberespionage are referred to the Federal Bureau of Investigation.

CHAPTER SUMMARY

This chapter examined various ways in which the nature of a computer crime can affect the process of forensically investigating the crime. It is imperative that you be aware of the different crimes and how to investigate them. For example, seeking e-mail evidence would be useful for investigating cyberstalking, but would not be useful for most denial of service attacks. It is important that forensic investigators have a working knowledge of how these attacks are committed in order to properly investigate them.

KEY CONCEPTS AND TERMS

Cyberstalking	Fraud	Three-way handshake
Denial of service (DoS) attack	Identity theft	Virus
Distributed denial of service (DDoS) attack	Logic bomb	
	Rainbow table	

CHAPTER 2 ASSESSMENT

1. When investigating a virus, what is the first step?

   A. Check firewall logs.

   B. Check IDS logs.

   C. Document the virus.

   D. Trace the origin of the virus.

2. Which of the following crimes is most likely to leave e-mail evidence?

   A. Cyberstalking

   B. DoS

   C. Logic bomb

   D. Fraud

3. Where would you seek evidence that Ophcrack had been used on a Windows Server 2008 machine?

   A. In the logs of the server; look for the reboot of the system

   B. In the logs of the server; look for the loading of a CD

   C. In the firewall logs

   D. In the IDS logs

4. Logic bombs are often perpetrated by _____.

   A. Identity thieves

   B. Disgruntled employees

   C. Terrorists

   D. Hackers

5. Spyware is legal.

   A. True

   B. False

6. It is legal for employers to monitor work computers.

   A. True

   B. False

7. What is the primary reason to take cyberstalking seriously?

   A. It can damage your system.

   B. It can be annoying and distracting.

   C. It can be a prelude to real-world violence.

   D. It can be part of identity theft.

8. What is the starting point for investigating denial of service attacks?

   A. Firewall logs

   B. E-mail headers

   C. System logs

   D. Tracing the packets

Forensic Methods and Labs

I N THIS CHAPTER, you will learn some specific approaches to forensic investigation. These methodologies provide a framework for your investigations. You will also learn the requirements for setting up a computer forensics lab. Finally, you will get a brief introduction to major computer forensics software.

Chapter 3 Topics

This chapter covers the following topics and concepts:

- What the methodologies used in forensic investigations are
- What the formal forensic approaches are
- What the proper documentation of methodologies and findings is
- What evidence-handling tasks are
- How to set up a forensic lab
- What the common forensic software programs are
- What the common forensic certifications are

Chapter 3 Goals

When you complete this chapter, you will be able to:

- Understand major forensic methodologies
- Set up a computer forensics lab
- Demonstrate an understanding of major forensic software

Forensic Methodologies

You will learn very specific techniques for computer forensics; however, it is important that you have a general framework for approaching forensics. This section examines general principles and specific methodologies you can apply to your own forensic investigations. First, here are some basic principles to consider.

Handle Original Data as Little as Possible

A forensic specialist should touch the original data as little as possible. Instead, information should be copied prior to examination. This means that the first step in any investigation is to make a copy of the suspected storage device. In the case of computer hard drives, you make a complete copy. That means a bit-level copy. Tools like EnCase and Forensic Toolkit will do this for you; it is also possible to do this with basic Linux commands. In addition, it is a common practice to make two copies of the drive. This gives you one to work with and a backup in the event you need it.

The idea of handling original information as little as possible is a critical philosophy that should permeate your approach to forensics. But the real question is, why? Why is it so important that you not touch the actual original evidence any more than you have to? The first answer to that question is that each time you touch digital information, there is some chance of altering it. Even such a simple thing as changing the time/date stamp on a file is altering it. And if you alter the file, you cannot be certain that the evidence you find is valid.

Another reason is that there may be a need for another investigator to do his or her own examination. If you have worked with the original information, you may have altered it so that another person cannot now do a fresh analysis. There are many situations in which another examiner will need to review the original information. The most obvious situation is when the opposing counsel hires his or her own expert who wants to do his or her own examination.

Comply with the Rules of Evidence

During an investigation, a forensic specialist should keep in mind the relevant rules of evidence. The chain of custody and the Daubert standard, for instance, are just two of these that you must follow.

Rules of evidence govern whether, when, how, and why proof of a legal case can be placed before a judge or jury. A forensic specialist should have a good understanding of the rules of evidence in the given type of court and jurisdiction.

As one example, the Federal Rules of Evidence (FRE) is a code of evidence law. The FRE governs the admission of facts by which parties in the U.S. federal court system may prove their cases. The FRE provides guidelines for the authentication and identification of evidence for admissibility under rules 901 and 902. The following is an excerpt from rule 901 of the FRE from Cornell University Law School (2011) with the portions relevant to computer forensics shown:

(a) In General. To satisfy the requirement of authenticating or identifying an item of evidence, the proponent must produce evidence sufficient to support a finding that the item is what the proponent claims it is....

> **(1) Testimony of a Witness with Knowledge.** Testimony that an item is what it is claimed to be....

> **(3) Comparison by an Expert Witness or the Trier of Fact.** A comparison with an authenticated specimen by an expert witness or the trier of fact....

> **(9) Evidence About a Process or System.** Evidence describing a process or system and showing that it produces an accurate result.

Item 1 refers to expert testimony. You as a forensic examiner may be called upon to authenticate evidence. Item 3 refers to a comparison between a given specimen and another item. This can be used to authenticate evidence. Item 9 is critical for computer forensics. Even if you use automated tools such as EnCase from Guidance Software or Forensic Toolkit from AccessData, you should understand how the tools work in detail so you can authenticate the process if need be.

Individual jurisdictions may have some additional rules particular to that jurisdiction. It is critical that you be aware of the rules in your jurisdiction as well as general rules of evidence.

Avoid Exceeding Your Knowledge

A forensic specialist should not undertake an examination that is beyond his or her current level of knowledge and skill. This might seem obvious, but it is a problem that you can observe not just in forensics, but in the IT industry in general. Most other professions are more than happy to refer a client to a specialist. For example, if you see your family doctor and she discovers an anomaly regarding your heart, she will refer you to a cardiologist. Certainly she studied cardiology in medical school, but she will still send you to someone who specializes in cardiology. However, IT professionals all too often believe that if they have a little knowledge, that is enough to proceed.

FYI

In the field of forensics, your reputation is the most important thing you have. If you overextend beyond your actual skills, it is likely to come out at trial. The opposing side might have experts advising them. And when the other side's attorney cross-examines you and your lack of knowledge becomes apparent, your reputation will be damaged. Consider adopting this standard: Never testify or write an expert report unless you are very sure of your expertise in the relevant technologies and very comfortable with the conclusions you are presenting. Even one occasion of being found to have been exaggerating, fabricating, or overextending yourself during testimony can ruin your reputation and your career.

This can be very problematic in forensics. Suppose you are a very skilled forensic examiner, and you have extensive experience with Microsoft Windows and Linux. But a computer is brought to you that runs Mac OS X. Now it is very likely that your skills would allow you to extract data. And it is true that OS X is based on a Linux-like system (FreeBSD). But is that enough? Very likely it is not. It is very likely that if you insist on doing the investigation yourself, you may miss key evidence or, at the very least, the opposition's attorney can claim in court that you have.

These basic principles should guide your forensic investigation. These are not specific procedures, but rather general philosophical approaches to investigation.

Create an Analysis Plan

Before you begin any forensic examination, you should have an analysis plan. This plan is a guide for your work. How will you gather evidence? Are there concerns about evidence being changed or destroyed? What tools are most appropriate for this specific investigation? Is this a federal or state case? Will this affect admissibility rules? You should address all of these issues in your data analysis plan. It is advisable to have a standard data analysis plan that you simply customize for specific situations.

Creating an Order of Volatility

Much of the evidence on a system does not last very long. Some evidence resides in storage that requires a consistent power supply. *Volatility* refers to how easy it is for data to change. Registers are very volatile, whereas a CD-ROM is not. Other evidence might sit in media locations that are continuously changing. You must start with collecting the most volatile evidence and proceed to the least volatile. To determine what evidence to collect first, draw up an order of volatility—a list of evidence sources ordered by their relative volatility. The following is an example of an order of volatility:

1. Registers and cache
2. Routing tables
3. ARP cache
4. Process table
5. Kernel statistics and modules
6. Main memory
7. Temporary file systems
8. Secondary memory
9. Router configuration
10. Network topology

Technical Information Collection Considerations

System forensics specialists must keep in mind three main technical data collection considerations. These are understanding the life span of information, collecting information quickly, and collecting bit-level information.

Considering the Life Span of Information

In planning collection efforts, a forensic specialist must be aware that information has a life span. **Life span** refers to how long information is valid. The term is related to volatility. More volatile information tends to have a shorter life span. The nature of the information as well as organizational policies and practices determine the information's life span. For example, data regarding network traffic and the messages themselves may exist only for the time the transmission is passing through a router. This may be only milliseconds. Information stored in computer memory may have a life span of a millisecond.

As information life spans increase, the life span determinant is typically related to organizational practice. For example, an organization may establish a policy that an e-mail message may be stored within the e-mail system for only 30 days. After 30 days, any message that is not moved to alternate storage is deleted. Log files may be retained for months or years, in accordance with an organization's audit policy. Finance and accounting information may have a multiple-year life span that corresponds with requirements established by state or federal governments.

In planning a collection effort, forensic specialists must be aware of the life span of the information with which they are working. They must use collection techniques appropriate to the information's life span.

Collecting Information Quickly

Once the collection effort is announced or in process, it is important to collect the evidence as quickly as possible. It is frequently not possible or practical to determine who made a change or when. In addition, the target of an investigation may try to conceal information, which further obscures changes. Networking systems also increase the potential for unauthorized changes. The person making a change on a network does not have to be local to the device on which the information is stored.

Collecting Bit-Level Information

To be useful, 1 and 0 bits must be converted through hardware and software into text, pictures, screen displays, videos, audio, or other usable formats. Investigators also look for whether unrelated bits were inserted, such as trade secrets buried within other files. Forensic specialists must therefore have tools that allow manipulation and evaluation of bit-level information. Use of bit-level tools also enables an investigator to reconstruct file fragments if files have been deleted or overwritten.

Basically, **bit-level information** is information at the level of actual 1s and 0s stored in memory or on the storage device, as opposed to going through the file system's interpretation. Whatever operating system is being used simply shows its representation of the data. Going to a bit-level view gives the most accurate view of how the information is actually stored on the hardware. If you use the file system to copy a suspect drive, you probably won't get slack space or hidden partitions. But you will get those items with a bit-level copy.

Formal Forensic Approaches

Several organizations have established formal guidelines for approaching a forensic investigation. You should become familiar with these guidelines. Depending on your work environment, you might implement one of these or use one of these as a base and adjust it to your own plan.

DoD Forensic Standards

The U.S. Department of Defense (DoD) coordinates and supervises agencies and functions of the government related to national security and the U.S. armed forces. The DoD uses system forensics to evaluate and examine data related to cyberattacks. The DoD estimates the potential impact of malicious activity. It also assesses the intent and identity of perpetrators. The DoD Cyber Crime Center (DC3) sets standards for digital evidence processing, analysis, and diagnostics. It is involved with DoD investigations that require computer forensics support to detect, enhance, or recover digital media. DC3 is also involved in criminal law enforcement forensics and counterintelligence. It assists in criminal, counterintelligence, counterterrorism, and fraud investigations. In addition, it supports safety investigations, commander-directed inquiries, and inspector-general investigations.

DC3 provides computer investigation training. It trains forensic examiners, investigators, system administrators, and others. It also ensures that defense information systems are secure from unauthorized use, criminal and fraudulent activities, and foreign intelligence service exploitation. DC3 partners with government, academic, and private industry computer security officials.

For more information on DC3, see *http://www.dc3.mil*.

The DFRWS Framework

The Digital Forensic Research Workshop (DFRWS) is a nonprofit volunteer organization. Its goal is to enhance the sharing of knowledge and ideas about digital forensics research.

DFRWS sponsors annual conferences, technical working groups, and challenges to help drive the direction of research and development. In 2001, the DFRWS developed a framework for digital investigation that is still useful. The DFRWS framework is a matrix with six classes:

- Identification
- Preservation
- Collection
- Examination
- Analysis
- Presentation

An Event-Based Digital Forensics Investigation Framework

In 2004, Brian Carrier and Eugene Spafford, researchers at the Center for Education and Research in Information Assurance and Security (CERIAS) at Purdue University, proposed a model that is more intuitive and flexible than the DFRWS framework.

This model has five primary phases, each of which may contain additional subphases. The primary phases are the Readiness phase, the Deployment phase, the Physical Crime Scene Investigation phase, the Digital Crime Scene Investigation phase, and the Presentation phase. The Readiness phase contains the Operations Readiness subphase, which involves training people and testing investigation tools, and the Infrastructure Readiness subphase, which involves configuring the equipment. The Deployment phase includes the Detection and Notification subphase, in which someone detects an incident and alerts investigators, and the Confirmation and Authorization subphase, in which investigators receive authorization to conduct the investigation.

Documentation of Methodologies and Findings

Documentation of forensic processing methodologies and findings is critical. Without proper documentation, a forensic specialist has difficulty presenting findings. When security or audit findings become the object of a lawsuit or a criminal investigation, the legal system requires proper documentation. Without documentation, courts are unlikely to accept investigative results. Thus, a system forensics specialist must know the ins and outs of computer evidence processing methodology. This methodology includes strong evidence-processing documentation and good chain-of-custody procedures.

Disk Structure

A system forensics specialist should have a good understanding of how computer hard disks and compact discs (CDs) are structured. A specialist should also know how to find data hidden in obscure places on CDs and hard disk drives.

File Slack Searching

A system forensics specialist should understand techniques and automated tools used to capture and evaluate file slack. A hard disk or CD is segmented into clusters of a particular size. Each cluster can hold only a single file or part of a single file. If you write a 1-kilobyte (KB) file to a disk that has a cluster size of 4 KB, the last 3 KB of the cluster are wasted. This unused space between the logical end of file and the physical end of file is known as **file slack** or **slack space**.

Most computer users have no idea that they're creating slack space as they use a computer. In addition, pieces of a file may remain even after you delete it. This residual information in file slack is not necessarily overwritten when you create a new file. File slack is therefore a source of potential security leaks involving passwords, network logons, e-mail, database entries, images, and word processing documents. A forensic specialist should know how to search file slack, identify what is and is not useful information, and document any findings.

Evidence-Handling Tasks

A system forensics specialist has three basic tasks related to handling evidence:

- **Find evidence**—Gathering computer evidence goes beyond normal data recovery. Finding and isolating evidence to prove or disprove allegations can be difficult. Investigators may need to investigate thousands of active files and fragments of deleted files to find just one that makes a case. System forensics has therefore been described as looking for one needle in a mountain of needles. Examiners often work in secure laboratories where they check for viruses in suspect machines and isolate data to avoid contamination.

- **Preserve evidence**—Preserving computer evidence is important because data can be destroyed easily. The 1s and 0s that make up data can be hidden and vanish instantly with the push of a button. As a result, forensic examiners should assume that every computer has been rigged to destroy evidence. They must proceed with care in handling computers and storage media.

- **Prepare evidence**—Evidence must be able to withstand judicial scrutiny. Therefore, preparing evidence requires patience and thorough documentation. Failing to document where evidence comes from and failing to ensure that it has not been changed can ruin a case. Judges have dismissed cases because of such failures.

Evidence-Gathering Measures

Here are principles to use when you gather evidence:

- **Avoid changing the evidence**—Photograph equipment in place as you find it before you remove it. Label wires and sockets so that you can put everything back as it was once you get computers and other equipment into your lab. Transport items carefully, and avoid touching hard disks or CDs. Make exact bit-by-bit copies and store them on a medium such as a write-once CD.

- **Determine when evidence was created**—You should create timelines of computer usage and file accesses. This can be difficult, because there are so many ways to falsify data. But timelines can make or break a case.
- **Trust only physical evidence**—The 1s and 0s of data are recorded at the physical level of magnetic materials. This is what counts in system forensics. Other items may be corrupt.
- **Search throughout a device**—You need to search at this level of 1s and 0s across a wide range of areas inside a computer.
- **Present the evidence well**—Forensic examiners must present computer evidence in a logical, compelling, and persuasive manner. A jury must be able to understand the evidence. In addition, the evidence should be solid enough that a defense counsel cannot rebut it.

Expert Reports

An expert report is a formal document that details the expert's findings. Often this is filed in a case prior to trial. If there are depositions, then the expert report will probably be used as the basis for some questions you are asked during deposition. When writing an expert report, you should consider several issues.

The first issue is the format of the report. You usually list all items, documents, and evidence you considered. You also detail tests you performed, analysis done, and your conclusion. You should list your entire curriculum vitae (CV)—an extensive document detailing your experience and qualifications for a position—in an appendix. Keep in mind that a CV is much more thorough than a résumé. You should list every publication, award, or credential you have earned. A CV should also include more detail on work history and educational history.

Another issue for your report is thoroughness. In most jurisdictions, if it is not in your report, you are not allowed to testify about it at trial. So be very thorough. Anything you leave out may become a problem at trial. It is critical that you be detailed in what you write and that you document all the analysis done. For example, if you performed three tests and all three support a specific conclusion, make sure you list all three tests. If you list just one, then that is the only test you can testify about at trial.

Finally, back up everything you say. Clearly, you are an expert in forensics or else you would not be asked to testify. But remember that there is an opposing counsel whose job it is to disagree with you. The opposing counsel may have his or her own expert who will testify to different conclusions. It's good to have at least three well-respected references to support any important claims you make. This way, it is not just your opinion, but rather your opinion along with the support of multiple credible sources.

How to Set Up a Forensic Lab

The detailed specifics of any given lab are based on the needs of the lab, the budget, and the types of cases that lab is likely to handle. A state law enforcement agency with a high volume of cases has different needs from a small forensic lab that deals only with civil matters. However, some general principles apply to all labs.

Equipment

First and foremost, you must have adequate equipment for the job. Among other things, this means adequate storage for the data. Remember, you might analyze a system, but it could be months before the case goes to trial. A server with the most storage you can afford is in order. And that server must have redundancy. It should have a bare minimum of RAID 1 (disk mirroring), but RAID 5 is recommended. And it should be backed up at least once per day. It is likely you will need multiple servers to accommodate your storage needs.

You also need a variety of computers capable of attaching various types of drives— for example, external universal serial bus (USB), internal Small Computer System Interface (SCSI), Enhanced Integrated Drive Electronics (EIDE), and Serial Advanced Technology Attachment (SATA) drives. The exact number depends on the workload expected for the lab. You should also have power connectors for all types of smartphones, laptops, routers, and other devices.

Security

Security is paramount for forensics. First and foremost, the machines being examined should not be connected to the Internet. You can have a lab network that is not attached to the Internet and is separate from your working network where you check e-mail and use the Internet. It is also important to have the lab in a room that is shielded from any electromagnetic interference. This means that cellular and wireless signals cannot penetrate the room housing the lab.

After you have established network and electronic security, physical security is the next concern. It is imperative to limit access to the lab. Allow only people with a legitimate need to enter the lab. It is recommended that the lab entrance have some sort of electronic method of recording who enters and when they enter. Swipe-card access is ideal for this. Furthermore, the room itself should be difficult to forcibly access. That means the windows and doors are very secure and would be extremely difficult to force open.

The lab also requires the means to secure evidence when it is not being used. An evidence safe is the best way to do this. The safe should be highly fire resistant as well, so that in case of fire the evidence is preserved.

In addition to the general guidelines already listed, you should consider various standards that exist.

American Society of Crime Laboratory Directors

The American Society of Crime Laboratory Directors (ASCLD) provides guidelines for managing a forensic lab. It also provides guidelines for acquiring crime lab and forensic lab certification. The ASCLD offers voluntary accreditation to public and private crime laboratories in the United States and around the world. It certifies computer forensics labs that analyze digital evidence and other criminal evidence, such as fingerprints and DNA samples. The ASCLD/LAB certification regulates how to organize and manage crime labs. Achieving ASCLD accreditation is a rigorous process. A lab must meet about 400 criteria to achieve accreditation. Typically, an unaccredited lab needs two to three years to prepare for accreditation. It spends this time developing policies, procedures, document controls, analysis validations, and so on. Then, the lab needs another year to go through the process. The lab manager submits an application. The lead assessor and a team spend one to two months reviewing the application and the policies and procedures to make sure the lab is ready. The assessment takes about a week. The assessment team generates findings that require corrective action. The lab typically requires several months to make corrections to the satisfaction of the lead assessor. Once the facility has made all corrections, the lead assessor recommends the lab to the board of directors for accreditation. Finally, the ASCLD/LAB board of directors votes on whether to accredit the lab.

The ASCLD/LAB program includes audits to ensure that forensic specialists are performing lab procedures correctly and consistently for all casework. The society performs these audits in computer forensics labs to maintain quality and integrity. One recommendation for labs is to follow the DoD guidelines on electromagnetic radiation (EMR). The U.S. Department of Defense shields computers from EMR detection under its TEMPEST program. You can find out more about TEMPEST at *http://www.gao.gov/products/NSIAD-86-132*. Shielding all computers would be impossible because of the high cost involved. To protect high-risk investigations, however, a lab might also consider implementing TEMPEST protection. TEMPEST certifies equipment that is built with shielding that prevents EMR. In some cases, TEMPEST can be applied to an entire lab. Shielding a lab is an extremely high-cost approach that includes the following measures:

- Lining the walls, ceiling, floor, and doors with specially grounded conductive metal sheets
- Installing filters that prevent power cables from transmitting computer emanations
- Installing special baffles in heating and ventilation ducts to trap emanations
- Installing line filters on telephones lines
- Installing special features at entrances and exits that prevent the facility from being open to the outside at all times

Creating and maintaining a TEMPEST-certified lab is expensive. Such a lab must be inspected and tested regularly. Only large regional computer forensics labs that demand absolute security from eavesdropping should consider complete TEMPEST protection. For smaller facilities, use of TEMPEST-certified equipment is often a more effective approach.

Common Forensic Software Programs

After setting up the lab and the equipment, the next thing to address is the software. Several software tools are available that you might want to use in your forensic lab. This section takes a brief look at several commonly used tools. However, this section gives extra attention to Guidance Software's EnCase and AccessData's Forensic Toolkit because these two programs are very commonly used by law enforcement.

EnCase

EnCase from Guidance Software is a very widely used forensic toolkit. This tool allows the examiner to connect an Ethernet cable or null modem cable to a suspect machine and to view the data on that machine. EnCase prevents the examiner from making any accidental changes to the suspect machine. This is important: Remember the basic principle of touching the suspect machine as little as possible. EnCase organizes information into "cases." This matches the way examiners normally examine computers. Figure 3-1 shows a sample case.

The EnCase concept is based on the evidence file. This file contains the header, the checksum, and the data blocks. The data blocks are the actual data copied from the suspect machine, and the checksum is done to ensure there is no error in the copying of that data and that the information is not subsequently modified. Any subsequent modification causes the new checksum not to match the original checksum. As soon as the evidence file is added to the case, EnCase begins to verify the integrity of the entire

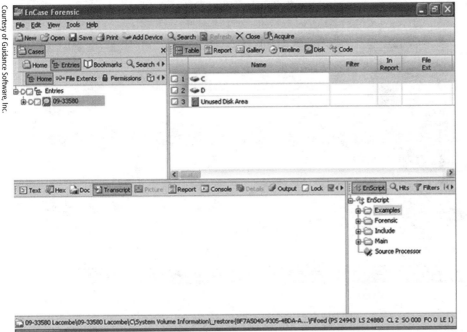

Courtesy of Guidance Software, Inc.

FIGURE 3-1

EnCase case file.

disk image. The evidence file is an exact copy of the hard drive. EnCase calculates an MD5 hash when the drive is acquired. This hash is used to check for changes, alterations, or errors. When the investigator adds the evidence file to the case, it recalculates the hash; this shows that nothing has changed since the drive was acquired.

You can use multiple methods to acquire the data from the suspect computer:

- **EnCase boot disk**—This method boots the system to EnCase using DOS mode rather than a GUI mode. You can then copy the suspect drive to a new drive to examine it.

- **EnCase network boot disk**—This is very similar to the EnCase boot disk, but it allows you to perform the process over a crossover cable between the investigator's computer and the computer being investigated.

- **LinEn boot disk**—This is specifically for acquiring the contents of a Linux machine. It operates much like the boot disk method, but is for target machines that are running Linux.

After you have acquired a suspect drive, you can then examine it using EnCase.

The EnCase Tree pane is like Windows Explorer. It lists all the folders and can expand any particular element in the tree (folders or subfolders). The Table pane lists the subfolders and files contained within the folder that was selected in the Tree pane. When you select an item, it is displayed in the View pane, as shown in Figure 3-2.

FIGURE 3-2

EnCase View pane.

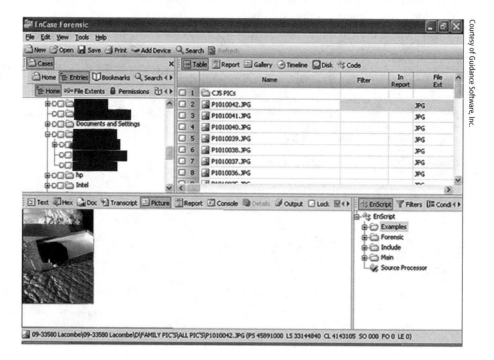

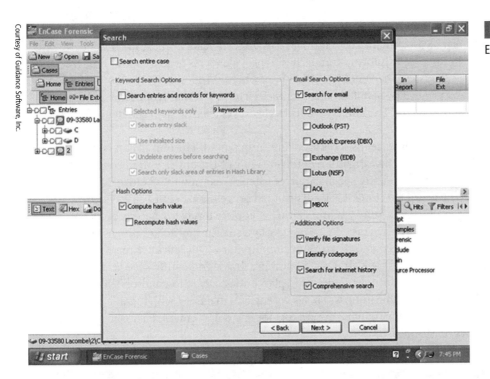

Courtesy of Guidance Software, Inc.

FIGURE 3-3

EnCase Search.

The Filter pane is a useful tool that can affect the data you view in the Table pane. It allows you to filter what you view, narrowing your focus to specific items of interest. You can also search data using the EnCase Search feature, shown in Figure 3-3.

This is just a very brief introduction to EnCase. It is a very popular tool with law enforcement, and the vendor, Guidance Software, offers training for its product. You can visit the vendor Web site for more details at *http://www.guidancesoftware.com/*.

Forensic Toolkit

The Forensic Toolkit (FTK) from AccessData is another widely used forensic analysis tool that is also very popular with law enforcement. You can get additional details at the company's Web site, *http://www.accessdata.com/products/digital-forensics*, but this section reviews some basics of the tool. With FTK, you can select which hash to use to verify the drive when you copy it, which features you want to use on the suspect drive, and how to search, as shown in Figure 3-4.

3

Forensic Methods
and Labs

Forensic Toolkit is particularly useful at cracking passwords. For example, password-protected Portable Document Format (PDF) files, Excel spreadsheets, and other documents often contain important information. FTK also provides tools to search and analyze the Windows Registry. The Windows Registry is where Windows stores all information regarding any programs installed. This includes viruses, worms, Trojan horses, hidden programs, and spyware. The ability to effectively and efficiently scan the Registry for evidence is critical.

FTK gives you a robust set of tools for examining e-mail. The e-mail can be arranged in a timeline, giving the investigator a complete view of the entire e-mail conversation and the ability to focus on any specific item of interest, as shown in Figure 3-5.

Another feature of this toolkit is its distributed processing. Scanning an entire hard drive, searching the Registry, and doing a complete forensic analysis of a computer can be a very time-intensive task. With AccessData's Forensic Toolkit, processing and analysis can be distributed across up to three computers. This lets all three computers perform the three parts of the analysis in parallel, thus significantly speeding up the forensic process. In addition, FTK has an Explicit Image Detection add-on that automatically detects pornographic images. This is very useful in cases involving allegations of pornography. This is a particularly useful tool for law enforcement. FTK is available for Windows or Macintosh.

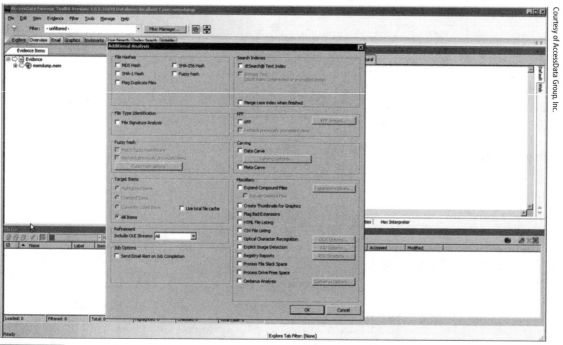

Courtesy of AccessData Group, Inc.

FIGURE 3-4

FTK features.

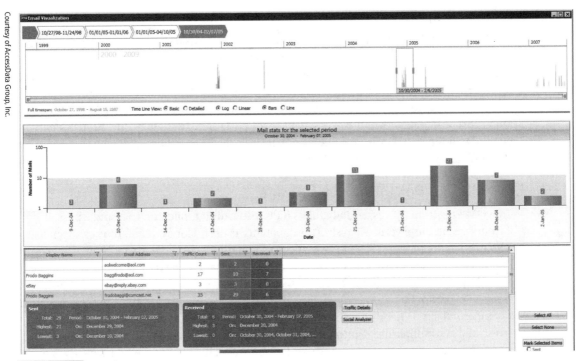

FIGURE 3-5

E-mail analysis.

Helix

Helix is a customized Linux Live CD used for computer forensics. The suspect system is booted into Linux using the Helix CDs and then the tools provided with Helix are used to perform the analysis. This product is robust and full of features, but simply has not become as popular as AccessData's FTK and Guidance Software's EnCase. For more information, check out their Web site at *http://www.e-fense.com/products.php*.

BackTrack

BackTrack is a Linux Live CD that you use to boot a system and then use the tools. BackTrack is a free Linux distribution, making it extremely attractive to schools teaching forensics or to laboratories on a strict budget. It is not used just for forensics, however, as it offers a wide number of general security and hacking tools. In fact, it is probably the most widely used collection of security tools available.

AnaDisk Disk Analysis Tool

AnaDisk, from New Technologies Incorporated (NTI), turns a PC into a sophisticated disk analysis tool. The software was originally created to meet the needs of the U.S. Treasury Department in 1991. AnaDisk scans for anomalies that identify odd formats, extra tracks, and extra sectors. It can be used to uncover sophisticated data-hiding techniques.

AnaDisk supports all DOS formats and many non-DOS formats, such as Apple Macintosh and UNIX TAR. If a disk will fit in a PC CD drive, it is likely that AnaDisk can be used to analyze it. For information on AnaDisk, see *http://www.retrocomputing.org/ cgi-bin/sitewise.pl?act=det&p=776&id=retroorg.*

CopyQM Plus Disk Duplication Software

CopyQM Plus from NTI essentially turns a PC into a disk duplicator. In a single pass, it formats, copies, and verifies a disk. This capability is useful for system forensics specialists who need to preconfigure CDs for specific uses and duplicate them. In addition, CopyQM Plus can create self-extracting executable programs that can be used to duplicate specific disks. CopyQM is an ideal tool for use in security reviews because once a CopyQM disk-creation program has been created, anyone can use it to make preconfigured security risk assessment disks. When the resulting program is run, the disk image of the original disk is restored on multiple disks automatically. The disk images can also be password-protected when they are converted to self-extracting programs. This is helpful when security is a concern, such as when disks are shared over the Internet. CopyQM Plus is particularly helpful in creating computer incident response toolkit disks.

CopyQM Plus supports all DOS formats and many non-DOS formats, such as Apple Macintosh and UNIX TAR. It copies files, file slack, and unallocated storage space. However, it does not copy all areas of copy-protected disks—extra sectors added to one or more tracks on a CD. AnaDisk software should be used for this purpose. For information on CopyQM Plus, see *http://vetusware.com/download/CopyQM%203.24/?id=6457.*

The Sleuth Kit

The Sleuth Kit is a collection of command-line tools that are available as a free download. You can get them from this site: *http://www.sleuthkit.org/sleuthkit/.* This toolset is not as rich nor as easy to use as EnCase or FTK, but can be a good option for a budget-conscious agency. The most obvious of the utilities included is ffind.exe.

There are options to search for a given file or to search for only deleted versions of a file. This particular utility is best used when you know the specific file you are searching for. It is not a good option for a general search. A number of utilities are available in Sleuth Kit; however, many people find using command-line utilities to be cumbersome. Fortunately, a graphical user interface (GUI) has been created for Sleuth Kit. That GUI is named Autopsy and is available at *http://www.sleuthkit.org/autopsy/download.php.*

Disk Investigator

This is a free utility that comes as a graphical user interface for use with Windows operating systems. You can download it from *http://www.theabsolute.net/sware/dskinv.html*. It is not a full-featured product like EnCase, but it is remarkably easy to use. When you first launch the utility, it presents you with a cluster-by-cluster view of your hard drive in hexadecimal form.

From the View menu, you can view directories or the root. The Tools menu allows you to search for a specific file or to recover deleted files.

Entire books could be written about the various forensic utilities available on the Internet. It is a good idea for any investigator to spend some time searching the Internet and experimenting with various utilities. Depending on your own skill set, technical background, and preferences, you might find one utility more suitable than another. It is also recommended that after you select a tool to use, you scan the Internet for articles about that tool. Make certain that it has widespread acceptance and that there are no known issues with its use. It can also be useful to use more than one tool to search a hard drive. If multiple tools yield the same result, this can preempt any objections the opposing attorney or his or her expert may attempt to present at trial. And remember—as always— to document every single step of your investigation process.

Forensic Certifications

You have a lab, you have software, but what about personnel? When considering potential candidates, looking for candidates who have taken a forensic class is a very good first step, but you should also look for candidates who have earned industry certifications. Before looking at specific certifications, let's discuss computer certifications in general.

Certifications have always been a controversial topic. Some people swear by them and won't even interview a candidate who does not have a few. Other people are convinced they are worthless. The issue stems from a misunderstanding of what a certification means. It is not meant to indicate the person is an expert or master in a specific field. It is meant to demonstrate a baseline of competence. Think about a medical degree. Simply having an MD does not guarantee the person is a brilliant physician. It just shows that the person achieved a certain minimum skill level. There is certainly a wide variation in skills among physicians. The same thing occurs with IT certifications. There are people with the Certified Information Systems Security Professional (CISSP®) credential from the International Information Systems Security Certification Consortium (ISC)²® who are brilliant security professionals with a very deep understanding of security and a wide set of skills. There are others with that credential who are only moderately competent.

Another issue with certifications is the boot camp. These programs are usually four or five days of intense study where the materials needed to pass a certification test are crammed into the students. On the final day, when it is all still fresh in their minds, they take the relevant certification test. This does lead to many boot camp attendees forgetting everything a few months later; however, this can be seen not as a failure of the training, but rather of the student. If you attend a boot camp, it is incumbent upon you to keep your skills up after the training is over.

Regardless of your personal feelings on certifications, it is a fact that they can only help your résumé as a forensic analyst. That doesn't mean, however, that you should ever hire any IT professional based solely on certifications. But they are one part of the total résumé. A combination of the right certifications along with formal education and experience make an ideal candidate.

So what are the right certifications? Forensics is a very broad topic, and requires analysts to have both a broad and deep knowledge. Some of this knowledge is obtained in a formal degree program, whereas some is obtained on the job. But anywhere you have a gap in your knowledge, or simply want to enhance your résumé, is a good place to add a certification. You need to know the following areas:

- **PC hardware**—This can be obtained in a basic hardware course at a college or via the CompTIA A+ certification.

- **Basic networking**—Most computer science–related degrees include a course in basic networking. This satisfies your needs as a forensic expert. However, you might consider the CompTIA Network+ or the Cisco Certified Network Associate certifications.

- **Security**—You must have a general knowledge of security. This can be best demonstrated with the (ISC)^2 CISSP certification or the CompTIA Security+ certification.

- **Hacking**—Yes, you do need to know what the hackers know. A few certifications for this area of study exist, but two of the most widely known and highly regarded are the EC Council Certified Ethical Hacker and several SANS white-hat hacker certifications. Ethical hacking training can be a perfect match for forensic training.

Now that you have learned about certifications in general, it's time to consider specific forensic certifications. The following sections examine two vendor certifications. Clearly, if your lab uses a specific tool, it is a good idea to have analysts who are certified in that tool. Subsequent sections explore a couple of general forensic certifications. These tests are about forensic methodologies rather than a specific tool.

EnCase Certified Examiner Certification

Guidance Software, the creator of EnCase, sponsors the EnCase Certified Examiner (EnCE) certification program. EnCE certification is open to the public and private sectors. This certification focuses on the use and mastery of system forensics analysis using EnCase. For more information on EnCE certification requirements, visit *http://www .guidancesoftware.com*.

AccessData Certified Examiner

AccessData is the creator of Forensic Toolkit (FTK). AccessData sponsors the AccessData Certified Examiner (ACE) certification program. ACE certification is open to the public and private sectors. This certification is specific to the use and mastery of FTK. Requirements for taking the ACE exam include completing the AccessData boot camp and Windows forensic courses. For more information on ACE certification, visit *http://www.accessdata.com*.

EC Council Certified Hacking Forensic Investigator

The EC Council Certified Hacking Forensic Investigator (CHFI) certification is a good general forensic certification. EC Council is more widely known for its Certified Ethical Hacker test, but its forensic test is a solid choice. It covers the general principles and techniques of forensics rather than specific tools like EnCase or FTK. This is a good starting point for learning forensics. You can learn more at their Web site at *http://www.eccouncil.org/Computer-Hacking-Forensic-Investigator/index.html*.

High Tech Crime Network Certifications

This specific certification is solid and well designed, but is not as widely known. High Tech Crime Network (HTCN) offers several levels of certification, with different requirements:

- Certified Computer Crime Investigator, Basic
- Certified Computer Crime Investigator, Advanced
- Certified Computer Forensic Technician, Basic
- Certified Computer Forensic Technician, Advanced

HTCN certification is open to anyone in a computing investigations profession.

HTCN requires a review of all related training. This includes training in one of its approved courses, a written test for the specific certification, and a review of the candidate's work history. It is the review of the candidate's work history that makes this certification stand out from the others. The HTCN Web site, *http://www.htcn.org*, specifies requirements for the various certification levels.

Global Information Assurance Certification Certifications

The Global Information Assurance Certification (GIAC) certifications are well respected in the IT industry. They have security, hacking, and forensic certifications. GIAC provides several levels of certification, beginning with the GIAC Certified Forensic Analyst (GCFA) and culminating with the GIAC Certified Forensic Examiner (GCFE). You can learn more about their certifications at the GIAC Web site at *http://www.giac.org/certification/certified-forensic-analyst-gcfa*.

CHAPTER SUMMARY

This chapter provided an overview of the forensic process. You examined general concepts as well as specific forensic frameworks. It is important that you fully understand these concepts before you move forward.

Then, this chapter looked at some widely used forensic tools. Even if you already have a tool that you prefer to use or that is mandated at your lab, it is worthwhile for you to at least have a basic familiarity with other forensic tools that are available. BackTrack, in particular, is a tool you should become familiar with because is it free to use.

KEY CONCEPTS AND TERMS

Bit-level information	**Rules of evidence**
File slack	**Slack space**
Life span	

CHAPTER 3 ASSESSMENT

1. To preserve digital evidence, an investigator should _____.

   A. Make two copies of each evidence item using a single imaging tool
   B. Make a single copy of each evidence item using an approved imaging tool
   C. Make two copies of each evidence item using different imaging tools
   D. Store only the original evidence item

2. Bob was asked to make a copy of all the evidence from the compromised system. Melanie did a DOS copy of all the files on the system. What would be the primary reason for you to recommend for or against using a disk-imaging tool?

   A. A disk-imaging tool would check for internal self-checking and validation and have an MD5 checksum.
   B. The evidence file format will contain case data entered by the examiner and encrypted at the beginning of the evidence file.
   C. A simple DOS copy will not include deleted files, file slack, and other information.
   D. There is no case for an imaging tool because it will use a closed, proprietary format that if compared with the original will not match up sector for sector.

3. It takes _____ occurrence(s) of overextending yourself during testimony to ruin your reputation.

   A. Only one if it is a major case
   B. Several
   C. Only one
   D. At least two

4. The MD5 message-digest algorithm is used to _____.

   A. Wipe magnetic media before recycling it
   B. Make directories on an evidence disk
   C. View graphics files on an evidence drive
   D. Hash a disk to verify that a disk is not altered when you examine it

5. You should make at least two bitstream copies of a suspect drive.

   A. True
   B. False

6. What is the purpose of hashing a copy of a suspect drive?

   A. To make it secure
   B. To remove viruses
   C. To check for changes
   D. To render it read-only

7. What is the most important reason that you not touch the actual original evidence any more than you have to?

   A. Each time you touch digital data, there is some chance of altering it.
   B. You might be accused of planting evidence.
   C. You might accidentally decrypt files.
   D. It can lead to data degradation.

## PART TWO

Technical Overview: System Forensics Tools, Techniques, and Methods

CHAPTER 4 **Collecting, Seizing, and Protecting Evidence** 80

CHAPTER 5 **Understanding Techniques for Hiding and Scrambling Information** 103

CHAPTER 6 **Recovering Data** 130

CHAPTER 7 **E-mail Forensics** 147

CHAPTER 8 **Windows Forensics** 166

CHAPTER 9 **Linux Forensics** 186

CHAPTER 10 **Macintosh Forensics** 209

CHAPTER 11 **Mobile Forensics** 221

CHAPTER 12 **Performing Network Analysis** 233

Collecting, Seizing, and Protecting Evidence

I N THIS CHAPTER, you see specific and practical steps that must be taken when seizing evidence, imaging drives, and preparing suspect drives for analysis. You are also introduced to some concepts such as forensic file formats.

Chapter 4 Topics

This chapter covers the following topics and concepts:

- How to use proper forensic procedure
- How to handle evidence appropriately
- What the different storage formats are
- What the process of forensically imaging a drive is
- How to acquire RAID

Chapter 4 Goals

When you complete this chapter, you will be able to:

- Properly seize a suspect computer
- Prepare that computer for forensic examination
- Understand the various storage formats
- Image a drive
- Acquire RAID drives

Proper Procedure

It is important to follow proper procedure when examining a suspect machine. This chapter covers specific details on the proper procedure to follow when collecting, seizing, and protecting evidence.

Shutting Down the Computer

The first step is usually shutting down the computer, but hold on. Before you do, you need to see what is currently running on the computer. Remember, you want to touch it as little as possible, so it is important to be careful. But you do need to find out if someone is currently accessing the computer—or if there is malware running on the computer—before you shut it down. Although the specifics may vary depending on the installed operating system, this section focuses on Windows because it is the most common desktop operating system.

The first thing to do is to check for running processes. In Windows (all versions), you press the Ctrl+Alt+Delete keys simultaneously, then select Task Manager. The Task Manager window opens; select the Processes tab. The Windows 8 version of this is shown in Figure 4-1.

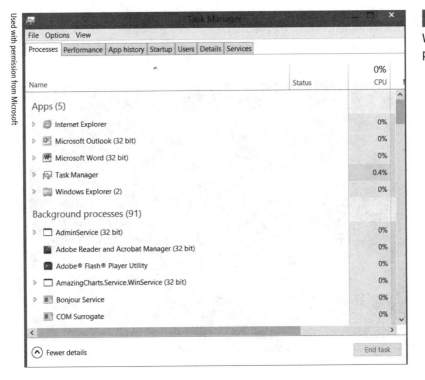

Used with permission from Microsoft

FIGURE 4-1

Windows 8 running processes.

4

Collecting, Seizing, and Protecting Evidence

Now take a picture of the screen so you have a record of the running processes. In this case, "take a picture" means taking an actual photo with a camera, not taking a screenshot. It's also a good idea to take a traditional analog photo because digital photos are so easily altered. (In some jurisdictions, this is mandatory.) In many cases, these photos are also subject to the rules of the chain of custody for evidence. Next, it is important to see if there are live connections to this system. Fortunately, there are built-in commands (most work in Linux as well as Windows) that will help you with that. The following sections cover a few of those commands.

Using netstat

The netstat command shows network statistics and any current connections. Normally, there are connections. For example, a Windows 7 computer that is part of a homegroup will have communications with other members of that group. What you are looking for are external connections, particularly ones from outside the local network. You can see an example of netstat in Figure 4-2.

Using net sessions

The net sessions command is actually more helpful than netstat. The netstat command shows even meaningless connections, such as your computer opening a Web browser. But net sessions shows only established network communication sessions, such as someone logging on to that system. You can see an example of net sessions in Figure 4-3.

FIGURE 4-2

Using netstat.

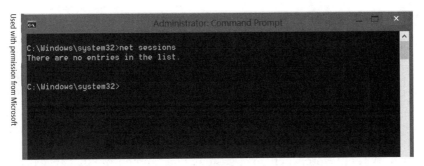

FIGURE 4-3

Using net sessions.

The openfiles Command

The openfiles command is very useful. It tells you if any shared files or folders are open and who has them open. Before shutting down the suspect machine, this is a critical command to run. You can see an example of openfiles in Figure 4-4.

You should run each of these commands and photograph the results before shutting down the machine. Also document that you ran them, the time, and the results. Then power down the machine. Most sources recommend you simply pull the plug. This may be contrary to how you usually power down a machine, but the idea is to interrupt normal operations. It is possible, though not likely, that there is some malware on the machine that would delete files, clear the swap, or otherwise destroy evidence during a normal power-down or the subsequent power up of a machine.

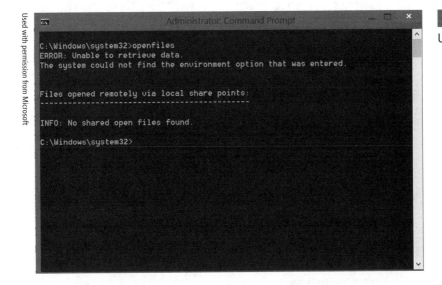

FIGURE 4-4

Using openfiles.

Transporting the Computer System to a Secure Location

Seized computers are often stored in less-than-secure locations. Both law enforcement agencies and corporations sometimes fail to transport and store suspect systems properly. It is imperative that you treat a subject computer as evidence and store it out of reach of curious computer users. Sometimes, individuals operate seized computers without knowing that they are destroying potential evidence and the chain of custody. A seized computer left unattended can easily be compromised. Someone could plant evidence or destroy crucial evidence. Lack of a proper chain of custody can make a savvy defense attorney's day. Without a proper chain of custody, you can't ensure that evidence was not planted on the computer after the seizure.

During the transport, you must be aware that this seized computer is evidence. It should be locked in a vehicle and the vehicle should be driven directly to the lab. This is not a time to stop for lunch. Any period of time that you cannot account for the evidence is a break in the chain of custody. And it is certainly possible for someone to break into the vehicle while you are stopped at your favorite lunch spot.

Preparing the System

If the device you have seized is a computer, you need to remove the drive(s) from the suspect machine even if the drive(s) is not currently attached to any cabling. Create a chain of custody form. You can see a sample evidence form in Figure 4-5.

FIGURE 4-5
Evidence form.

Single Evidence Form

Case No. | Evidence No.

PLEASE COMPLETE FORM IN UPPERCASE

Section B: Evidence Collection	
Date/Time Collected DD/MM/YY HH:MM	Collected by
Site Address	

Section C: Evidence Details	
Date/Time Stored DD/MM/YY HH:MM	
Storage Location	
Device Type	Capacity
Manufacturer	Model
Serial No.	
MD5 Sum	
SHA-1 Sum	
Additional Information ...	
Note any damage, marks and scratches	Digital Image Taken ☐ Yes ☐ No

Section D: Image Details	
Date/Time Imaged DD/MM/YY HH:MM	Imaged by
Storage Location	
Image Filename	Image Size (inc. unit)
Additional Information ...	

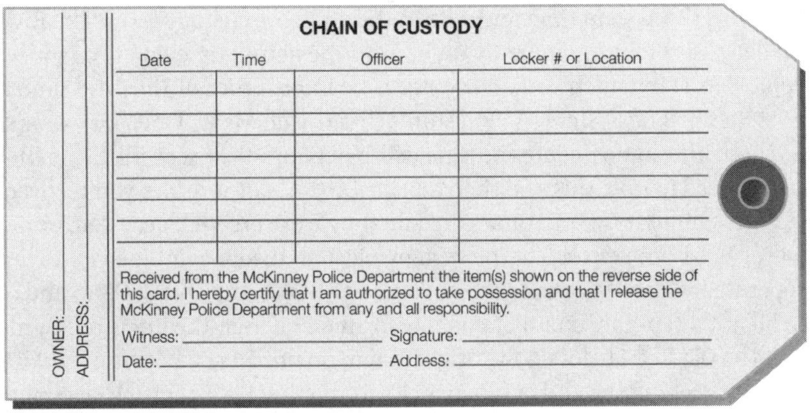

CHAIN OF CUSTODY

Date	Time	Officer	Locker # or Location

Received from the McKinney Police Department the item(s) shown on the reverse side of this card. I hereby certify that I am authorized to take possession and that I release the McKinney Police Department from any and all responsibility.

Witness: ________ Signature: ________

Date: ________ Address: ________

OWNER: ________

ADDRESS: ________

FIGURE 4-6

Chain of custody form.

Some forensic examiners have a separate chain of custody form. Figure 4-6 shows one from an actual police department.

Now the specifics of your chain of custody form will vary depending on your jurisdiction and your organizational policies. You typically need to use a separate chain of custody form for each drive you have removed. Depending on your level of comfort in reliably describing and re-creating the technology present in the suspect system, you may want to take photographs of all of the drive connections, cable connections to the case, and general work area for future use. Photos, however, are not required for admittance into court. But you should take photographs whenever possible. Anytime you can use photographs to enhance your investigation or your reporting, you should do so. You can also leave the drives in the system and acquire them with some forensically safe boot disks, CD-ROMs, or thumb drives.

In the case of phones, it is often necessary to remove the SIM card (though this is not always required). It is possible to examine a phone without removing the SIM card, and some modern phone forensic devices allow you to simply dock the phone into the device.

Documenting the Hardware Configuration of the System

Before dismantling the computer, it is important to take pictures of the computer from all angles to document the system hardware components and how they are connected. Labeling each wire is also important, so that you can easily reconnect each one when the system configuration is restored to its original condition. You should also record BIOS (basic input/output system) information. At this point, the drives are removed and you have identified and removed the media from the system. You can now safely boot up the system to check the BIOS information. In the chain of custody form, enter information about the BIOS of the system; you can typically access this information by pressing Esc, Delete, F2, F9, F10, or F11 (the specific key depends on the system, but F2 seems to be the most common) during the initial boot screen. But this varies depending on the system manufacturer, so always try to search the system manufacturer's Web site ahead of time to determine how to access this information. Once you've accessed the BIOS information, you need to record the system time and date in the chain of custody form. The BIOS time is important because it can significantly differ from the actual time and time zone set for the geographical area in which you are located. The importance of the BIOS time varies by the file system (NT File System [NTFS] stores Greenwich Mean Time, for example) and operating system, and some update the time using network time servers. If the BIOS time is different, you need to note this and then adjust the times of any files you recover from the image to determine the actual time and date they were created, accessed, or modified. After the power has been restored to the system, eject all media contained in drives that cannot be operated without power (such as some CD-ROMs and DVD-ROMs) and remove them. Then fill out a separate chain of custody form for each of the items removed. If you forget to eject the CD-ROM before powering it down, do not worry, because most CD-ROMs can be opened by sticking the end of a paper clip in the tiny hole near the eject button.

Mathematically Authenticating Data on All Storage Devices

You must be able to prove that you didn't alter any of the evidence after taking possession of a suspect computer. Such proof helps rebut allegations that the investigator changed or altered the original evidence. After imaging any drive, you must always create a hash of the original and the copy. Compare the hashes. If they do not match exactly, then something was altered. You must also document what hashing algorithm you used (SHA1 is the most common) and what the results were. Linux has built-in tools for hashing, but many forensic tools such as EnCase and Forensic Toolkit (FTK) hash the suspect drive after it is imaged to check for copy errors.

In Linux, the following command hashes a partition:

```
md5sum /dev/hda1
```

FYI

What is a hash? Although you might already have some knowledge of hashing algorithms, it is important to make certain you are completely clear on what a hash is. A hash is not encryption. There are three criteria for an algorithm to be considered a **hash**:

1. It must be nonreversible. Things are so scrambled they cannot be "unhashed." You don't "decrypt" or "dehash" a hash. You can compare it with another hash to see if it matches.

2. Variable-length input produces fixed-length output. No matter how much you put in, the hash is always the same size and the size of the resulting hash value depends on the specific hashing algorithm.

3. There are few or no collisions. It should be extremely rare that you can put in two different values and get the same hash. Ideally, this should never occur.

MD5 has been a popular hash for many years. SHA1 and SHA2 are currently the most widely used hashing algorithms.

This assumes the partition is hda1. If your partition is different, then substitute your partition name. If you want to send that hash to a target machine (such as your forensic server), use this command:

```
md5sum /dev/hda1 | nc 192.168.0.2 8888 -w 3
```

This says to create the hash of the partition, then use netcat to send it to IP 192.168.0.2 port 8888. Obviously, your IP address and port could be different.

Handling Evidence

Once you have appropriately transported the device and prepared it for forensic examination, you have to handle the evidence. There are specific steps to utilize.

Preserving computer evidence requires planning and training in incident discovery procedures. The following sections describe tasks related to handling evidence and measures to take when gathering evidence. To review, a system forensics specialist has three basic tasks related to handling evidence:

- Find evidence
- Preserve evidence
- Prepare evidence

Collecting Data

There are three primary types of data that a forensic investigator must collect: volatile data, temporary data, and persistent data. As an investigator, you must attempt to avoid permanently losing data. Therefore, you must carefully secure the physical evidence. Then you can collect volatile and temporary data. Such data is lost whenever a system is used. You should collect it first to minimize corruption or loss. The following are examples of **volatile data**:

- **Swap file**—The swap file is used to optimize the use of random access memory (RAM). Data is frequently found in the swap file. The details on how to extract data from the swap file vary depending on the installed operating system.
- **State of network connections**—This data is captured before the system is shut down.
- **State of running processes**—This data is captured before the system is shut down.

After collecting volatile data, you collect **temporary data**—data that an operating system creates and overwrites without the computer user taking a direct action to save this data. The likelihood of corrupting temporary data is less than that of volatile data. But temporary data is just that—temporary—and you must collect it before it is lost. Only after collecting volatile and temporary data should you begin to collect persistent data.

Documenting Filenames, Dates, and Times

From an evidence standpoint, filenames, creation dates, and last modified dates and times can be relevant. Therefore, it is important to catalog all allocated and "erased" files. Sort the files based on the filename, file size, file content, creation date, and last modified date and time. Such sorted information can provide a timeline of computer usage. The output should be in the form of a word processing–compatible file to help document computer evidence issues tied to specific files.

Identifying File, Program, and Storage Anomalies

Encrypted, compressed, and graphics files store data in binary format. As a result, text search programs can't identify text data stored in these file formats. These files require manual evaluation, which may involve a lot of work, especially with encrypted files. Depending on the type of file, view and evaluate the content as potential evidence. Reviewing the partitioning on seized hard disk drives is also important. Evaluate hidden partitions for evidence and document their existence. With Windows operating systems, you should also evaluate the files contained in the Recycle Bin. The Recycle Bin is the repository of files selected for deletion by the computer user. The fact that they have been selected for deletion may have some relevance from an evidentiary standpoint. If you find relevant files, thoroughly document the issues involved. Those issues can include the following:

- How did you find the files?
- What condition were they in (i.e., did you recover the entire file or just part of the file)?
- When was the file originally saved?

Remember that the more information you document about evidence, the better.

Evidence-Gathering Measures

Forensic specialists should take the following measures when gathering evidence:

- **Avoid changing the evidence**—Before removing any equipment, forensic specialists should photograph equipment in place and label wires and sockets so that computers and peripherals can be reassembled in a laboratory exactly as they were in the original location. When transporting computers, peripherals, and media, forensic specialists must be careful to avoid heat damage, jostling, or touching original computer hard disks and compact discs (CDs). Forensic specialists should also make exact bit-by-bit copies, storing the copies on an unalterable medium, such as a CD-ROM.

- **Determine when evidence was created**—Timelines of computer usage and file accesses can be valuable sources of computer evidence. The times and dates when files were created, last accessed, or modified can make or break a case. However, forensic specialists should not trust a computer's internal clock or activity logs. It is possible that the internal clock is wrong, that a suspect tampered with logs, or that simply turning on the computer changes a log irrevocably. Before logs disappear, an investigator should capture the time a document was created, the last time it was opened, and the last time it was changed. The investigator can then calibrate or recalibrate evidence, based on a time standard, and work around log tampering.

- **Search throughout a device**—Forensic specialists must search at the bit level (the level of 1s and 0s) across a wide range of areas inside a computer. This includes e-mail, temporary files, swap files, logical file structures, and slack and free space on the hard drive. They must also search software settings, script files, Web browser data caches, bookmarks and history, and session logs. Forensic specialists can then correlate evidence to activities and sources.

- **Determine information about encrypted and steganized files**—Investigators should usually not attempt to decode encrypted files. Rather, investigators should look for evidence in a computer that tells them what is in the encrypted file. Frequently, this evidence has been erased, but unencrypted traces remain and can be used to make a case. For steganized information, concealed within other files or buried inside the 1s and 0s of a picture, for example, an investigator can tell if the data is there even though it is inaccessible. The investigator can compare nearly identical files to identify minute differences.

- **Present the evidence well**—Forensic examiners must present computer evidence in a logical, compelling, and persuasive manner. The jury must be able to understand the evidence and the evidence must be solid enough that a defense counsel cannot rebut it. The forensic examiner must be able to create a step-by-step reconstruction of actions, with documented dates and times. In addition, the forensic examiner must prepare charts, graphs, and exhibits that explain both what was done and how it was done as well as be able to withstand scrutiny. The forensic examiner's testimony must explain simply and clearly what a suspect did or did not do. The forensic examiner should remember that the jury and judge are rarely savvy computer technologists, and the ability of a forensic examiner to explain technical points clearly in plain English can make or break a case.

This chapter has so far discussed general preparations involved in the initial seizing, duplication, and finding of digital evidence. There's much more to learn, especially about examining data to find *incriminating evidence*—evidence that shows, or tends to show, a person's involvement in an act, or evidence that can establish guilt. One of the three techniques of forensic analysis is live analysis, which is the recording of any ongoing network processes. The remaining two techniques are physical analysis and logical analysis, which both deal with hard drive structures and file formats.

Physical analysis is offline analysis conducted on an evidence disk or forensic duplicate after booting from a CD or another system. **Logical analysis** involves using the native operating system, on the evidence disk or a forensic duplicate, to peruse the data. Put another way, physical analysis is looking for things that may have been overlooked, or are invisible, to the user. Logical analysis is looking for things that are visible, known about, and possibly controlled by the user.

Physical Analysis

Two of the easiest things to extract during physical analysis are a list of all Web site uniform resource locators (URLs) and a list of all e-mail addresses on the computer. The user may have attempted to delete these, but you can reconstruct them from various places on the hard drive. Next, you should index the different kinds of file formats.

The file format you start with depends on the type of case. For example, you might want to start with graphics file formats or document formats in a pornography or forgery case. There are lots of other file formats: multimedia, archive, binary, database, font, game, and Internet related. Computers generally save things in file formats beyond the user's control. For example, all graphics files have header information. Collectors of pornography usually don't go to the trouble of removing this header information, so it's an easy matter of finding, for example, one graphics header at the beginning of a JPEG (Joint Photographic Experts Group) file and doing a string search for all other graphics of that type.

The following sections describe some of the places that an investigator must physically analyze.

 NOTE

Of most interest forensically is the fact that swap files are not erased when the system shuts down. They work on a queue system. Data stays in the swap file and is not overwritten until that space is needed. That means it is possible to find data in the swap file that was live in memory and not stored on the suspect drive.

The swap file. You read briefly about the swap file earlier in this chapter. A swap file is the most important type of ambient data. Windows uses a swap file on each system as a "scratch pad" to write data when additional RAM is needed. A swap file is a virtual memory extension of RAM. Most computer users are unaware of the existence of swap files. The size of these files is usually about 1.5 times the size of the physical RAM in the machine. Swap files contain remnants of word processing documents, e-mails, Internet browsing activity, database entries, and almost any other work that has occurred during past Windows sessions. Swap files can be temporary or permanent, depending on the version of Windows installed and the settings selected by the computer user. Permanent swap files are of the greatest forensic value because they hold larger amounts of information for longer periods of time. However, temporary, or dynamic, swap files are more common. These files shrink and expand as necessary. When a dynamic swap file reduces its size close to zero, it sometimes releases the file's content to unallocated space, which you can also forensically examine.

Unallocated (free) space. **Unallocated space**, or free space, is the area of a hard drive that has never been allocated for file storage, or the leftover area that the computer regards as unallocated after file deletion. It's where the hard disk often sends fragments of files when someone deletes or removes files. The only way to clean unallocated space is with cleansing devices known as **sweepers** or **scrubbers**. However, few commercial products scrub free space to Department of Defense (DoD) standards. The fragments of old files in free space can be anywhere on the disk, even on a different partition, but they tend to fall next to partition headers, file allocation tables (FAT), and the last sectors of a cluster.

Logical Analysis

You must examine the logical file and directory structure to reconstruct what the user was doing with his or her computer. Rarely does an investigator run across a signed confession in the My Documents folder. Most perpetrators are smarter than that. They use various tactics to hide what they've been doing. For example, perpetrators often use unusual file paths. In addition, many try to thwart investigators by using encryption to scramble information or steganography to hide information, or both together. Or they may use metadata to combine different file formats into one format. You can also expect to find lots of deleted, professionally scrubbed data.

> **NOTE**
>
> What is metadata? *Metadata* is essentially data about the data. In the case of files, it can include creation time/date, size, last modified date, and even file header information. If a criminal is skilled, he or she can combine the metadata from different files to hide information. For example, someone can take a text file and alter its metadata so it appears to be a system dynamic-link library (DLL).

An investigator hopes to trace the uses that a suspect computer has been set up for. Certain types of criminals optimize their systems for different uses. For example, a programmer optimizes for speed, a pornographer for storage, and a stalker for messaging. You must go about logical analysis methodically. Divide the data on the hard drive into layers and try to find evidentiary information at each layer. Look for peculiarities on each layer and then choose the right extraction tool.

Creating a Timeline

To reconstruct the events that led to corruption of a system, create a timeline. This can be particularly difficult when it comes to computers. Clock drift, delayed reporting, and different time zones can create confusion. Never change the clock on a suspect system. Instead, record any clock drift and the time zone in use.

Storage Formats

Working with forensics, you need to be familiar with a variety of storage formats. Specifically, you should be familiar with the various hard drive types, file systems, and journaling. This section reviews a variety of storage and file formats and explores additional issues with storage formats.

Magnetic Media

Although mobile devices, like smartphones and tablets, are a growing part of forensic work, computers are still the biggest target of forensic investigations. Most computers utilize magnetic media. Hard drives and floppy drives are types of magnetic media. Essentially, the data is organized by sectors and clusters, which are in turn organized in tracks around the platter. A typical sector is 512 bytes and a cluster can be from 1 to 128 sectors.

Because the data is stored magnetically, the drives are susceptible to magnetic interference. This can include being demagnetized. If a drive has been demagnetized, there is no way to recover the data. You should transport drives in special transit bags that reduce electrostatic interference. This reduces the chance of inadvertent loss of data.

There are five types of magnetic drives:

- Integrated Drive Electronics (IDE)
- Extended Integrated Drive Electronics (EIDE)
- Parallel Advanced Technology Attachment (PATA)
- Serial Advanced Technology Attachment (SATA)
- Serial SCSI

These drive types refer to the connection between the drive and the motherboard as well as the total capacity of the drive, but they are all magnetic drives.

It is important to remember that because magnetic drives have moving parts in them, they are also susceptible to physical damage. If you drop a drive, you may render the data inaccessible. This is why you must take care when handing magnetic drives.

Solid-State Drives

Solid-state drives (SSDs) use microchips, which retain data in non-volatile memory chips and contain no moving parts. Most SSDs use Negated AND (NAND) gate–based flash memory, which retains memory even without power. Because there are no moving parts, these drives are usually less susceptible to physical damage than magnetic drives are. However, they are still more expensive than magnetic drives and usually have a lower capacity.

One reason these drives are so popular is because they generally require one-half to one-third the power of hard disk drives (HDDs). The start-up time for SSDs is usually much faster than for magnetic storage drives. They are often used in tablets and in some laptops. This means that you are likely to encounter them at some point in your forensic career.

If these drives are internal, they can use the same interfaces magnetic drives use, including SCSI and SATA. However, if connected externally, it is most common for them to have a universal serial bus (USB) connection.

Both magnetic and solid state drives include a few features that are important for forensics:

- **Host protected area (HPA)**—This was designed as an area where computer vendors could store data that is protected from user activities and operating system utilities, such as delete and format. To hide data in the HPA, a person would need to write a program to access the HPA and write the data.

- **Master boot record (MBR)**—This requires only a single sector, leaving 62 empty sectors of MBR space for hiding data.

- **Volume slack**—This is the space that remains on a hard drive if the partitions do not use all the available space. For example, suppose that two partitions are filled with data. When you delete one of them, the data is not actually deleted. Instead, it is hidden.

- **Unallocated space**—An operating system can't access any unallocated space in a partition. That space can contain hidden data.

- **Good blocks marked as bad**—Suppose that someone manipulates the file system metadata to mark unusable blocks as bad. The operating system will no longer access these blocks. These blocks can then be used to hide data.

- **File slack**—File slack is the unused space that is created between the end of file and the end of the last data cluster assigned to a file.

Digital Audio Tape Drives

Although many organizations are moving from electronic backups to optical media or even direct network backups to an off-site location, digital audio tape (DAT) drives are still widely used. DAT drives are among the most common type of tape drives. DAT uses 4-mm magnetic tape enclosed in a protective plastic shell. Even though this looks very similar to audio tapes, the recording is digital rather than analog.

From a forensic point of view, it is important to remember that these tapes do wear out, just like audio tapes. If you are old enough to remember cassette or 8-track tapes, you'll recall that these tapes would, from time to time, become stretched and worn and no longer usable. The same thing happens with the DAT tapes. In fact, network administrators are admonished to replace them periodically.

When working with DAT drives, most likely they will contain archived/backup data that you need to analyze. Make certain you first forensically wipe the target drive so you can be sure that there is no residual data on that drive. You then need to restore it to the target hard drive (magnetic or solid state) in order to analyze it.

Digital Linear Tape and Super DLT

Digital Linear Tape (DLT) is another type of tape storage, more specifically a magnetic tape. The DLT technology relies on a linear recording method. The tape itself has either 128 or 208 total tracks. This technology was first invented by Digital Electronics Corporation (DEC). This tape, like DAT, is used primarily to store archived data. So, as with DAT, you need to make sure you have a forensically wiped hard drive to restore the data to and then restore the data to that hard drive in order to analyze it.

Optical Media

Like hard disks, optical media such as CD-ROMs use high and low polarization to set the bits of data; however, CDs have reflective pits that represent the low bit. If the pit is nonexistent, the data is a 1; if the pit exists, it's a 0. The laser mechanism actually detects the distance the light beam has traveled in order to detect the presence or absence of a pit. This is why scratches can be problematic for optical media.

Since the advent of the original compact disc, there have been enhancements. These enhancements still utilize the same optical process, but have larger capacity. The DVD (or digital video disc) can hold 4.7 gigabytes (GB) for a one-sided DVD and 9.4 GB for a double-sided DVD. This technology uses a 650-nm wavelength laser diode light as opposed to 780 nm for CDs. The smaller wavelength allows DVDs to use smaller pits, thus increasing storage capacity.

Blu-ray discs are the successor to the DVD and store up to 25 GB per layer, with dual-layer discs storing up to 50 GB. There are also triple- and quadruple-layer discs such as the Blu-ray Disc XL that allow up to 150 GB of storage. Although Blu-ray discs are primarily associated with movies, you can certainly store data on them. And for smaller organizations, the Blu-ray disc can be an attractive backup medium.

Just like all other storage devices, a Blu-ray device should be forensically copied to a clean, forensically wiped drive for analysis. No matter what the media, you never work with the original suspect storage if it is at all possible to avoid it.

Using USB Drives

USB, or universal serial bus, is actually a connectivity technology, not a storage technology. And USB can be used to connect to external drives that can be either magnetic or solid state. Small USB flash drives, also known as thumb drives, are also quite common. These drives can be easily erased or overwritten. It is important to copy the data from the USB drive to a target forensic drive for analysis. You must, of course, document the copying process and ensure nothing was missed or altered.

USB thumb drives have no moving parts. Each bit is set by using a two-transistor cell, and the value is changed in each cell using a technique called Fowler-Nordheim tunneling. The memory bank then communicates with the computer using a controller and USB interface, much like a hard disk communicates over IDE or SCSI. Because there are no moving parts, these drives are resilient to shock damage (i.e., dropping them probably won't hurt them). From a forensic point of view, you should remember that many of these drives come with a small switch to put them in read-only mode. Use this whenever you are extracting data for investigation. If the drive is in read-only mode, it is unlikely you will accidentally alter the data.

File Formats

In addition to physical means of storing data, there are a variety of file formats for storing forensic data on a given storage device. It is important that you have a working knowledge of these formats for forensic analysis.

The Advanced Forensic Format

This file format (abbreviated AFF) was invented by Basis Technology. It is an open file standard with three variations: AFF, AFM, and AFD. The AFF variation stores all data and metadata in a single file. The AFM variation stores the data and the metadata in separate files. The AFD variation stores the data and metadata in multiple small files. The AFF file format is part of the AFF Library and Toolkit, which is a set of open-source computer forensics programs. Sleuth Kit and Autopsy both support this file format.

EnCase

The EnCase format is a proprietary format that is defined by Guidance Software for use in its EnCase tool to store hard drive images and individual files. It includes a hash of the file to ensure nothing was changed when it was copied from the source.

The Generic Forensic Zip

Gfzip is another open-source file format used to store evidence from a forensic examination.

IXimager

This is a proprietary file format that is used by the iLook tool. This tool was developed by the U.S. Internal Revenue Service (IRS) and is restricted to law enforcement and government use only.

Forensic Imaging

Once you have acquired a physical storage medium of some type, you need to image it. You always work with an image whenever possible. Even if the medium is an optical storage device like a Blu-ray disc, you should make a forensic image of the drive and work with the image. It is possible to create a forensic image utilizing open-source tools, specifically Linux commands. This section explains all the details behind each step.

First, you must forensically wipe the target drive (which is the drive to which you will copy the suspect drive contents) to ensure there is no residual data left from a previous case. You can do this with the Linux dd command:

```
dd if=/dev/zero of=/dev/hdb1 bs=2048
```

This command is literally using /dev/zero as an input file and writing its contents out to the partition hdb1 as the output file. If you are not familiar with Linux, the /dev/zero is a special file on UNIX-like systems that reads out as many nulls as are required. So this command is overwriting everything on the target drive with null values.

If your partition is different, you can use fdisk -l to list the partitions on your system.

> **NOTE**
>
> Many Linux distributions have dd and netcat, so you do not have to utilize BackTrack. However, BackTrack is designed for computer security. This Linux distribution has a host of security, hacking, and forensic tools on it. It is a very good idea to start getting comfortable with BackTrack early in your forensic training.

The primary propose of dd, a common UNIX program, is the low level copying and conversion of raw data. Low-level copying means at the bit level. If you do your copy through the file system/operating system, then you can see only the data that the operating system sees. You won't get deleted files or slack space. That is why a basic file system copy is inadequate for forensic analysis. You must get a bit-level copy, and the dd utility is perfect for that.

You also need to use netcat to set up the forensic server to listen, so you have a BackTrack CD boot up the suspect drive to copy it to the forensic server. At this point, both the suspect drive and the target forensic server have been booted into Linux using BackTrack.

The netcat command reads and writes bits over a network connection. The command to run on the forensic server is as follows:

```
# nc -l -p 8888 > evidence.dd
```

This sets up the listen process on the forensic server prior to sending the data from the subject's computer. The process listens (the –l flag) on port 8888 (the –p 8888 command) and takes all input and writes to a file called evidence.dd. You can always use another port or another filename if necessary. You must ensure the target drive is at least as big as the suspect drive.

> **NOTE**
>
> Even if you use automated forensic systems, it is critical that you know how to perform all forensic processes manually. If if you don't know how the process works, then during cross-examination, you will appear to have too little knowledge of the forensic process to be able to validate that the evidence is correct and has not been tampered with.

On the suspect computer, use the dd command to read the first partition:

```
# dd if=/dev/hda1 | nc 192.168.0.2 8888 -w 3
```

You then pipe the output of the dd command to netcat, which sends the bits over the network to the specified network address and port on the listening forensic computer. The argument –w 3 indicates that netcat should wait 3 seconds before closing the connection upon finding no more data. This assumes that the suspect partition is hda1, but it might be a different partition.

This process can be accomplished with most major forensic tools, including EnCase from Guidance Software and Forensic Toolkit from AccessData.

Imaging with EnCase

EnCase is a forensic tool that is widely used by law enforcement. Once you have the suspect's hard drive disconnected from the suspect machine, you can connect that drive to the forensic computer. In some cases, you first connect to a device that prevents writing to the suspect device. FastBlock and Tableau are two such devices that are widely used in forensics.

At the top of the EnCase window, click New on the toolbar to start the new case you will be working. The Case Options dialog box opens, as shown in Figure 4-7.

FIGURE 4-7

EnCase Case Options
dialog box.

This dialog box allows you to type in the case name and the examiner's name. Tracking evidence by case and examiner is one convenient feature of EnCase that helps make it popular with law enforcement agencies. The text boxes are filled in automatically, but you have to click on the button on the right side next to each of the lower text boxes to select the paths. After selecting the paths, click the Finish button.

Now that you have created the case, you need to save it by clicking the Save icon on the EnCase toolbar. Select a path for the save location when prompted. Now, you are ready to acquire evidence. On the EnCase toolbar, click the Add Device button. The Add Device window appears in EnCase, asking which device to add, as shown in Figure 4-8.

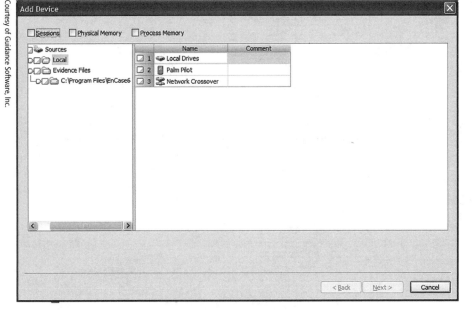

FIGURE 4-8

EnCase Add Device
window.

4

**Collecting, Seizing, and
Protecting Evidence**

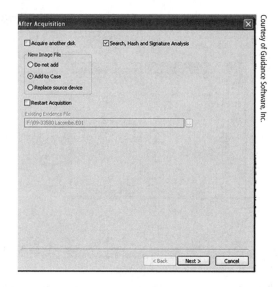

FIGURE 4-9

EnCase After Acquisition
dialog box.

The left pane lists devices with subfolders, Local and Evidence Files. The right pane lists Local Drives, Palm Pilot, Parallel Port, and Network Crossover (note these options may differ on different systems). In this procedure, you check the Local Drives in the right pane. After EnCase reads the local drives, another window appears. Once you have added the device, it shows in the case, as shown in Figure 4-9.

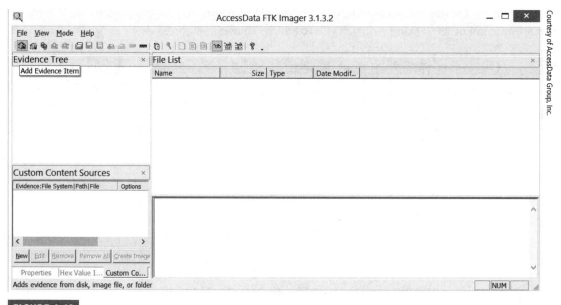

FIGURE 4-10

FTK: adding evidence.

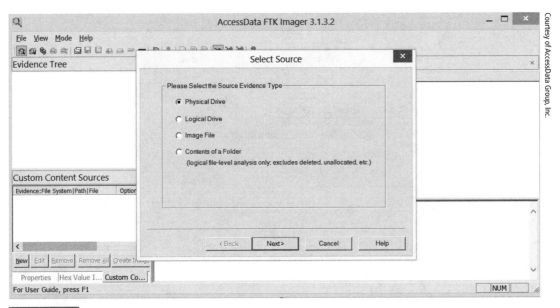

Courtesy of AccessData Group, Inc.

FIGURE 4-11

FTK Select Source dialog box.

One of the first things you should note is that you can add multiple devices to a single case. This makes sense because many cases will have more than one device that is seized and requires examination.

Imaging with the Forensic Toolkit

The Forensic Toolkit (FTK) from AccessData is another popular forensic tool that is widely used by law enforcement. Once you have connected the suspect drive to the forensic machine, you simply have to add evidence, as shown in Figure 4-10.

You now have to select specifically what you want to image. As you can see in Figure 4-11, FTK offers a number of choices. The most common choice is a physical drive, but you can also add folders, logical drives, and even drive images, such as those made with the dd and netcat commands earlier in this chapter. Select one of the Source Evidence Type options and then click the Next button.

Next, from the Select Drive drop-down, choose the specific drive you want to acquire and then click Finish. FTK mounts the drive; you can then see it in the evidence tree, as shown in Figure 4-12.

> **NOTE**
>
> Both EnCase and FTK routinely come out with new versions of their software. These new versions invariably have a host of new features and tools. If you work in law enforcement, it is very likely you will be working with FTK or EnCase. These are the two tools most often encountered in law enforcement computer forensics.

4

Collecting, Seizing, and Protecting Evidence

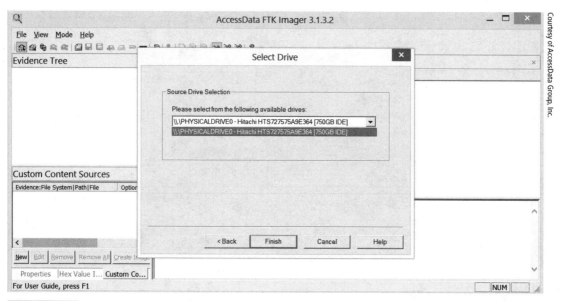

FIGURE 4-12

Evidence acquired.

RAID Acquisitions

You may already be comfortable with the concept of RAID; however, if you are not, this section provides a brief overview.

RAID stands for "redundant array of independent disks." The most common RAID levels are as follows:

- RAID 0 (disk striping) distributes data across multiple disks in a way that gives improved speed for data retrieval.

- RAID 1 mirrors the contents of the disks. The disk is completely mirrored so there is an identical copy of the drive running on the machine.

- RAID 3 or 4 (striped disks with dedicated parity) combines three or more disks in a way that protects data against loss of any one disk. Fault tolerance is achieved by adding an extra disk to the array and dedicating it to storing parity information. The storage capacity of the array is reduced by one disk.

- RAID 5 (striped disks with distributed parity) combines three or more disks in a way that protects data against the loss of any one disk. It is similar to RAID 3, but the parity is not stored on one dedicated drive; instead, parity information is interspersed across the drive array. The storage capacity of the array is a function of the number of drives minus the space needed to store parity.

- RAID 6 (striped disks with dual parity) combines four or more disks in a way that protects data against loss of any two disks.

- RAID 1+0 (or 10) is a mirrored data set (RAID 1), which is then striped (RAID 0), hence the "1+0" name. A RAID 1+0 array requires a minimum of four drives: two mirrored drives to hold half of the striped data, plus another two mirrored drives for the other half of the data.

No matter what version of RAID you are using (except for RAID 1), what you have is an array of disks with the same data on them.

Acquiring a RAID array has some challenges that are not encountered when acquiring a single drive. Some people recommend acquiring each disk separately. This is fine for RAID 1. Each disk is a separate entity. However with RAID 0, 3, 4, 5, and 6, there is data striping. The data is striped across multiple disks. In these situations, acquiring the disks separately is not recommended. Instead, make a forensic image of the entire RAID array. This requires a rather large target drive to copy it to.

 NOTE
Both FTK and EnCase provide built-in tools for acquiring RAID arrays.

 CHAPTER SUMMARY

In this chapter, you were introduced to some very specific procedures. These procedures govern how you will seize evidence, transport it, and prepare it for analysis. When you perform forensic analysis on drives, you gather very specific information and/or evidence. However, if the procedures outlined in this chapter are not followed carefully, any evidence subsequently gathered may be suspect. Failure to properly seize, transport, and handle evidence may even render the evidence inadmissible in a court of law.

 KEY CONCEPTS AND TERMS

Hash	Sweeper
Logical analysis	Temporary data
Physical analysis	Unallocated space
Scrubber	Volatile data

4

Collecting, Seizing, and Protecting Evidence

CHAPTER 4 ASSESSMENT

1. _____ is the most commonly used hashing algorithm.

2. What Linux command can be used to create a hash?
   - A. SHA
   - B. MD5
   - C. MD5sum
   - D. Sha3sum

3. What Linux command can be used to wipe a target drive?
   - A. Del
   - B. Delete
   - C. nc
   - D. dd

4. RAID 4 should be acquired as individual disks.
   - A. True
   - B. False

5. Which of the following drives would be least susceptible to damage when dropped?
   - A. SCSI
   - B. SSD
   - C. IDE
   - D. SATA

6. It is acceptable, when you have evidence in a vehicle, to stop for a meal, if the vehicle is locked.
   - A. True
   - B. False

7. A _____ might contain data that was live in memory and not stored on the hard drive.

Understanding Techniques for Hiding and Scrambling Information

REALLY TECHNICALLY SAVVY CRIMINALS will try to hide or scramble evidence on their computers. Sometimes they will hide scrambled information and sometimes they will scramble hidden information. Sometimes they will scramble and not hide, or hide and not scramble. That way, even if the computer is seized and searched, investigators are less likely to find the evidence. This chapter introduces the two ways of hiding and scrambling information: *steganography* and *encryption*. These techniques predate modern computers. In fact, they are so old that they can trace their origins to ancient Greece. Steganography comes from the Greek *steganos*, meaning covered or protected. Cryptography comes from the Greek *kryptos*, to hide. Encrypted information is clearly scrambled, and not hidden, per se.

Chapter 5 Topics

This chapter covers the following topics and concepts:

- What you need to understand about using and detecting steganography
- What you need to know about encryption

Chapter 5 Goals

When you complete this chapter, you will be able to:

- Understand steganography
- Use steganography
- Detect steganography
- Understand basic cryptography
- Utilize basic cryptography
- Understand general cryptanalysis techniques

Steganography

Steganography is the art and science of writing hidden messages. The goal is to hide information so that even if it is intercepted, it is not clear that information is hidden there. The most common method today is to hide messages in pictures. This is done using the **least significant bit (LSB)** method (when the last bit or least significant bit is used to store data). The LSB method depends on the fact that computers store things in bits and bytes. Now consider for a moment an 8-bit byte. For example, consider 11111111. If you convert this to decimal numbers, it equals 255. Now if you change the first 1 to a 0, you get 01111111. This equals 127 in decimal numbers, which is a pretty major change.

However, what if—instead of changing the first 0—you change the last 0? That would give you 11111110, which is equal to 254 in decimal numbers. This is a trivial change. That is why this last bit is called the least significant bit. Changing the least significant bit from a 0 to a 1 or from a 1 to a 0 makes the smallest change in the original information. Also consider that if the steganographic software overwrites the least significant bit with a 0 and it was already a 0, or overwrites the least significant bit with a 1 and it was already a 1 then there is no change to the original information.

Colored pixels in a computer are stored in bits. In Windows, for example, 24 bit is the normal color resolution. If you examine the Windows color palette, you'll find that you define a color by selecting three values between 0 and 255 in the Red, Green, and Blue text boxes shown in Figure 5-1.

Now consider what happens if you change just one bit. In Figure 5-2, you see a color that is defined by three numbers: 252, 101, and 100.

You can change the 101 by just one bit and make it 100, as you see in Figure 5-3.

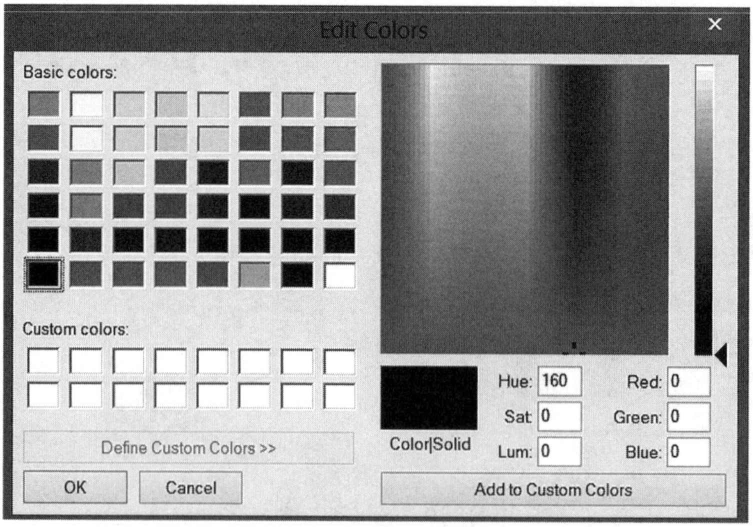

FIGURE 5-1

The Windows color palette in the Edit Colors dialog box.

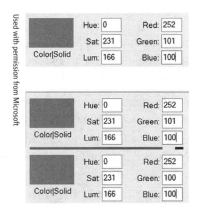

Used with permission from Microsoft

Used with permission from Microsoft

FIGURE 5-2

Windows color.

FIGURE 5-3

Windows color changed by one bit.

Your eye cannot really tell the difference; even if this book were in color, the difference would be impossible to detect. This is the basis for modern image steganography. If you change the least significant bit in a pixel, the image still looks the same. But a picture is made up of thousands—sometimes millions—of pixels. So by changing the least significant bit of many pixels, you can hide data in an image. If someone finds the image, even by using a tool such as Photoshop or GIMP (GNU Image Manipulation Program) to magnify the image, that person will not be able to see that data is hidden in it. Only by comparing the original image, bit by bit, to the steganized image can it be determined that information *may* be hidden within. And it is even more difficult to determine if there is hidden information if the hidden information has also been scrambled using encryption. As mentioned earlier, steganography and encryption can be used together.

It used to be the case that steganography required someone to be able to write specific computer program code to manipulate the bits in an image. This took training and skill; therefore, steganography was used only by computer professionals. However, a number of tools are now available on the Web that will hide information within an image for you:

- **QuickStego**—Is very easy to use, but very limited
- **Invisible Secrets**—Is much more robust, with both a free and a commercial version
- **MP3Stego**—Hides payload in MP3 files
- **Stealth Files 4**—Works with sound files, video files, and image files
- **Snow**—Hides data in white space
- **StegVideo**—Hides data in a video sequence

The following are some basic steganography terms you should know:

- **Payload** is the information to be covertly communicated. In other words, it is the message you want to hide.
- The **carrier** or carrier file is the signal, stream, or file in which the payload is hidden.
- The **channel** is the type of medium used. This may be a passive channel, such as photos, video, or sound files, or even an active channel, such as a Voice over IP (VoIP) voice call or streaming video connection.

5

Information-Hiding Techniques

Historical Steganography

Obviously, using digital images and files to hide messages did not exist prior to the advent of modern computers. However, hiding messages is not new. It has been done since ancient times. The following methods were once used to hide messages:

- The ancient Chinese wrapped notes in wax and swallowed them for transport. This was a crude but effective method of hiding messages.

- In ancient Greece, a messenger's head might be shaved, a message written on his head, then his hair was allowed to grow back. Obviously, this method required some time to work effectively.

- The German scholar Johannes Trithemius (1462–1516) wrote a book on cryptography and described a technique where a message was hidden by having each letter taken as a word from a specific column.

- During World War II, the French Resistance sent messages written on the backs of couriers using invisible ink.

NOTE

It is a common practice for pornographers, cybercriminals, terrorists, and others to cache steganized files on the servers or file stores of unsuspecting third parties and to use such locations as dead drops unbeknown to the third party.

NOTE

A *dead drop* is a location where one person drops off an item, and then a second person picks it up. For example, this is common in espionage. A spy drops off film with classified information near a bench in a park, and his contact picks it up later. In this way, the spy and his contact are never even seen together.

Steganophony

Steganophony is a term for hiding messages in sound files. This can be done with the LSB method. However, another method to use with steganophony is the echo method. This method adds extra sound to an echo inside an audio file. It is that extra sound that contains information. Steganophony can be used with static files, such as MP3 files, but can also be used dynamically with VoIP and similar multimedia technologies, also utilizing the LSB method and imperceptibly changing the sound being transmitted.

Video Steganography

Information can also be hidden in video files, a practice called video steganography. There are various ways to do this, including the LSB method. Whatever method is used, it is important to realize that video files are obviously larger than other file types. This provides a great deal of opportunity for hiding information.

Steganalysis

Steganalysis is the process of analyzing a file or files for hidden content. It is a difficult task. At best, it can show a likelihood that a given file has additional information hidden in it. A common method for detecting LSB steganography is to examine close-color pairs. Close-color pairs consist of two colors whose binary values differ only in the LSB. If this is seen too frequently in a given file, it can indicate that steganographically hidden messages may be present.

There are several methods for analyzing an image to detect hidden messages. The raw quick pair method is one. It is based on statistics of the numbers of unique colors and close-color pairs in a 24-bit image. Basically, it performs a quick analysis to determine if there are more close-color pairs than would be expected.

Another option uses the chi-square method from statistics. Chi-square analysis calculates the average LSB and builds a table of frequencies and a second table with pairs of values. Then it performs a chi-square test on these two tables. Essentially, it measures the theoretical versus the calculated population difference. When analyzing audio files, you can use steganalysis, which involves examining noise distortion in the carrier file. Noise distortion could indicate the presence of a hidden signal.

Many modern forensic tools also check for the presence of steganographically hidden messages. Forensic Toolkit (FTK) and EnCase both check for steganography, and FTK has an entire image detection engine devoted to this task. Details about this feature of FTK can be found at *http://marketing.accessdata.com/acton/attachment/4390/f-01ba/1/-/-/-/-/file.pdf*.

There are several free or inexpensive tools for detecting steganography:

- Outguess Xdetect is one tool: *http://www.outguess.org/detection.php*
- Steg Secret is another tool: *http://stegsecret.sourceforge.net/*
- StegSpy has fewer limitations than StegDetect: *http://www.spy-hunter.com/stegspydownload.htm*

But be aware that none of these methods is perfect. A great deal depends on the size of the payload compared with the size of the carrier file. This determines what percentage of the bits need to be changed. For example, if you have a 10-Kb text message in a 2-megabyte image file, it will be hard to detect. However, if you hide a 1-megabyte image in a 2-megabyte image, it will be easier to find.

It is also the case that the specific steganographic tool you use will determine how reliable steganalysis tests are. Some stego tools are more efficient than others. Depending upon how well information has been hidden, and if it is encrypted, it may be impossible to detect.

Invisible Secrets

A forensic examiner must be very familiar with steganography. This means you should be able to do steganography. Many tools are available on the Web. In this section, you learn Invisible Secrets. This tool is very inexpensive and a free trial version is available. It is also easy to use.

You can download Invisible Secrets from *http://www.invisiblesecrets.com/*. First, you must choose whether you want to hide a file or extract a hidden file. For this example, suppose you want to hide a file. You select your chosen option in the Invisible Secrets Select Action dialog box, shown in Figure 5-4, and then click the Next button.

Now select an image you want to use as the carrier file. You can see this in Figure 5-5. Select the file you want to hide. It can be a text file or another image file. You can also choose to encrypt as well as hide. This is shown in Figure 5-6.

FIGURE 5-4

Choose to hide a file or extract a hidden file in the Invisible Secrets Select Action dialog box.

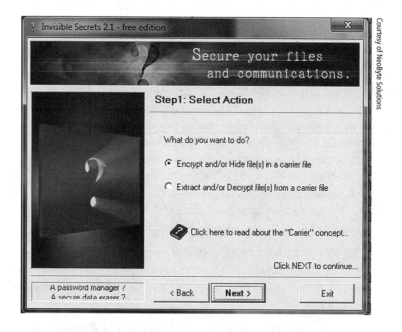

FIGURE 5-5

Select an image to use as the carrier file in the Invisible Secrets Select a Carrier File dialog box.

Now, select a password for your hidden file, as shown in Figure 5-7.

Next, pick a name for the resulting file that contains your hidden file, as shown in Figure 5-8.

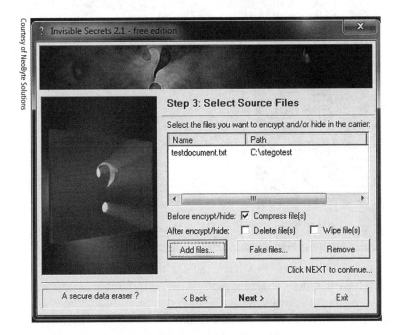

Courtesy of NeoByte Solutions

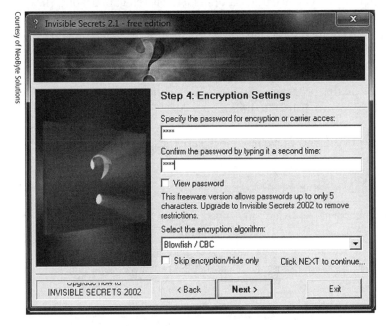

Courtesy of NeoByte Solutions

5

Information-Hiding
Techniques

FIGURE 5-8

Name the new file in the Invisible Secrets Target File Settings dialog box.

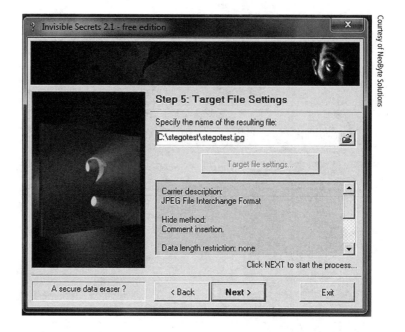

That's it. You have just done steganography. Now consider this for just a moment. If it is that easy and tools are available on the Internet, then this is something many criminals probably use. Fortunately, not all criminals are tech savvy, so you will still find many computers with evidence that is not hidden with steganography. However, during your career as a forensic examiner, you will come across steganography from time to time, and more often in complex cases involving organized crime, spying, and terrorism.

MP3Stego

You can download this program from *http://www.petitcolas.net/fabien/steganography/ mp3stego/*. This program is used to hide data in MP3 files. It takes the information (usually text) and combines it with a sound file to create a new sound file that contains the hidden information. From the MP3Stego readme file are these instructions:

FYI

During the raid on Osama Bin Laden's compound, which resulted in his death, a number of computer hard drives were found. On those hard drives, a number of pornographic videos were discovered. It was later determined, using computer forensics, that these videos contained steganographically hidden messages. It is clear that Bin Laden was communicating with terrorist cells via steganography.

- `encode -E data.txt -P pass sound.wav sound.mp3`—Compresses sound.wav and hides data.txt. This produces the output called sound.mp3. The text in data.txt is encrypted using `pass`.

- `decode -X -P pass sound.mp3`—Uncompresses sound.mp3 into sound.mp3. pcm and attempts to extract hidden information. The hidden message is decrypted, uncompressed, and saved into sound.mp3.

This is a very simple program to use and it is freely available on the Internet.

Additional Resources

This is enough steganography for you to work as a forensic examiner, but if you want to learn more, you might find the following resources of value:

- **An Australian Broadcasting Corporation story on steganography**— *http://www.abc.net.au/catalyst/stories/s1320215.htm*

- **A technical paper on steganography**—*http://www.jjtc.com/stegdoc/*

- **A ComputerWorld article on steganography**—*http://www.computerworld.com/s/article/71726/Steganography_Hidden_Data*

- **An RQP paper**—*http://www.ws.binghamton.edu/fridrich/Research/acm_2001_03.pdf*

- **A paper on the detection of LSB steganography**—*http://www.cecs.uci.edu/~papers/icme06/pdfs/0001377.pdf*

- **A paper on the detection of audio steganography**—*http://www.ece.ucdavis.edu/~yliu/pub/papers/Tracy_ISC08.pdf*

Encryption

Cryptography is not so much about hiding a message, as with steganography, but rather about obfuscating the message so that it cannot be read. In other words, with steganography, the examiner may not even be aware a message is present. With cryptography, it is obvious there is a message present, but the examiner cannot easily decipher the message. The word cryptography is derived from word *kryptós*, which means *hidden*, and the verb *gráfo*, which means *write*. Therefore, cryptography is the study of writing secret messages.

> **NOTE**

Although professional cryptographers have distinctions between terms like *cryptography*, *cryptology*, and *encryption*, for the purposes of this discussion, this chapter ignores those technical distinctions and you will see the words used interchangeably.

FYI

Cryptography is an area in which many security professionals, including forensic examiners, are weak. Even the major security certifications give only a cursory coverage of cryptography. It is particularly important for forensic examiners to be more knowledgeable about cryptography. This section provides a thorough introduction to the field.

5

Information-Hiding Techniques

The History of Encryption

Encrypting communications is almost as old as writing. Throughout history, people have wanted to keep their communications private. Although for much of human history this has been a requirement primarily for governments, militaries, and businesses, in modern times private individuals also have had a need for cryptography.

The concept of cryptography is actually pretty simple. Messages must be changed in such a way that they cannot be read easily by any party that intercepts them but can be decoded easily by the intended recipient. Modern methods usually depend on some combination of mathematics and information theory. First, it is a good idea to start with examining a few historical methods of encryption. Keep in mind that these historical methods are no longer considered secure. They can be cracked in seconds by modern computers. But they are very useful for the novice to begin learning the encryption process.

The Caesar Cipher

The **Caesar cipher** is purported to have been used by the ancient Roman Caesars, such as Julius Caesar, hence the name. This method is also referred to as a substitution cipher. Almost every introductory cryptography book in existence mentions the Caesar cipher. It is even mentioned in the course material for several prominent network security certifications. It is actually quite simple to do. You choose some number by which to shift each letter of a text and substitute the new alphabetic letter for the letter you are encrypting. For example, if the text is

A CAT

And you choose to shift by two letters; then *C* replaces *A*, *E* replaces *C*, *C* replaces *A*, and *V* replaces *T* and the encrypted message is

C ECV

Or, if you choose to shift by three letters, the encrypted message becomes

D FDW

You can choose to shift by any number of letters, either left or right. If you choose to shift 2 to the right, that would be a $+2$; if you choose to shift 4 to the left, that would be a -4. If you get to the end of the alphabet, just keep going back to the beginning. So if you are shifting to the right, and need to go past Z, just start over at A. Julius Caesar was reputed to have used a shift of three to the right.

Because this is a very simple method to understand, it is a good place to start your study of encryption. It is, however, extremely easy to crack using the two major forms of attacking text for decryption. The first is a **brute-force attack**. If a Caesar cipher is suspected, modern computers can simply try all possible combinations and see if recognizable text emerges. The second is an academic, or knowledge-based, attack. The Caesar cipher is easy to crack using an academic approach because of letter and word frequency.

Any language has a certain letter and word frequency, meaning that some letters are used more frequently than others. In the English language, the most common single-letter word is *a*. The most common three-letter word is *the*. Those two rules alone could help you decrypt a Caesar cipher. For example, if you saw a string of seemingly nonsense letters and noticed that a three-letter word was frequently repeated in the message, you might easily surmise that this word was *the* and the odds are highly in favor of this being correct. Furthermore, if you frequently noticed a single-letter word in the text, it is most likely the letter *a*. You now have found the substitution scheme for *a, t, h,* and *e*. You can now either translate all of those letters in the message and attempt to guess the rest or simply analyze the substitute letters used for *a, t, h,* and *e* and derive the substitution cipher that was used for this message.

Decrypting a message of this type does not even require a computer. Someone with no background in cryptography could do it in less than 10 minutes using pen and paper. There are other rules that help make cracking this code even easier. For example, in the English language, the two most common two-letter combinations are *ee* and *oo*. That gives you even more to work with.

The substitution scheme you choose (e.g., +2, +1) is referred to as a substitution alphabet (i.e., *b* substitutes for *a, u* substitutes for *t,* and so on). Thus, the Caesar cipher is also referred to as a monoalphabet or single-alphabet substitution method, meaning that it uses a single substitution for the encryption. That just means that all letters in the plaintext are shifted by the same number.

In any cryptographic algorithm, be it a simple one like the Caesar cipher or a more modern one, the number that is used by the algorithm to encrypt or decrypt a message is called the key because it unlocks the scrambled information. In the case of the Caesar cipher, it is a single digit (like +2), and in the case of modern algorithms like Advanced Encryption Standard (AES), it is a 128-bit number. Even though the Caesar cipher may have a much simpler algorithm (shift the letters by whatever number and direction is in the key) and a smaller key (a single digit, or at most two digits, as in +12 or −11), it is still an example of the basic concepts you see in more sophisticated modern cryptographic algorithms.

The Caesar cipher also introduces two more basic concepts of cryptography. The text you want to encrypt is referred to as the plaintext. After it has been subjected to the algorithm and key, the resultant text is called the ciphertext. So, although simple, the Caesar cipher introduces cryptography algorithms, keys, plaintext, and ciphertext.

This gives you a primitive introduction to cryptography and encryption. It must be stressed that this is no longer a secure method of encrypting messages, but it is an interesting exercise to begin introducing the basic concepts of encryption.

The Atbash Cipher

Hebrew scribes copying the book of Jeremiah used this cipher. This cipher is very simple—just reverse the alphabet. This is, by modern standards, a very primitive and easy-to-break cipher. But it will help you get a feel for how cryptography works.

The Atbash cipher is a Hebrew code that substitutes the first letter of the alphabet for the last letter and the second letter for the second-to-last letter, and so forth. It simply reverses the alphabet. This, like the Caesar cipher, is a single-alphabet substitution cipher. A becomes Z, B becomes Y, C becomes X, and so on.

The ROT13 Cipher

This is another single-alphabet substitution cipher. It is, in fact, the simplest of all of them. It is really just a permutation of the Caesar cipher. All characters are rotated 13 characters through the alphabet. The phrase

A CAT

becomes

N PNG

It is essentially the Caesar cipher, but always using a rotation or shift of 13 characters. This is very simple and not sophisticated enough for any real security. But, again, it can be done with pen and paper, or with a simple computer program.

The Scytale Cipher

The *scytale*, which rhymes with Italy, is a cylinder or baton used by the Greeks, and is often specifically attributed to the Spartans. This physical cylinder was used to encrypt messages. Turning the cylinder produced different ciphertexts. Although it is not clear exactly how old this cipher is, it was first mentioned in the 7th century BC by the Greek poet Archilochus. The recipient used a rod of the same diameter as the one used to create the message. He then wrapped the parchment to read the message. To encrypt, he simply wrote across a leather strip attached to a rod. To decrypt, the recipient would just wrap the leather strip around the rod and read across. This was a simple process; it just required both parties have the same size rod and the leather "key."

Multialphabet Substitution

Eventually, a slight improvement on the Caesar cipher was developed, called multi-alphabet substitution. In this scheme, you select multiple numbers by which letters in the plaintext will be shifted; in other words, multiple substitution alphabets are created. For example, if you select three substitution alphabets ($+2, -2, +3$), then A CAT becomes C ADV. Notice that the fourth letter starts over with another $+2$, and you can see that the first *A* was transformed to *C* and the second *A* was transformed to *D*. This makes it more difficult to decipher the underlying text. Although this is harder to decrypt than a Caesar cipher, it is not overly difficult. It can be done with simple pen and paper and a bit of effort. It can be cracked very quickly by a computer. In fact, no one would use such a method today to send any truly secure message because this type of encryption is considered very weak.

	A	B	C	D	E	F	G	H	I	J	K	L	M	N	O	P	Q	R	S	T	U	V	W	X	Y	Z
A	A	B	C	D	E	F	G	H	I	J	K	L	M	N	O	P	Q	R	S	T	U	V	W	X	Y	Z
B	B	C	D	E	F	G	H	I	J	K	L	M	N	O	P	Q	R	S	T	U	V	W	X	Y	Z	A
C	C	D	E	F	G	H	I	J	K	L	M	N	O	P	Q	R	S	T	U	V	W	X	Y	Z	A	B
D	D	E	F	G	H	I	J	K	L	M	N	O	P	Q	R	S	T	U	V	W	X	Y	Z	A	B	C
E	E	F	G	H	I	J	K	L	M	N	O	P	Q	R	S	T	U	V	W	X	Y	Z	A	B	C	D
F	F	G	H	I	J	K	L	M	N	O	P	Q	R	S	T	U	V	W	X	Y	Z	A	B	C	D	E
G	G	H	I	J	K	L	M	N	O	P	Q	R	S	T	U	V	W	X	Y	Z	A	B	C	D	E	F
H	H	I	J	K	L	M	N	O	P	Q	R	S	T	U	V	W	X	Y	Z	A	B	C	D	E	F	G
I	I	J	K	L	M	N	O	P	Q	R	S	T	U	V	W	X	Y	Z	A	B	C	D	E	F	G	H
J	J	K	L	M	N	O	P	Q	R	S	T	U	V	W	X	Y	Z	A	B	C	D	E	F	G	H	I
K	K	L	M	N	O	P	Q	R	S	T	U	V	W	X	Y	Z	A	B	C	D	E	F	G	H	I	J
L	L	M	N	O	P	Q	R	S	T	U	V	W	X	Y	Z	A	B	C	D	E	F	G	H	I	J	K
M	M	N	O	P	Q	R	S	T	U	V	W	X	Y	Z	A	B	C	D	E	F	G	H	I	J	K	L
N	N	O	P	Q	R	S	T	U	V	W	X	Y	Z	A	B	C	D	E	F	G	H	I	J	K	L	M
O	O	P	Q	R	S	T	U	V	W	X	Y	Z	A	B	C	D	E	F	G	H	I	J	K	L	M	N
P	P	Q	R	S	T	U	V	W	X	Y	Z	A	B	C	D	E	F	G	H	I	J	K	L	M	N	O
Q	Q	R	S	T	U	V	W	X	Y	Z	A	B	C	D	E	F	G	H	I	J	K	L	M	N	O	P
R	R	S	T	U	V	W	X	Y	Z	A	B	C	D	E	F	G	H	I	J	K	L	M	N	O	P	Q
S	S	T	U	V	W	X	Y	Z	A	B	C	D	E	F	G	H	I	J	K	L	M	N	O	P	Q	R
T	T	U	V	W	X	Y	Z	A	B	C	D	E	F	G	H	I	J	K	L	M	N	O	P	Q	R	S
U	U	V	W	X	Y	Z	A	B	C	D	E	F	G	H	I	J	K	L	M	N	O	P	Q	R	S	T
V	V	W	X	Y	Z	A	B	C	D	E	F	G	H	I	J	K	L	M	N	O	P	Q	R	S	T	U
W	W	X	Y	Z	A	B	C	D	E	F	G	H	I	J	K	L	M	N	O	P	Q	R	S	T	U	V
X	X	Y	Z	A	B	C	D	E	F	G	H	I	J	K	L	M	N	O	P	Q	R	S	T	U	V	W
Y	Y	Z	A	B	C	D	E	F	G	H	I	J	K	L	M	N	O	P	Q	R	S	T	U	V	W	X
Z	Z	A	B	C	D	E	F	G	H	I	J	K	L	M	N	O	P	Q	R	S	T	U	V	W	X	Y

FIGURE 5-9

Vigenère table.

The Vigenère Cipher

One of the most widely known multialphabet ciphers was the **Vigenère cipher**. This cipher was invented in 1553 by Giovan Battista Bellaso. It is a method of encrypting alphabetic text by using a series of different monoalphabet ciphers selected based on the letters of a keyword. This algorithm was later misattributed to Blaise de Vigenère, and so it is now known as the Vigenère cipher, even though Vigenère did not really invent it.

You use the table (shown in Figure 5-9) along with a keyword you have selected. Match the letter of your keyword on the top with the letter of your plaintext on the left to find the ciphertext.

Using the table shown in Figure 5-9, if you are encrypting the word *cat* and your keyword is *horse*, then the ciphertext is *jok*.

Multialphabet ciphers are more secure than single-alphabet substitution ciphers. However, they are still not acceptable for modern cryptographic usage. Computer-based cryptanalysis systems can crack historical cryptographic methods (both single-alphabet and multialphabet) very easily. This chapter presents the single-alphabet substitution and multialphabet substitution ciphers just to show you the history of cryptography and to help you get an understanding of how cryptography works.

The Enigma Machine

In World War II, the Germans made use of an electromechanical rotor-based cipher system known as the Enigma machine. The Enigma machine is pivotal in the history of cryptography. It is a multialphabet substitution cipher using machinery to accomplish the encryption. There are multiple variations on this machine.

The machine was designed so that when the operator pressed a key, the encrypted ciphertext for that plaintext was altered each time. So, if the operator pressed the *A* key, he or she might generate an *F* in the ciphertext, and the next time it might be a *D*. Essentially, this was a multialphabet cipher, consisting of 26 possible alphabets.

Allied cipher machines used in World War II included the British TypeX and the American SIGABA. Both of these were quite similar to the Enigma machine, but with improvements that made them more secure. The Enigma machine and its variations were essentially mechanical implementations of multialphabet substitution.

Modern Cryptography

The earlier "The History of Encryption" section was designed to give you a feel for cryptography. Some forms, like the Caesar cipher, can even be done with pen and paper. Modern cryptography methods, as well as computers, make decryption a rather advanced science. Therefore, encryption must be equally sophisticated to have a chance of success. It is also important to realize that cryptographic methods have evolved quite a bit since the days of these ancient ciphers.

Modern cryptography is separated into two distinct groups: symmetric cryptography and asymmetric cryptography. Symmetric cryptography uses the same key to encrypt and decrypt the plaintext, while asymmetric cryptography uses different keys to encrypt and decrypt the plaintext. In this section, you learn about both methods.

Beware of Algorithms Too Good to Be True

As you discover in this chapter, the basic concepts of encryption are very simple. Anyone with even rudimentary programming skills can write a program that implements one of the simple encryption methods examined here. However, these methods are not secure and are only included to illustrate fundamental encryption concepts.

From time to time, someone new to encryption discovers these basic methods, and in his enthusiasm attempts to create his own encryption method by making some minor modifications. Although this can be a very stimulating intellectual exercise, it is only that. Users without training in advanced math or cryptography are extremely unlikely to stumble across a new encryption method that is effective for secure communications.

Amateurs frequently post claims that they have discovered the latest, unbreakable encryption algorithm on the Usenet newsgroup sci.crypt (if you are not familiar with Usenet, those groups are now accessible via the Groups link on *http://www.google.com*). Their algorithms are usually quickly broken. Unfortunately, some people implement such methods into software products and market them as secure.

Some distributors of insecure encryption methods and software do so out of simple greed and are intentionally defrauding an unsuspecting public. Others do so out of simple ignorance, honestly believing that their method is superior. Methods for evaluating encryption claims are discussed later in this chapter.

Kerckhoffs's Principle

This principle states that the security of a cryptographic algorithm depends only on the secrecy of the key, not the algorithm itself. For practical purposes, this means that the details of a cryptographic algorithm can be made public. In fact, all the major algorithms discussed here are published. You can get all the details online or in books. This does not undermine the security of the algorithm. In fact, it enhances it. Publishing the algorithm allows cryptographic researchers to analyze the algorithm and to search for flaws in it. The opposite of Kerckhoffs's principle is an application of the principle of "security by obscurity" to the underlying cryptographic algorithm: The algorithm is kept secret. Although this is a fairly common practice, it does not contribute to the secrecy of encrypted information—in fact, quite the opposite.

Symmetric Cryptography

Symmetric cryptography refers to those methods where the same key is used to encrypt and decrypt the plaintext. One step that has been used widely is to use two different encryption keys, one from sender to receiver and one from receiver to sender. This is still symmetric cryptography because the same key is used for encryption as is used for decryption—having different keys in both directions just provides additional security if the keys are learned or disclosed. This is historically the type of encryption that has been used exclusively until recently.

Substitution and transposition. **Substitution** is changing some part of the plaintext for some matching part of ciphertext. The Caesar and Atbash ciphers are simple substitution ciphers. The Vigenère cipher is a bit more complex, but is still a substitution cipher. In fact, all of the historical examples examined in this chapter are called simple substitution. They are substitution ciphers because each single character of plaintext is converted into a single character of ciphertext.

    Transposition is the swapping of blocks of ciphertext. For example, if you have the text "I like ice cream," you could transpose or swap every three-letter sequence (or block) with the next and get:

    "ikeI l creiceam"

Of course, modern transposition is at the level of bits, or rather blocks, or contiguous groups, of bits. However, this illustrates the concept. All modern block-cipher algorithms use both substitution and transposition. The combination of substitution and transposition increases the security of the resultant ciphertext.

Block ciphers and stream ciphers. There are two types of symmetric algorithms: block ciphers and stream ciphers. A **block cipher** literally encrypts the data in blocks; 64-bit blocks are quite common, although some algorithms (like AES) use larger blocks. For example, AES uses a 128-bit block. **Stream ciphers** encrypt the data as a stream, one bit at a time.

5

There are a few basic facts that are generally applicable to all block ciphers. Assuming the actual algorithm is mathematically sound, then the following is true:

- Larger block sizes increase security.
- Larger key sizes increase security against brute-force attack methods.
- If the round function is secure, then more rounds increase security to a point.

Now the real caveat here is the "assuming the algorithm is mathematically sound" part. If the algorithm is mathematically sound, these facts hold true. If the algorithm is not sound, a larger block size or larger key size may have little impact on security. This takes us back to the previously mentioned Kerckhoff's principle. It is important that any cryptographic algorithm be rigorously examined by mathematicians and cryptographers to ensure that it is sound.

The Feistel function. This function is named after its inventor, the German-born physicist and cryptographer Horst Feistel. At the heart of many block ciphers is a **Feistel function**. So this makes it a good place to start your study of symmetric algorithms. This function forms the basis for many, if not most, block ciphers. This makes it one of the most influential developments in symmetric block ciphers. It is also known as a Feistel network or a Feistel cipher. Any block cipher that is based on Feistel will essentially work in the same manner; the differences will be what is done in the round function.

This function starts by splitting the block of plaintext data (often 64 bits) into two parts (traditionally termed L_0 and R_0). Usually the split is equal—both sides are the same size. However, there are variations where this is not the case.

The round function F is applied to one of the halves. The term *round function* simply means a function performed with each iteration, or round, of the Feistel cipher. The details of the round function F can vary with different implementations. Usually these are relatively simple functions, to allow for increased speed of the algorithm.

The output of each round function F and the remaining half of the data are then run through the exclusive OR (XOR) function. This means, for example, that you take L_0, pass it through the round function F, then take the result and XOR it with R_0.

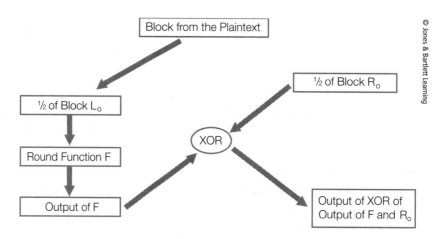

FIGURE 5-10

Feistel function.

Block from the Plaintext

½ of Block R_0

½ of Block L_0

Round Function F

XOR

Output of F

Output of XOR of Output of F and R_0

Then, the halves are transposed, or their positions switched. This means L_0 gets moved to the right and R_0 gets moved to the left. This process is repeated a given number of times. The main difference between different cryptographic algorithms that are Feistel ciphers is the exact nature of the round function F and the number of iterations. A simple diagram of this process is shown in Figure 5-10.

A Brief Review of Binary Operations

When working with binary numbers, there are three logical operations not found in normal math: AND, OR, and XOR operations. Each is illustrated below.

AND

To perform the AND operation, you take two binary numbers and compare them one place at a time. If both numbers have a 1 in both places, then the resultant number is a 1. If not, then the resultant number is a 0, as you see here:

```
1 1 0 1
1 0 0 1
_____
1 0 0 1
```

OR

The OR operation checks to see whether there is a 1 in either or both numbers in a given place. If so, then the resultant number is 1. If not, the resultant number is 0, as you see here:

```
1 1 0 1
1 0 0 1
_____
1 1 0 1
```

XOR

The exclusive OR (XOR) operation affects your study of encryption the most. It checks to see whether there is a 1 in a number in a given place, but not in both numbers at that place. If it is in one number but not the other, then the resultant number is 1. If not, the resultant number is 0, as you see here:

```
1 1 0 1
1 0 0 1
_____
0 1 0 0
```

The XOR function has a very interesting property in that it is reversible. If you XOR the resultant number with the second number, you get back the first number. And if you XOR the resultant number with the first number, you get the second number.

```
0 1 0 0
1 0 0 1
_____
1 1 0 1
```

Data Encryption Standard (DES). One of the oldest of the modern symmetric ciphers is the Data Encryption Standard (DES). DES was developed by IBM in the early 1970s. DES is a block cipher. It was a U.S. government standard until the 1990s. IBM had originally developed a cipher called Lucifer, which was designed by Horst Feistel. When the U.S. government began seeking a standardized encryption algorithm, IBM worked with the National Security Agency (NSA) to alter Lucifer to fit the government's needs, thus DES was created. As you may guess, DES is a Feistel cipher.

The basic concept of DES, is as follows:

1. Data is divided into 64-bit blocks.
2. That data is then manipulated by 16 separate steps of encryption involving substitutions, bit-shifting, and logical operations using a 56-bit key.
3. Data is then further scrambled using a swapping algorithm.
4. Data is finally transposed one last time.

Those four steps provide a simplified, high-level view of DES. As you can see, it works on splitting the block into two sections, as with all Feistel ciphers. The idea is to continually scramble the underlying message to make it appear as random as possible.

To generate the keys for each round, the 56-bit key is split into two 28-bit halves and those halves are circularly shifted after each round by 1 or 2 bits. In other words, the halves are first subjected to a round function, then the keys are shifted by 1 to 2 bits each time so they can be used in the next round as a different key. Then 48 bits from those two halves are selected and permuted to form the round key. This means there is a different round key for each round. But, it is related to the previous round key. In fact, it is derived from the previous round key.

DES uses eight S-boxes. The term *S-boxes* means substitution boxes. They are simply lookup tables. Each S-box basically has a table that determines, based on the bits passed into it, what to substitute for those bits. Each item passed into the box is substituted with the item that matches it in the lookup table. This is a very common tactic in symmetric key

The Vulnerabilities of DES

DES is no longer considered secure but is still widely used, or at least is a common choice, for encryption. DES uses short keys compared with later algorithms and is therefore considered vulnerable to brute-force attacks. A brute-force attack is one in which the attacker tries to decrypt a message by simply applying every possible key in the keyspace. Modern computers can attempt 256 different possibilities in a reasonably short period of time. It is also interesting that the number of possible key combinations doubles for each bit added; therefore, a 57-bit key actually has twice the number of possible combinations as a 56-bit key. It was not known for sure until the late 1990s, but was widely hypothesized, that the reason why the NSA steered IBM toward using a 56-bit key instead of the original 64-bit key of Lucifer was so that the NSA could crack DES encryption.

algorithms. Each one of the DES S-boxes takes in 6 bits and produces 4 bits. The middle 4 bits of the 6-bit input are used to look up the 4-bit replacement.

The round F function works as follows:

1. Expand the 32-bit half that was input to 48 bits; this is done by replicating some bits.
2. XOR the resultant 48 bits with the 48-bit round key.
3. Split the result into eight 6-bit sections.
4. Pass each of these 6-bit portions through a different S-box. Each S-box produces a 4-bit output, giving a total of 32 output bits. Note in Step 1 the expansion of the 32 bits into 48; it's now taken back to just 32 bits, which demonstrates yet another way to scramble the resultant ciphertext.
5. Transpose the output bits.

This is done for each round of DES. DES has 16 rounds. So this is an effective way to scramble the plaintext.

The only reason DES is no longer considered secure is the short key. The 56-bit key is simply not long enough to prevent brute-force attacks. Brute force is trying every possible key. DES has a total number of possible keys (also called **keyspace**) of 2^{56}. A modern computer system can break this in a reasonable amount of time.

> **NOTE**
>
> In the early days of cryptanalysis, much of the work was done manually and then by computer once computers were invented. It is now a very common practice for multiple computers to be used in parallel to break a code, which cuts what used to take weeks down to something that can be accomplished in minutes.

Triple DES (3DES). Eventually, it became obvious that DES would no longer be secure. The U.S. federal government began a contest seeking a replacement cryptography algorithm. However, in the meantime Triple Des (3DES) was created as an interim solution. Essentially, it does DES three times, with three different keys.

3DES uses a "key bundle," which comprises three DES keys, K1, K2, and K3. Each key is a standard 56-bit DES key. It then applies the following process:

DES encrypt with K_1, DES *decrypt* with K_2, then DES encrypt with K_3.

FYI

You might ask, "If DES was the first DES and 3DES is currently popular, what happened to 2DES and is there a 4DES?" Whereas 3DES basically does DES three times, there was an interim step, which was to do DES twice. This was called 2DES; however, it was not much more secure than DES and it took more time and computer resources to implement, so it was not widely used. On the other hand, 4DES was never implemented because early simulations indicated that 4DES was too scrambled—so scrambled, in fact, that blocks of the original plaintext appeared in the final ciphertext. This was one of the driving factors behind searching for a new algorithm not in the DES line.

There are three options for the keys. In the first option, all three keys are independent and different. In the second options, K_1 and K_3 are identical. In the third option, all three keys are the same. So you are literally applying the exact same DES algorithm three times, with the same key. Option 1 is the most secure, with Option 3 being the least secure.

Advanced Encryption Standard (AES). The Advanced Encryption Standard (AES) is also known as the Rijndael block cipher. It was officially designated as a replacement for DES in 2001 after a five-year process involving 15 competing algorithms. AES is designated as Federal Information Processing Standard 197 (FIPS 197).

AES can have three different key sizes:128, 192, or 256 bits. The three different implementations of AES are referred to as AES 128, AES 192, and AES 256. All three operate on a block size of 128 bits.

The AES algorithm was developed by two Belgian cryptographers, Joan Daemen and Vincent Rijmen. Unlike both DES and 3DES, AES is not based on a Feistel network. AES uses a substitution-permutation matrix instead. AES operates on a 4×4 column matrix of bytes, termed the state (versions of AES with a larger block size have additional columns in the state). The general steps of AES are as follows:

1. **Key expansion**—Round keys are derived from the cipher key using Rijndael's key schedule. The specifics of that key schedule are not important for this book, but essentially it generates a different key each round, based on the original key. This is much like DES.

2. **Initial round**

   a. **AddRoundKey**—Each byte of the state is combined with the round key using bitwise XOR. In other words, the plaintext is arrayed bit by bit in a matrix that is XOR'd with the key.

3. **Rounds**

   a. **SubBytes**—A nonlinear substitution step where each byte is replaced with another according to a lookup table. Basically, each byte in the matrix is then fed into a substitution box. However, with AES, this box also transposes the bits as well as substituting them, so it is called a permutation box.

   b. **ShiftRows**—A transposition step where each row of the state is shifted cyclically a certain number of steps.

   c. **MixColumns**—A mixing operation that operates on the columns of the state, combining the 4 bytes in each column.

   d. **AddRoundKey**—A step where the key is XOR'd with the matrix again.

4. **Final round (no MixColumns)**

   a. **SubBytes**—Same as above

   b. **ShiftRows**—Same as above

   c. **AddRoundKey**—Same as above

Some details about these steps are as follows:

- In the SubBytes step, each byte in the matrix is substituted for another byte using an 8-bit substitution box, called the Rijndael S-box.
- The ShiftRows step works by shifting the bytes in each row by a certain amount. The first row is left unchanged. The second row is shifted one to the left, the third row is shifted by two, and so on.
- In the MixColumns step, the columns are mixed, similar to the shifting rows. However, rather than just shifting them, they are actually mixed together.
- In the AddRoundKey step, the subkey is XOR'd with the state. For each round, a subkey is derived from the main key using Rijndael's key schedule; each subkey is the same size as the state.

This algorithm is a bit more complex than DES or 3DES.

AES can use three different key sizes: a 128-bit, a 192-bit, or a 256-bit key. The longer the key, the more resistant the resultant ciphertext will be to brute-force attacks. The National Security Agency has approved 256-bit AES for use with Top Secret data; therefore, it is secure enough for commercial applications.

Other symmetric algorithms. There are many other symmetric algorithms. A few examples include the following:

- Blowfish
- Serpent
- Skipjack

However, AES is the most commonly used symmetric algorithm today, and DES is one of the most widely known and an excellent example of a Feistel cipher. If you study these two, you will be reasonably well informed on symmetric ciphers.

Asymmetric Cryptography

Asymmetric cryptography is cryptography wherein two keys are used: one to encrypt the message and another to decrypt it.

> **WARNING**
>
> Federal law prohibits the exportation of encryption beyond a certain strength. This means that if you are in the United States, you cannot market any product outside the United States if that product has any encryption technology that exceeds the federal limits. The exact limit is currently being contested in various court cases. It is also illegal to carry encryption tools beyond a certain strength out of the United States or into certain other countries.

RSA. This algorithm was publicly described in 1977 by Ron Rivest, Adi Shamir, and Leonard Adleman at MIT. The letters RSA are the initials of their surnames. RSA is perhaps the most widely used public key cryptography algorithm in existence today.

It is based on some interesting relationships of prime numbers. The security of RSA derives from the fact that it is difficult to factor a large integer composed of two or more large prime factors.

To create the key, two large random primes, p and q, of approximately equal size are generated. Now two numbers are chosen so that when multiplied together the product will be the desired size—for example, 1,024 bits, 2,048 bits, and so on.

Now *p* and *q* are multiplied to get *n*.

The next step is to multiply Euler's Totient for each of these primes. **Euler's Totient** is the total number of coprime numbers. Two numbers are considered coprime if they have no common factors. For example, if the original number is 7, then 5 and 7 would be coprime. It just so happens that for prime numbers, this is always the number minus 1. For example, 7 has six numbers that are co-prime to it. Therefore,

$$m = (p-1)(q-1)$$

NOTE

Modulo refers to dividing two numbers and returning the remainder. For example, 8 modulo 3 would be 8/2 with a remainder of 2. The modulo would, therefore, be 2.

Now another number is selected. This number is called *e* and *e* is coprime to *m*.

At this point, the key is almost generated. Now a number *d* is calculated that when multiplied by *e* and modulo *m* would yield a 1.

Find *d*, such that $de \bmod(m) = 1$

Now you have the public keys, *e* and *n*, and the private, or secret, keys, *d* and *n*. To encrypt, you simply take your message raised to the *e* power and modulo *n*.

$$= M^e \bmod(n)$$

To decrypt, you take the ciphertext, raise it to the *d* power modulo *n*, or

$$P = C^d \bmod(n)$$

Then, you can get a better understanding of RSA by walking through the algorithm utilizing small integers. Normally, RSA would be done with very large integers.

RSA is based on large prime numbers. Now you might think, couldn't someone take the public key and use factoring to derive the private key? Hypothetically, yes. However, factoring really large numbers into their prime factors is difficult. There is no efficient algorithm for doing it. RSA can use 1,024-, 2,048-, 4,096-bit and larger keys. Those make for some huge numbers. Of course, should anyone ever invent an efficient algorithm that will factor a large number into its prime factors, RSA would be obsolete.

Diffie-Hellman. The Diffie-Hellman algorithm is a cryptographic protocol that allows two parties to establish a shared key over an insecure channel. In other words, Diffie-Hellman is often used to allow parties to exchange a symmetric key through some insecure medium, such as the Internet. It was developed by Whitfield Diffie and Martin Hellman in 1976. An interesting twist is that the method had actually already been developed by Malcolm J. Williamson of the British Intelligence Service, but it was classified and, therefore, could not be publicly disclosed at the time of its creation. Diffie-Hellman enabled all secure communications between parties that did not have a preestablished relationship, such as e-commerce, and facilitated communications even between parties with a preestablished relationship, such as e-banking.

Other asymmetric algorithms. RSA is the most widely used asymmetric algorithm, so it is the only one this chapter covers in detail. However, you can study other asymmetric algorithms if you desire:

- MQV
- Elliptic Curve
- DSA

Each of these is based on some aspect of number theory.

Breaking Encryption

Cryptanalysis is using techniques other than brute force to attempt to uncover a key. This is also referred to as academic or knowledge-based code breaking. In some cases, cryptographic techniques are used to test the efficacy of a cryptographic algorithm. Such techniques are frequently used to test hash algorithms for collisions. Any attempt to crack a nontrivial cryptographic algorithm is simply an attempt. There is no guarantee of any method working. And whether it works or not, it will probably be a long and tedious process. If cracking encryption were a trivial process, then encryption would be useless.

Frequency Analysis

This is the basic tool for breaking most classical ciphers. In natural languages, certain letters of the alphabet appear more frequently than others. By examining those frequencies, you can derive some information about the key that was used. This method is very effective against classic ciphers like Caesar, Vigenère, and so on. It is not effective against modern methods of cryptography. Remember, in English, the words *the* and *and* are the two most common three-letter words. The most common single letter words are *a* and *I*. If you see two of the same letters together in a word, it is most likely *ee* or *oo*.

Kasiski

Kasiski examination was developed by Friedrich Kasiski in 1863. It is a method of attacking polyalphabetic substitution ciphers, such as the Vigenère cipher. This method can be used to deduce the length of the keyword used in a polyalphabetic substitution cipher. Once the length of the keyword is discovered, the ciphertext is lined up in *n* columns, where *n* is the length of the keyword. Then, each column can be treated as a monoalphabetic substitution cipher and each column can be cracked with simple frequency analysis. The method simply involves looking for repeated strings in the ciphertext. The longer the ciphertext, the more effective this method will be. This is sometimes also called Kasiski's test or Kasiski's method.

Modern Methods

Cracking modern cryptographic methods is a nontrivial task. In fact, the most likely outcome is failure. However, with enough time and resources (i.e., computational power, sample cipher/plaintexts, etc.), it is possible. Following are some techniques that can be employed in this process:

- **Known plaintext attack**—This method is based on having a sample of known plaintexts and their resulting ciphertexts, and then using this information to try to ascertain something about the key used. It is easier to obtain known plaintext samples than you might think. Consider e-mail. Many people use a standard signature block. If you intercept encrypted e-mails, you can compare a known signature block with the end of the encrypted e-mail. You would then have a known plaintext and the matching ciphertext to work with.

- **Chosen plaintext attack**—In this attack, the attacker obtains the ciphertexts corresponding to a set of plaintexts of his own choosing. This can allow the attacker to attempt to derive the key used and thus decrypt other messages encrypted with that key. This can be difficult but is not impossible.

- **Ciphertext-only**—The attacker only has access to a collection of ciphertexts. This is much more likely than known plaintext, but also the most difficult. The attack is completely successful if the corresponding plaintexts can be deduced, or even better, the key. But obtaining any information at all about the underlying plaintext in this situation is still considered a success.

- **Related-key attack**—This attack is like a chosen plaintext attack, except the attacker can obtain ciphertexts encrypted under two different keys. This is actually a very useful attack if you can obtain the plaintext and matching ciphertext.

There are other methods based on more advanced cryptanalysis techniques—for example, differential and integral cryptanalysis. However, this section should give any forensic examiner a good basic understanding of cryptanalysis.

Tools

A number of tools can aid in cracking passwords and encrypted data. Remember that if the encryption was implemented correctly and is strong, you may not be able to crack it. But passwords can often be cracked (encrypted information less often). It is also possible to obtain keys or copies of information before encryption via a number of nontechnical means that fall in the category of **social engineering**, which includes going through the trash, also known as dumpster diving; lying to a person to obtain the keys, passwords, phrases, or unencrypted information; or even getting a job at the target company and stealing the desired information.

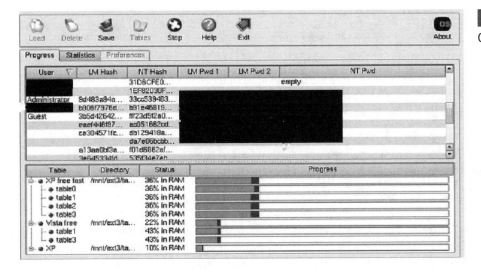

FIGURE 5-11

Ophcrack.

Rainbow tables. In 1980, Martin Hellman described a cryptanalytic time-memory tradeoff, which reduces the time of cryptanalysis by using precalculated data stored in memory. Essentially, these types of password crackers work with precalculated hashes of all passwords available within a certain character space, be that a–z or a–zA–z or a–zA–Z0–9, etc. These files are called rainbow tables because they contain every letter combination "under the rainbow." They are particularly useful when trying to crack hashes. Because a hash is a one-way function, the way to break it is to attempt to find a match. The attacker takes the hashed value and searches the rainbow tables seeking a match to the hash. If one is found, then the original text for the hash is found. Popular hacking tools like Ophcrack depend on rainbow tables. Ophcrack is usually very successful at cracking Windows local machine passwords. The steps are very simple:

1. Download Ophcrack and burn the image to a CD.
2. Put the CD in the target computer and boot through the CD.
3. Wait as it boots as Linux grabs the Windows password file, then uses cracking tools to crack that file and produces a text file with usernames and passwords.

You can see Ophcrack in use in Figure 5-11. Note, this is from a live machine so some information has been redacted.

John the Ripper. John the Ripper is another password cracker that is very popular with both network administrators and hackers. It can be downloaded free of charge from *http://www.openwall.com/john/*. This product is completely command-line based and has no Windows interface. It enables the user to select text files for word lists to attempt cracking a password. Although John the Ripper is less convenient to use because of its command-line interface, it has been around for a long time and is well regarded by both the security and hacking communities. Interestingly, there is a tool available at *http://www.openwall.com/passwdqc/* that ensures your passwords cannot easily be cracked by John the Ripper.

CHAPTER SUMMARY

This chapter introduced two complex topics: steganography and cryptography. Steganography is widely utilized to hide data, particularly from forensic examination. As you saw in this chapter, it is easy to implement and has even been used by terrorist organizations for covert communications.

Cryptography is used to systematically scramble information such that it can be unscrambled by use of a key. Scrambled information may be hidden, or hidden information may be scrambled, or steganography or encryption may be used by themselves.

This chapter is meant to provide a general overview of cryptography. Any truly good forensic examiner should be very familiar with the historical methods presented, and at least have a basic understanding of the modern symmetric and asymmetric cryptography algorithms as well as of some of the fundamentals of cryptanalysis.

KEY CONCEPTS AND TERMS

Asymmetric cryptography	Feistel function	Steganophony
Block cipher	Kasiski examination	Symmetric cryptography
Brute-force attack	Keyspace	Stream cipher
Caesar cipher	Least significant bit (LSB)	Substitution
Carrier	Payload	Transposition
Channel	Social engineering	Vigenère cipher
Cryptanalysis	Steganalysis	
Euler's Totient	Steganography	

CHAPTER 5 ASSESSMENT

1. The Caesar cipher is the oldest known encryption method.

A. True
B. False

2. An improvement on the Caesar cipher that uses more than one shift is called a(n) _____.

A. DES encryption
B. Multialphabet substitution
C. IDEA
D. Triple DES

3. What type of encryption uses a different key to encrypt the message than it uses to decrypt the message?

A. Private key
B. Asymmetric
C. Symmetric
D. Secure

4. Which of the following is an asymmetric cryptography algorithm invented by three mathematicians in the 1970s?

A. PGP
B. DES
C. DSA
D. RSA

5. Which of the following encryption algorithms uses three key ciphers in a block system and uses the Rijndael algorithm?

A. DES
B. RSA
C. AES
D. NSA

6. What is the key length used for DES?

A. 56
B. 64
C. 128
D. 256

7. Which of the following is an example of a multialphabet cipher?

A. Caesar
B. Vigenère
C. Atbash
D. ROT13

8. How many rounds does DES have?

A. 64
B. 56
C. 16
D. 4

9. Hiding messages inside another medium is referred to as _____.

A. Cryptography
B. Cryptology
C. Steganalysis
D. Steganography

10. In steganography, the _____ is the data to be covertly communicated. In other words, it is the message you want to hide.

A. Payload
B. Carrier
C. Signal
D. Channel

11. In steganography, the _____ is the stream or file into which the data is hidden.

A. Payload
B. Carrier
C. Signal
D. Channel

12. The most common way steganography is accomplished is via _____.

A. MSB
B. ASB
C. RSB
D. LSB

Recovering Data

A COMPUTER USER MAY MAKE AN EFFORT TO DELETE information. But the file or remnants of the information may still be available to the forensic examiner. This chapter reviews practical, hands-on steps that you can take to recover deleted data. It discusses undeleting files in Windows, Linux, and Macintosh.

Chapter 6 Topics

This chapter covers the following topics and concepts:

- How to undelete data
- What you need to know about recovering information from damaged drives

Chapter 6 Goals

When you complete this chapter, you will be able to:

- Recover deleted files in Windows
- Recover deleted files in Linux
- Recover deleted files in Macintosh
- Recover files from damaged drives

Undeleting Data

It is common for people to delete files from their computers. And even criminals who are not very technically savvy think that deleting a file will keep authorities from discovering it. So you should expect that evidence will frequently be deleted from computers you examine. For this reason, one of the most fundamental tasks a forensic examiner will conduct is to retrieve deleted data.

This chapter does not dive into the specifics of the three major operating systems—Windows, Linux, and Macintosh. Instead, the focus is simply on recovering files from them.

Windows

Windows is a very common operating system. In fact, it would be quite a challenge to find any office that did not have any computers running Windows. PCs running Windows also account for the overwhelming majority of home computers. So recovering deleted Windows files is the first skill you learn in this chapter.

You can recover deleted files from the Windows operating system because of the way the file system works. Older versions of Windows use FAT (either FAT16 or FAT32), and newer versions (since Windows 2000) use primarily NTFS. This section explores FAT and NTFS file systems in relationship to recovering deleted files. In both file systems, a table is used to map files to specific clusters where they are stored on the disk.

FAT

In FAT16 and FAT32, the table used to store cluster/file information is the file allocation table (FAT), thus the name of the file system. The file allocation table is really a list of entries that map to each cluster on the disk partition. Each entry records one of five things:

1. The cluster number of the next cluster for this file is recorded.
2. If this cluster is the end of a chain, then it has a special end of cluster chain (EOC) entry.
3. Bad clusters have a special entry in the file allocation table.
4. Reserved clusters have a special entry in the file allocation table.
5. Open, or available, clusters are also marked in the file allocation table.

When a file is deleted, the data is not actually removed from the drive. Rather, the FAT is updated to reflect that those clusters are no longer in use. If new information is saved to the drive, it may be saved to those clusters overwriting the old information. What this means from a forensic point of view is that the more recently a file was deleted, the more likely you will be able to recover the file. Over time, it becomes more likely that those clusters have had other information saved in them. In fact, the cluster may have been deleted and saved over several times. Because of this, recovering a deleted file is not always an all-or-nothing procedure. It is possible to recover just a portion of a file.

NTFS

Starting with Windows 2000, NTFS has been the preferred file system for Windows operating systems. NFTS is an acronym for New Technology File System. From a forensic point of view, there are two fundamental files that are part of NTFS that are of most interest. These are the Master File Table (MFT), which some sources call the Meta File Table, and the cluster bitmap. The MFT describes all files on the volume, including filenames, timestamps, security identifiers, and file attributes, such as read-only, compressed, encrypted, and so on. This file contains one base file record for each file and directory on an NTFS volume. It serves the same purpose as the file allocation table does in FAT and FAT32. The cluster bitmap file is a map of all the clusters on the hard drive. This is an array of bit entries where each bit indicates whether its corresponding cluster is allocated/used or free/unused.

When files are deleted from an NTFS system, the process is similar to what occurs in FAT. The main difference is that clusters are first marked as deleted, thus "moved" to the Recycle Bin. In NTFS prior to Vista, the Recycle Bin resides in a hidden directory called RECYCLER. In Vista and Windows 7, the name of the directory was changed to $recycle. bin. Only when you empty the Recycle Bin is the cluster marked as fully available. More specifically, when a file is deleted, the filename in the MFT is marked with a special character that signifies to the computer that the file has been deleted. Just as with FAT systems, clusters in an NTFS system are more likely to be overwritten as more time elapses after deletion.

Windows Tools

A number of tools are available to recover deleted files from Windows computers. This section introduces a few of these tools. You should definitely take the time to explore the various tools available and select the one you prefer. Simply using your favorite search engine to look for "how to recover deleted Windows files" will result in a number of tools you can try. Many are free, and those that are not usually have a trial version with which you can experiment.

DiskDigger. DiskDigger (*http://diskdigger.org/*) is an easy-to-use tool. It can be downloaded free of charge and is fully functional. But when recovering files in the free version, you have to recover them one at a time. If you pay for the commercial version, you can recover as many files at one time as you want. The interface is very easy to use. When you launch the program, you see a screen like the one shown in Figure 6-1.

Then you select the drive you want to examine, and choose Dig Deep or Dig Deeper, as shown in Figure 6-2. The difference is the level of recovery.

Once recovery is done, you will see a screen like the one shown in Figure 6-3. You can select any file and recover it. On your screen the files will be in color. For files in green, you should get the entire file back. Gray indicates a partial file, and red indicates very little of the file is left.

Forensically Scrubbing a File or Folder

Many Web pages report that DOD 5220.22-M recommends that data be overwritten with random characters seven times to ensure it is completely wiped (*http://www .wipingdata.com/index.html*). That is accurate, but incomplete. There is actually a matrix of how to sanitize different types of media (*http://recycleyourmedia.com/webuytape/ compliance/d-o-d-data-sanitization-matrix/*). Note: key appears on following page.

MEDIA	CLEAR	SANITIZE
Magnetic Tape1		
Type I	a or b	a, b, or m
Type II	a or b	b or m
Type III	a or b	m
Magnetic disk		
Bernoullis	a, b, or c	m
Floppies	a, b, or c	m
Nonremovable rigid disk	c	a, b, d, or m
Removable rigid disk	a, b, or c	a, b, d, or m
Optical Disc		
Read many, write many	c	m
Read-only		m, n
Write once, read many (Worm)		m, n
Memory		
Dynamic random access memory (DRAM)	c or g	c, g, or m
Electronically alterable PROM (EAPROM)	l	j or m
Electronically erasable PROM (EEPROM)	l	h or m
Flash EPROM (FEPROM)	l	c then i, or m
Programmable ROM (PROM)	c	m
Magnetic core memory	c	a, b, e, or m
Magnetic plated wire	c	c and f, or m
Magnetic resistive memory	c	m
Non-volatile RAM (NOVRAM)	c or g	c, g, or m

continued

MEDIA	CLEAR	SANITIZE
Read-only memory ROM		m
Static random access memory (SRAM)	c or g	c and f, g, or m
Equipment		
Cathode ray tube (CRT)	g	q
Printers		
Impact	g	p then g
Laser	g	o then g

a. Degauss with a Type I degausser.

b. Degauss with a Type II degausser.

c. Overwrite all addressable locations with a single character.

d. Overwrite all addressable locations with a character, its complement, and then a random character, and then verify.

e. Overwrite all addressable locations with a character, its complement, and then a random character.

f. Each overwrite must reside in memory for a period longer than the classified data resided.

g. Remove all power to include battery power.

h. Overwrite all locations with a random pattern, all locations with binary zeros, and all locations with binary ones.

i. Perform a full chip erase as per manufacturer's data sheets.

j. Perform i, then c, a total of three times.

k. Perform an ultraviolet erase according to manufacturer's recommendation.

l. Perform k, but increase time by a factor of three.

m. Destroy—disintegrate, incinerate, pulverize, shred, or melt.

n. Destruction required only if classified information is contained.

o. Run five pages of unclassified text (font test acceptable).

p. Ribbons must be destroyed. Platens must be cleaned.

q. Inspect and/or test screen surface for evidence of burned-in information. If present, the cathode ray tube must be destroyed.

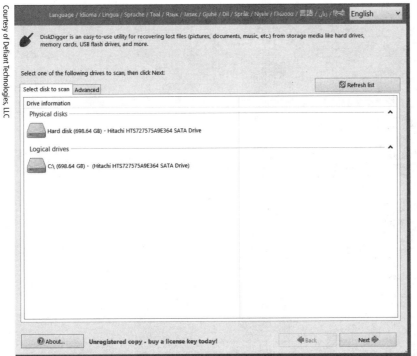

FIGURE 6-1

DiskDigger main screen.

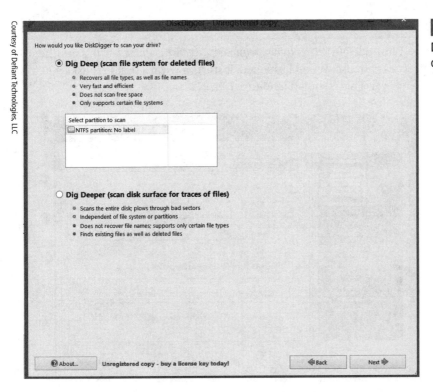

FIGURE 6-2

DiskDigger starting data recovery.

FIGURE 6-3

Recovering an individual
file using DiskDigger.

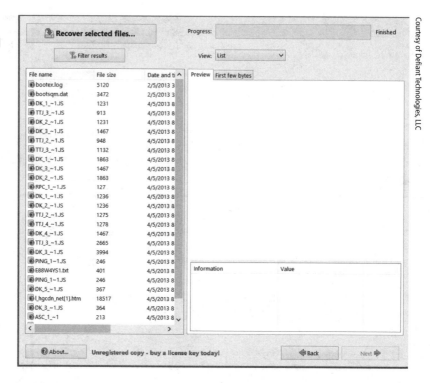

You can view and recover individual files from this screen.

WinUndelete. WinUndelete (*http://www.winundelete.com/download.asp*) is another tool that is relatively easy to use. When launched, it starts a wizard that first asks you to select what drive to recover. This is shown in Figure 6-4.

FIGURE 6-4

WinUnDelete Wizard
Step 1: selecting a drive.

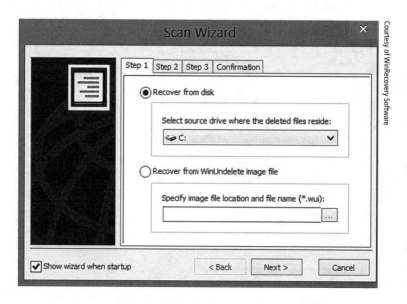

Step 2 allows you to select the file types you want to recover. This is shown in Figure 6-5.

The third step is to select a folder to place recovered files in. You can see this in Figure 6-6.

When WinUndelete has completed running the recovery process, you can go to that folder to see the files.

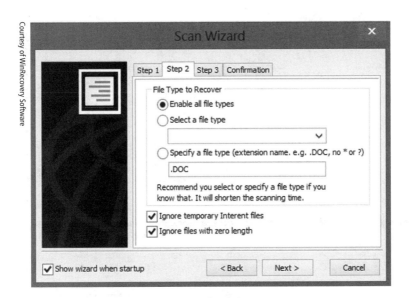

FIGURE 6-5

WinUndelete Step 2: selecting file types.

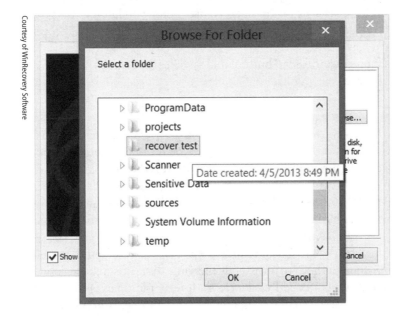

FIGURE 6-6

WinUndelete Step 3: selecting a restore file location.

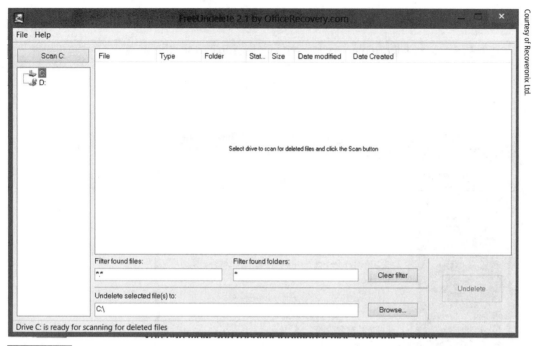

Courtesy of Recoveronix Ltd.

FIGURE 6-7

FreeUndelete selecting a drive.

FreeUndelete. FreeUndelete (*http://www.officerecovery.com/freeundelete/*) is free for personal use. There is a fee for commercial use. When you launch this program, the first screen requires you to select the drive from which you want to recover files. This is shown in Figure 6-7.

Then you simply click the Scan button, and any files that can be fully or partially recovered will be listed.

Linux

With Linux, you have the option of using prepackaged tools or some built-in Linux commands. In this section, you see both, but first you need to understand the ext file system. Linux can run on multiple file systems, but ext is the most common. The most recent version of ext is ext4; however, many Linux distributions still use ext3.

First consider how Linux stores files. The content of files is stored in contiguous blocks. The exact size of these blocks depends on the parameters used with the command to create that partition (for example, mke2fs can be used to make ext2 partitions). The size can be 1,024, 2,048, or 4,096 bytes. You can think of these blocks as something similar to the clusters in NTFS, though they are not exactly the same thing, just related conceptually.

Hard drives that run Linux address blocks, or integer multiples of blocks, at a time. The specific block size is stored in the superblock. The entire partition is divided into an integral number of blocks, starting at 0.

Blocks are divided into groups. Each group uses one block as a bitmap to keep track of which block inside that group is allocated (used); thus, there can be at most 32,768 (4,096 * 3 = 32,768) normal blocks per group. Another block is used as a bitmap for the number of allocated inodes. Inodes are data structures of 128 bytes that are stored in a table, (4,096/128 = 32 inodes per block) in each group. An **inode** is a data structure in the file system that stores all the information about a file except its name and its actual data.

An inode can refer to a file or a folder/directory. In either case, the inode is really a link to the file. This is important because there are basically two types of links. The first type is the *hard link.* A hard link is an inode that links directly to a specific file. The operating system keeps a count of references to this link. When the reference count reaches zero, the file is deleted. In other words, you can have any number of names referencing a file, but if that number of references reaches zero (i.e., there is *no* name that references that file), then the file is deleted.

The second type of file link is called a *soft link* or *symbolic link.* In this case, the link is not actually a file itself, but rather a pointer to another file or directory. You can think of this as the same thing as a shortcut, such as you might find in Windows.

Because there are at most 32,768 bits in the bitmap, that means that there will be a maximum of 32,768 inodes per group, and thus 1,024 blocks (32,768 / 32 = 1,024) blocks in the inode table of each group. The actual size of the inode table is given by the actual number of inodes per group, which is also stored in the superblock.

The inodes in the inode table of each group contain metadata for each type of data that the file system can store. This type might be a symbolic link, in which case only the inode is sufficient; it might be a directory, a file, and so on. In the case of files and directories, the real data is stored in the file.

Manual Recovery

This method depends on manually recovering deleted files using Linux commands. It does not require external tools. Unfortunately, there are variations between the Linux distributions, so there is no guarantee that this process will work on your specific Linux installation.

The first step is to move the system to single-user mode. If this is a network system, you should probably notify network users first. This can be done with the `wall` command, which sends messages to all logged-in users.

Then, you can move to single-user mode, using the `init` command:

```
init 1
```

The Linux/UNIX command `grep` can be used to search for files, contents of files, and just about anything you may want to search for. The **grep** command is very flexible and quite popular with Linux users. For example: `grep -b 'search-text' /dev/partition >` `file.txt` will search for 'search-text' in a given partition and output the results to file.txt.

You can also use this syntax:

```
grep -a -B[size before] -A[size after] 'text' /dev/[your_partition]
> file.txt
```

Using `init` to Change Run Levels in Linux

Linux run levels determine at what level the operating system is running.

MODE	DIRECTORY	RUN LEVEL DESCRIPTION
0	/etc/rc.d/rc0.d	Halt
1	/etc/rc.d/rc1.d	Single-user mode
2	/etc/rc.d/rc2.d	Not used (user-definable)
3	/etc/rc.d/rc3.d	Full multiuser mode without GUI
4	/etc/rc.d/rc4.d	Not used (user-definable)
5	/etc/rc.d/rc5.d	Full multiuser mode with GUI
6	/etc/rc.d/rc6.d	Reboot

The `init` command allows you to change run level.

To recover a text file starting with the word *forensics* on /dev/sda2, you can try the following command:

```
# grep -i -a -B10 -A100 'forensics' /dev/sda2 > file.txt
```

In this case, `grep` is searching for this phrase, ignoring case, looking through binary files, and essentially looking to find the text, even if the file has a reference count of zero (i.e., has been deleted). Of course, if the file blocks have been overwritten enough times, then it will be irrecoverable.

The `extundelete` Utility

The `extundelete` utility (*http://extundelete.sourceforge.net/*) works with both ext3 and ext4 partitions. This product works via shell commands, and they are relatively simple. For example, if you want to restore all deleted files from the sda1 partition, just use this command:

```
extundelete /dev/sda4 --restore-all
```

The Web site documents all the various options you can utilize with this tool.

FYI

A few `grep` flags of use in these searches:

- `-i`—Ignore case distinctions in both the PATTERN and the input files; that is, match both uppercase and lowercase characters.
- `-a`—Process a binary file as if it were text.
- `-B`—Print number lines/size of leading context before matching lines.
- `-A`—Print number lines/size of trailing context after matching lines.

Scalpel

This tool works with both Linux and Mac OS, and it is even possible to compile the source code to work in Windows. However, it is easiest to install and work with in Linux. For example, if you are using Ubuntu Linux, this is all it takes to install:

```
sudo apt-get install scalpel
```

Next is some text editing—the configuration file is /etc/scalpel/scalpel.conf. You will find that everything has been commented out—uncomment the specific file format that you want to recover. For example, if you want to recover deleted Zip files, then you need to uncomment the .zip file section in scalpel.conf.

Next, in a terminal, run the following command:

```
sudo scalpel [device/directory/file name] -o [output directory]
```

The output directory, in which you want to store recovered files, should be empty before running Scalpel; otherwise, you will get an error.

> **NOTE**
>
> If you are unfamiliar with Linux, some of these commands might seem odd to you. It is recommended that if you are unfamiliar with an operating system, you leave forensics for that system to someone who is better qualified. However, given the number of open source forensic tools that work with Linux, it is advised that you learn at least the fundamentals of Linux.

Macintosh

Starting with OS X, Macintosh is actually based on FreeBSD, which is a UNIX clone, much like Linux. In fact, if you go to a terminal window in Mac OS X, what you actually get is a shell where you can run UNIX shell commands. This means that some of the techniques that work for Linux also work with Macintosh. However, there are also some tools you can use that are made specifically for Macintosh.

You should also be aware that Macintosh has its own file system. Mac OS X uses HFS+, or Hierarchical File System Plus. Earlier versions of Macintosh used HFS. You can get details on HFS and HFS+ at *http://www.osxbook.com/book/bonus/ancient/ whatismacosx/arch_fs.html*.

MacKeeper

MacKeeper (*http://mackeeper.zeobit.com/recover-deleted-files-on-mac*) is a useful tool for recovering deleted files on a Macintosh computer. There is a free, fully functional trial version. Once you download and install this tool, you can recover files in just a few easy steps:

1. Open the Files Recovery tool. Select the volume where your lost files were and start the scan. This is shown in Figure 6-8.

2. Then select Undelete, shown in Figure 6-9.

That is it. This tool is remarkably simple to use.

FIGURE 6-8

MacKeeper Step 1.

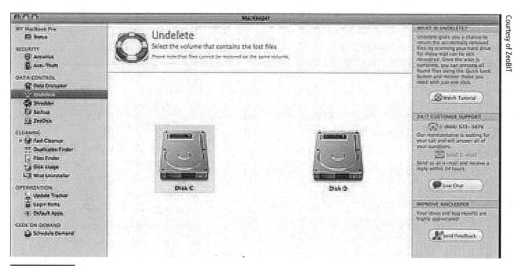

FIGURE 6-9

Files Recovery Tool.

There are certainly other tools that can recover Macintosh deleted files. You should experiment with various tools and find the one(s) that are most useful for you. As always, you should be comfortable with a given operating system before attempting forensic analysis of that operating system.

Recovering Information from Damaged Media

A wide variety of failures cause **physical damage** to storage media. Compact discs (CDs) can have their metallic substrate or dye layer scratched. Hard disks can suffer any of several mechanical failures, such as head crashes and failed motors. Tapes can simply break. Physical damage always causes some data loss, and in many cases, the file system's logical structures sustain damage as well. This results in logical damage that must be dealt with before any files can be salvaged from the failed media.

> **NOTE**
>
> A **clean room** is an environment that has a controlled level of contamination, such as from dust, microbes, and other particles.

End users can't repair most physical damage. Generally, they don't have the hardware or technical expertise required to make physical repairs. Further, end users' attempts to repair physical damage often increase the damage. Normally you shouldn't attempt to repair physical media. You may try a number of techniques to recover data from damaged media. However, only organizations with specialized equipment and facilities, such as clean rooms, should attempt repair or enhanced data recovery.

Physical Damage Recovery Techniques

Recovering data from a hard drive should start with the assumption that, unless the case is visibly damaged, the drive itself is still operable. Today's hard disks are built to be rugged enough to protect against damage. Thus, when presented with a "failed hard drive," use the following techniques to evaluate the drive and retrieve needed data:

1. Remove the drive from the system on which it is installed and connect it to a **test system**—a compatible system that is functional. Make the connection without installing the drive but only connecting the data and power cables.

2. Boot the test system from its own internal drive. Listen to the failed drive to determine whether the internal disks are spinning. If the disks are spinning, it generally means the disk has not experienced a catastrophic failure. Therefore, you can likely recover the data.

3. Determine whether the failed drive is recognized and can be installed as an additional disk on the test system. If the drive installs, copy all directories and files to a hard drive on the test system. If a drive fails on one system but installs on another, the drive may be usable. The drive may have failed because of a power supply failure, corruption of the operating system, malicious software, or some other reason. If you can operate the drive, run a virus check on the recovered data and test for directory and file integrity.

4. If the hard drive is not spinning or the test system does not recognize it, perform limited repair. You may be able to get the hard drive to start and it may be recognized by the test system. If you can repair the drive, use specialized software to image all data bits from the failed drive to a recovery drive. Use the extracted raw image to reconstruct usable data. Try open source tools such as DCFLdd (this is an enhanced version of the dd utility) to recover all data except for data in physically damaged sectors.

5. If necessary, send the device to data recovery specialists, who may be able to apply extraordinary recovery techniques.

It is possible that the data is deemed "lost," and there will be no increased loss if you attempt local repair and fail. If so, you can try the following:

1. Remove the printed circuit board and replace it with a matching circuit board from a known healthy drive.

2. Change the read/write head assembly with matching parts from a known healthy drive.

3. Remove the hard disk platters from the original drive and install them into a known healthy drive.

Recovering Data After Logical Damage

Logical damage to a file system is more common than physical damage. Logical damage may prevent the host operating system from mounting or using the file system. Power outages can cause logical damage, preventing file system structures from completely writing information from memory to the storage medium. Even turning off a machine while it is booting or shutting down can lead to logical damage. Errors in hardware controllers—especially RAID (redundant array of inexpensive disks) controllers—and drivers and system crashes can have the same effect.

Logical damage can cause a variety of problems, such as system crashes or actual data loss. It can result in intermittent failures. It can also trigger other strange behavior, such as infinitely recursing directories and drives reporting negative free space remaining. Some programs can correct the inconsistencies that result from logical damage. Most operating systems provide a basic repair tool for their native file systems. Microsoft Windows has chkdsk, for example; Linux comes with the fsck utility; and Mac OS X provides Disk Utility. A number of companies have developed products to resolve logical file system errors, such as the Sleuth Kit (*http://www.sleuthkit.org*). Third-party products may be able to recover data even when the operating system's repair utility doesn't recognize the disk. TestDisk (*http://www.cgsecurity.org/wiki/TestDisk*) is one example. It can recover lost partitions and reconstruct corrupted partition tables.

Preventing Logical Damage

Journaling file systems, such as NTFS (NT File System) 5.0 and ext3, help to reduce the incidence of logical damage. In the event of system failure, you can roll these file systems back to a consistent or stable state. The information most likely to be lost will be in the drive's cache at the time of the system failure.

Using a consistency checker should be a routine part of system maintenance. A consistency checker protects against file system software bugs and storage hardware design incompatibilities. For example, a disk controller may report that file system structures have been saved to disk, but the data is actually still in the write cache. If the computer loses power while this data is in the cache, the file system may be left in an inconsistent or unstable state. To avoid this problem, use hardware that does not report the data as written until it actually is written. Another solution is to use disk controllers with battery backups. When the power is restored after an outage, the pending data is written to disk. For greater protection, use a system battery backup to provide power long enough to shut down the system safely.

Logical Damage Recovery Techniques

Two techniques are common for recovering data after logical damage: consistency checking and zero-knowledge analysis. Use these techniques to either repair or work around most logical damage. However, applying data recovery software doesn't guarantee that no data loss will occur. For example, when two files claim to share the same allocation unit, one of the files is almost certain to lose data.

Consistency checking. **Consistency checking** involves scanning a disk's logical structure and ensuring that it is consistent with its specification. For instance, in most file systems, a directory must have at least two entries: a dot (.) entry that points to itself and a dot-dot (..) entry that points to its parent. A file system repair program reads each directory to ensure that these entries exist and point to the correct directories. If they do not, the program displays an error message, and you can correct the problem. Both chkdsk and fsck work in this fashion. However, consistency checking has two major problems:

- A consistency check can fail if the file system is highly damaged. In this case, the repair program may crash, or it may believe the drive has an invalid file system.

- The chkdsk utility might automatically delete data files if the files are out of place or unexplainable. The utility does this to ensure that the operating system can run properly. However, the deleted files may be important and irreplaceable user files.

The same type of problem occurs with system restore disks that restore the operating system by removing the previous installation. Avoid this problem by installing the operating system on a separate partition from the user data.

Zero-knowledge analysis. Zero-knowledge analysis is the second technique for file system repair. With **zero-knowledge analysis**, few assumptions are made about the state of the file system. The file system is rebuilt from scratch using knowledge of an undamaged file system structure. In this process, scan the drive of the affected computer, noting all file system structures and possible file boundaries. Then match the results to the specifications of a working file system.

Zero-knowledge analysis is usually much slower than consistency checking. You can use it, however, to recover data even when the logical structures are almost completely destroyed. This technique generally does not repair the damaged file system but allows you to extract the data to another storage device.

CHAPTER SUMMARY

In this chapter, you learned the essentials of file recovery in the three major operating systems. The most attention was given to Windows due to how widely it is used. It is important that you be comfortable with these undeletion techniques. You should also be familiar with how to utilize any undeletion functionality in your preferred forensic toolkit (such as EnCase or Forensic Toolkit).

KEY CONCEPTS AND TERMS

Clean room	Logical damage
Consistency checking	Physical damage
grep	Test system
Inode	Zero-knowledge analysis

CHAPTER 6 ASSESSMENT

1. Which of the following is the Linux equivalent of a shortcut?

A. Hard link

B. Symbolic link

C. Partial link

D. Faux link

2. What file system does Windows 7 use?

A. FAT

B. FAT32

C. NTFS

D. HPFS

3. What file system does OS X use?

A. HPFS

B. HFS+

C. NTFS

D. EXT3

4. Why can you undelete files in Windows 7?

A. Nothing is deleted; it is just removed from MFT.

B. Nothing is deleted; it is just removed from FAT.

C. Fragments might exist, even though the file is deleted.

D. You cannot.

E-mail Forensics

A GREAT MANY COMPUTER CRIMES involve e-mail. In fact, many noncomputer crimes, and even civil litigation, can require extracting evidence from e-mail. Electronic communication is so ubiquitous that e-mail communications can often shed light on issues. In civil lawsuits, subpoenas for all e-mail correspondence are common. But it is also possible to spoof e-mail addresses and hide the real sender. It is important to be able to track and appropriately analyze e-mails.

Chapter 7 Topics

This chapter covers the following topics and concepts:

- How e-mail clients and servers work
- What you need to know about e-mail headers
- How to trace e-mails
- What you need to know about e-mail server forensic examination
- What the laws that are relevant to e-mail forensics are

Chapter 7 Goals

When you complete this chapter, you will be able to:

- Understand the functionality of e-mail and e-mail protocols
- Obtain the full e-mail headers for a variety of e-mail clients
- Read and understand the contents of e-mail headers
- Trace e-mail to its origin
- Work with e-mail servers
- Understand the laws related to e-mail investigations

How E-mail Works

You might already have a strong working knowledge of how e-mail works. If you don't, this section provides a common base of knowledge, which allows you to get the most from this chapter.

Different types of devices and methods generate e-mails. Most commonly, a user composes a message on his or her computer and then sends it to his or her mail server. At this point, the user's computer is finished with the job, but the mail server still has to deliver the message. A mail server is like an electronic post office: It sends and receives electronic mail. Most of the time, the mail server is separate from the computer where the mail was composed.

The sender's mail server forwards the message through the organization's network and/or the Internet to the recipient's mail server. The message then resides on that second mail server and is available to the recipient. The software program used to compose and read e-mail messages is the e-mail client.

Depending on how the recipient's e-mail client is configured, copies of the message may exist in a number of places. The recipient's and sender's computers, another electronic device such as a smartphone or a tablet, and the mail server or servers and their backups may all hold copies of the message. In addition, any of the servers that relay the message from the sender to the recipient may retain a copy of the e-mail message. This is shown in Figure 7-1.

The number of relay "hops" may be only one if the sender and recipient are on the same network. Transmitting a message to a remotely located recipient might require many hops.

A forensic investigation of e-mail might reveal information such as the following:

- E-mail messages related to the investigation
- E-mail addresses related to the investigation
- Sender and recipient information
- Information about those copied on the e-mail
- Content of the communications
- Internet Protocol (IP) addresses

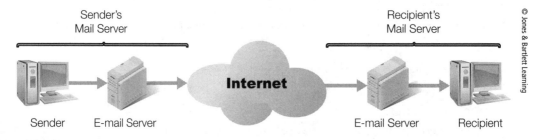

FIGURE 7-1

Delivering e-mail.

FYI

Consider in how many places an e-mail might be saved. It could be saved on the sender's machine, on the recipient's machine, on either the sender's or recipient's e-mail server, or both, and on backup media for either server. If you consider the many places an e-mail could reside, that should indicate to you that it is rare that an e-mail is ever truly deleted. It may be quite hard to find, but it probably exists somewhere. This is one reason why e-mail forensics is so important.

- Date and time information
- User information
- Attachments
- Passwords
- Application logs that show evidence of spoofing

It is also important to keep in mind that the content of e-mail can be very important even in non–computer crime cases. Given how common e-mail communications are, it should not surprise you to find that criminals often communicate via e-mail. Some crimes, like cyberstalking, usually include an e-mail element. Other crimes, such as drug trafficking and terrorism, can also utilize e-mail communication.

In financial crimes, such as insider trading, as well as in discrimination lawsuits, e-mail is often a critical piece of evidence. Keep in mind that the sender and perhaps even the recipient may have deleted the e-mail. But it could still reside on an e-mail server or in the backup media for that server.

E-mail Protocols

The **Simple Mail Transfer Protocol (SMTP)** is a protocol used to send e-mail. SMTP typically operates on port 25. For many years, **Post Office Protocol version 3 (POP3)** was the only means for retrieving e-mail. However, in recent years, POP3 has begun to be replaced by the **Internet Message Access Protocol (IMAP)**. IMAP operates on port 143. The main advantage of IMAP over POP3 is it allows the client to download only the e-mail headers to the machine, so that the user can choose which messages are to be downloaded

FYI

Think about the last time you were on a plane. It is likely that you had your phone in "airplane mode" during the flight. When the flight landed—if you are like many frequent travelers— you immediately turned your phone off of airplane mode so you could get your messages. There might have been a great number of messages. In this type of situation, if you are using POP3, your phone downloads all of the messages (even if many are e-mails you would rather ignore, or even spam). However, if you are using IMAP, your phone only downloads the headers, and doesn't try to download the full e-mail until you select it.

completely. This is particularly useful for smartphones and any wireless devices where bandwidth may be at a premium.

Faking E-mail

Criminals may fake their e-mail messages. Some of them use e-mail programs that strip the message header from the message before delivering it to the recipient. Or they may bury the message header within the e-mail program. In other cases, the "From:" line in a message header is fake.

In addition to manipulating the e-mail header, perpetrators may simply set up a temporary, bogus e-mail account. For example, free e-mail accounts, as offered by Yahoo!, Gmail, and Hotmail, are easy to set up, and you can use any desired and available name.

Spoofing

Spoofing involves making an e-mail message appear to come from someone or someplace other than the real sender or location. The e-mail sender uses a software tool that is readily available on the Internet to cut out his or her IP address and replace it with someone else's IP address. However, the first machine to receive the spoofed message records the machine's real IP address. Thus, the header contains both the faked IP and the real IP address—unless, of course, the perpetrator is clever enough to have also spoofed his or her actual IP address.

Anonymous Remailing

Anonymous remailing is another attempt to throw tracing or tracking attempts off the trail. A suspect who uses anonymous remailing sends an e-mail message to an anonymizer. An anonymizer is an e-mail server that strips identifying information from an e-mail message before forwarding it with the anonymous mailing computer's IP address.

FYI

The issue of spoofing e-mails, IP addresses, and similar identifying information brings up the question of the sophistication of computer criminals. E-mail spoofing is just like any other crime. There are a few very sophisticated criminals—and a host of unsophisticated criminals. The more sophisticated a criminal, the harder it is to find evidence. For example, if you wanted to send an e-mail that you did not want traced to you, you could start by finding a free public Wi-Fi in an area at least one hour from your home. Then you could spoof both your IP address and MAC address. Finally, you could send the e-mail through an anonymous e-mail account set up for that purpose. It is, however, very common for criminals to actually send e-mails from their own computers without even bothering to spoof their IP address or MAC address. Even computer-savvy criminals, who think to spoof their IP addresses, might not think to spoof the MAC address. In addition, keep in mind that e-mail address spoofing is only one kind of spoofing. In this section, you also saw MAC and IP spoofing.

To find out who sent remailed e-mail, try to look at any logs maintained by remailer or anonymizer companies. However, these services frequently do not maintain logs. In addition, you can closely analyze the message for embedded information that might give clues to the user or system that sent the message.

There are many Web sites that let someone send an e-mail and choose any "from" address he or she wants. Here are just a few:

- *http://sendanonymousemail.net/*
- *http://theanonymousemail.com/*
- *http://send-email.org/*

 NOTE

TOR, *https://www.torproject.org/*, is an anonymous network of proxy servers. You can use the TOR network to send any sort of network traffic, including e-mails. This makes tracing the traffic back to its source extremely difficult.

Valid E-mails

It is also very common for an e-mail to arrive, often from a trusted friend, colleague, or family member, that is valid in every respect except for the content of the message. The e-mail passes all of the normal validity checks, such as header structure and content, and even comes from a known nonspam e-mail server that is not blacklisted with any of the blacklist services such as SPAM Cop. However, the message is suspect and the Web site uniform resource locator (URL) pointed to is usually a hacker or phishing site. The message may read something like "Wow! Check out this great Web site: *www.hackersite.com*." These messages usually contain no hidden URL, pictures, or attachments and are very short. However, clicking the URL can unleash all sorts of malicious software or other negative results.

E-mail Headers

One of the first things to learn about e-mails is that they have headers. The header for an e-mail message tells you a great deal about the e-mail. The standard for e-mail format, including headers, is RFC 2822. It is important that all e-mail uses the same format. That is why you can send an e-mail from Outlook on a Windows 8 PC and the recipient can read it from a Hotmail account on an Android phone that runs Linux. This is because all e-mail programs use the same e-mail format, regardless of what operating system they run on.

Make sure that any e-mail you offer as evidence includes the message, any attachments, and the full e-mail header. The header keeps a record of the message's journey as it travels through the communications network. As the message

NOTE

RFC 2822 supplements the older RFC 822 with a few notable enhancements. RFC 822 was originally designed for the standard for text messages sent over the ARPANET network, which was the precursor to the modern Internet. You can check out *http://tools.ietf.org/html/rfc822* for more details.

is routed through one or more mail servers, each server adds its own information to the message header. Each device in a network has an Internet Protocol (IP) address that identifies the device and can be resolved to a location address. A forensic investigator may be able to identify IP addresses from a message header and use this information to determine who sent the message.

Most e-mail programs normally display only a small portion of the e-mail header along with a message. This usually is information that the sender puts in the message, such as the "To" address, subject, and body of the message. You can view and examine the full header record by using tools available in the e-mail client.

An e-mail investigation begins with a review of an e-mail message followed by a detailed examination of the message header information. Look at the header in more detail to find additional information associated with the e-mail message. The message header provides an audit trail of every machine through which the e-mail has passed.

Consider the specifications for e-mail format given in RFC 2822:

- The message header must include at least the following fields:
  - **From**—The e-mail address and, optionally, the name of the sender
  - **Date**—The local time and date when the message was written
- The message header should include at least the following fields[:
  - **Message-ID**—An automatically generated field
  - **In-Reply-To**—The message-ID of the message that this is a reply to; used to link related messages together

RFC 3864 describes message header field names. Common header fields for e-mail include the following:

- **To**—The e-mail address and, optionally, name of the message's primary recipient(s)
- **Subject**—A brief summary of the topic of the message
- **Cc**—Carbon copy; a copy is sent to secondary recipients
- **Bcc**—Blind carbon copy; a copy is sent to addresses added to the SMTP delivery list while the Bcc address remains invisible to other recipients
- **Content-Type**—Information about how the message is to be displayed, usually a Multipurpose Internet Mail Extensions (MIME) type
- **Precedence**—Commonly with values "bulk," "junk," or "list"; used to indicate that automated "vacation" or "out of office" responses should not be returned for this mail, for example, to prevent vacation notices from being sent to all other subscribers of a mailing list
- **Received**—Tracking information generated by mail servers that have previously handled a message, in reverse order (last handler first)
- **References**—Message-ID of the message to which this is a reply
- **Reply-To**—Address that should be used to reply to the message
- **Sender**—Address of the actual sender acting on behalf of the author listed in the From field

There is a wealth of information in these headers so examining them is very important.

Getting Headers in Outlook 2010

With a specific message open, you select File and then Info, as shown in Figure 7-2. Then select Properties and you will be able to view the headers, as shown in Figure 7-3.

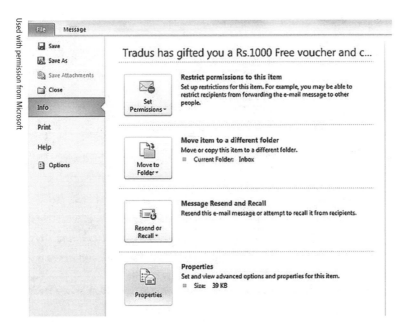

Used with permission from Microsoft

FIGURE 7-2

Outlook 2010 headers Step 1.

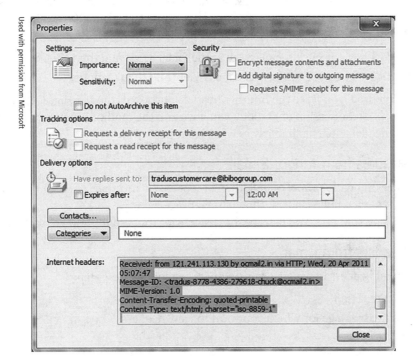

Used with permission from Microsoft

FIGURE 7-3

Outlook 2010 headers Step 2.

7

E-mail Forensics

FIGURE 7-4

Outlook headers.

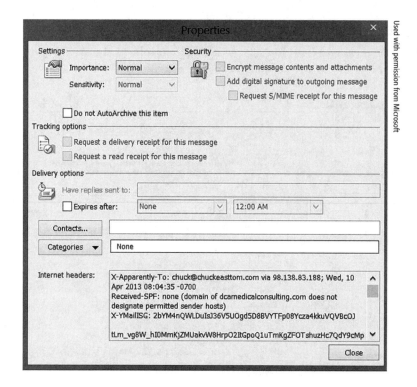

You can see it is relatively easy to view the headers using Outlook. Older versions of Outlook have a different method to get to headers. With Outlook 2000/2003/2007, there are two methods:

- **Method #1**—Right-click the message in the folder view, and then choose Options.
- **Method #2**—In an open message, choose View and then Options.

With either method, you'll see the Internet headers portion of the Message Options dialog box. Regardless of the version of Outlook you have and the method you use to view the headers, the headers appear similarly to what is shown in Figure 7-4.

Getting Headers from Yahoo! E-mail

If you are working with Yahoo! e-mail, then first open the message. On the lower right, there is a link named Full Headers, shown in Figure 7-5.

If you click on that link, you can see the headers for that e-mail, shown in Figure 7-6.

Getting Headers from Gmail

Viewing e-mail headers in Gmail is fairly simple; just follow these steps:

1. Log on to Gmail.
2. Open the message for which you want to view headers.

3. Click the down arrow next to Reply, at the top of the message pane. Be certain you click the arrow *next* to Reply—not the Reply button itself.

4. Select Show Original.

This is shown in Figure 7-7.

| Select Message Encoding | <u>Full Headers</u> |

Courtesy of Yahoo!

FIGURE 7-5

Find Yahoo! headers.

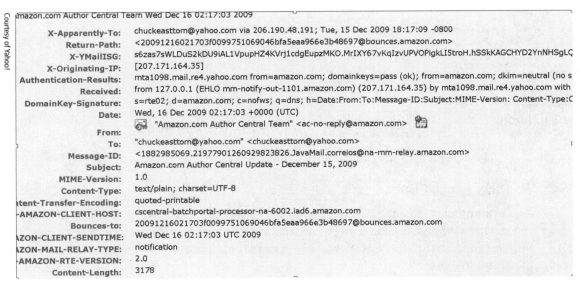

Amazon.com Author Central Team Wed Dec 16 02:17:03 2009

X-Apparently-To:	chuckeasttom@yahoo.com via 206.190.48.191; Tue, 15 Dec 2009 18:17:09 -0800
Return-Path:	<20091216021703f0099751069046bfa5eaa966e3b48697@bounces.amazon.com>
X-YMailISG:	s6zas7sWLDuS2kDU9iAL1VpupHZ4KVrj1cdgEupzMKO.MrIXY67vKqIzvUPVOPigkLI5troH.hSSkKAGCHYD2YnNHSgLQ
X-Originating-IP:	[207.171.164.35]
Authentication-Results:	mta1098.mail.re4.yahoo.com from=amazon.com; domainkeys=pass (ok); from=amazon.com; dkim=neutral (no s
Received:	from 127.0.0.1 (EHLO mm-notify-out-1101.amazon.com) (207.171.164.35) by mta1098.mail.re4.yahoo.com with
DomainKey-Signature:	s=rte02; d=amazon.com; c=nofws; q=dns; h=Date:From:To:Message-ID:Subject:MIME-Version:Content-Type:C
Date:	Wed, 16 Dec 2009 02:17:03 +0000 (UTC)
From:	"Amazon.com Author Central Team" <ac-no-reply@amazon.com>
To:	"chuckeasttom@yahoo.com" <chuckeasttom@yahoo.com>
Message-ID:	<1882985069.21977901260929823826.JavaMail.correios@na-mm-relay.amazon.com>
Subject:	Amazon.com Author Central Update - December 15, 2009
MIME-Version:	1.0
Content-Type:	text/plain; charset=UTF-8
Content-Transfer-Encoding:	quoted-printable
X-AMAZON-CLIENT-HOST:	cscentral-batchportal-processor-na-6002.iad6.amazon.com
Bounces-to:	20091216021703f0099751069046bfa5eaa966e3b48697@bounces.amazon.com
X-AMAZON-CLIENT-SENDTIME:	Wed Dec 16 02:17:03 UTC 2009
X-AMAZON-MAIL-RELAY-TYPE:	notification
X-AMAZON-RTE-VERSION:	2.0
Content-Length:	3178

Courtesy of Yahoo!

FIGURE 7-6

View Yahoo! headers.

FIGURE 7-7

Find Gmail headers.

Google and the Google logo are registered trademarks of Google Inc., used with permission

```
Delivered-To: chuckeasttom007@gmail.com
Received: by 10.182.25.137 with SMTP id c9csp84759obg;
        Wed, 23 May 2012 13:58:23 -0700 (PDT)
Return-Path: <3b0-9Tw8KD4Ykn6yln2-xylozv8qyyqvo.mywmr4muok233ywAAHqwksv.myw@scoutcamp.bounces.google.com>
Received-SPF: pass (google.com: domain of 3b0-9Tw8KD4Ykn6yln2-xylozv8qyyqvo.mywmr4muok233ywAAHqwksv.myw@scoutcamp.bounces.google.com designates 10.50.40
Authentication-Results: mr.google.com; spf=pass (google.com: domain of 3b0-9Tw8KD4Ykn6yln2-xylozv8qyyqvo.mywmr4muok233ywAAHqwksv.myw@scoutcamp.bounces.go
Received: from mr.google.com ([10.50.40.230])
        by 10.50.40.230 with SMTP id a6mr20555688igl.2.1337806703082 (num_hops = 1);
        Wed, 23 May 2012 13:58:23 -0700 (PDT)
DKIM-Signature: v=1; a=rsa-sha256; c=relaxed/relaxed;
        d=google.com; s=20120113;
        h=date:from:to:cc:subject:reply-to:x-google-ads-sender:message-id
         :x-trak-extra-language:mime-version:content-type;
        bh=XekTgcS1iYSkFAHQTAJcm7aGSzICw8DGRTeLhcUe8M8=;
        b=H6rb7OD+xtuyUTc1NCDwh+e3H1JphFiN1BO431WP2SkZuYqn3BT/2XJ2muJslF+7A0
         g716xr4Q/a+pquw0lyOQyMCfRQVBZFxThD90f6HdYHje/9GiMdu/YS+LrDbYhlWmgKqJ
         nV9CMQyjAjlcOFkAqAOcd9EIDqJ8elnTGan8U+r18OUrKtL83R4rauiXIObnpdBrDF3t
         ykwzmC42LXMELs53FCjM+Abn/geyxEB4wKmAfmvpxBbOOUC8Slbzs6PgqURKjll2VlXb
         rcvDOazwpdqhLlPRND8a9PfFv2RHzWtPnl3thYQdljmkBl/vEIvVV9XMHGbelj9StGy6
         1PNA==
Date: Wed, 23 May 2012 20:58:23 +0000
Received: by 10.50.40.230 with SMTP id a6mrl1939917igl.2.1337806703051;
        Wed, 23 May 2012 13:58:23 -0700 (PDT)
From: Google AdWords <adwords-noreply@google.com>
To: chuckeasttom007@gmail.com
Cc:
Subject: =?utf-8?q?Only_days_left_to_get_=24100_=26_tips_from_Google_AdWords=2E_En?=
 =?utf-8?q?ds_May_31=2E?=
Reply-To: adwords-noreply@google.com
X-Google-Ads-Sender: auto_adsense_emails
Message-ID: <29060e2c.1337806701.000000.53518.1.EN_US.2f59020b@google.com>
X-Trak-Extra-Language: EN_US
MIME-Version: 1.0
Content-Type: multipart/alternative; boundary="===============0825779531=="
```

FIGURE 7-8

View Gmail headers.

The headers appear in a separate window and look similar to Figure 7-8.

Other E-mail Clients

A vast number of e-mail clients are available for people to use. It is not beneficial to you to go through each and every one separately. By now, you should be noticing some similarities in the processes. However, you can see the basic steps for many of these clients in this section.

Hotmail

Hotmail is similar to Gmail:

1. Select Inbox from the menu on the left.
2. Right-click the message for which you want to view headers and select View Message Source.
3. The full headers will appear in a new window.

Apple Mail

Apple Mail is pretty straightforward:

1. Open Apple Mail.
2. Click on the message for which you want to view headers.
3. Go to the View menu.
4. Select Message, then Long Headers.
5. The full headers will appear in the window below your Inbox.

You can get a list of other e-mail clients from Google Support at *http://support.google.com/mail/answer/22454?hl=en.*

Of course, you can always use your favorite search engine to search for the e-mail client you are using. It is usually quite easy to find out how to view headers.

E-mail Files

Local storage archives are any archives that have an independent archive format from a mail server. Examples of these types of archives include the following:

- .pst (Outlook)
- .ost (Offline Outlook Storage)
- .mbx or .dbx (Outlook Express)
- .mbx (Eudora)
- .emi (common to several e-mail clients)

You need to know how to find these files and how to view them. For example, in Outlook a clever criminal might have a second .pst file containing e-mail messages that he loads only when committing his nefarious activities. If his computer is seized and you simply look in Microsoft Outlook, you won't see any incriminating evidence. If you search the suspect drive and find an additional .pst file, you can easily mount it in Outlook by selecting File, Open, and Open Outlook Data File, as shown in Figure 7-9.

There are tools that allow you to convert from one e-mail file format to another. For example, the accused's e-mail file could be an EML file, but you use Outlook. It would be helpful to translate that file into an Outlook .pst format. Transend Migrator (*http://www.transend.com/*) is a tool that will do this for you.

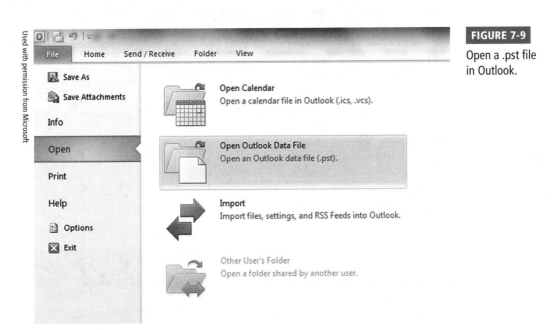

FIGURE 7-9

Open a .pst file in Outlook.

In addition, a number of forensic tools can examine the e-mail files for you. A few examples include the following:

- **Paraben's E-mail Examiner**—This tool is meant specifically to analyze e-mail. It is available at *http://www.paraben.com/email-examiner.html*.
- **Guidance Software's EnCase**—This is a general-purpose forensic tool. You can find more information about EnCase at *http://www.guidancesoftware.com*.
- **AccessData's Forensic Toolkit (FTK)**—This is another general-purpose forensic tool. You can find more details about FTK at *http://www.accessdata.com/products/digital-forensics*.
- **LibPST package**—This is an open source tool. You can get this tool from *http://www.five-ten-sg.com/libpst/*.

Paraben's E-mail Examiner

Although there are many tools available that may be used with e-mail forensics, this tool is exclusively for e-mail forensics, so it merits a closer look. Paraben works like the more complete forensic suites (Forensic Toolkit and EnCase) in that evidence is grouped by case. When you first start Paraben, you select New and then create a new case, as shown in Figure 7-10.

Paraben will also associate information about the investigator along with the case information. This is shown in Figure 7-11.

Next, you select the type of e-mail database you are going to be working with. The major e-mail clients are all represented, as you can see in Figure 7-12.

FIGURE 7-10

A new Paraben case.

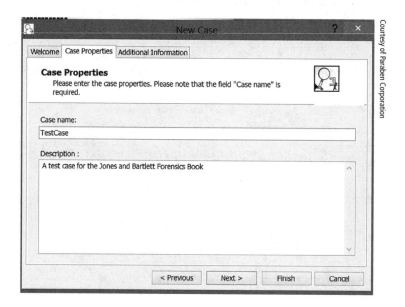

Courtesy of Paraben Corporation

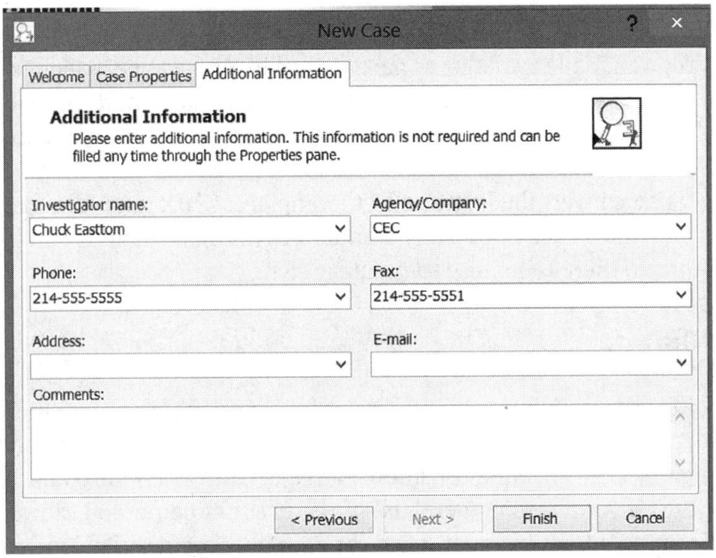

FIGURE 7-11

The investigator.

Courtesy of Paraben Corporation

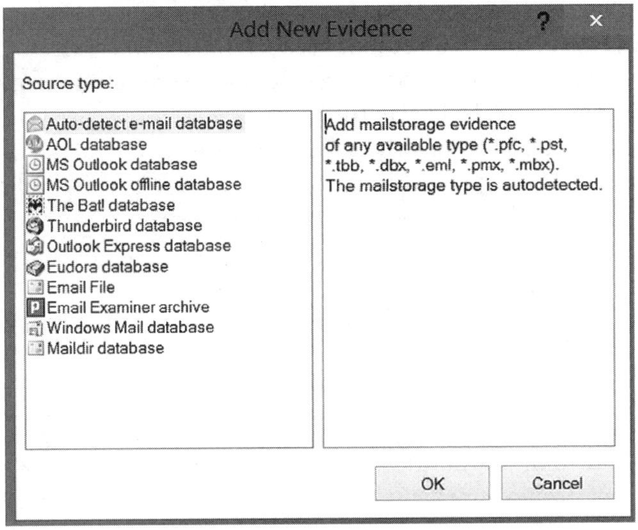

FIGURE 7-12

Select your e-mail database.

At this point, you select the database you want to work with and it is added to the case. From within Paraben, you can sort, search, scan, and otherwise work with the e-mail data. Paraben can also generate reports of the data showing whatever data is most relevant to your case—or all the e-mail data, if you prefer.

ReadPST

ReadPST is a program made available as part of the libPST package, which is available at *http://alioth.debian.org/projects/libpst/*. You will need to download and compile it because it is not available in precompiled format. Once you have done so, you can run it and use it to examine PST files.

ReadPST will first convert the PST into RFC-compliant UNIX mail. You can access the extracted mail and attachments with any standard UNIX mail client. If you have access to Microsoft Outlook, there is no need to use ReadPST.

Tracing E-mail

E-mail tracing involves examining e-mail header information to look for clues about where a message has been. This will be one of your more frequent responsibilities as a forensic investigator. You will often use audits or paper trails of e-mail traffic as evidence in court. Many investigators recommend use of the `tracert` command. However, because of the dynamic nature of the Internet, `tracert` does not provide reliable, consistent, or accurate routing information for an e-mail. To prove this, you can simply compare the routing from the e-mail header to the results shown by `tracert`. The results are likely different, and the greater the distance between sender and receiver, the bigger the difference between the theoretical `tracert` results and the results determined from the actual routing information embedded in the header.

It may be useful to determine the ownership of the source e-mail server for a message. If you need to manually find out to whom a given IP address is registered, a number of whois databases are available on the Web. Here are just a few:

- *http://www.whois.net*
- *http://www.networksolutions.com/whois/index.jsp*
- *http://www.who.is*
- *http://www.internic.net/whois.html*
- *http://cqcounter.com/whois/*

After a suspect comes to the authorities' attention, your organization may ask you to monitor that person's traffic. For example, administrators might request security checks on an employee who appears to be disgruntled or who has access to sensitive information. This employee's e-mail logs and network usage may, for example, show him or her sending innocent family photos to a Hotmail account, but no traffic coming back from that Hotmail account. These seemingly innocent photos might carry a steganographically hidden message, and so provide evidence of the employee's part in corporate espionage.

Forensic e-mail tracing is similar to traditional gumshoe detective work. It involves looking at each point through which an e-mail passed. You work step by step back to the originating computer and, eventually, the perpetrator.

E-mail Server Forensics

At some point, you need to check the e-mail server. Both the sender and the recipient could have deleted the relevant e-mails. But there is a good chance a copy is still on the e-mail server. Many servers have a retention policy, which may be governed by law in certain industries. When you examine an e-mail server, be aware that there are a variety of e-mail server programs that could be in use. Microsoft Exchange is a very common server. Lotus Notes and Novell GroupWise are also popular e-mail server products.

The file extensions associated with the most widely used e-mail server software are listed here:

- Exchange Server (.edb)
- Exchange Public Folders (pub.edb)
- Exchange Private Folders (priv.edb)
- Streaming Data (priv.stm)
- Lotus Notes (.nsf)
- GroupWise (.db)
- GroupWise Post Office Database (wphost.db)
- GroupWise User Databases (userxxx.db)
- Linux E-Mail Server Logs/var/log/mail.*

Obviously, tools like Forensic Toolkit and EnCase allow you to add these files to a case and to work with them. You can also manually examine these files provided that you have access to the relevant software (for example, Exchange or Lotus Notes).

E-mail and the Law

There are specific laws in the United States that are applicable to e-mail investigations. It is critical that you be aware of the relevant laws. Failure to adhere to the legal guidelines can render evidence inadmissible.

The Fourth Amendment to the U.S. Constitution

If an e-mail message resides on a sender's or recipient's computer or other device, the Fourth Amendment to the U.S. Constitution and state requirements govern the seizure and collection of the message. Determine whether the person on whose computer the evidence resides has a reasonable expectation of privacy on that computer. The Fourth Amendment requires a search warrant or one of the recognized exceptions to the search warrant requirements, such as consent from the device owner.

The Electronic Communications Privacy Act

If an Internet service provider (ISP) or any other communications network stores an e-mail, retrieval of that evidence must be analyzed under the Electronic Communications Privacy Act (ECPA). The ECPA creates statutory restrictions on government access to such evidence from ISPs or other electronic communications service providers.

The ECPA requires different legal processes to obtain specific types of information:

- **Basic subscriber information**—This information includes name, address, billing information including a credit card number, telephone toll billing records, subscriber's telephone number, type of service, and length of service. An investigator can obtain this type of information with a subpoena, court order, or search warrant.

- **Transactional information**—This information includes Web sites visited, e-mail addresses of others with whom the subscriber exchanged e-mail, and buddy lists. An investigator can obtain this type of information with a court order or search warrant.

- **Content information**—An investigator who has a search warrant can obtain content information from retrieved e-mail messages and also acquire unretrieved stored e-mails.

- **Real-time access**—To intercept traffic as it is sent or received, an investigator needs to obtain a wiretap order.

The CAN-SPAM Act

The CAN-SPAM Act of 2003 was the first law meant to curtail unsolicited e-mail, often referred to as spam. However, the law has many loopholes. For example, you do not need permission before sending e-mail. This means that unsolicited e-mail, what most people consider spam to be, is not prohibited. The second issue is that it applies only to commercial e-mails—e-mails that are trying to sell some product or service. Therefore, mass e-mailings for political, religious, or ideological purposes are not covered by the CAN-SPAM Act.

The only requirement of CAN-SPAM is that the sender must provide some mechanism whereby the receiver can opt out of future e-mails and that method cannot require the receiver to pay in order to opt out.

The law defines commercial e-mail as "any electronic mail message the primary purpose of which is the commercial advertisement or promotion of a commercial product or service (including content on an Internet website operated for a commercial purpose)." This means that any mass e-mails that have no commercial purpose are not covered by this law.

All commercial e-mail is required to offer ways for the recipient to opt out. Those methods must meet the following guidelines:

- A visible and operable unsubscribe mechanism is present in all e-mails.
- Consumer opt-out requests are honored within 10 days.
- Opt-out lists, also known as suppression lists, can be used only for compliance purposes, not to be sold to other vendors/senders.

There are also restrictions on how the sender can acquire the recipient's e-mail address and how the sender can actually transmit the e-mail. Those requirements are as follows:

- A message cannot be sent through an open relay.
- A message cannot be sent to a harvested e-mail address.
- A message cannot contain a false header.

This is important because these are the methods often used by people who send spam e-mail. Spam is one crime that obviously lends itself to e-mail forensics. Tracking down the original sender of the e-mail is the first step in investigating spam. Unfortunately, the e-mail is sometimes sent from offshore sites or relayed through an innocent third party's servers. This makes prosecuting spam very difficult, and even if a judgment is obtained, in most cases it is impossible to enforce.

18 U.S.C. 2252B

You might already be at least somewhat familiar with the laws already discussed in this chapter. However, this law is less well known. To begin, read the actual law. Findlaw.com (2013) details the law as:

(a) Whoever knowingly uses a misleading domain name on the Internet with the intent to deceive a person into viewing material constituting obscenity shall be fined under this title or imprisoned not more than 2 years, or both.

(b) Whoever knowingly uses a misleading domain name on the Internet with the intent to deceive a minor into viewing material that is harmful to minors on the Internet shall be fined under this title or imprisoned not more than 4 years, or both.

(c) For the purposes of this section, a domain name that includes a word or words to indicate the sexual content of the site, such as "sex" or "porn," is not misleading.

(d) For the purposes of this section, the term "material that is harmful to minors" means any communication, consisting of nudity, sex, or excretion, that, taken as a whole and with reference to its context—

(1) predominantly appeals to a prurient interest of minors;

(2) is patently offensive to prevailing standards in the adult community as a whole with respect to what is suitable material for minors; and

(3) lacks serious literary, artistic, political, or scientific value for minors.

(e) For the purposes of subsection (d), the term "sex" means acts of masturbation, sexual intercourse, or physical contact with a person's genitals, or the condition of human male or female genitals when in a state of sexual stimulation or arousal.

This law is about perpetrators who attempt to hide the pornographic nature of their Web site, often to make it more accessible to minors. This is a very serious concern, and one that sometimes arises in child predator cases.

The Communication Assistance to Law Enforcement Act

The Communication Assistance to Law Enforcement Act (CALEA), not to be confused with the law enforcement standards certification of the same name, is a U.S. wiretapping law passed in 1994.

CALEA's purpose is to allow law enforcement and intelligence agencies to lawfully conduct electronic surveillance. It requires that telecommunications carriers and manufacturers of telecommunications equipment modify and design their equipment, facilities, and services to ensure that they have built-in surveillance capabilities, allowing federal agencies to monitor all telephone, broadband Internet, and VoIP traffic in real time. CALEA is widely used, and a basic awareness of CALEA should be a part of every forensic investigator's base knowledge.

The Foreign Intelligence Surveillance Act

The **Foreign Intelligence Surveillance Act (FISA)** of 1978 is a U.S. law that prescribes procedures for the physical and electronic surveillance and collection of "foreign intelligence information" between foreign powers and agents of foreign powers, which may include American citizens and permanent residents suspected of espionage or terrorism. The law does not apply outside the United States but may be encountered by a forensic investigator in researching intelligence even if it does not specifically regard espionage or terrorism. The law is an important part of many agencies' approaches to information gathering. It has been amended frequently, so it is important to stay current on the latest revisions and court cases.

The USA Patriot Act

The **USA Patriot Act** of 2001 incorporates in its name a 10-letter acronym standing for Uniting (and) Strengthening America (by) Providing Appropriate Tools Required (to) Intercept (and) Obstruct Terrorism. The act was passed into law as a response to the terrorist attacks of September 11, 2001. It significantly reduced restrictions on law enforcement agencies' gathering of intelligence within the United States; expanded the Secretary of the Treasury's authority to regulate financial transactions, particularly those involving foreign individuals and entities; and broadened the discretion of law enforcement and immigration authorities in detaining and/or deporting immigrants suspected of terrorism and related acts. The act also expanded the definition of terrorism to include domestic terrorism, thus enlarging the number of activities to which the USA Patriot Act's expanded law enforcement powers can be applied.

In May 2011, President Barack Obama signed the Patriot Sunsets Extension Act of 2011, which is a four-year extension of three key provisions in the Patriot Act: roving wiretaps, searches of business records, and conducting surveillance of individuals suspected of terrorist-related activities who are not linked to terrorist groups, and so are known as lone wolves. The Patriot Act gives law enforcement dramatically enhanced powers for information gathering and should be a part of a comprehensive knowledge base for any forensic investigator.

CHAPTER SUMMARY

In this chapter, you learned the process of e-mail forensics. You examined e-mail headers, learned about file formats, and worked with a few e-mail tools. You also learned about laws relevant to e-mail forensics. You should be very comfortable with the material in this chapter because e-mail evidence is common to many cases.

KEY CONCEPTS AND TERMS

Anonymous remailing
Foreign Intelligence
    Surveillance Act (FISA)
Internet Message Access
    Protocol (IMAP)

Post Office Protocol version 3
    (POP3)
Simple Mail Transfer Protocol
    (SMTP)
Spoofing
USA Patriot Act

CHAPTER 7 ASSESSMENT

1. What is the file format .edb used with?

  A. GroupWise
  B. Microsoft Exchange
  C. Microsoft Outlook
  D. Linux e-mail

2. IMAP uses port 143.

  A. True
  B. False

3. Which of the following types of mass e-mails are *not* covered by the CAN-SPAM Act?

  A. E-mails advertising products
  B. E-mails advertising legal services
  C. E-mails advertising a church event
  D. E-mails advertising stock prices

4. What is the .ost file format used for?

  A. Microsoft Outlook mailbox
  B. Microsoft Outlook offline storage
  C. Microsoft Lotus Notes
  D. Microsoft Outlook Express

5. Lotus Notes uses the _____ file format.

7

E-mail Forensics

Windows Forensics

M ICROSOFT WINDOWS IS A VERY COMMONLY USED operating system. Therefore, it is important that you be very familiar with conducting forensics on Windows machines. In this chapter, you learn how to perform forensic examination of a Windows computer. That includes examining the Registry, the index.dat, the swap file, and more.

Chapter 8 Topics

This chapter covers the following topics and concepts:

- What the details of Windows are
- What you need to know about evidence in volatile data
- What the Windows swap file is
- What the Windows logs are
- What the Windows directories are
- What you need to know about index.dat
- What you need to know about the Windows Registry

Chapter 8 Goals

When you complete this chapter, you will be able to:

- Understand the workings of the Windows operating system
- Gather evidence from the Registry
- Retrieve evidence from logs
- Examine directories for evidence
- Check the index.dat file for evidence

Windows Details

Before delving deeply into Windows forensics, it is a good idea to get a better idea of the operating system itself. In this section, you learn about the history of Windows and its structure. This gives you a context within which to learn Windows forensics. For deeper coverage of Windows internals, refer to the book *Windows Sysinternals Administrator's Reference* by Mark E. Russinovich and Aaron Margosis.

Windows History

Most people became familiar with Windows with the release of version 3.1 in 1992. It was then that the Windows system became widely popular. At that time, Windows was a graphical user interface, and not really an operating system. The operating system was **Disk Operating System (DOS)**. Windows provided a visual interface for interacting with the operating system by means of mouse clicks, rather than typing in DOS commands.

During the early 1990s, you could use other, non-Microsoft user interfaces to work with DOS. You could also install Windows on systems running some non-Microsoft operating systems, such as Dr. DOS (an alternative to DOS). There were also several competing operating systems for PCs, including OS2 and OS2 Warp from IBM.

For servers and serious professionals, Microsoft had Windows NT Versions 3.1, 3.51, and 4.0, which were widely used. Each version had both workstation and server editions. The NT version of Windows was widely considered more stable and more secure than Windows 3.1.

The release of Windows 95 in 1995 marked a change in Windows. At this point, the underlying operating system and the **graphical user interface (GUI)**—a point-and-click user interface—were fused into one single, coherent product. This meant that you could not choose some non-Windows GUI. Shortly after the release of Windows 95, Windows NT 4.0 was released. Many consider Windows 98 just an intermediate step, an improvement on Windows 95. The interface looked very much the same as Windows 95, but the performance was vastly improved. Windows 95 and 98 used the FAT32 file system.

Windows 2000 was widely considered a major improvement in the Windows line. Essentially, the days of separate NT and Windows lines were over. Now there would simply be different editions of Windows 2000. There were editions for home users, for professional users, and for servers. The differences among the editions were primarily in the features available and the capacity, such as how much random access memory (RAM) could be addressed. Windows 2000 was also the version of Windows wherein Microsoft began to recommend NTFS over FAT32 as a file system.

Windows XP was the next milestone for Microsoft, and Windows Server 2003 was released the same year. This marked a return to the approach of having a separate server and desktop system (unlike Windows 2000). The interface was not very different, but there were structural improvements.

Windows Vista and Windows 7 did not have significantly different user interfaces from XP. There were feature changes and additional capabilities, but essentially the interface was moderately tweaked with each version. The same can be said of the relationship between Windows Server 2008 and Windows Server 2003. Someone comfortable with Windows Server 2003 would have no problem working with Windows Server 2008.

Windows 8 was a radical change. The operating system is meant to be more like that of a tablet. You can get to a desktop that looks much like Windows 7, but the default behavior of Windows 8 is tablet-like.

Not all the differences in Windows versions are pertinent to forensics. However, certain issues are, such as the following: Does the Windows version in question support 64-bit processing? Does it have a firewall—XP was the first Windows version to have one—and if so, is the firewall automatically on, as in Windows XP Service Pack 1? Does the version of Windows support the Encrypted File System (EFS), which allows the user to encrypt specific files and folders? This was first introduced with Windows 2000, but starting with Vista, this feature is available only on professional/business or higher editions.

64 Bit

What exactly does 64 bit mean? Why is it so important? First of all, the term refers to how the central processing unit (CPU) and the operating system process information. Basically, 64-bit systems can use 64-bit addressing. That means that a 32-bit system can address up to 4,294,967,295 bytes, with each byte having its own address. That is why 32-bit systems were limited to 4 gigabytes (GB) of RAM. A 64-bit system can address up to 18,446,744,073,709,551,616 bytes. Literally, millions of billions of bytes. This is a huge number. So, you can clearly see that a 64-bit processor and a 64-bit operating system have significant advantages over a 32-bit system.

A Brief History of Windows

1985 Windows 1.0 opened

1990 Windows 3.0

1992 Windows 3.1

1995 Windows 95

1996 Windows NT 4.0

1998 Windows 98

2000 Windows 2000

2001 Windows XP (first 64-bit version)

2003 Windows XP with Windows Server 2003

2007 general release of Windows Vista

2008 Windows Vista Home Basic, Home Premium, Business, and Ultimate; Windows Server 2008

2009 Windows 7 and Windows Server 2008 R2

2012 Windows 8 and Windows Server 2012

Just as important to forensics is how Windows handles 32-bit programs. You can install 32-bit programs on a 64-bit system. However, they usually are installed into the Program Files (x86) directory. Windows uses x86 to refer to 32-bit versions of programs, files, and so on.

The Boot Process

A forensic examiner needs to understand the Windows boot process for many reasons. A virus might infect a suspect drive at a specific point in the boot process. It is also the case that hard drive encryption programs operate during the boot process of the system. The following is a summary of the basic process:

1. The BIOS conducts the **power-on self test (POST)**. This is when the system's **basic input/output system (BIOS)** checks to see if the drives, keyboard, and other key items are present and working. This occurs before any operating system components are loaded.

2. The computer reads the **master boot record (MBR)** and partition table.

3. The MBR locates the boot partition. This is the partition that has the operating system on it.

4. The MBR passes control to the boot sector on the boot partition.

5. The boot sector loads NTLDR. NTLDR is the NT loader; it is the first part of the Windows operating system and is responsible for preparing and loading the rest of the operating system.

6. Note that if instead of being shut down, Windows has been put in the hibernation state, the contents of *hiberfil.sys* are loaded into memory and the system resumes at the previous state.

7. NTLDR switches from real mode to 32-bit memory or 64-bit depending on the system. Real mode is the default for x86 systems. It provides no support for memory protection, multitasking, or code privilege levels.

8. NTLDR starts minimal file system drivers (FAT, FAT32, NTFS).

9. NTLDR reads boot.ini and displays the boot loader menu. If there are multiple operating systems, they will be displayed.

10. NTLDR loads NTOSKRNL and passes hardware information. The NTOSKRNL is the actual kernel for the Windows operating system. This is the end of the *boot phase* and the beginning of the *load phase*.

11. NTLDR loads hal.dll (hardware abstraction layer).

12. NTLDR loads the system hive (i.e., the Registry) and reads in settings from it.

13. Kernel initialization begins (the screen turns blue).

14. The services load phase begins.

15. The Win32 subsystem start phase begins.

16. The user logs on.

Knowing the boot order can allow you to diagnose issues that might prevent booting the system, understand when encryption is implemented, and more. Some viruses infect the boot sector and, thus, are loaded when the system loads and can affect how the system loads. These are all good reasons to understand the boot order, at least in a general way.

Important Files

Windows has a number of files. If you look at the Task Manager, you see many processes/programs running. Clever virus and spyware writers give their malware a name that is similar to these system processes. This makes a casual observer think these are part of the operating system. A few of the more important Windows files are listed here:

- **Ntdetect.com**—A program that queries the computer for basic device/config data like time/date from CMOS, system bus types, disk drives, ports, and so on
- **Ntbootdd.sys**—A storage controller device driver
- **Ntoskrnl.exe**—The core of the operating system
- **Hal.dll**—An interface for hardware
- **Smss.exe**—A program that handles services on your system
- **Winlogon.exe**—The program that logs you on
- **Lsass.exe**—The program that handles security and logon policies
- **Explorer.exe**—The interface the user interacts with, such as the desktop, Windows Explorer, and so on
- **Crss.exe**—The program that handles tasks like creating threads, console windows, and so forth

Of particular interest in forensics are those programs that are named similarly to the system processes. If you see a running process with a similar name (for example, Lsassx .exe), that could indicate the presence of malware.

Volatile Data

Volatile memory analysis is a live system forensic technique in which you collect a memory dump and perform analysis in an isolated environment. Volatile memory analysis is similar to live response in that you must first establish a trusted command shell. Next, you establish a data collection system and a method for transmitting the data. However, you would only acquire a physical memory dump of the compromised system and transmit it to the data collection system for analysis. In this case, VMware allows you to simply suspend the virtual machine and use the .vmem file as a memory image.

As in other forensic investigations, you would also compute the hash after you complete the memory capture. Unlike with traditional hard drive forensics, you don't need to calculate a hash before data acquisition. Due to the volatile nature of running memory, the imaging process involves taking a snapshot of a "moving target."

The primary difference between this approach and live response is that you don't need any additional evidence from the compromised system. Therefore, you can analyze the evidence on the collection system.

To produce digital data from a live system as evidence in court, it is essential to justify the validity of the acquired memory data. One common approach is to acquire volatile memory data in a dump file for offline examination. A **dump** is a complete copy of every bit of memory or cache recorded in permanent storage or printed on paper. You can then analyze the dump electronically or manually in its static state.

Programmers have developed a number of toolkits to collect volatile memory data. These automated programs run on live systems and collect transient memory data. These tools suffer from one critical drawback: If run on a compromised system, such a tool heavily relies on the underlying operating system. This could affect the collected data's reliability. Some response tools may even substantially alter the digital environment of the original system and cause an adverse impact on the dumped memory data.

As a result, you may have to study those changes to determine whether the alterations have affected the acquired data. Data in memory is not consistently maintained during system operation. This issue poses a challenge for computer forensics.

Maintaining **data consistency** is a problem with live system forensics in which data is not acquired at a unified moment and is thus inconsistent. If a system is running, it is impossible to freeze the machine states in the course of data acquisition. Even the most efficient method introduces a time difference between the moment you acquire the first bit and the moment you acquire the last bit. For example, the program may execute Function A at the beginning of the memory dump and execute Function B at the end.

The data in the dump may correspond to different execution steps somewhere between Function A and Function B. Because you didn't acquire the data at a unified moment, data inconsistency is inevitable in the memory dump.

When dumping memory, it is useful for the forensic examiner to be aware of the fact that there are actually two types of memory:

- **Stack (S)**—Memory in the **stack (S)** segment is allocated to local variables and parameters within each function. This memory is allocated based on the last-in, first-out (LIFO) principle. When the program is running, program variables use the memory allocated to the stack area again and again. This segment is the most dynamic area of the memory process. The data within this segment is discrepant and influenced by the program's various function calls.

- **Heap (H)**—Dynamic memory for a program comes from the **heap (H)** segment. A process may use a memory allocator such as malloc to request dynamic memory. When this happens, the address space of the process expands. The data in the heap area can exist between function calls. The memory allocator may reuse memory that has been released by the process. Therefore, heap data is less stable than the data in the data segment.

When a program is running, the code, data, and heap segments are usually placed in a single contiguous area. The stack segment is separated from the other segments. It expands within the memory allocated space. Indeed, the memory comprises a number of processes of the operating system or the applications it is supporting. Memory can be viewed as a large array that contains many segments for different processes. In a live system, process memory grows and shrinks, depending on system usage and user activities.

This growth and shrinking of memory is either related to the growth of heap data or the expansion and release of stack data. The data in the code segment is static and remains intact at all times for a particular program or program segment. Data in the growing heap segment and stack segment causes inconsistency in the data contained in memory as a whole. The stack data has a greater effect than the heap data. Nevertheless, the code segment contains consistent data. Consistent data is usually dormant and not affected when a process is running in memory. When you obtain a process dump of a running program, data in the code segment remains unchanged.

Tools

A number of tools and even some Windows utilities are available that can help you to analyze live data on a Windows system. This section looks at some of the more widely used tools and utilities.

PsList

Use PsList to view process and thread statistics on a system. Running PsList lists all running processes on the system. However, it does not reveal the presence of the rootkit or the other processes that the rootkit has hidden. PsList is a part of a suite of tools, PsTools, available as a free download from *http://technet.microsoft.com/en-us/sysinternals/bb896682.aspx*. You can see this tool used in Figure 8-1.

PsInfo

This tool is also from the PsTools suite. It can tell you system uptime (time since last reboot), operating system details, and other general information about the system. This is good background information to put into your forensic report. This tool is shown in Figure 8-2.

ListDLLs

ListDLLs allows you to view the currently loaded dynamic-link libraries (DLLs) for a process. Running ListDLLs lists the DLLs loaded by all running processes. However, ListDLLs cannot show the DLLs loaded for hidden processes. Using a Trojan horse to compromise a program or system DLL, however, is a common attack vector. So this tool can be important to your forensic investigation. This tool is also available online for free. You can download it from *http://technet.microsoft.com/en-us/sysinternals/bb896656.aspx*. You can see this utility in use in Figure 8-3.

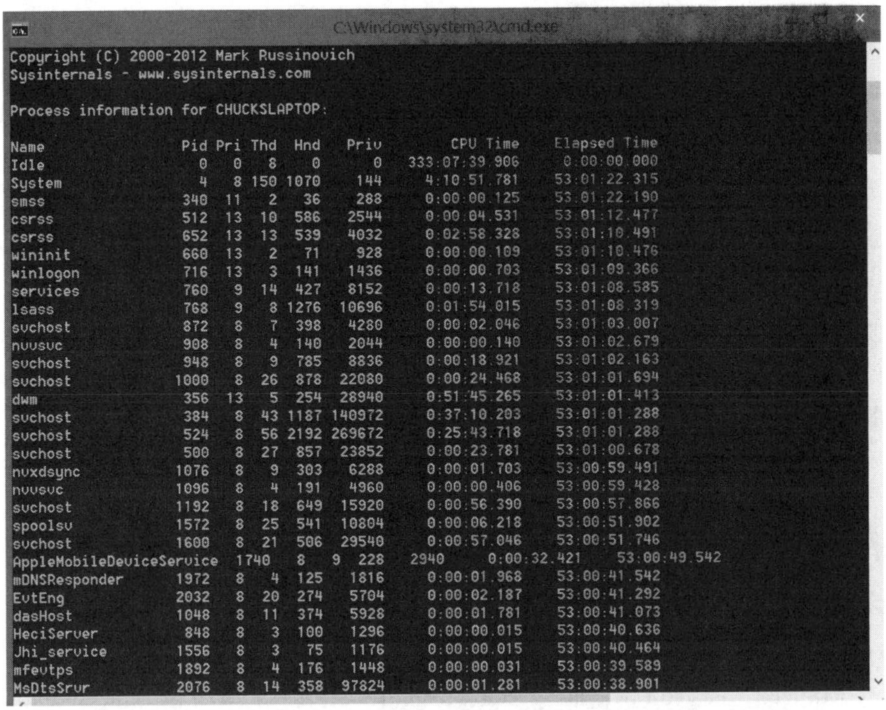

```
C:\Windows\system32\cmd.exe
Copyright (C) 2000-2012 Mark Russinovich
Sysinternals - www.sysinternals.com

Process information for CHUCKSLAPTOP:

Name                  Pid Pri Thd  Hnd   Priv        CPU Time    Elapsed Time
Idle                    0   0   8    0      0  333:07:39.906     0:00:00.000
System                  4   8 150 1070    144    4:10:51.781    53:01:22.315
smss                  340  11   2   36    288    0:00:00.125    53:01:22.190
csrss                 512  13  10  586   2544    0:00:04.531    53:01:12.477
csrss                 652  13  13  539   4032    0:02:58.328    53:01:10.491
wininit               660  13   2   71    928    0:00:00.109    53:01:10.476
winlogon              716  13   3  141   1436    0:00:00.703    53:01:09.366
services              760   9  14  427   8152    0:00:13.718    53:01:08.585
lsass                 768   9   8 1276  10696    0:01:54.015    53:01:08.319
svchost               872   8   7  398   4280    0:00:02.046    53:01:03.007
nvvsvc                908   8   4  140   2044    0:00:00.140    53:01:02.679
svchost               948   8   9  785   8836    0:00:18.921    53:01:02.163
svchost              1000   8  26  878  22080    0:00:24.468    53:01:01.694
dwm                   356  13   5  254  28940    0:51:45.265    53:01:01.413
svchost               384   8  43 1187 140972    0:37:10.203    53:01:01.288
svchost               524   8  56 2192 269672    0:25:43.718    53:01:01.288
svchost               500   8  27  857  23852    0:00:23.781    53:01:00.678
nvxdsync             1076   8   9  303   6288    0:00:01.703    53:00:59.491
nvvsvc               1096   8   4  191   4960    0:00:00.406    53:00:59.428
svchost              1192   8  18  649  15920    0:00:56.390    53:00:57.866
spoolsv              1572   8  25  541  10804    0:00:06.218    53:00:51.902
svchost              1600   8  21  506  29540    0:00:57.046    53:00:51.746
AppleMobileDeviceService  1740   8   9  228   2940    0:00:32.421    53:00:49.542
mDNSResponder        1972   8   4  125   1816    0:00:01.968    53:00:41.542
EvtEng               2032   8  20  274   5704    0:00:02.187    53:00:41.292
dasHost              1048   8  11  374   5928    0:00:01.781    53:00:41.073
HeciServer            848   8   3  100   1296    0:00:00.015    53:00:40.636
Jhi_service          1556   8   3   75   1176    0:00:00.015    53:00:40.464
mfevtps              1892   8   4  176   1448    0:00:00.031    53:00:39.589
MsDtsSrvr            2076   8  14  358  97824    0:00:01.281    53:00:38.901
```


FIGURE 8-1

PsList.

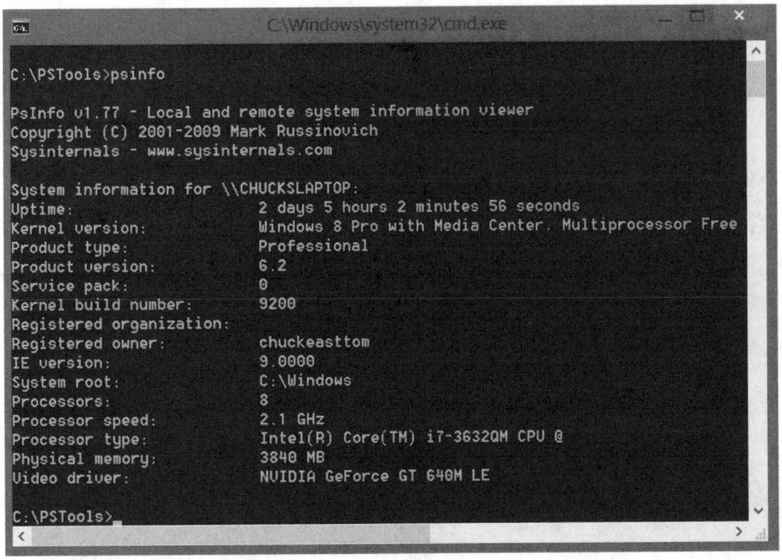

```
C:\Windows\system32\cmd.exe

C:\PSTools>psinfo

PsInfo v1.77 - Local and remote system information viewer
Copyright (C) 2001-2009 Mark Russinovich
Sysinternals - www.sysinternals.com

System information for \\CHUCKSLAPTOP:
Uptime:                    2 days 5 hours 2 minutes 56 seconds
Kernel version:            Windows 8 Pro with Media Center, Multiprocessor Free
Product type:              Professional
Product version:           6.2
Service pack:              0
Kernel build number:       9200
Registered organization:
Registered owner:          chuckeasttom
IE version:                9.0000
System root:               C:\Windows
Processors:                8
Processor speed:           2.1 GHz
Processor type:            Intel(R) Core(TM) i7-3632QM CPU @
Physical memory:           3840 MB
Video driver:              NVIDIA GeForce GT 640M LE

C:\PSTools>
```


FIGURE 8-2

PsInfo.

FIGURE 8-3

ListDLLs.

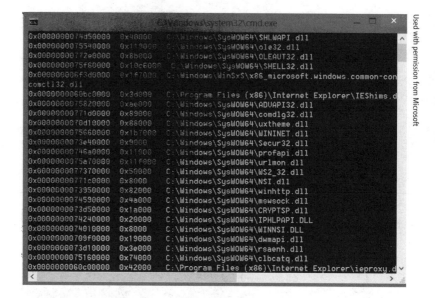

PsLoggedOn

PsLoggedOn helps you discover users who have logged on both locally and remotely. Of most importance, it tells you who is logged on to shares on the current machine. This is also part of the PsTools suite available from Microsoft TechNet. This utility is shown in Figure 8-4.

FIGURE 8-4

PsLoggedOn.

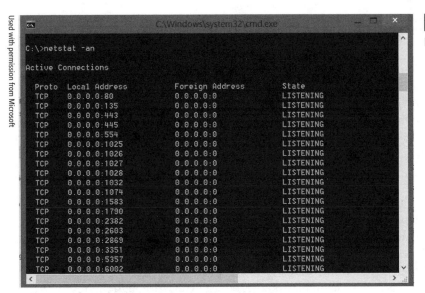

FIGURE 8-5

Netstat.

Using netstat

This utility is important in the context of checking live system data. Remember that netstat is a command-line tool that displays both incoming and outgoing network connections. It also displays routing tables and a number of network interface statistics. It is available on UNIX, UNIX-like, and Windows-based operating systems.

Use the netstat utility to view the network connections of a running machine. Running netstat with the an option will show all ports, list what they are doing (listening or sending), and list them in numerical order. This can be useful information in your forensic analysis, particularly if the suspected crime uses spyware or a botnet. You can see netstat in Figure 8-5.

Using Fport

Fport is a free tool formerly available from Foundstone, now distributed by McAfee, which you can find at *http://www.mcafee.com/us/downloads/free-tools/fport.aspx*. Fport allows you to view all open TCP and UDP ports and maps those to specific processes. This lets

FYI

One issue with extracting live data is slurred images. A **slurred image** is similar to a photograph of a moving object. A slurred image, in the context of live forensic acquisition, is the result of acquiring a file as it is being updated. Even a small file modification can cause a problem because the operating system reads the metadata section of the hard disk before accessing any file. If a file or metadata folder in the file system changes after the operating system has read the metadata but before it acquires the data, the metadata and data sectors may not totally agree.

8

Windows Forensics

you know which process is using which port. This tool is similar in function to running `netstat -an`.

Userdump

Userdump is a command-line tool for dumping basic user info from Windows-based systems. With Userdump, you can extract the memory dumps of running processes for offline analysis. This is a free tool from Microsoft, which you can download from *http://www.microsoft.com/en-us/download/details.aspx?id=4060*. This tool is used primarily to dump data to an external file, so you need to specify where to dump the data.

PTFinder

PTFinder, by Andreas Schuster, is a Perl script memory analysis tool; you can find more information at *http://computer.forensikblog.de/en/2007/11/ptfinder_0_3_05.html*. It supports analysis of Windows operating system versions.

PTFinder enumerates processes and threads in a memory dump. It uses a brute-force approach to enumerating the processes and uses various rules to determine whether the information is either a legitimate process or just bytes. Although this tool does not reveal anything new in terms of malware, it does enable repeatability of the results, which is an important benefit in volatile memory analysis. The No Threads option in PTFinder provides a list of processes found in a memory dump. This is an open source graphics language that provides a visual representation of the relationships between threads and processes.

There are certainly other tools that you can use to examine a live system forensically. However, these tools are the ones most commonly used.

Windows Swap File

The Windows swap file is used to augment the RAM. Essentially, it is a special place on the hard drive where items from memory can be temporarily stored for fast retrieval. For example, you might have five programs open at one time, but you are only using one at a time. If the system is running low on RAM, it can take the program or file that has been inactive the longest and move it to the swap file.

FYI

A common situation you may encounter during a live forensic investigation is the use of virtual environments. A virtual machine is a software program that appears to be a physical computer and executes programs as if it were a physical computer. You commonly use a virtual machine when you need to run an operating system on another computer. For example, you can run one or more Linux virtual machines on a computer running a Microsoft Windows operating system. Virtual machines are popular in organizations that want to save IT costs by running several virtual machines on a single physical computer. Two of the most popular software packages that implement virtual machines are VMware and VirtualBox.

The Windows swap file used to end in a .swp extension; since Windows XP, however, it ends in pagefile.sys. It is typically found in the Windows root directory. The swap file is a binary file. Given that the swap file is used to augment RAM, it is often referred to as virtual memory.

Windows Logs

All versions of Windows support logging. However, the method to get to the log can vary from one version to another. With Windows 7 and Windows Server 2008, you find the logs by clicking on the Start button in the lower-left corner of the desktop and then clicking Control Panel. You then select Administrative Tools and then Event Viewer. You would check for the following logs:

- **Security log**—This is probably the most important log from a forensic point of view. It has both successful and unsuccessful logon events.

- **Application log**—This log contains various events logged by applications or programs. Many applications record their errors here in the Application log.

- **System log**—The System log contains events logged by Windows system components. This includes events like driver failures. This particular log is not as interesting from a forensic perspective as the other logs are.

- **ForwardedEvents log**—The ForwardedEvents log is used to store events collected from remote computers. This has data in it only if event forwarding has been configured.

- **Applications and Services logs**—This log is used to store events from a single application or component rather than events that might have systemwide impact.

> **NOTE**
>
> Logging is not turned on by default, so not all systems will have logs to examine. However, it is rare to find a server that does not have logging turned on.

You can view logs, as shown in Figure 8-6.

Windows servers have similar logs. However, it is also possible that the logs will be empty. For example, the tool auditpol.exe can turn logging on and off. Savvy criminals might turn the logging off while they do their misdeeds, then turn it back on. In addition, the tool WinZapper allows you to selectively erase individual records in the log. So it is possible that the logs will yield no evidence, even if a crime did take place.

Another type of tool that is often used on PCs, servers, routers, switches, and other devices is Tripwire, which you can find at *http://www.tripwire.com*. A newer tool is CimTrak, which you can find at *http://www.fileintegritymonitoring.com/cimtrak-home*, and related software. These programs store a secure hash of files and the static part of device memory and monitor for changes to the files and/or memory. Security practitioners can use the tools to harden their defenses and make their systems "aware" of attacks when they occur. They can also allow files or memory to be checkpointed and restored to a preattack condition. This class of tool can also be very important to the forensic examiner, as a large amount of information is made available due to different generations of files as well as multiple log files.

FIGURE 8-6

Viewing Windows logs.

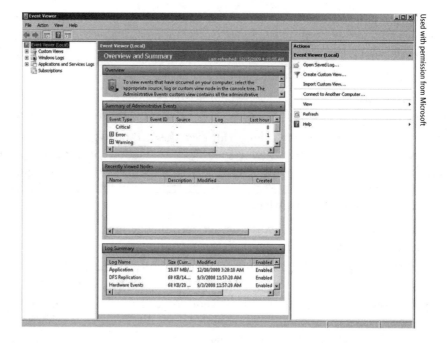

Windows Directories

There are certain directories in Windows that are more likely than others to contain evidence. Obviously, a technically savvy criminal can erase evidence. However, not all criminals are technically savvy, and even those who are might have missed something. Or the computer might have been seized before they could erase the incriminating evidence. Although there are many directories on a computer, the following are the most forensically interesting:

- **C:\Windows documents and settings**—This folder is the default location to save documents. A criminal can save documents anywhere on the computer; however, it is a good idea to check this folder.

- **C:\users**—This is where you will find user profile information, documents, pictures, and more for all users, not just the one currently logged on.

- **C:\Program Files**—By default, programs are installed in subdirectories of this directory.

- **C:\Program Files (x86)**—In 64-bit systems, 32-bit programs are installed here.

- **C:\Users\username\Documents**—The current user's Documents folder. This is a very important place to look.

And, of course, you should do a general search of the entire suspect drive—not just these specific folders and directories.

UserAssist

UserAssist is a feature of Windows 2000 and later that is not well documented or well understood by the public. Basically, it tracks what happens on the computer, including programs launched. Unless it is disabled, for example by changing the Registry setting for it, there will be a record of everything done on that computer.

According to an article on BetaNews.com by Mike Williams (2011), "What's not quite as well known, though, is that Windows also maintains a longer and separate history of all the programs launched on your computer, including details like the number of times they've been run and the last execution date and time. This information is stored in the Registry (HKEY_CURRENT_USER\Software\Microsoft\Windows\CurrentVersion\Explorer\UserAssist), but it's encrypted, so you'll need something like the free UserAssist tool to find out more."

You can get the UserAssist tool free from *http://www.downloadcrew.com/article/23805 -userassist*. An example of this tool is shown in Figure 8-7.

As you can see, this gives a lot of information as to what programs were run, and when.

Key	Index	Name	Unkno...	Sessi...	Counter	Last	Last UTC	Focus count...	Fc
{CEBF...	0	UEME_CTLCUACount.ctor			0			0	
{CEBF...	1	Microsoft.Windows.Explorer			0			533	
{CEBF...	2	UEME_CTLSESSION							
{CEBF...	3	Microsoft.Windows.ControlPanel			0			24	
{CEBF...	4	Microsoft.InternetExplorer.Default			43	4/19/2013 1:42:33 PM	4/19/2013 6:42:33 PM	860	
{CEBF...	5	C:\Users\chuckeasttom\AppData\Local\Microsoft\Windows\Te...			0	1/30/2013 5:00:07 PM	1/30/2013 11:00:07 PM	0	
{CEBF...	6	C:\Users\chuckeasttom\AppData\Local\Amazon\Kindle\applica...			2	4/19/2013 12:10:08 PM	4/19/2013 5:10:08 PM	16	
{CEBF...	7	D:\SETUP.EXE			8	4/16/2013 10:13:54 AM	4/16/2013 3:13:54 PM	0	
{CEBF...	8	{1AC14E77-02E7-4E5D-B744-2EB1AE5198B7}\rundll32.exe			0	4/14/2013 9:10:46 PM	4/15/2013 2:10:46 AM	0	
{CEBF...	9	Microsoft.DSUI.Device.{D71920D5-657D-5146-8B6F-5B9A7BF6...			0			0	
{CEBF...	10	D:\autorun.exe			0	4/14/2013 9:06:15 PM	4/15/2013 2:06:15 AM	0	
{CEBF...	11	{7C5A40EF-A0FB-4BFC-874A-C0F2E0B9FA8E}\Common Files\I...			0			0	
{CEBF...	12	C:\Users\chuckeasttom\AppData\Local\Temp\{06F80017-8F98-...			0			0	
{CEBF...	13	Microsoft.AutoGenerated.{1F6B0A56-09D4-8DF1-3FB9-959287B...			0			0	
{CEBF...	14	Microsoft.AutoGenerated.{923DD477-5846-686B-A659-0FCCD73...			0			8	
{CEBF...	15	{7C5A40EF-A0FB-4BFC-874A-C0F2E0B9FA8E}\Microsoft Office...			8	4/19/2013 1:41:33 PM	4/19/2013 6:41:33 PM	1006	
{CEBF...	16	microsoft.windowsphotos_8wekyb3d8bbwe!Microsoft.WindowsL...			0			0	
{CEBF...	17	{1AC14E77-02E7-4E5D-B744-2EB1AE5198B7}\WWAHost.exe			0			0	
{CEBF...	18	{1AC14E77-02E7-4E5D-B744-2EB1AE5198B7}\OpenWith.exe			0			0	
{CEBF...	19	{7C5A40EF-A0FB-4BFC-874A-C0F2E0B9FA8E}\Microsoft Office...			13	4/19/2013 9:09:37 AM	4/19/2013 2:09:37 PM	52	
{CEBF...	20	{7C5A40EF-A0FB-4BFC-874A-C0F2E0B9FA8E}\Microsoft Office...			56	4/19/2013 2:53:32 PM	4/19/2013 7:53:32 PM	528	
{CEBF...	21	Microsoft.Windows.ControlPanel.Taskbar			0			0	
{CEBF...	22	{1AC14E77-02E7-4E5D-B744-2EB1AE5198B7}\SystemPropertie...			0			0	
{CEBF...	23	Microsoft.AutoGenerated.{8ABD94FB-E7D6-84A6-A997-C918E...			0	2/2/2013 2:05:29 PM	2/2/2013 8:05:29 PM	0	
{CEBF...	24	{1AC14E77-02E7-4E5D-B744-2EB1AE5198B7}\msconfig.exe			0	3/26/2013 10:41:01 AM	3/26/2013 3:41:01 PM	0	
{CEBF...	25	Apple.iTunes			0			85	
{CEBF...	26	Microsoft.DSUI.Device.{0C9DEDE0-3428-5A1C-8029-FB940833...			0			0	
{CEBF...	27	Microsoft.DSUI.Device.{A343F791-6C8A-11E2-BE75-C8F7331D...			0			0	
{CEBF...	28	{7C5A40EF-A0FB-4BFC-874A-C0F2E0B9FA8E}\iTunes\iTunes....			0	3/18/2013 1:24:31 PM	3/18/2013 6:24:31 PM	0	
{CEBF...	29	{1AC14E77-02E7-4E5D-B744-2EB1AE5198B7}\FileHistory.exe			0			0	
{CEBF...	30	{1AC14E77-02E7-4E5D-B744-2EB1AE5198B7}\DevicePairingW...			0	2/3/2013 8:34:18 PM	2/4/2013 2:34:18 AM	0	
{CEBF...	31	{1AC14E77-02E7-4E5D-B744-2EB1AE5198B7}\mblctr.exe			0			0	

FIGURE 8-7

UserAssist.

Unallocated/Slack Space

You will need to search the entire disk to locate all relevant documents, logs, e-mails, and more in most of your cases. At times, though, you may want to find relevant data only in the unallocated space. To do so, you would search the unallocated space for keywords. Tools such as AccessData's Forensic Toolkit (FTK) allow an investigator to take an entire image and try to identify all of the documents in the file system, including the unallocated space. If you want to search the entire disk many times over, tools such as FTK can help you build a full-text index. Full-text indexing allows you to build a binary tree-based dictionary of all the words that exist in an image, and you can search the entire image for those words in seconds.

Alternate Data Streams

This is a clever way that a criminal can hide things on the target computer. Alternate data streams are essentially a method of attaching one file to another file, using the NTFS file system.

According to Irongeek.com, "Alternative Data Stream support was added to NTFS (Windows NT, Windows 2000 and Windows XP) to help support Macintosh Hierarchical File System (HFS), which uses resource forks to store icons and other information for a file. While this is the intended use (as well as a few Windows internal functions) there are other uses for Alternative Data Streams that should concern system administrators and security professionals. Using Alternative Data Streams a user can easily hide files that can go undetected unless closely inspected. This tutorial will give basic information on how to manipulate and detect Alternative Data Streams."

For example, if a criminal wants to attach a script to a text file, the following command will attach that script using alternate data streams:

```
type somescript.vbs> ADSFile.txt:somescript.vbs
```

A number of tools are available that will detect whether files are attached via alternate data streams. One of the most widely known is List Alternate Data Streams. You can download it free from *http://www.heysoft.de/en/software/lads.php?lang=EN*.

Index.dat

The browser can be a source of both direct evidence and circumstantial or supporting evidence. Obviously, in cases of child pornography, the browser might contain direct evidence of the specific crime. You may also find direct evidence in the case of cyber-stalking. However, if you suspect someone of creating a virus that infected a network, you would probably find only indirect evidence, such as evidence of the suspect having searched virus creation or programming-related topics.

Even if the suspect's browsing history has been erased, it is still possible to retrieve it if he or she was using Internet Explorer. Index.dat is a file used by Microsoft Internet Explorer to store Web addresses, search queries, and recently opened files. So if a file is on a universal serial bus (USB) device but was opened on the suspect machine, index.dat would contain a record of that file.

You can download a number of tools from the Internet that will allow you to retrieve and review the index.dat file. Here are a few:

- *http://www.eusing.com/Window_Washer/Index_dat.htm*
- *http://www.acesoft.net/index.dat%20viewer/index.dat_viewer.htm*
- *http://download.cnet.com/Index-dat-Analyzer/3000-2144_4-10564321.html*

You can see Window Washer in Figure 8-8.

Whatever tool you choose to use, the index.dat is a fantastic source of forensic information that cannot be overlooked in your forensic investigation.

The Registry

What is the Registry? It is a repository of all the information on a Windows system. When you install a new program, its configuration settings are stored in the Registry. When you change the desktop background, that is also stored in the Registry.

According to a Microsoft TechNet article by Joan Bard, "With few exceptions, all 32-bit Windows programs store their configuration data, as well as your preferences, in the Registry, while most 16-bit Windows programs and MS-DOS programs don't—they favor the outdated INI files (text files that 16-bit Windows used to store configuration data) instead. The Registry contains the computer's hardware configuration, which includes Plug and Play devices with their automatic configurations and legacy devices. It allows

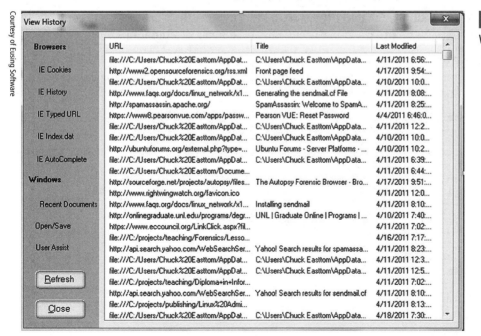

FIGURE 8-8

Window Washer.

8

Windows Forensics

the operating system to keep multiple hardware configurations and multiple users with individual preferences. It [The Registry] allows programs to extend the desktop with such items as shortcut menus and property sheets. It supports remote administration via the network. Of course, there's more. But this serves as a good introduction to what the Registry does."

As you see in this section, there is a great deal of forensic information you can gather from the Registry, which is why it is important to have a thorough understanding of Registry forensics. But, first, how do you get to the Registry? The usual path is through the tool regedit. In Windows 7 and Server 2008, you select Start, then Run, then type in regedit. In Windows 8, you need to go to the applications list, select All Apps, and then find regedit.

The Registry is organized into five sections referred to as **hives**. Each of these sections contains specific information that can be useful to you. The five hives are described here:

1. **HKEY_CLASSES_ROOT (HKCR)**—This hive stores information about drag-and-drop rules, program shortcuts, the user interface, and related items.

2. **HKEY_CURRENT_USER (HKCU)**—This hive is very important to any forensic investigation. It stores information about the currently logged-on user, including desktop settings, user folders, and so forth.

3. **HKEY_LOCAL_MACHINE (HKLM)**—This hive can also be important to a forensic investigation. It contains those settings common to the entire machine, regardless of the individual user.

4. **HKEY_USERS (HKU)**—This hive is very critical to forensic investigations. It has profiles for all the users, including their settings.

5. **HKEY_CURRENT_CONFIG (HCU)**—This hive contains the current system configuration. This might also prove useful in your forensic examinations.

You can see these five hives in Figure 8-9.

As you move forward in this section and learn where to find certain critical values in the Registry, keep in mind the specific hive names.

FIGURE 8-9

The Windows Registry.

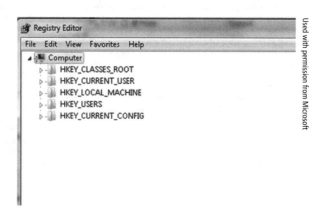

All Registry keys contain a value associated with them called LastWriteTime. You can think of this like the modification time on a file or folder. Looking at the LastWriteTime tells you when this Registry value was last changed. Rather than be a standard date/time, this value is stored as a FILETIME structure. A FILETIME structure represents the number of 100 nanosecond intervals since January 1, 1601.

Before you learn about specific evidence found in the Registry, consider a few general settings that can be useful. Auto-run locations are Registry keys that launch programs automatically during boot-up. It is common for viruses and spyware to be automatically run at start-up. Another setting to look at is the MRU, or most recently used. These are program specific. For example, Microsoft Word might have an MRU describing the most recently used documents.

USB Information

One important thing you can find is any USB devices that have been connected to the machine.

The Registry key HKEY_LOCAL_MACHINE\System\ControlSet\Enum\UBSTOR lists USB devices that have been connected to the machine. It is often the case that a criminal will move evidence or exfiltrate other information to an external device and take it with him or her. This could indicate to you that there are devices you need to find and examine. Often, criminals attempt to move files offline onto an external drive. This Registry setting tells you about the external drives that have been connected to this system.

Wireless Networks

Think, for just a moment, about connecting to a Wi-Fi network. You probably had to enter some passphrase. But you did not have to enter that passphrase the next time you connected to that Wi-Fi, did you? That information is stored somewhere on the computer, but where? It is stored in the Registry.

When an individual connects to a wireless network, the service set identifier (SSID) is logged as a preferred network connection. This information can be found in the Registry in the HKEY_LOCAL_MACHINE \SOFTWARE\Microsoft\WZCSVC\Parameters\ Interfaces key.

The Registry key HKLM\SOFTWARE\Microsoft\Windows NT\CurrentVersion\ NetworkList\Profiles\ gives you a list of all the Wi-Fi networks to which this network interface has connected. The SSID of the network is contained within the Description key. When the computer first connected to the network is recorded in the DateCreated field.

The Registry key HKLM\SOFTWARE\Microsoft\WindowsNT\CurrentVersion\ NetworkList\Signatures\Unmanaged \{ProfileGUID} stores the MAC address of the wireless access point to which it was connected.

Associated Drives

The user of the suspect computer might have mounted some drive, even if it is not a USB drive. There is a Registry key, HKEY_LOCAL_MACHINE \SYSTEM\MountedDevices, that stores a list of mounted volumes that are used by the NTFS file system.

Tracking Word Documents in the Registry

Many versions of Word store a PID_GUID value in the Registry—for example, something like: { 1 2 3 A 8 B 2 2 - 6 2 2 B - 1 4 C 4 - 8 4 A D - 0 0 D 1 B 6 1 B 0 3 A 4 }. The string 0 0 D 1 B 6 1 B 0 3 A 4 is the MAC address of the machine on which this document was created. In cases involving theft of intellectual property, espionage, and similar crimes, tracking the origin of a document can be very important. This is a rather obscure aspect of the Windows Registry that is not well known, even among forensic analysts.

Malware in the Registry

If you search the Registry and find HKLM\SOFTWARE\Microsoft\Windows NT\ CurrentVersion\Winlogon, it has a value named Shell with default data Explorer.exe. Basically, it tells the system to launch Windows Explorer when the logon is completed. Some malware appends the malware executable file to the default values data, so that the malware will load every time the system launches. It is important to check this Registry setting if you suspect malware is an issue.

The key HKLM\SYSTEM\CurrentControlSet\Services\ lists system services. There are several examples of malware that installs as a service, particularly backdoor software. So again, check this key if you suspect malware is an issue.

A good resource for more information on the Windows Registry can be found at the Sans Institute online Reading Room, which you can find at *http://www.sans.org/reading _room/whitepapers/auditing/wireless-networks-windows-registry-computer-been_33659*.

CHAPTER SUMMARY

This chapter introduced you to the details of forensic analysis of a Microsoft Windows system. You should pay particular attention to the Registry and the forensic data you can extract from it. Also important to your forensic investigation is the index.dat file. These two are the most important items to learn in this chapter.

Additional topics in this chapter, such as examining the swap file and extracting data from a live system, are also important to any forensic examination of a Windows computer. But they may not yield quite as much information as examining index.dat and the Registry.

KEY CONCEPTS AND TERMS

Basic input/output system (BIOS)	Graphical user interface (GUI)	Slurred image
Data consistency	Heap (*H*)	Stack (*S*)
Disk Operating System (DOS)	Hives	Volatile memory analysis
Dump	Master boot record (MBR)	
	Power-on self test (POST)	

CHAPTER 8 ASSESSMENT

1. _____ was the first Windows operating system to support FAT32.

2. How many hives are in the Windows Registry?
   A. 1
   B. 2
   C. 5
   D. 8

3. Stack memory is stored in a first-in, last-out format.
   A. True
   B. False

4. Which of the following is a concern for capturing live data that is caused by data being changed as it is being captured?
   A. Slurred image
   B. Corrupt image
   C. Data corruption
   D. Memory fragmenting

5. In Windows 7, the swap file ends with what extension?
   A. .sys
   B. .swp
   C. .swap
   D. .vmem

Linux Forensics

I N THIS CHAPTER, you learn about forensics on a Linux system. Assuming you may not have a good working knowledge of Linux, this chapter spends a significant amount of time giving you the basic background in Linux required to do forensics. Then, you learn about specific shell commands, directories, and logs that are important to a forensic investigation of a Linux system.

Chapter 9 Topics

This chapter covers the following topics and concepts:

- What you need to know about Linux
- What you need to know about Linux file systems
- What to look for in the system logs
- What forensically interesting directories are
- What the important shell commands are
- How to undelete files from Linux

Chapter 9 Goals

When you complete this chapter, you will be able to:

- Understand the Linux operating system
- Retrieve logs from Linux
- Utilize important shell commands
- Understand what directories are important in a Linux forensic investigation
- Undelete files from Linux

Linux Basics

Before you can conduct forensics on a Linux machine, you need to have a basic understanding of how Linux works. If you do have a good working knowledge of Linux, feel free to skim over this section anyway as it provides a common background knowledge level for all learners.

Linux History

A good way to get an overview of Linux is to begin by studying the history of Linux. And the first, most important, thing to know about the history of Linux is that it is actually a clone of UNIX. That means that the history of Linux includes the history of UNIX. So that is where this examination of Linux history begins: with the birth of UNIX.

The UNIX operating system was created at Bell Laboratories. Bell Labs is famous for a number of major scientific discoveries. It was there that the first evidence of the Big Bang was found and it was there that the C programming language was born. So innovation is nothing new for Bell Labs.

By the 1960s computing was spreading, but there was no widely available operating system. Bell Labs had been involved in a project called Multics (Multiplexed Information and Computing Service). Multics was a combined effort of Massachusetts Institute of Technology, Bell Labs, and General Electric to create an operating system with wide general applicability. Due to significant problems with the Multics project, Bell Labs decided to pull out. A team at Bell Labs, consisting of Ken Thompson, Dennis Ritchie, Brian Kernighan, Douglas McElroy, and Joe Ossanna, decided to create a new operating system that might have wide usage. They wanted to create an operating system that would run on a range of types of hardware. The culmination of their project was the release of the UNIX operating system in 1972. Even though that was more than 40 years ago, UNIX is still considered a very stable, secure operating system today. That should be an indication of how successful they were.

The original name of the project was Unics, a play on the term Multics. Originally, UNIX was a side project for the team, as Bell Labs was not providing financial support for the project. However, that changed once the team added functionality that could be used on other Bell computers. Then the company began to enthusiastically support the project. In 1972, after the C programming language was created, UNIX was rewritten entirely in C. Before this time, all operating systems were written in assembly language.

In 1983, Richard Stallman, one of the fathers of the open source movement, began working on a UNIX clone. He called this operating system GNU (an acronym for GNU's Not UNIX). His goal was simply to create an open source version of UNIX. He wanted it to be as much like UNIX as possible, despite the name of GNU's Not UNIX. However, Stallman's open source UNIX variant did not achieve widespread popularity, and it was soon replaced by other, more robust variants.

In 1987, a university professor named Andrew S. Tanenbaum created another UNIX variant, this one called Minix. Minix was a fairly stable, functional, and reasonably good UNIX clone. Minix was completely written in C by Professor Tanenbaum. He created it primarily as a teaching tool for his students. He wanted them to learn operating systems by being able to study the actual source code for an operating system. The source code for Minix was included in his book *Operating Systems: Design and Implementation*. Placing the source code in a textbook that was widely used meant a large number of computer science students would be exposed to this source code.

Though Minix failed to gain the popularity of some other UNIX variants, it was an inspiration for the creator of Linux. The story of the Linux operating system is really the story of Linus Torvalds. He began his work on Linux when he was a graduate student working toward his Ph.D. in computer science. Linus decided to create his own UNIX clone. The name derives from his name (Linus) combined with the word UNIX. Linus had extensive exposure to both UNIX and Minix, which made creating a good UNIX clone more achievable for him.

Linux Shells

Now that you have a grasp of the essential history of Linux, the next step is to look at what is arguably the most important part of Linux, the shell. Many Linux administrators work entirely in the shell without ever using a graphical user interface (GUI). Linux offers many different shells. Each shell is designed for a different purpose. The following list details the most common shells:

- **Bourne shell (sh)**—This was the original default shell for UNIX. It was first released in 1977.
- **Bourne-again shell (Bash)**—This is the most commonly used shell in Linux. It was released in 1989.
- **C shell (csh)**—This shell derives its name from the fact that it uses very C-like syntax. Linux users who are familiar with C will like this shell. It was first released for UNIX in 1978.
- **Korn shell (ksh)**—This is a popular shell developed by David Korn in the 1980s. The Korn shell is meant to be compatible with the Bourne shell, but to also incorporate true programming language capabilities.

There are other shells, but these are the most common. And of these Bash is the most widely used. Most Linux distributions ship with Bash. You do not have to be a master of Linux in order to perform some basic Linux forensics. However, there are some essential shell commands you should know, which are shown in Table 9-1.

If you need more training on Linux shell commands, the following Web sites could be helpful:

- *http://linuxcommand.org/learning_the_shell.php*
- *http://lowfatlinux.com/linux-basics.html*
- *http://www.cyberciti.biz/tips/linux-unix-commands-cheat-sheets.html*

TABLE 9-1 Linux shell commands.	
LINUX COMMAND	**EXPLANATION AND EXAMPLE**
`ls`	The `ls` command lists the contents of the current directory. Example: `ls`
`cp`	The `cp` command copies one file to another directory. Example: `cp filename.txt directoryname`
`mkdir`	The `mkdir` command creates a new directory. Example: `mkdir directoryname`
`cd`	The `cd` command is used to change directories. Example: `cd directory name`
`rm`	The `rm` command is used to delete or remove a file. Example: `rm filename`
`rmdir`	The `rmdir` command is used to remove or delete entire directories. Example: `rmdir directoryname`
`mv`	The `mv` command is used to move a file. Example: `mv myfile.txt myfolder`
`diff`	The `diff` command performs a byte-by-byte comparison of two files and tells you what is different about them. Example: `diff myfile.txt myfile2.txt`
`cmp`	The `cmp` command performs a textual comparison of two files and tells you the difference between the two. Example: `cmp myfile.txt myfile2.txt`
`>`	This is the redirect command. Instead of displaying the output of a command like `ls` to the screen, it redirects it to a file. Example: `ls > file1.txt`
`ps`	The `ps` command lists all currently running processes that the user has started. Any program or daemon is a process. Example: `ps`
`top`	The `top` command lists all currently running processes, whether the user started them or not. It also lists more detail on the processes. Example: `top`
`fsck`	This is a file system check. The `fsck` command can check to see whether a given partition is in good working condition. Example: `fsck /dev/hda1`

continued

9

Linux Forensics

TABLE 9-1 Linux shell commands, *continued.*	
`fdisk`	The `fdisk` command lists the various partitions. Example: `fdisk -l`
`mount`	The `mount` command mounts a partition, allowing you to work with it. Example: `mount /dev/fd0 /mnt/floppy`

It is a good idea to be comfortable working with shell commands. In the next section, you will be briefly introduced to the graphical user interfaces that are available in Linux. You will find that these interfaces are fairly intuitive and not that dissimilar to Windows. However, many forensic commands and utilities work primarily from the shell. You might recall that you can make a forensic copy of a disk using the dd command. That is a shell command, and only one of many you will want to be familiar with.

Graphical User Interface

Although Linux aficionados prefer the shell, and a great deal of forensics can be done from the shell, Linux does have a graphical user interface. In fact, there are several you can choose from. The most widely used are GNOME and KDE.

GNU Network Object Model Environment (GNOME)

There is no doubt that GNOME (*http://www.gnome.org/*) is one of the two most popular GUIs for Linux. Most Linux distributions include GNOME, or a choice between GNOME and some other desktop environment. In fact the popular Ubuntu distribution ships only with GNOME. GNOME, which is built on GTK+, is a cross-platform toolkit for creating graphical user interfaces. The name GNOME is an acronym of GNU Network Object Model Environment. You can see the GNOME desktop in Figure 9-1.

K Desktop Environment (KDE)

> **NOTE**
> KDE has changed the name of the desktop environment to "Plasma Desktop." In fact, the KDE Web site has this section at *http://kde.org/workspaces/plasmadesktop/*. However, you will still find a lot of Linux users who simply refer to it as KDE.

KDE (*http://www.kde.org/*) is the other of the two most popular Linux GUIs available. Most Linux distributions ship with either KDE or GNOME, or both. For example, the Kbuntu distribution is essentially Ubuntu with KDE. KDE was founded in 1996 by Matthias Ettrich. At the time of KDE's creation, Ettrich was, like Linus Torvalds, a computer science student. The name KDE was intended as a word play on the Common Desktop Environment (CDE) available for UNIX systems. Today, the K stands for nothing and the acronym stands for K Desktop Environment. KDE is built on the Qt framework. Qt is a multiplatform GUI framework written in C++. KDE is shown in Figure 9-2.

FIGURE 9-1

GNOME.

FIGURE 9-2

KDE.

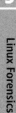

9

Linux Forensics

Although KDE and GNOME are the most widely known and used graphical user interfaces for Linux, there are certainly others. A couple of the more widely used are listed and briefly described here:

- **Common Desktop Environment (CDE)**—The CDE (*http://www.opengroup.org/cde/*) was originally developed in 1994 for UNIX systems. At one time it was the default desktop for Sun Solaris systems. CDE is based on HP's Visual User Environment (VUE).

- **Enlightenment**—This desktop is rather new and is meant specifically for graphics developers. You can learn more at *http://www.enlightenment.org/*.

Linux Boot Process

It is important to understand the Linux boot process because some crimes, including malware attacks, can affect the boot process.

Linux is often used on embedded systems, even smartphones. In such cases, when the system is first powered on, the first step is to load the bootstrap environment. The **bootstrap environment** is a special program, such as U-Boot or RedBoot, that is stored in a special section of flash memory. On a PC, booting Linux begins in the BIOS (basic input/output system) at address 0xFFFF0.

Just as with Windows, the first sector on any disk is called the boot sector. It contains executable code that is used in the boot process. A boot sector also has the hex value 0xaa55 in the final two bytes. Also, as in Windows, after the BIOS has been loaded and the power-on self test (POST) has completed, the BIOS locates the master boot record (MBR) and passes control to it.

The MBR then loads up a boot loader program, such as **LILO (Linux Loader)** or **GRUB (Grand Unified Bootloader)**. GRUB is the more modern and much more widely used boot loader. Often boot loaders are larger than a single sector, so they are loaded in stages. When a bootable device is found, the first-stage boot loader is loaded into random access memory (RAM) and executed.

In Linux, there are actually two boot loaders. The first boot loader is rather small, only 512 bytes. The first 446 bytes are the primary boot loader, which contains both executable code and error message text. The next 64 bytes are the partition table, which contains a record for each of four partitions. Each is just 16 bytes. The first boot loader is terminated

---

FYI

You can view what is in the MBR. Just type the following two lines in the shell of your choice:

```
# dd if=/dev/hda of=mbr.bin bs=512 count=1
# od -xa mbr.bin
```

When forensically examining a Linux machine, you may want to examine the master boot record to see if it has been altered.

with 2 bytes that are defined as the magic number (0xAA55). This boot loader is less than 512 bytes in length (a single sector), and its job is to load the second-stage boot loader. The second boot loader is responsible for loading the Linux kernel.

When the second-stage boot loader is loaded into RAM and executing, a splash screen is commonly displayed. At this point, the Linux image is loaded into RAM. When the images are loaded, the second-stage boot loader passes control to the kernel image and the kernel is decompressed and initialized.

At this point, the second-stage boot loader checks the system hardware and any attached peripherals. Once the devices are enumerated, the second-stage boot loader can attempt to mount the root device and load the necessary kernel modules.

The second-stage boot loader loads the kernel image. This is called the kernel stage of the boot process. The kernel must initialize any devices the system has. Even devices that have been initialized by the BIOS must be reinitialized. The system then switches the CPU from real mode to protected mode. The system now loads the compressed kernel and calls the decompress_kernel( ) function. It is at this point that you may see the "Uncompressing Linux..." message displayed on the screen. Now the start_kernel( ) function is called, and the uncompressed kernel displays a large number of messages on the screen as it initializes the various hardware items and processes such as the scheduler.

> **NOTE**
>
> Unlike in Windows, the boot messages are displayed on the screen and you can see everything. However, this often happens too fast to follow. After the system is booted up, you can use the dmesg command from the shell to see what boot messages were displayed.

Once the kernel is initialized, the first user program starts. In PC-based Linux systems, that first process is called init. The kernel_thread( ) function is called next to start init. The kernel goes into an idle loop and becomes an idle thread with process ID 0. The process init() begins high-level system initialization. Note that unlike PC systems, embedded systems have a simpler first user process than init.

The boot process then inspects the /etc/inittab file to determine the appropriate run level. As a reference, the Linux run levels are listed in Table 9-2.

TABLE 9-2   Typical default active services.

MODE	DIRECTORY	RUN LEVEL DESCRIPTION
0	/etc/rc.d/rc0.d	Halt
1	/etc/rc.d/rc1.d	Single-user mode
2	/etc/rc.d/rc2.d	Not used (user-definable)
3	/etc/rc.d/rc3.d	Full multiuser mode without GUI
4	/etc/rc.d/rc4.d	Not used (user-definable)
5	/etc/rc.d/rc5.d	Full multiuser mode with GUI
6	/etc/rc.d/rc6.d	Reboot

Based on the run level, the init process then executes the appropriate start-up script. Those scripts are located in subdirectories of the /etc/rc.d directory. Scripts used for run levels 0 to 6 are located in subdirectories /etc/rc.d/rc0.d through /etc/rc.d/rc6.d, respectively. The default boot run level is set in the file /etc/inittab with the initdefault variable. At this point, the boot process is over, and Linux is up and running!

Linux Distributions

Linux is open source. That means the source code is available for anyone who wants to modify, repackage, and distribute it. Therefore a lot of different distributions are available. They are all Linux, they all have the same Linux shells, but each has some differences. For example, some use KDE by default, whereas others use GNOME. Some ship with lots of additional open source tools, whereas others don't have quite as many tools, or have different tools. A few of the more common distributions include the following:

- **Ubuntu**—Very popular with beginners
- **Red Hat Enterprise Linux (RHEL)**—Often used with large-scale servers
- **OpenSuse**—A popular, general-purpose Linux distribution
- **Debian**—Another popular, general-purpose Linux distribution
- **Slackware**—Becoming more popular

BackTrack is the one most interesting to forensic analysts. BackTrack is replete with tools for hacking, security, and forensics. It is a very good idea to become at least basically familiar with BackTrack. There are some great tutorials for BackTrack at *http://www .backtrack-linux.org/tutorials/*. The company also has a Facebook fan page you might want to check out at *https://www.facebook.com/BackTrack.Fan.Page?fref=ts*.

The Web site *http://www.DistroWatch.com* has a list of 100 best-selling distributions.

Linux File Systems

This section provides details about Linux file systems.

 NOTE

All operating systems must connect to a device or partition and assign it some designation, such as a drive letter, so it can be accessed by the user. Linux and all UNIX-like operating systems assign a device name to each device. This usually happens automatically but Linux has a mount command that allows you to manually mount devices and partitions.

Ext

Although there are other file systems, the Extended File System (ext) is the one most commonly used with Linux. The current version is 4. The ext4 file system can support volumes with sizes up to 1 exabyte (10^{18} bytes or 1 billion gigabytes) and single files with sizes up to 16 terabytes. These sizes are extremely large, indicating that there will not be a need for an update to ext anytime soon.

The first two versions of ext did not support journaling. Ext3 was the first to support journaling. Ext3 and ext4 support three specific types of journaling. The most secure and safe level is called *journal*. With the journal level, metadata and file contents are written to the journal before being written to the main file system. The next level, slightly less secure than journal, is called *ordered*. With the ordered level only metadata is written to the journal; however, changes to files are not journaled until they have been committed to the disk. Finally, the least secure level is *writeback*. With the writeback level, only metadata is written to the journal, and it might be written to the journal before or after it is actually committed. Ext4 added checksums in the journal to prevent errors.

The Reiser File System

The Reiser File System (ReiserFS) was first introduced as a part of the Linux kernel version 2.4.1. ReiserFS has always supported journaling. ReiserFS performs very well when the hard drive has a large number of smaller files. In fact, tests have shown that when you are dealing with files that are under 4 KB in size, ReiserFS outperforms ext2 and ext3.

The Berkeley Fast File System

The Berkeley Fast File System is also known as the UNIX File System. It was developed at University of California, Berkeley specifically for use with Linux. Berkeley uses a bitmap to track free clusters, indicating which clusters are available and which are not.

Linux Logs

Like Windows, Linux has a number of logs that can be very interesting for a forensic investigation. This section provides a brief description of each of the major Linux logs and the forensic relevance of that log.

The /var/log/faillog Log

This log file contains failed user logins. This can be very important when tracking attempts to crack into the system. Usually, a normal user might occasionally have one or two failed login attempts. Numerous failed login attempts, or even frequent failed login attempts that occur at diverse times, can be an indicator of someone trying to compromise access to the system. It is also worth noting the times of failed login attempts. If an employee normally works from 8:00 a.m. to 5:00 p.m. and there are failed login attempts at 11:00 p.m., that may be a warning sign.

The /var/log/kern.log Log

This log file is used for messages from the operating system's kernel. This log is less interesting forensically. It is more likely to show systemwide problems. However, it is entirely possible for someone to mistake system issues for some intrusion or malware. If you have odd behavior on a target system and find related messages in the kern.log, it may allow you to rule out malware.

The /var/log/lpr.log Log

This is the printer log. It can give you a record of any items that have been printed from this machine. That can be useful in many cases. To begin with, corporate espionage cases often involve the criminal printing out sensitive documents. Having a record of exactly what was printed when and which user printed it can be very useful.

The /var/log/mail.* Log

This is the mail server log and can be very useful in any computer crime investigation. E-mail can be useful in many different criminal investigations. It is obviously very useful in cyberstalking cases, as well as many civil litigation cases.

The /var/log/mysql.* Log

This log records activities related to the MySQL database server. These are of most interest in crimes involving database attacks. For example, SQL injection attacks might leave a record in the database log.

The /var/log/apache2/* Log

If this machine is running the Apache Web server, then this log shows related activity. This can be very useful in tracking attempts to hack into the Web server. You can examine the log to see attempts at buffer overflow attacks, denial of service attacks, and a variety of other attacks.

FYI

Snort is an open source **intrusion detection system (IDS)**. Intrusion detection systems monitor network traffic looking for suspicious activity. There are two types of intrusion detection systems: passive and active.

A passive IDS will simply log suspicious activity and perhaps notify a network administrator. Active IDSs (also called intrusion prevention systems [IPSs]) also log the activity, but then shut down the suspected attack. The problem is that all systems get false positives—traffic that appears to be an attack but is not. For example, suppose Jane usually works from 8:00 a.m. to 5:00 p.m. and uses no more than 50 megabytes of bandwidth per hour. Suddenly, the system shows Jane logged on at 11:00 p.m. and using 300 megabytes of bandwidth per hour. The active IDS assumes this is an attack and blocks the traffic. However, in reality, Jane is working late on an important presentation that is due tomorrow.

The issue of active versus passive is one for the organization's security administrator to deal with. From a forensic point of view, the IDS log is the important issue. If an organization is using an IDS, any IDS, you should absolutely view those logs.

The /var/log/lighttpd/* Log

If this machine is running the Lighttpd Web server, then this log shows related activity. This can be very useful in tracking attempts to hack into the Web server.

The /var/log/apport.log Log

This log records application crashes. Sometimes these can reveal attempts to compromise the system or the presence of malware. Of course, it can also simply reveal a buggy application. That is the real challenge with computer forensics: determining what is evidence of an actual crime.

Other Logs

Any other applications running on the Linux computer that store logs can be useful in your forensic examination. For example, if you are using an intrusion detection system (IDS) such as Snort, it keeps logs of all suspicious traffic. That can be very useful in your investigation.

Viewing Logs

With Linux, you can use a variety of shell commands to view a log. You can also simply use your favorite text editor within your preferred graphical user interface. Using the Linux dmesg command is the preferred way to view logs from the shell. It works like this:

```
dmesg | lpr
```

Or, you can use any of these methods as well:

```
# tail -f /var/log/lpr.log
# less /var/log/ lpr.log
# more -f /var/log/ lpr.log
```

As you can see, there are a number of methods for viewing logs in Linux.

Linux Directories

In any operating system, there are key directories that are important to the functioning of that operating system. In Linux, these directories are important places to seek out evidence. Knowing the general purpose of the major directories, as well as their potential forensic importance, is useful in conducting a forensic analysis of a Linux system.

The /root Directory

The /root directory is the home directory for the root user. The root in Linux is the same as the administrator in Windows. This directory is where any data for the administrator will be located.

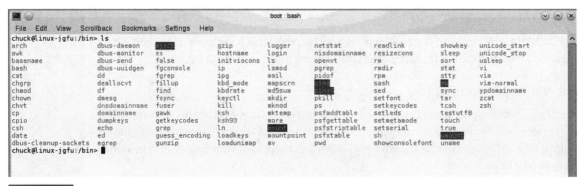

FIGURE 9-3

The /bin directory.

The /bin Directory

The /bin directory holds binary or compiled files. This means programs, including some malware, may be found here. You absolutely should examine this directory. You can see an example of this directory in Figure 9-3.

The /sbin Directory

This directory is similar to /bin, but it contains binary files that are not intended for the average computer user. For example, the mke2fs command, a file system utility that is usually utilized by administrators, is in this directory.

The /etc Folder

The /etc folder contains configuration files. Most applications require some configuration when they start up. The Web servers, boot loaders (LILO and GRUB), and many other applications have configuration files. Obviously, an intruder into a system may want to change how a given application behaves. Web server, boot loader, and security software configuration files would be attractive targets for any hacker.

The /etc/inittab File

This is where the boot-up process and operation is set. For example, the init level for the system on start-up is set in this file. Again, a sophisticated attacker might want to change the inittab to change the behavior of the system. Even some advanced malware might alter your inittab.

The inittab has a number of entries. Each is defined by four fields separated by colons. Those fields include the following:

- **label**—A unique identification label of up to four characters.
- **run_level**—The init level at which the entry is executed.
- **action:a**—A keyword indicating the action that init is to take on the process.

- **process**—The process init executes upon entering the specified run level.
- **boot**—Starts the process and continues to the next entry without waiting for the process to complete. When the process dies, init does not restart the process.
- **bootwait**—Starts the process once and waits for it to terminate before going on to the next inittab entry.
- **initdefault**—Determines which run level to enter initially, using the highest number in the run_level field. If there is no initdefault entry in inittab, then init requests an initial run level from the user at boot time.
- **sysinit**—Starts the process the first time init reads the table and waits for it to terminate before going on to the next inittab entry.

The /dev Directory

This directory contains device files. Device files are really interfaces to devices, including drives. Storage devices, sound devices, and, in fact, all of your devices should have a device file located in this directory. Some naming conventions can help you navigate this directory. For example, all hard drives start with hd, floppy drives start with fd, and CD drives start with cd. So, the main hard drive might be named /dev/hd0. The floppy drive would be called /dev/fd0.

The /mnt Directory

Many devices, such as floppy and CD-ROM drives, are mounted in the /mnt directory. Any drive must be mounted prior to its use. The process of mounting a drive simply involves the operating system accessing it and loading it into memory. Modern Linux distributions do this for you. From a forensic perspective, checking this directory lets you know what things are currently mounted on the system.

The /boot Directory

The boot directory contains those files critical for booting. Your boot loader (whether it is LILO or GRUB) looks in this directory. It is a common practice to keep kernel images in this directory.

The /usr Directory

This directory contains the subdirectories for individual users. In cases of suspected corporate espionage, these directories might contain valuable evidence.

The /var Directory

The /var directory contains data that is changed during system operation. This directory is only useful on a live system. Once you shut down the system, the contents of this directory will be different the next time the system is booted up.

```
                                          sys : bash
 File   Edit   View   Scrollback   Bookmarks   Settings   Help
chuck@linux-jgfu:/proc> ls
1       1246  1720  20     2242  26    3     4061  556   asound       dri           kcore          misc          self          tty
10      13    1750  2021   2254  2613  339   4062  57    buddyinfo    driver        kdb            modules       slabinfo      uptime
1029    1343  1763  2052   229   2636  3584  4072  58    bus          execdomains   key-users      mounts        softirqs      version
1031    1370  18    21     23    28    3618  4222  59    cgroups      fb            kmsg           mtrr          splash        vmallocinfo
11      1377  181   21992  2355  2915  3638  4223  6     cmdline      filesystems   kpagecount     net           stat          vmstat
1116    1378  1901  21994  2357  2949  3687  4224  66    config.gz    fs            kpageflags     pagetypeinfo  swaps         zoneinfo
1154    14    1906  22     2395  2965  3741  4225  67    cpuinfo      interrupts    latency_stats  partitions    sys
1160    1478  1912  22044  24    2966  3750  4226  7     crypto       iomem         loadavg        reserve_info  sysrq-trigger
1163    15    1951  22145  2478  2969  3787  4227  8     devices      ioports       locks          sched_debug   sysvipc
12      16    1978  222    2489  2976  4     5     9     diskstats    irq           mdstat         schedstat     timer_list
120     17    2     223    25    2988  4036  542   acpi  dma          kallsyms      meminfo        scsi          timer_stats
chuck@linux-jgfu:/proc> █
```

FIGURE 9-4

The /proc directory.

The /var/spool Directory

This directory contains the print queue, so it can be very important if something is currently in the print queue.

The /proc Directory

The /proc directory is different from any other directory in that it is not really stored on your hard disk. It is created in memory and keeps information about currently running processes. If you have a live Linux system and you want to see what is running on that system, before powering it down, the contents of this directory can be very useful. You can see an example of the contents of a /proc directory in Figure 9-4.

This directory has subdirectories that can be used to recover files and evidence. Consider this scenario: Assume that an intruder has downloaded a password cracker and is attempting to crack system passwords. The tool is attempting a number of passwords in a text file called pass. The intruder subsequently deletes both the executable and the text file, but the process is still running in memory. You can use ps or pstree to find the running processes and get the process ID. Assume the process ID is 3201. Now in the /proc directory, you can find /proc/3201. If you simply copy the executable from /proc to some other directory, it recovers that deleted executable. Of course, this works only on a live system, prior to shutting it down.

Shell Commands for Forensics

There are hundreds of shell commands, and earlier in this chapter you were given a few links to some shell tutorials. Many of those commands are basic file/directory navigation, network administration, and general commands. In this section, you are introduced to a few Linux shell commands that can be very useful in your forensic investigations.

The dmesg Command

When your system boots up, you see a lot of information telling you what processes are starting, what processes failed, what hardware is being initialized, and more. This can be invaluable information to a forensic investigation. You can use the dmesg command to view all the messages that were displayed during the boot process.

The command dmesg displays the messages for you. However, it does tend to fill up multiple screens. It is recommended that you simply pipe the output to some file (for example, dmesg>myfile.txt) and then search that file. You can see some sample output of dmesg in Figure 9-5.

The fsck Command

Hard drives eventually age and begin to encounter problems. It is also possible that a suspect hard drive may have some issues preventing a full forensic analysis. You can use fsck (file system check) to help with that. There are several related commands, such as e2fsck.

Be aware, however, that you should try all other forensic methods before using any file system utility. It is possible that a file system utility will erase some data and lose some evidence—particularly evidence hidden in slack space.

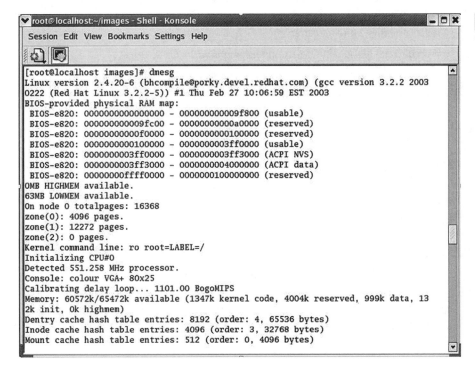

FIGURE 9-5

The dmesg command.

The `grep` Command

This is the single most popular search command for Linux. It allows you to search for a wide range of parameters. For example, you might use `dmesg>myfile.txt`, then `grep myfile.txt` for specific data. Here are some specific examples of using `grep`:

- Find all instances of the word *corrupt* in a file named somefile:

   `grep file na' somefile`

- Look for the same data in the same file, but ignore case:

   `grep -i ep for t' somefile`

- Look for words beginning with *c* and ending with *t* in file somefile:

   `grep ile ' somefile`

- Count the number of accounts that have /bin/false as the shell:

   `grep -c false /etc/passwd`

As you can see, this can be very useful in searching both files and directories. As you gain more experience with Linux, you will most likely find yourself using `grep` very regularly. There are some great tutorials on the Web to help you learn about `grep` and about variants of `grep`, such as those in the following list:

- *http://beginnerlinuxtutorial.com/help-tutorial/basic-linux-commands/linux-grep-command/*
- *http://www.uccs.edu/~ahitchco/grep/*
- *http://www.cyberciti.biz/faq/howto-use-grep-command-in-linux-unix/*

The first tutorial in the preceding list is ideal for people who are new to Linux. You can also find tutorials about other Linux commands on that site.

The `history` Command

The `history` command allows you to see the commands that have previously been entered. By default, this command returns the last 500 shell commands. This command can be very useful on a live system. When you first locate a Linux machine that is suspect, this is one of the commands you might want to run and record the results of before powering down the system.

The `mount` Command

The `mount` command is used to mount a new file system. When you add drives, they must be mounted. You will use this command frequently, specifically when you have a suspect drive you want to mount on your forensic workstation. Most of the commercial forensic tools like Forensic Toolkit (FTK) and EnCase can mount drives for you; however, many forensic analysts work completely with open source tools. In that case, you will need to mount the drives yourself.

The `ps` Command

The `ps` command shows the currently running processes for the current user. By default, `ps` selects all processes with the same user ID as the current user and associated with the same terminal as the invoker. It displays the process ID (PID), the terminal associated with the process (TTY), the cumulated CPU time in dd-hh:mm:ss format, and the executable name. There are flags you can add to this command to get more details about processes. Here are a few examples:

```
ps -aux
```

Display more info:

```
ps –ef
```

This is another command you will want to run on the live suspect system, before powering it down.

The `pstree` Command

The `pstree` command is very similar to the `ps` command, except it shows all the processes in the form of a tree structure. The tree format gives more information particular to a given forensic investigation. Not only will you know what processes are running, but also what process initiated those processes. You can see an example of `pstree` in Figure 9-6.

```
test@debian:~$ pstree
init─┬─NetworkManager───{NetworkManager}
     ├─NetworkManagerD
     ├─acpid
     ├─anacron───run-parts───apt───sleep
     ├─apache2───5*[apache2]
     ├─atd
     ├─avahi-daemon───avahi-daemon
     ├─bonobo-activati───{bonobo-activati}
     ├─cron
     ├─cupsd
     ├─2*[dbus-daemon]
     ├─dbus-launch
     ├─dhcdbd───dhclient
     ├─exim4
     ├─gconfd-2
     ├─gdm───gdm─┬─Xorg
     │           └─x-session-manag─┬─bluetooth-apple
     │                             ├─gnome-panel
     │                             ├─gnome-settings-───{gnome-settings-}
     │                             ├─kerneloops-appl
     │                             ├─metacity
     │                             ├─nautilus
     │                             ├─nm-applet
     │                             ├─seahorse-agent
     │                             ├─system-config-p
     │                             ├─update-notifier
     │                             └─{x-session-manag}
     ├─6*[getty]
     ├─gnome-keyring-d
     ├─gnome-power-man
     ├─gnome-screensav
     ├─gnome-terminal─┬─bash───pstree
     │                ├─gnome-pty-helpe
     │                └─{gnome-terminal}
     ├─gnome-vfs-daemo
     ├─gnome-volume-ma
     ├─hald───hald-runner─┬─hald-addon-acpi
     │                    ├─hald-addon-inpu
     │                    └─hald-addon-stor
     ├─kerneloops
     ├─mapping-daemon
     ├─mixer_applet2───{mixer_applet2}
     ├─notification-da
     ├─portmap
     ├─postgres───4*[postgres]
     ├─rpc.statd
     ├─rsyslogd───2*[{rsyslogd}]
```

FIGURE 9-6

The `pstree` command.

The pgrep Command

The pgrep command takes the name you provide it and returns the ID for that process. It can even work with partial names. This is useful as many other commands require the process ID, so pgrep can help you retrieve that if you know the name of a process.

The top Command

The top command is similar to the ps command, except it lists the processes in the order of how much CPU time the process is utilizing. When examining a drive for the presence of malware, this can be a useful command. A virus or worm may be using up an excessive amount of CPU time, thus slowing down the infected machine.

The kill Command

The kill command is perhaps the simplest command of all. You simply type in the word *kill* followed by the process ID (PID) to halt a running process. An example is as follows:

```
kill 1045
```

The file Command

The file command can tell you exactly what a file is regardless of whether or not it has been renamed or had its extension changed. This can be very important in a forensic investigation. The criminal may have changed the file extension to make the file appear to be something other than what it is. The file command will help you with this. An example of the file command is shown in Figure 9-7.

The su Command

At times, you may be at a Linux machine where someone has logged in, and you need to perform some task that requires the privileges of the root user. Logging out, then logging back in as the root, can be tedious. Fortunately, you don't have to do that. You can simply invoke the super user mode. If you type in su at the shell, you are asked for the root password. If you can successfully supply it, you will then have root privileges.

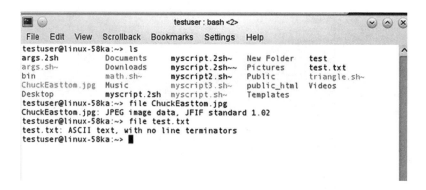

FIGURE 9-7

The file command.

The `who` Command

The `who` command tells you all the users currently logged in to the system. This is useful only if you run it on the live suspect machine prior to shutting it down.

The `finger` Command

The `finger` command is used to get back information regarding a specific user. This is often useful for a system administrator. For example, if you run `top`, and see that one specific user is spawning several processes on your server, and those processes are consuming resources, then you may want to find out about that user. This is great to use along with `who`. After you know who is on your system, you can find out specific information about that user.

The `dd` Command

The `dd` command can be used to make a forensic copy of a suspect drive. But that is not all `dd` can do for you. You can use `dd` to make a physical image of what is live in memory. Linux physical memory is accessible via two files, the /dev/mem file and the /proc/kcore file. The following command is one example of making an image of memory:

```
dd if=/dev/mem of=/evidence/image.memory1
```

This command takes whatever is in /dev/mem and sends it to the evidence partition, creating an image of it.

The `ls` Command

`ls` is a simple file management command. It lists the contents of the current directory. But `ls` can also be used to quickly catalog a suspect drive. For example, if you want to create a text file that has a listing of all directories and subdirectories, then try this command:

> **NOTE**
> Note that when you use the `ls` command with the −i option, you get the inode number for the files that are listed.

```
ls -R > directories.txt
```

The -R flag causes a recursive listing of all subdirectories. The `> directories.txt` writes the output of `ls` to the directories.txt file.

Can You Undelete in Linux?

This section expands on the details of Linux files and discusses a method for recovering deleted files.

Whenever you refer to a file by name, the operating system uses the filename to look up the corresponding inode, which then enables the system to obtain the information it needs about the file to perform further operations. An inode is a data structure in the file system that stores all the information about a file except its name and its actual data. Inodes can refer to either files or directories.

From the operating system's perspective, a filename is really just an entry in a table with inode numbers. The name is not directly associated with the file. The name is just a human-readable method of locating the inode number.

The inode is really a link to the file. The operating system keeps a count of references to this link. When the reference count reaches zero, the file is deleted. This is why deleted files can sometimes be recovered.

Manual Method

In Linux, a file is deleted when its internal inode link count reaches zero. Just follow these steps to retrieve the deleted file:

1. Move the system to single-user mode. The `init` command can be used for this purpose.

2. Once you have moved to single user mode, there are several methods you might use. The following is a rather traditional UNIX/Linux method using the `grep` command. Use the following `grep` syntax:

   ```
   grep -b 'search-text' /dev/partition > file.txt
   ```

   or

   ```
   grep -a -B[size before] -A[size after] 'text' /dev/[your_partition] > file.txt
   ```

   The flags used are defined as follows:

   - `-i`—Ignore case distinctions in both the PATTERN and the input files; that is, match both uppercase and lowercase characters.
   - `-a`—Process a binary file as if it were text.
   - `-B`—Print number lines/size of leading context before matching lines.
   - `-A`—Print number lines/size of trailing context after matching lines.

   For example, to recover a text file starting with "criminalevidence" on /dev/sda1, you can try the following command:

   ```
   # grep -i -a -B10 -A100 'criminalevidence' /dev/sda1 > file.txt
   ```

3. Next use any command-line text editor you like to see file.txt. You can then save that file.

This is only one of many methods for recovering deleted files in Linux.

CHAPTER SUMMARY

In this chapter, you were given a general introduction to the Linux operating system, along with basic forensics. You learned which logs to look at for specific types of evidence and how to retrieve those logs. You also learned about specific directories and shell commands that are useful in a forensic investigation. Furthermore, you were introduced to recovering data from a file system. You may also want to check out specific Web sites devoted to Linux forensics. A great one is *http://www.linux -forensics.com/.*

KEY CONCEPTS AND TERMS

Bootstrap environment
GRUB (Grand Unified
   Bootloader)
Intrusion detection system (IDS)
LILO (Linux Loader)

9

Linux Forensics

CHAPTER 9 ASSESSMENT

1. Where are the start-up scripts defined?

A. etc/init.d

B. /etc/scripts

C. /etc/start

D. /etc/inittab

2. Which of the following file systems *cannot* be mounted by using the `mount` command?

A. ext2

B. swap

C. fat

D. ReiserFS

3. Which of the following is a file system that provides system statistics? It doesn't contain real files but provides an interface to run-time system information.

A. /proc

B. /var

C. /home

D. /boot

4. _____ is a commonly used name for a command-line utility that provides disk partitioning functions in an operating system. It can list the partitions on a Linux system.

A. mkfs

B. parted

C. fdisk

D. format

5. What single shell command will tell you the home directory, current user, and current history size?

A. `who`

B. `whois`

C. `env`

D. `logname`

6. Use the _____ command to see running processes as a tree.

7. The `dmesg` command can be used to see the Linux boot messages.

A. True

B. False

Macintosh Forensics

MACINTOSH COMPUTERS MAY NOT BE as ubiquitous as Microsoft-based PCs, but they represent a significant portion of personal computers. For this reason, it is important that you have at least a basic understanding of the Macintosh operating system and how to conduct forensics on it. In this chapter, you will learn some history of the Macintosh operating system as well as some operating system basics. You will also learn some basic forensic techniques to use on a Macintosh.

Chapter 10 Topics

This chapter covers the following topics and concepts:

- What the basic knowledge you need to know about Macintosh is
- Where to find the logs in Macintosh
- What forensically interesting directories are
- What some forensic techniques for Macintosh are
- How to undelete files in Macintosh

Chapter 10 Goals

When you complete this chapter, you will be able to:

- Understand the basics of Macintosh and its history
- Know where to find logs in a Macintosh system
- Be able to examine the virtual memory of a Macintosh
- Be able to undelete Macintosh files

Mac Basics

It is important that you have a working understanding of the Mac operating system before attempting forensics. As with Linux, however, it is common *not* to have a good working knowledge of Macintosh systems. So this section first shows you the history of the Macintosh and then discusses the operating system fundamentals. This will establish a baseline of knowledge to help you understand Apple systems.

Mac History

Apple began with Steve Wozniak and Steve Jobs collaborating while working from their homes. In 1975, they finished the prototype of the first Apple computer. Steve Wozniak worked for Hewlett-Packard and his employment contract required him to give his employer first right of refusal on any new inventions he came up with. However, Hewlett-Packard was not interested and released the technology to Steve Wozniak. This led to the formation of Apple Computer in April 1976. The company's three founders were Steve Jobs, Steve Wozniak, and Ronald Wayne. The first computer was the Apple I, created by Wozniak.

That computer had an 8-bit microprocessor running at just below 1 MHz. The Apple I had a built-in video terminal, sockets for 8 kilobytes of onboard random access memory (RAM), a keyboard, and a cassette board meant to work with regular cassette recorders.

Apple II

It wasn't long before the team came up with the Apple II. This computer was based on the same microprocessor but came in a plastic case with the keyboard built in. It was also the first personal computer with color graphics. This was followed by a series of enhancements to the Apple II: Apple II+, IIe, IIc, IIc+, IIe Enhanced, and IIe Platinum. In 1986, the Apple IIGS was released; this computer was 16-bit rather than 8-bit.

There were multiple operating systems for the Apple II, including the following:

- **Apple DOS (Disk Operating System)**—The first edition was released as Apple DOS 3.1 in 1978. It had no relationship to Microsoft DOS.

- **Apple Pascal**—This was based on the p-system, an operating system developed at UC San Diego. It was basically a virtual machine running p-code, and Pascal was the most popular language for it. Apple Pascal was a similar design released in 1979.

- **Apple SOS**—This operating system was developed for the Apple III. The acronym stands for Sophisticated Operating System. Every program that used SOS loaded the operating system into memory as well. A SOS application disk consisted of a kernel (SOS.kernel), an interpreter (SOS.Interp), which was often the application itself, and a set of drivers (SOS.Driver).

- **ProDOS**—This was meant as a replacement for Apple DOS 3.3 and was based on SOS. It had more support for programming, including assembly and BASIC. Eventually, this led to a 16-bit version called ProDOS 16.

- **Lisa OS**—This operating system had a full graphical user interface with a file browser that was navigated with mouse clicks. It also came with some basic office programs.

Beyond the Apple II

After the Apple II, the company changed the name to Macintosh and took a new direction with its computers. The main points in that evolution are as follows:

- **The Macintosh**—Although today many people may think of Apple and Macintosh as synonymous, the Macintosh was actually released by Apple in January 1984. It had an 8-MHz Motorola processor, a black-and-white monitor, and a 3.5-inch floppy drive. The operating system for Macintosh was System 1. This eventually led to the Macintosh II running System 7.

- **System 7**—This system allowed text dragging between applications, viewing and switching applications from a menu, a control panel, and cooperative multitasking.

- **Mac OS for PowerPC**—This Mac introduced the System 7.1.2 operating system.

- **AIX for PowerPC**—In 1996, Apple had a product called Apple Network Server that used a variation of the IBM AIX system. It also used the Common Desktop Environment, a graphical user interface that is popular in the UNIX world. This product did not do well in the market and was discontinued in 1997.

Mac OS X

The next major change was the introduction of Mac OS X, which is still used in Macintosh computers today. The public beta version of the product was named Kodiak. The real change with OS X was that the operating system was based on FreeBSD, a UNIX clone. When using Mac OS X, you can navigate to a shell and run UNIX/Linux shell commands. The initial release of OS X was followed by periodic improvements, each with an animal name:

- Mac OS X v10.0, named Cheetah, was released in March 2001.

- Mac OS X v10.1 was released the same year and was named Puma.

- The next release was Mac OS X v10.2 in 2002, called Jaguar. This release included improved graphics and iChat messaging.

- In 2003, Apple released Mac OS X v10.3, named Panther.

- Mac OS X v10.4, named Tiger, was released in 2005. This release had built-in support for FireWire, and it had a new dashboard and updated mail program.

- Mac OS X v10.5, called Leopard, was released in 2007. It had over 300 new features, support for Intel x86 chips, and support for the new G3 processor.

- In 2009, Apple released Mac OS X v10.6, Snow Leopard. Most of the changes in this release were performance enhancements, rather than new features. For example, Snow Leopard had support for multicore processors.
- Mac OS X 10.7 was released in 2011 and code-named Lion. The major interface change with this release was to make it more like the iOS interfaces used on iPhone and iPad.
- Mac OS X 10.8, named Mountain Lion, was released in 2012. This release had built-in support for iCloud, to support cloud computing.

The Mac OS X desktop is shown in Figure 10-1.

When performing forensics on an Apple system, you are most likely to encounter OS X, as it is the most widely used Apple operating system today. In fact, it is the only operating system still supported by Apple.

Mac File Systems

In this section, you will learn details about the Hierarchical File System and other file systems used by Macintosh operating systems.

Macintosh File System

Macintosh File System (MFS) is an older Apple technology that has not been used in over 15 years. You are unlikely to encounter it. It has long since been replaced, first with HFS then with HFS+. It shipped with the first Macintosh in 1984.

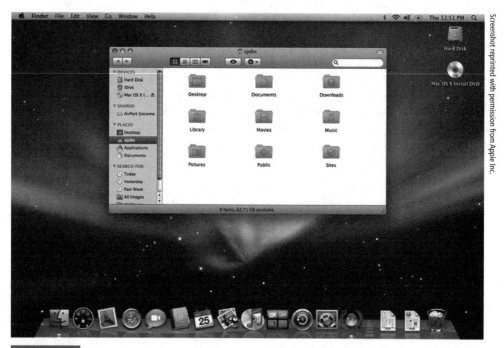

FIGURE 10-1

Mac OS X.

Hierarchical File System

The Hierarchical File System (HFS) was used on the Macintosh Plus. But with Mac OS 8.1, it was replaced by HFS+. Because HFS was the standard for Macintosh, it became known as *HFS Standard*, while HFS+ became known as *HFS Extended*. Apple introduced this file system in 1985, specifically to support its new Apple hard drive. It replaced the earlier Macintosh File System.

Hierarchical File System Plus

This is an enhancement of the HFS file system. HFS+ is the preferred file system on Mac OS X. Most important, it supports journaling. Journaling is basically the process whereby the file system keeps a record of what file transactions take place so that in the event of a hard drive crash, the files can be recovered. Journaling file systems are fault tolerant because the file system logs all changes to files, directories, or file structures. The log in which changes are recorded is referred to as the file system's journal—thus, the term journaling file systems.

It also supports disk quotas. That allows the administrator to limit the amount of disk space a given user can use, keeping that user from taking up all the space. HFS+ also has hard and soft links. There are basically two types of links. The first type is the hard link. A hard link is an inode that links directly to a specific file. A soft link or symbolic link is essentially a shortcut.

HFS+ is architecturally similar to HFS, which is not surprising as it is an enhancement to HFS. However, there are some key differences. One such difference is that HFS+ uses 32 bits for allocation blocks, rather than 16 bits. HFS+ also supports long filenames, up to 255 characters. Furthermore, HFS+ uses **Unicode**, which is the international standard for information encoding (for file naming), rather than **ASCII (American Standard Code for Information Interchange)**, which is a set of codes defining all the various keystrokes you could make, including letters, numbers, characters, and even the spacebar and return keys.

For forensic examinations, one of the more important differences in HFS+ to keep in mind is aliases. Aliases are like symbolic links; they allow you to have multiple references to a single file or directory. HFS+ also has a very interesting optimization scheme. It essentially does defragmentation on a per-file basis. The following conditions are checked, and if met, the file is defragmented when it is opened:

- The file is less than 20 megabytes in size.
- The file is not already in use.
- The file is not read-only.
- The file is fragmented.
- The system uptime is at least three minutes.

This means an HFS+ volume is routinely defragmenting itself!

Because HFS+ is the preferred file system for Mac OS X, it is one you will likely encounter when doing forensic examinations of Apple computers.

ISO9660

ISO9660 is the file system used by compact discs (CDs). ISO9660 is not Macintosh specific, but Apple does have its own set of ISO9660 extensions. Although a CD may be readable on either a PC—Windows or Linux—or a Macintosh, the files on that CD may require a specific operating system in order to be read.

Microsoft Disk Operating System

Mac OS X includes support for Microsoft Disk Operating System (MS-DOS) file systems FAT12, FAT16, and FAT32. This allows a Macintosh machine to read floppy disks (FAT12) as well as files created with DOS/Windows 3.1.

New Technology File System

Mac OS X includes read-only support for the New Technology File System (NFTS). This means if you have a portable drive that is NTFS, Mac OS X can read that partition. But like ISO9660, the files on that drive may be operating system specific.

Universal Disk Format

Universal Disk Format (UDF) is the file system used by DVD-ROM discs (both video and audio). Like ISO9660, this only guarantees that Mac OS X can read the partition or drive; it does not guarantee that Mac OS X can read the files.

UNIX File System

UNIX File System (UFS) is the file system used by FreeBSD and many other UNIX variants. Being based on FreeBSD, Mac OS X can read UFS volumes.

Partition Types

Partition types are referred to in Apple documents as partition schemes. The partition type determines how the partition is organized on the drive. Apple directly supports three different partition schemes: the GUID, the Partition Table, the Apple Partition Map, and the master boot record. The partition types are described in this section.

GUID Partition Table

The GUID Partition Table (GUID stands for "globally unique identifier") is used primarily with computers that have an Intel-based processor. It requires OS X v10.4 or later. Intel-based Macintosh machines can boot only from drives that use the GUID Partition Table.

Apple Partition Map

The Apple Partition Map is used with any PowerPC-based Mac. Intel-based Macs can mount and use a drive formatted with the Apple Partition Map, but cannot boot from the device. PowerPC-based Macs can both mount and use a drive formatted with the Apple Partition Map, and can also use it as a start-up device.

Master Boot Record

The master boot record (MBR), contained in the boot sector, is used when DOS- or Windows-based computers start up. The MBR contains important information such as a partition table, bootstrap code, and other information.

Macintosh Logs

One of the first steps in any forensic examination should be to check the logs. Remember that logs are very important when examining a Windows or a Linux computer. They are just as important when examining a Macintosh computer. This section examines the Macintosh logs and what is contained in them.

The /var/log Log

The name of this log should suggest that it is a general repository for a lot of information. The naming structure should also seem familiar. Remember that Mac OS X is based on FreeBSD, so seeing file structures similar to Linux should be no surprise.

This directory has many logs in it. The /var/log/daily.out contains data on all mounted volumes, including the dates they were mounted. This is very important in cases involving stolen data. You can see what devices have been attached and get data from them.

This folder includes data on removable media, including serial numbers.

The /var/spool/cups Folder

In this folder, you will also find information about printed documents. If you need to know what documents have been printed from this Macintosh, this folder can give you that information. This includes the name of the document printed and the user who printed it.

The /Library/Receipts Folder

This folder contains information about system and software updates. It is less useful for a forensic investigation than some of the other folders; however, it can be useful to know if a given patch was applied and when it was applied. This might be of some interest in investigating malware crimes.

The /Users/<user>/.bash_history Log

As you know, Mac OS X is based on FreeBSD, a UNIX variant. When you launch the terminal window, what you actually get is a Bash shell. So this particular log can be very interesting. It will show you a variety of commands. You might look for commands such as rm, which would be removing or deleting something, or commands like dd, indicating the user might have tried to make an image of the drive.

The var/vm Folder

In this folder, you will find a subfolder named app profile. This will contain lists of recently opened applications as well as temporary data used by applications. Both of these can be very interesting in a forensic examination.

The /Users/ Directory

This is where various users' files are stored. It is always a good idea to check in this directory to find out if users have saved data here that could be used as evidence.

The /Users/<user>/Library/Preferences/ Folder

As you probably suspect, this folder contains user preferences. This might not seem that interesting for a forensic investigation, except for one small issue. This folder even maintains the preferences of programs that have been deleted. This could be a very valuable place to get clues about programs that have been deleted from the system.

Directories

As with Windows and Linux, Macintosh has a number of directories. Some are more important than others. You must know the ones in the following sections in order to do an effective forensic examination of a Macintosh machine.

The /Volumes Directory

This directory contains information about mounted devices. You will find data here regarding hard disks, external disks, CDs, digital video discs (DVDs), and even virtual machines. This is a very important directory in your forensic examination.

The /Users Directory

This directory contains all the user accounts and associated files. This is clearly critical to your investigation of a Macintosh machine.

The /Applications Directory

This directory is where all applications are stored. Particularly in cases of malware, this is a critical directory to check.

The /Network Directory

This directory contains information about servers, network libraries, and network properties.

The /etc Directory

Just as in Linux, this is where configuration files are located. Obviously, configuration files can be quite interesting in a forensic investigation. It is often true that cybercriminals like to adjust the system's configuration. Sometimes this is done in order to facilitate the criminal's return to the system later.

The /Library/Preferences/SystemConfiguration/dom.apple.preferences.plist File

This file contains the network configuration data for each network card. This is important information to document before beginning your search for evidence.

Macintosh Forensic Techniques

This section covers some general forensic techniques to use on Macintosh systems. In the preceding sections, you learned about the Macintosh operating system, and you learned where to look for important logs, which is a valuable step in any forensic investigation. Now, you will learn a variety of forensic techniques.

Target Disk Mode

One of the most fundamental steps in forensics is to create a bit-level copy of the suspect drive. If the suspect drive is a Macintosh, all the techniques you know from Linux or Windows can still be used. You can utilize the dd command along with netcat to make a forensic copy. You can also use the imaging tools within EnCase or Forensic Toolkit. However, Macintosh provides another way to make a forensically sound copy of a drive. You begin by placing the suspect computer into Target Disk Mode. When you put the computer in that mode, it cannot be written to, so there is no chance of altering the source disk. Then simply connect to the suspect computer with universal serial bus (USB) or FireWire and image the disk.

Also, Target Disk Mode allows you to preview the computer on-site. This allows investigators to do a quick inspection before disconnecting and transporting the computer to a forensic lab. This is important because, just like with Windows or Linux, you will want to check running systems' processes before shutting the machine down. You simply have to reboot the machine in Target Disk Mode, as shown in Figure 10-2.

> **NOTE**
>
> Because Mac OS X is based on FreeBSD, Linux commands can be used here. So before shutting the suspect Macintosh down, you will want to run netstat to see any connections the system has. You may also want to run ps, pstree, and top to check running processes.

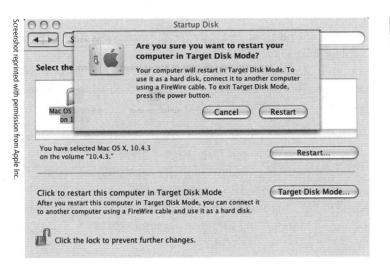

Screenshot reprinted with permission from Apple Inc.

FIGURE 10-2

Target Disk Mode.

Searching Virtual Memory

Checking virtual memory is just as important with a Macintosh as it is with a Windows or Linux computer. With Macintosh OS X, the swap file/virtual memory is located in the folder /var/vm/. You can check it with simple Linux commands like ls (for listing files). A good option is ls -al, which gives you a listing of all the files in virtual memory as well as of who launched the program and when. The best news is that you can use the grep search tool to search in the virtual memory folder.

Shell Commands

Because Mac OS X is based on FreeBSD, you can use shell commands to extract information. A number of commands can be quite useful in your forensic examination. Some additional commands are available that are specific to Macintosh.

The date Command

The date command returns the current date and time zone. It is good for documenting when exactly you begin your forensic examination. If you need the date in Coordinated Universal Time (UTC), then use the date -u version of the command.

The ls /dev/disk? Command

This command lists the current device files that are in use. You should document this information before shutting the system down for transport to the forensic lab.

The /hdiutil partition /dev/disk0 Command

This command lists the partition table for the boot drive. Clearly, it is important to know the partitions the machine recognizes upon boot-up.

The system_profiler SPHardwareDataType Command

This command returns the hardware information for the host system. This provides information useful for the basic documentation of the system prior to beginning your forensic examination. There are related commands, such as system_profiler SPSerialATADataType. This command gives information on all the attached Serial Advanced Technology Attachment (SATA) devices.

 NOTE

There is an interesting trick you can do to circumvent passwords in Macintosh. If you change the amount of physical memory, the firmware password is automatically reset. So simply add or remove RAM, then reboot.

The system_profiler SPSoftwareDataType Command

Related to system_profiler SPHardwareDataType, this command returns information about the operating system. This is also important for documenting the system prior to starting the forensic examination.

Can You Undelete in Mac?

Recall that in Windows systems, deleting actually just removes a file from the master file table (MFT) or file allocation table (FAT) and marks those clusters as available. The file's data is still there and can be recovered. What happens when a file is deleted on an HFS or HFS+ volume? Although the details are a bit different, a similar thing occurs. The references to the file are gone and the clusters might be used and overwritten. But, depending on how soon after the deletion you attempt to recover data, you may be able to recover some or all of the data. Even if the data is overwritten, data may still exist in unallocated space and in index nodes. When a file is deleted in Macintosh, it is moved to the trash folder—much like the Recycle Bin in Windows. The trash is represented on the file system as a hidden folder, .Trash, on the root directory of the file system. You can list the contents with a shell command, as shown here:

```
$/.Trash ls -al
total 764
drwx------ 7 pc pc 306 Oct 30 15:05 .
drwxr-xr-x 30 pc pc 1054 Oct 30 12:44 ..
-rw------- 1 pc pc 6148 Oct 30 14:38 .DS_Store
-rw-r--r-- 1 pc pc 187500 Oct 27 15:41 Resume.pdf
-rw-r--r-- 1 pc pc 108382 Oct 27 15:43 VacationPIC.jpg
-rw-r--r-- 1 pc pc 108382 Oct 27 15:43 Report.pdf
```

Now files in the trash directory can be recovered just by copying or moving them to any other location.

Note that the Trash (.Trash folder) contains four files, each of which can be recovered by simply copying or moving it to an alternate location. There are tools that will recover files, even after the trash bin has been emptied. A few are given here:

- Mac Keeper at *http://mackeeper.zeobit.com/mac-undelete*
- Mac Undelete at *http://www.macundelete.com/*
- Free Undelete Mac at *http://www.freeundeletemac.com/*

Any of these tools can aid you in recovering deleted Macintosh files.

CHAPTER SUMMARY

In this chapter, you learned the fundamentals of the Macintosh operating system. It is important to have a working understanding of any operating system before attempting forensics on that system. You also learned where to look for log files and what is contained in those logs.

The shell commands that you learned in this chapter are critical. It is important that you remember those and be able to use them on Macintosh computers you examine. It is also important that you understand imaging a suspect Macintosh computer and recovering deleted files.

KEY CONCEPTS AND TERMS

American Standard Code for
    Information Interchange
    (ASCII)
ISO9660

Unicode
Universal Disk Format (UDF)

CHAPTER 10 ASSESSMENT

1. Which partition type is used to boot Intel-based Macintosh machines?

    A. GUID
    B. APM
    C. MBR
    D. HFS

2. What is the preferred file system used in Mac OS X?

    A. NTFS
    B. ReiserFS
    C. EXT3
    D. HFS+

3. Where would you look for configuration files on a Macintosh computer?

    A. /etc
    B. /var
    C. /tmp
    D. /cfg

4. You can undelete files in Macintosh.

    A. True
    B. False

Mobile Forensics

MOBILE DEVICES OF ALL TYPES are everywhere. It is almost guaranteed that everyone reading this has a smartphone. It is also very likely that many readers have a tablet of some type. These devices are ubiquitous. There are some experts who think they are the wave of the future, and the PC will soon be gone. Whether that is true or not, it is a fact that mobile devices are a central part of our modern life. This means they are an important topic for forensics. Mobile devices can be a veritable treasure trove of forensic evidence. In this chapter, you will learn the basics of mobile devices and how to extract evidence from them.

Chapter 11 Topics

This chapter covers the following topics and concepts:

- What the cellular device concepts are
- What the evidence that you can obtain from a mobile device is
- How to seize evidence from a mobile device

Chapter 11 Goals

When you complete this chapter, you will be able to:

- Understand cellular concepts and terminology
- Understand what evidence to look for on mobile devices
- Seize evidence from an iPhone, iPod, or iPad
- Seize evidence from an Android phone
- Seize evidence from a BlackBerry

Cellular Device Concepts

As with the Windows, Linux, and Macintosh operating systems, it is important that you fully understand the technology of cell phones and other devices before you explore the forensic analysis of the devices. In this section, you will learn the essential concepts and technologies used in mobile devices. This section introduces you to some basic concepts that you need to understand in order to be able to conduct forensics on cellular devices.

Terms

The first place to start is with terminology. This section introduces a number of terms—along with brief definitions—that are relevant to mobile technology. It is important that you be comfortable with the terms in this section.

Mobile Switching Center

A **mobile switching center (MSC)** is the switching system for the cellular network. MSCs are used in 1G, 2G, 3G, and Global System for Mobile (GSM) communications networks. You will learn about 3G and GSM networks later in this section. The MSC processes all the connections between mobile devices and between mobile devices and landline phones. The MSC is also responsible for routing calls between base stations and the public switched telephone network (PSTN).

Base Transceiver Station

The **base transceiver station (BTS)** is the part of the cellular network responsible for communications between the mobile phone and the network switching system. The base station system (BSS) is a set of radio transceiver equipment that communicates with cellular devices. It consists of a BTS and a base station controller (BSC). The BSC is a central controller coordinating the other pieces of the BSS.

> **NOTE**
>
> SIM cloning occurs when a SIM card's identifying information is copied to a different SIM card. That card can then be used in a new phone but will operate as if it were the original phone. SIM cloning is illegal, happens frequently, and is done fairly easily with a minimum of technical knowledge and very little specialized equipment.

Home Location Register

The **home location register (HLR)** is a database used by the MSC that contains subscriber data and service information. It is related to the **visitor location register (VLR)**, which is used for roaming phones.

Subscriber Identity Module

The **subscriber identity module (SIM)** is a memory chip that stores the International Mobile Subscriber Identity (IMSI). It is intended to be unique for each phone and is what you use to identify the phone. Many modern phones have removable SIMs, which means you could change out the SIM and essentially have a different phone with a different number.

A SIM card contains its unique serial number—the ICCID—the IMSI, security authentication, and ciphering information. The SIM will also usually have network information, services the user has access to, and two passwords. Those passwords are the **personal identification number (PIN)** and the personal unlocking code (PUK).

Electronic Serial Number

Electronic serial numbers (ESNs) are unique identification numbers developed by the United States Federal Communications Commission (FCC) to identify cell phones. They are now used only in code division multiple access (CDMA) phones, whereas GSM and later phones use the **International Mobile Equipment Identity (IMEI) number**. The first 8 bits of the ESN identify the manufacturer, and the subsequent 24 bits uniquely identify the phone. The IMEI is used with GSM and Long Term Evolution (LTE) as well as other types of phones.

Personal Unlocking Code

The **personal unlocking code (PUK)** is a code used to reset a forgotten PIN. Using the code returns the phone to its original state, causing loss of most forensic data. If the code is entered incorrectly 10 times in a row, the device becomes permanently blocked and unrecoverable.

Integrated Circuit Card Identifier

Each SIM is identified by its **integrated circuit card identifier (ICCID)**. These numbers are engraved on the SIM during manufacturing. This number has subsections that are very important for forensics. This number starts with the issuer identification number (IIN), which is a seven-digit number that identifies the country code and issuer, followed by a variable-length individual account identification number to identify the specific phone, and a check digit.

Networks

Although this section covers terms as well, they are terms specific to networks. Therefore, they are listed separately. Knowing the types of networks used may be the most fundamental part of understanding mobile devices. The network-specific terms are as follows:

- **Global System for Mobile (GSM) communications**— **Global System for Mobile (GSM) communications** is a standard developed by the European Telecommunications Standards Institute (ETSI). Basically, GSM is the 2G network.

- **Enhanced Data Rates for GSM Evolution (EDGE)**—**Enhanced Data Rates for GSM Evolution (EDGE)** does not fit neatly into the 2G-3G-4G continuum. It is technically considered 2G+, but was an improvement on GSM (2G), so it can be considered a bridge between 2G and 3G technologies.

 NOTE

The real differentiator between 3G and 4G is speed. To be considered 4G, a wireless communication technology must have a speed of 100 megabits per second (Mbps) for mobile communications (such as when you are in a car) and 1 gigabit per second (Gbps) for stationary users.

- **Universal Mobile Telecommunications System (UMTS)**—Universal Mobile Telecommunications System (UMTS) is a 3G standard based on GSM. It is essentially an improvement of GSM.
- **Long Term Evolution (LTE)**—Long Term Evolution (LTE) is a standard for wireless communication of high-speed data for mobile devices. This is what is commonly called 4G.
- **Wireless fidelity (Wi-Fi)**—Most cellular phones and other mobile devices today are able to connect to Wi-Fi networks. Wireless networking has become the norm and free Wi-Fi hotspots can be found in restaurants, coffee shops, hotels, homes, and many other locations.

Operating Systems

Today's mobile devices are complex computer systems. Whether you prefer an Android, Windows, or Apple phone, the phone will have an operating system. The same is true for tablets. Therefore, it is important to have some basic understanding of the major operating systems used on mobile devices.

iOS

The iOS operating system is used by iPhone, iPod, and iPad. It is a relatively new operating system, originally released in 2007 for the iPod Touch and the iPhone. The user interface is based all on touching the icons directly. It supports what Apple calls gestures: swipe, drag, pinch, tap, and so on. The iOS operating system is derived from OS X.

There are four layers to iOS. The first is the Core OS layer. This is the heart of the operating system. Next is the Core Services layer. The Core Services layer is how applications interact with the iOS. Next is the Media layer, which is responsible for music, video, and so on. Finally, there is the Cocoa Touch layer, which responds to the aforementioned gestures.

In normal operations, iOS uses the HFS+ file system, but it can use FAT32 when communicating with a PC. The iOS contains several elements in the data partition:

- Calendar entries
- Contacts entries
- Note entries
- iPod_control directory (this directory is hidden)
- iTunes configuration
- iTunes music

Of particular interest to forensic investigation is the folder iPod_control\device\sysinfo. This folder contains two very important pieces of information:

- Model number
- Serial number

The iOS runs on iPhones, iPods, and iPads. This means that once you are comfortable with the operating system on one Apple device, you should be comfortable with any Apple device. This applies not just to the features that users interact with, but also to the operating system fundamentals. Thus, if you have experience with forensics on an iPhone, you will have no problem conducting a forensic analysis of an iPad.

Android

The Android operating system is a Linux-based operating system and it is completely open source. If you have a programming and operating systems background, you may find it useful to examine the Android source code from *http://source.android.com/*.

Android was first released in 2003 and is the creation of Rich Miner, Andy Rubin, and Nick Sears. Google acquired Android in 2005, but still keeps the code open source. The versions of Android have been named after sweets:

- Version 1.5 Cupcake
- Version 1.6 Donut
- Version 2.0–2.1 Éclair
- Version 2.2 Froyo
- Version 2.3 Gingerbread
- Version 3.1–3.2 Honeycomb
- Version 4.0 Ice Cream Sandwich
- Version 4.1–4.2 Jelly Bean

The differences from version to version usually involve adding new features, not a radical change to the operating system. This means that if you are comfortable with version 1.6 (Donut), you will be able to do forensic examination on version 4.2 (Jelly Bean).

In 2010, Google launched its Nexus series of devices. This is a series of devices, including smartphones and tablets, that all run the same Android operating system. This makes the smartphone and tablet identical in function and features. It is also worth noting that the new Google Glass uses Android as its operating system. Although this device is in its infancy, forensic analysts would do well to pay attention to its development. Should it achieve even moderately widespread use, it will be seen in forensic examinations in the future.

 NOTE
Many cell phone manufacturers take the base Android code that is publicly available and add their own items to it. This means that even if you are well versed in the public Android code, you may not know every nuance of the code actually running on a given Android phone.

Windows

Microsoft has produced several variations of Windows aimed at the mobile market. The company's first foray into the mobile operating system market was Windows CE. That operating system was also released as the Pocket PC 2000, which was based on Windows CE version 3. In 2008, Windows Phone was released. It had a major drawback in that it was not compatible with many of the previous Windows Mobile apps. In 2010, Microsoft released Windows Phone 7.

More recently, Microsoft has moved in the same direction as Apple with Windows 8 being its primary operating system. Windows 8 is shipped on PCs, laptops, phones, and tablets. This means that once you are comfortable with the operating system on one device, you are going to be able to conduct forensic examinations on other devices running Windows 8.

The BlackBerry

The first BlackBerry device was a pager capable of receiving e-mail pages, and it was released in 1999. BlackBerry uses its own proprietary operating system, BlackBerry 10. It is based on the QRNX operating system. BlackBerry supports the major features that other mobile phones support, such as drag and drop and gestures.

In recent years, the market share for BlackBerry has been steadily decreasing. However, you will still find BlackBerry devices in use, and they may be relevant to your forensic investigation.

What Evidence You Can Get from a Cell Phone

A cell phone, or tablet, can be a treasure trove of forensic information. This is one area of digital forensics that definitely extends well beyond the scope of computer crimes. With mobile devices, the evidence found can be relevant to any crime.

Items you should attempt to recover from a mobile device include the following:

- Call history
- E-mails, texts, and/or other messages
- Photos and video
- Phone information
- Global positioning system (GPS) information
- Network information

The call history lets you know who the user has spoken to and for how long. Yes, this is easily erasable, but many users don't erase their call history. Or perhaps the suspect

---

FYI

One good example of the evidence that can be derived from a mobile device is the contacts list. This does not mean guilt by association. However, consider your own phone for a moment. You are learning computer forensics. You probably have several contacts who are also in some aspect of computer science. If someone got your contacts list, it is likely it would contain other IT professionals or students. Certainly not every one of your contacts would be involved in computers, but some would. The same holds true for criminals. If you seize the phone of a drug dealer, it is not the case that everyone in his or her contacts list is a supplier or customer. But it is almost certain that some of those contacts are.

intended to delete this data and simply did not get to it yet. In either case, call history does not provide direct evidence of a crime—with the exception of cyberstalking cases. In a cyberstalking case, the call history can show a pattern of contact with the victim. However, in other cases, it provides only circumstantial evidence. For example, if John Smith is suspected of drug dealing and his call history shows a pattern of regular calls to a known drug supplier, by itself this is not adequate evidence of any crime. However, it aids the investigators in getting an accurate picture of the entire situation.

Many phones allow sending and receiving of e-mails and messages in SMS or other formats. Gathering this evidence from a mobile device can be very important. Both the parties that the suspect is communicating with and the actual content of the communications are very important.

Photos and video can provide direct evidence of a crime. In the case of child pornography cases, the relevance is obvious. However, it may surprise you to know that it is not uncommon for some criminals to actually photograph or videotape themselves committing serious crimes. This is particularly true of young criminals conducting unplanned crimes or conducting crimes under the influence of drugs or alcohol.

Information about the phone should be one of the first things you document in your investigation. This will include model number, serial number of the SIM card, operating system, and other similar information. The more detailed, descriptive information you can document, the better.

Global positioning system information has become increasingly important in a variety of cases. So many individuals have devices with GPS enabled, it would seem negligent for a forensic analyst not to retrieve this information. GPS information has begun to play a significant role in contentious divorces, for instance. If someone suspects a spouse of being unfaithful, determining that the spouse's phone and his or her car were at a specific motel when he or she claimed to be at work can be important.

Network information is also important. What Wi-Fi networks does the phone recognize? This might give you an indication of where the phone has been. For example, if the phone belongs to someone suspected of stalking a victim, and the suspect's phone network records show he or she has frequently been using Wi-Fi networks in close proximity to the victim's home, this can be important evidence.

Types of Information

The National Institute of Standards and Technology (NIST) guidelines at *http://csrc.nist .gov/publications/nistpubs/800-72/sp800-72.pdf*, list four different states a mobile device can be in when you extract data:

Nascent State—Devices are in the nascent state when received from the manufacturer—the device contains no user data and has its original factory configuration settings....

Active State—Devices that are in the active state are powered on, performing tasks, and able to be customized by the user and have their filesystems populated with data....

Quiescent State—The quiescent state is a dormant mode that conserves battery life while maintaining user data and performing other background functions. Context information for the device is preserved in memory to allow a quick resumption of processing when returning to the active state....

Semi-Active State—The semi-active state is a state partway between active and quiescent. The state is reached by a timer, which is triggered after a period of inactivity, allowing battery life to be preserved by dimming the display and taking other appropriate actions.

You should document what state the device is in when you conduct your investigation and analysis. If you change state—for example, by turning on the device—that should also be documented.

Seizing Evidence from a Mobile Device

Once you are ready to seize evidence from the mobile device, remember the following rules:

- If you are going to plug the phone into a computer, make sure the phone does not synchronize with the computer. This is particularly important with the iPhone, which routinely auto-syncs.
- Follow the same advice you follow for PCs. Make sure you touch the evidence as little as possible, and document what you do to the device.

One of the most important things to do is to make sure you don't accidentally write data to the mobile device. For example, if you plug an iPhone into your forensic workstation, you want to make sure you don't accidentally write information from your workstation to the iPhone.

If the forensic workstation is a Windows machine, you can use the Windows Registry to prevent the workstation from writing to the mobile device. Before connecting to a Windows machine, find the Registry key HKEY_LOCAL_MACHINE\System\CurrentControlset\StorageDevicePolicies, set the value to 0x00000001, and restart the computer. This prevents that computer from writing to mobile devices that are connected to it.

Although Forensic Toolkit and EnCase can both image a phone for you, there are other products made specifically for phone forensics:

- **Data Doctor**—This product recovers all Inbox and Outbox data and all contact data, and has an easy-to-use interface. Most important, it has a free trial version, but there is a cost for the full version. It is available from *http://www.simrestore.com/*.
- **Sim Card Data Retrieval Utility**—This product is available from *http://shareme.com/details/sim-card-data-retrieval-utility.html*. It retrieves Inbox and sent message data as well as contact data. It runs on various Windows versions, but has not yet been tested with Windows 7, as of this writing. There is a license fee associated with this product.

- **Device Seizure**—This is available from Paraben Software at *http://www.paraben .com/*. There is a license fee associated with this product. Paraben makes a number of forensic products.

- **Forensic SIM Cloner**—This tool is used to clone SIM cards, allowing you to perform forensic analysis of the SIM card.

Forensics for a Windows 8 phone is done in much the same way forensics for a Windows 8 PC or laptop is done. The only issue is to make certain the phone does not synchronize with the forensic workstation. A similar issue arises with the Android. Because it is based on Linux, many of the same forensic techniques can be applied. Keep in mind that a handheld portable device probably will not have all the same logs that a PC or server has, but if the operating system is the same, then the forensics will be largely the same.

The iPhone

There are automated processes for breaking an iPhone passcode. XRY is one such tool, which can be found at *http://news.cnet.com/8301-1023_3-57405580-93/iphone-passcode -cracking-is-easier-than-you-think/*. Keep in mind that the iPhone has only a four-digit pin, which means there are 10,000 possible combinations of the digits 0–9.

If you are using a forensic workstation with iTunes, you can simply plug the iPhone (or iPad/iPod) into the workstation and use iTunes to extract a great deal of information about the phone. This is shown in Figure 11-1.

FIGURE 11-1

Apple iPhone iTunes display.

You can immediately notice three important items to document:

1. The iOS version number
2. The phone number
3. The serial number

Notice you can also see where the phone is backed up. That can indicate yet another place you should search during your forensic investigation. Some information in Figure 11-1 has been redacted because this image was taken from an actual phone.

If you have imaged the phone and you then search for information, you may have to look more closely to find some data.

For example, Library_CallHistory_call_history.db has the entire call history. If you cannot view that directly on the phone itself, the database file has all call information. Cookies can be found in the file Library_Cookies_Cookies.plist. This can give you a history of the phone user's Internet activities. These, and other files, are actually copied to a PC during synchronization. Here are a few of those files:

- Library_Preferences_com.apple.mobileipod.plist
- Library_Preferences_com.apple.mobileemail.plist
- Library_Preferences_com.apple.mobilevpn.plist

The mobileemail.plist file has obvious forensic evidence. It will give you information about e-mail sent and received from the phone. The mobilevpn.plist file can also be interesting. If the user has utilized the phone to communicate over a VPN, this file will have information about that.

> **NOTE**
>
> The fact that these files are downloaded to the computer during synchronization allows you another method for gathering information. If you do not have access to a suspect iPhone, but you do have access to the computer it was synchronized with, you can retrieve a snapshot of the phone at the time of the synchronization.

Deleted Files

When a file is deleted on the iPhone, iPad, or iPod, it is actually moved to the .Trashes\501 folder. Essentially, the data is still there until it is overwritten, so recently deleted files can be retrieved.

Tools

There are tools specifically for the iOS devices. These can be a useful addition to your forensic toolset. Here are few widely used tools:

- **Pwnage**—This utility allows you to unlock a locked iPod Touch and is available from *http://wikee.iphwn.org/*.

- **Recover My iPod**—This utility allows you to recover files deleted from an iPod and is available from *http://www.recovermyipod.com/*.

- **Wolf**—This utility is a full-featured iPhone forensic tool available from *http://www.mysecured.com/?p=206*.

BlackBerry

First, you should download and install BlackBerry Desktop Manager. Use the following link to select and download the install file that fits your system or version: *https://www. blackberry.com/Downloads/entry.do?code=A8BAA56554F96369AB93E4F3BB068C22.* Then, you install the Desktop Manager. Once that is done, the steps for imaging the device are rather easy:

1. Open BlackBerry's Desktop Manager. Click Options then Connection Settings.
2. If the Desktop Manager hasn't already done so, select USB-PIN: Device # for connection type. Click OK.
3. Select Backup and Restore.
4. Click the Back Up button for a full backup of the device or use the Advanced section for specific data.
5. Select your destination and save the .ipd file.

This creates a complete backup image of the BlackBerry phone. Once you have that backup to your workstation, you can now examine the data and perform a forensic analysis.

CHAPTER SUMMARY

In this chapter, you were introduced to fundamental mobile terms and concepts. It is important that you fully understand these and commit them to memory. You were also shown mobile device forensic concepts. This chapter also gave you a look at each of the major phones, and you learned how to extract data from those devices.

Of at least as much importance, you learned what data is important and how phone forensics can provide a treasure trove of data.

KEY CONCEPTS AND TERMS

Base transceiver station (BTS)
Electronic Serial Number (ESN)
Enhanced Data Rates for GSM Evolution (EDGE)
Global System for Mobile (GSM) communications
Home location register (HLR)

Integrated circuit card identifier (ICCID)
International Mobile Equipment Identity (IMEI) number
Long Term Evolution (LTE)
Mobile switching center (MSC)
Personal identification number (PIN)

Personal unlocking code (PUK)
Subscriber identity module (SIM)
Universal Mobile Telecommunications System (UMTS)
Visitor location register (VLR)

CHAPTER 11 ASSESSMENT

1. It important to write-block a phone before doing forensic analysis to make certain data is not copied to the phone.

A. True
B. False

2. Which of the following is a 4G standard?

A. EDGE
B. GSM
C. LTE
D. GSM4

3. Where is the data for roaming phones stored?

A. VLR
B. HLR
C. BTS
D. GSM

4. All devices are in the _____ state when received from the manufacturer.

Performing Network Analysis

I N THIS CHAPTER, YOU WILL LEARN about network forensics. The main topic is network packet analysis. However, you will also explore network traffic analysis, router forensics, and firewall forensics. Unlike other forensics tasks, some of these tasks will be performed on live systems. For example, network analysis is done, at least in part, on a live network with actual traffic. Router forensics is usually done on an active router.

<u>**Chapter 12 Topics**</u>

This chapter covers the following topics and concepts:

- What the basics of network packet analysis are
- What you need to know about traffic analysis
- What router forensics is
- What firewall forensics is

<u>**Chapter 12 Goals**</u>

When you complete this chapter, you will be able to:

- Understand network packets
- Perform network analysis
- Analyze routers for forensic evidence
- Examine firewall logs for evidence

Network Packet Analysis

It is important for any forensic analyst to be able to analyze network traffic. Many attacks are live attacks on a network, such as denial of service (DoS) attacks. In this section, you will learn more about network packets, network-based attacks, and tools for analyzing network traffic.

Network Packets

Information that is sent across a network is divided into chunks, called packets. Technically speaking, packets exist in the OSI model at Layer 3 and are typically formatted according to the Internet Protocol—though many other protocols and their unique formats may also be encountered. Packets are divided into two parts, the header and the payload. If you think in terms of an envelope, the header contains the address information (to and from and any special handling) and the payload contains the content of the letter.

Packet Header

A unit of information being transferred can have several headers put on by different protocols at different layers of the OSI model. There is usually an Ethernet header from Layer 2, an IP header from Layer 3, a Transmission Control Protocol (TCP) header from Layer 5, and then appropriate higher-layer headers above that. Each contains different information. Combined, they have several pieces of information that will interest forensic investigations:

- The Ethernet header has the source and destination MAC address.

- The IP header contains the source IP address, the destination IP address, and the protocol number of the protocol in the IP packet's payload. These are critical pieces of information.

- The TCP header contains the source port, destination port, a sequence number, and several other fields. The sequence number is very important to network traffic; for example, knowing this is packet 4 of 10 is important. The TCP header also has synchronization bits that are used to establish and terminate communications between both communicating parties.

- It is also possible that certain types of traffic will have a User Datagram Protocol (UDP) header instead of a TCP header. A UDP header still has a source and destination port number, but it lacks a sequence number and synchronization bits.

The issue of synchronization bits in the TCP header can also yield interesting forensic data. Here are the bits most often used and what they indicate:

- **URG (1 bit)**—Traffic is marked as urgent, though this bit is rarely used. It is more common that the IP precedence bits are used for priority when there is a need.
- **ACK (1 bit)**—This bit acknowledges the attempt to synchronize communications.
- **RST (1 bit)**—The RST bit resets the connection.
- **SYN (1 bit)**—This bit synchronizes sequence numbers.
- **FIN (1 bit)**—This bit indicates there is no more data from the sender.

A normal network conversation starts with one side sending a packet with the SYN bit turned on. The target responds with both SYN and ACK bits turned on. Then, the other end responds with just the ACK bit turned on. Then, communication commences. When it is finished sending information, the connection is terminated by sending a packet with the FIN bit turned on.

There are some attacks that depend on sending malformed packets. For example, some session hijacking attacks begin with sending an RST packet to attempt to reset the connection so the attacker can take over. The SYN flood DoS attack is based on flooding the target with SYN packets but never responding to the SYN/ACK that is sent back.

Also keep in mind that most skilled hackers start by performing reconnaissance on the target system. One of the first steps in that process is to do a port scan. Many port-scanning tools are available on the Web. The most primitive of these just send an Internet Control Message Protocol (ICMP) packet to each port in order to see if they respond. But because this is rather obviously a port scan, and some administrators block incoming ICMP packets, hackers have become more sophisticated. There are several stealthier scans, based on manipulating the aforementioned bit flags in packet headers. Seeing incoming packets destined for well-known ports, like the ones listed previously, with certain flags (bits) turned on, is a telltale sign of a port scan. Here are some of the more common scans briefly described so you will know what to look for:

- **FIN scan**—A packet is sent with the FIN flag turned on. If the port is open, this generates an error message. Remember that FIN indicates the communication is ended. Because there was no prior communication, an error is generated telling the hacker that this port is open and in use.
- **Christmas tree scan**—The Christmas tree scan sends a TCP packet to the target with the URG, PUSH, and FIN flags set. This is called a Christmas tree scan because of the alternating bits turned on and off in the flags byte.
- **Null scan**—The null scan turns off all flags, creating a lack of TCP flags in the packet. This would never happen with real communications. It, too, normally results in an error packet being sent.

This means when you are examining TCP/IP packet headers, you need to look at the ports, IP address, and bit flags. You may also find useful information in the MAC address in the lower-layer part of the information transfer unit. This is in addition to searching the actual data in the packets.

12

Performing
Network Analysis

Payload

The payload is the body or information content of a packet. This is the actual content that the packet is delivering to the destination. If a packet is fixed length, the payload may be padded with blank information or a specific pattern to make it the right size.

Trailer

The TCP (OSI model Layer 4) and IP (OSI model Layer 3) portions of a unit of information transfer contain only a header and payload. However, if the Layer 2 portion of a unit of information transfer is analyzed, then in addition to a header and payload, there is also a part at the end called the trailer. The trailer may be part of the Ethernet or Point-to-Point Protocol (PPP) frame or other Layer 2 protocol, often called Data Link Layer protocol. An Ethernet frame, for instance, has 96 bits that tell the receiving device that it has reached the end of the transmission. A Layer 2 frame also has error checking.

Ethernet uses a 32-bit cyclic redundancy check (CRC). The sender calculates the CRC using a very complex calculation on the source address, destination address, length, payload, and pad, if any. The four-octet (32-bit) result is stored in the trailer by the sender and the frame is transmitted. The receiving device repeats the exact same calculation as the sender and compares the result with the value stored in the trailer. If the values match, the frame is good and the frame is processed. But if the values do not match, the receiving device has a decision to make. The decision is made consistently based upon the protocol involved. In the case of Ethernet, the receiver discards the errored frame and sends no indication whatsoever that the frame has been discarded. The receiver usually does, however, update some internal counter, which can be queried to say how many frames were discarded. There is also a counter that says how many frames arrived and passed the CRC check.

Ethernet relies on the fact that an upper-layer protocol may or may not request a retransmission of the errored frame or may or may not do something else, based on how the protocol works. In the case of Internet Protocol, there is, likewise, not a retransmission request for an errored or missing frame, nor is there a retransmission request in the UDP protocol. TCP, on the other hand, does request a retransmission. If a frame does not pass the CRC check of Ethernet, it is discarded. TCP knows that Ethernet discarded a frame because of the sequence number in the TCP header. If a lower-level frame is discarded, and therefore is missing from the sequence, then TCP will request a retransmission. It will also usually request a retransmission in the case of a sequence error.

Ports

A port is a number that identifies a channel in which communication can occur. Just as your television may have one cable coming into it, but many channels you can view, your computer may have one cable coming into it, but many network ports you can communicate on. There are 65,635 possible ports, divided into three distinct types, and some are used more often than others. There are certain ports a forensic analyst should know on sight. Knowing what port a packet was destined for (or coming from) will tell you what protocol it was using, which can be invaluable information. The IP address concatenated with a port number is called a socket and will be unique for the duration of a connection. The following is a list of the ports you should memorize and the protocols that normally use those ports:

- 20 and 21—Use FTP (File Transfer Protocol) for transferring files between computers. Port 20 is for information; 21 is for control.
- 22—Uses SSH (Secure Shell) to remotely and securely log on to a system. You can then use a command prompt or shell to execute commands on that system. This port is popular with network administrators and more secure than Telnet.
- 23—Uses Telnet to remotely log on to a system. You can then use a command prompt or shell to execute commands on that system. This port is popular with network administrators but less common. SSH is preferred for its greater security.
- 25—Uses SMTP (Simple Mail Transfer Protocol) to send e-mail.
- 43—Uses Whois, a command that queries a target IP address for information.
- 53—Uses DNS (Domain Name Service) to translate uniform resource locators (URLs) into Web addresses and possibly retrieve other information about the system that matches the URL.
- 69—Uses TFTP (Trivial File Transfer Protocol), which is a faster version of FTP.
- 80—Uses HTTP (Hypertext Transfer Protocol) to display Web pages.
- 88—Uses Kerberos authentication.
- 110—Uses POP3 (Post Office Protocol Version 3) to retrieve e-mail.
- 137–138, 139—Use NetBIOS.
- 161 and 162—Use SNMP (Simple Network Management Protocol).
- 179—Uses BGP (Border Gateway Protocol).
- 194—Uses IRC (Internet Relay Chat) chat rooms.
- 220—Uses the IMAP (Internet Message Access Protocol) e-mail service.
- 389—Uses LDAP (Lightweight Directory Access Protocol) user authentication.
- 443—Uses HTTPS (Hypertext Transfer Protocol Secure) secure Web page display.
- 445—Uses Active Directory/SMB (Server Message Block) protocol.
- 464—Uses Kerberos change password.
- 465—Uses SMTP over SSL (Simple Mail Transfer Protocol over Secure Sockets Layer) to secure e-mail sending.
- 636—Uses LDAPS (SSL or TLS) (Lightweight Directory Access Protocol, Secure).
- 31337—Uses Back Orifice.
- 54320/54321—Use BO2K.
- 6666—Uses Beast.
- 23476/23477—Use Donald Dick.
- 43188—Uses Reachout.
- 407—Uses Timbuktu.

Why should you know these ports? Consider the information you gather from them. Assume you capture traffic going to and from a database server on port 21. This means someone is using FTP to upload or download files with that server. But you query the network administrator and find he or she doesn't use FTP on his or her database server. This is likely a sign of an intruder or, at the very least, of an insider who is not adhering to system policy. Or perhaps you see frequent attempts to connect to a Web server on port 23 (Telnet). An old hacker trick is to attempt to telnet into a Web server and grab the server's banner or banners. This allows the hacker to determine the exact operating system and Web server running unless the system administrator has modified the banner to avoid such a well-known hacker trick.

The last six items on the preceding list (starting with Back Orifice) may seem strange. The names are certainly a bit odd. These are all utilities that give an intruder complete access to the target system. Only one of them, Timbuktu, has any legitimate use. Timbuktu is an open source alternative to PC Anywhere. It allows program users to log on to a remote system and work just like they were sitting in front of the desktop. It is possible that technical support personnel are using Timbuktu to make support calls more efficient. But it is also possible that an intruder is logging on and taking over the system. The other five items are simply examples of backdoor hacker software with no legitimate use. The list is not intended to be exhaustive—there are many more hacker programs and new ones appear every day.

As you can see, just knowing ports and seeing the ports in the TCP or UDP headers can yield very valuable evidence. The next step is to start tracking down the source IP address. Assuming it is not a spoofed IP address, this may lead you directly to the culprit.

FYI

You might think that tracing back a source IP address is a waste of time. After all, it is not particularly difficult to spoof an IP address; you can even find instructions on how to do it on YouTube. So surely any cybercriminal would take the obvious step of hiding his or her real IP address. Consider more traditional crimes. Surely anyone committing a murder with a gun would immediately destroy the gun and dispose of the parts? However, law enforcement officers routinely find the gun used in a crime, still in the suspect's possession. The same thing occurs with spoofing an IP. It is surprising how often criminals don't take this obvious step. And even if they do spoof their IP, they may not know to spoof their MAC address. So absolutely take the time to trace back the origins of suspect packets using the information you find in the headers—a little effort could prove very fruitful.

Network Attacks

There are certain computer attacks that actually strike at the network itself rather than at a specific machine that is attached to the network. In some cases, these attacks are directed at a specific machine or machines but have an impact on the network itself. A few of those attacks are discussed here.

Denial of Service

This is the classic example of a network attack. A DoS attack can be targeted at a given server, but usually the increased traffic affects the rest of the target network. In a DoS attack, the attacker uses one of three approaches. The attacker can damage the target machine's ability to operate, overflow the target machine with too many open connections at the same time, or use up the bandwidth to the target machine. In a DoS attack, the attacker usually floods the network with malicious packets, preventing legitimate network traffic from passing. The following sections discuss specific types of DoS attacks.

Ping of death attack. In a ping of death attack, an attacker sends an ICMP echo packet of a larger size than the target machine can accept. At one time, this form of attack caused many operating systems to lock or crash, until vendors released patches to deal with ping of death attacks. Firewalls can be configured to block incoming ICMP packets completely or to block ICMP packets that are malformed or of an improper length, which is typically 84 bytes, including the IP header.

Ping flood. Related to the ping of death is the ping flood. The ping flood simply sends a tremendous number of ICMP packets to the target, hoping to overwhelm it. This attack is ineffective against modern servers. It is just not possible to overwhelm a server, or even most workstations, with enough pings to render the target unresponsive. But when executed by a large number of coordinated source computers against a single target computer, this attack can be very effective. This second variety of ping flood falls into the category called a distributed denial of service (DDoS) attack.

Teardrop attack. In a teardrop attack, the attacker sends fragments of packets with bad values in them, which cause the target system to crash when it tries to reassemble the fragments. Like the ping of death attack, the teardrop attack has been around long enough for vendors to have released patches to avoid it.

SYN flood attacks. In a SYN flood attack, the attacker sends unlimited synchronize (SYN) requests to the host system. The SYN requests, which are the first step in initiating communication, are supposed to be responded to by the attacker's system but aren't. Essentially, the attacker sends the target the starting SYN request. This causes the server to set up some resources to handle the connection, and respond to the client with both the SYN and ACK bits turned on, acknowledging the synchronization request. The attacker is supposed to respond with the ACK bit turned on. In this attack, the attacker just floods the target with SYN packets, never responding. This can overwhelm the target system with phantom connection requests and render it unable to respond to legitimate requests.

Most modern firewalls can block this attack. This is because most modern firewalls look at the entire "conversation" between client and server, not just each individual packet. So while a single packet with the SYN bit turned on from a specific client is totally normal traffic, 10,000 such packets in under five minutes is not, and will be blocked. However, in the game of chess that is modern cybersecurity, the attacker can change the IP address and even the MAC address of his or her attack information to get around such blocking. Remember that the objective is to tie up resources on the target system such that a target system cannot process legitimate requests in a timely fashion or cannot process them at all.

> **NOTE**
>
> The type of firewall technology that allows blocking of SYN floods is called stateful packet inspection (SPI). Although many operating system firewalls provide just standard packet-filtering, most routers, even inexpensive routers for home use, will support SPI.

Land attacks. In a land attack, the attacker sends a fake TCP SYN packet with the same source and destination IP addresses and ports as the target computer. Basically, the computer is tricked into thinking it is sending messages to itself because the packets coming in from the outside are using the computer's own IP address.

Smurf attacks. A smurf attack generates a large number of ICMP echo requests from a single request, acting like an amplifier. This causes a traffic jam in the target network. Worse still, if the routing device on the target network accepts the requests, computers on that network will reply to each echo, increasing the traffic jam.

Fraggle attacks. A fraggle attack is similar to a smurf attack, except that it uses spoofed UDP packets instead of ICMP echo replies. Fraggle attacks can often bypass a firewall.

Packet mistreating attacks. A packet mistreating attack occurs when a compromised router mishandles packets. This type of attack results in congestion in a part of the network.

Network Traffic Analysis Tools

A **sniffer** is computer software or hardware that can intercept and log traffic passing over a digital network. Sniffers are used to collect digital evidence. Commonly applied sniffers include Tcpdump—see *http://www.tcpdump.org/tcpdump_man.html*—for various UNIX platforms and WinDump—see *http://www.winpcap.org/windump/*—which is a version of Tcpdump for Windows. These programs extract network packets and perform a statistical analysis on the dumped information.

Use them to measure response time, the percentage of packets lost, and TCP/UDP connection start-up and end.

The following are some other popular tools for network analysis:

- Wireshark can be found at *http://www.wireshark.org*.
- CommView can be found at *http://www.tamos.com/products/commview/*.
- Softperfect Network Protocol Analyzer can be found at *http://www.softperfect.com*.
- HTTP Sniffer can be found at *http://www.effetech.com/sniffer/*.
- ngrep can be found at *http://sourceforge.net/projects/ngrep/*.
- OmniPeek can be found at *http://www.wildpackets.com*.

Some software tools for investigating network traffic include the following:

- NetWitness can be found at *http://www.netwitness.com*.
- NetResident can be found at *http://www.tamos.com/products/netresident/*.
- InfiniStream can be found at *http://www.netscout.com/products/service_provider/ nSAS/sniffer_analysis/Pages/InfiniStream_Console.aspx*.
- Snort can be found at *http://www.snort.org*.
- Nmap can be found at *http://www.nmap.org*.

When collecting evidence on a network, it is vital to document what you've collected. Specifically, note in detail who collected the evidence, when it was collected, where it was collected, and how it was collected. Then analyze the evidence to construct a clearer picture of all activities that have occurred. If possible, organize the evidence by time and function.

A few of these tools bear a closer look.

Wireshark

Wireshark is a widely used packet sniffer. It is a free download at *http://www.wireshark.org* and available for several operating systems. It is very easy to use. The user simply selects an interface, or network card, then starts the process.

Figure 12-1 shows the address the packets are either coming from or going to, protocols, timing, and many other useful pieces of information. At any time, you can stop the packet-capture process and view the individual packets. Clicking on any given packet displays the details of that particular packet, an example of which is shown in Figure 12-2.

You can immediately see the source and destination MAC address, protocol, source and destination IP addresses—if appropriate—and much more. In fact, if you look at the bottom of the screen, you can see the data in the packet. The data won't always be readable, however. If the packet is an image file, for instance, or is encrypted, you won't be able to read much of what is displayed.

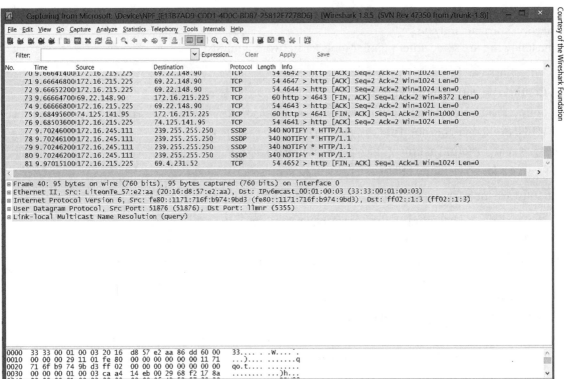

FIGURE 12-1

Wireshark packet capture.

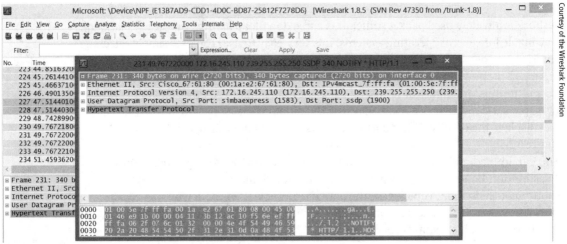

FIGURE 12-2

Wireshark packet details.

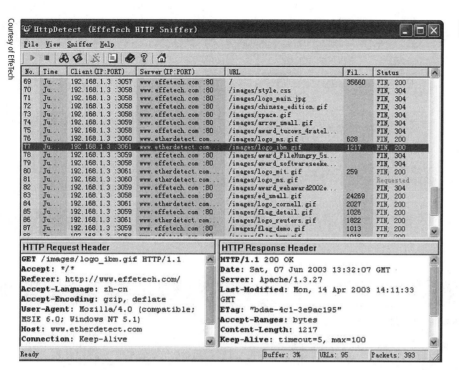

Courtesy of EffeTech

FIGURE 12-3

HTTPSniffer.

HTTPSniffer

Much like Wireshark, this product is easy to use and has a free trial version. It is used specifically to capture Web traffic. You can see all the HTTP commands going to the server and the responses from the server.

This is a very simple and intuitive product, as seen in Figure 12-3. To properly interpret this data, you need to understand the basic HTTP commands as well as the response codes. The HTTP commands are described in Table 12-1.

The most common are GET, HEAD, PUT, and POST. In fact, you might see only those four during most of your analysis of Web traffic.

FYI

There is sometimes some confusion over HTTP GET and POST commands. The HTML specifications define the difference between GET and POST: GET means that form data is to be encoded by a browser into a URL, whereas POST indicates that the form data is to appear inside a message body. They both actually send data to the server. Neither is getting data from the server. There are some great articles on the Web that describe the technical nuances of these two commands, one of which is at *http://www.diffen.com/difference/Get_vs_Post*.

TABLE 12-1 HTTP commands.

HTTP COMMAND	DESCRIPTION
GET	Request to read a Web page
HEAD	Request to read just the head section of a Web page
PUT	Request to write a Web page
POST	Request to append to a page
DELETE	Remove the Web page
LINK	Connects two existing resources
UNLINK	Breaks an existing connection between two resources

TABLE 12-2 HTTP response message.

MESSAGE RANGE	MEANING
100–199	These are just informational. The server is giving your browser some information, most of which will never be displayed to the user. For example, when you switch from HTTP to HTTPS, a 101 message goes to the browser telling it that the protocol is changing.
200–299	These are basically "OK" messages, meaning that whatever the browser requested, the server successfully processed.
300–399	These are redirect messages telling the browser to go to another URL. For example, 301 means that the requested resource has permanently moved to a new URL, whereas message 307 indicates the move is temporary.
400–499	These are client errors, and the ones most often shown to the end user. You may be puzzled—how is a file not found a client error? It is because the client requested a page that does not exist. The server processed the request without problem, but the request was invalid.
500–599	These are server-side errors. For example, 503 means the service requested is down, possibly overloaded. You will see this error frequently in DoS attacks.

Courtesy of Nmap.org

FIGURE 12-4

Nmap.

12

Performing
Network Analysis

The response codes are just as important. You have probably seen "Error 404 file not found," but there are a host of messages going back and forth, most of which you don't see. The messages are shown in Table 12-2.

The vendor also supplies an online Flash tutorial, which goes through the nuances of using this product. The tutorial can be found at *http://www.effetech.com/sniffer/tutorial.htm*.

Nmap

Nmap is popular with both network security administrators and hackers; an example is shown in Figure 12-4. It allows the user to map out what ports are open on a target system and what services are running. Nmap is a command-line tool, but has a Windows interface that is available for free.

This tool is popular with hackers because it can be configured to operate rather stealthily and determine all open ports on an individual machine, or for all machines in an entire range of IP addresses. It is popular with administrators because of its ability to discover open ports on the network. Such ports could indicate spyware, a backdoor, or many other attacks.

Snort

Snort is primarily used as an open source intrusion detection system. But it can also function as a robust packet sniffer with a lot of configuration options. For full installation instructions, visit *http://www.snort.org*. They also offer a free manual at *http://www.snort .org/assets/82/snort_manual.pdf*. For network analysis, you want to run snort as a packet sniffer and configure it to log verbose data.

NetWitness

This is a product from RSA that has a freeware version at *http://www.emc.com/security/ rsa-netwitness.htm#!freeware*. It is definitely worth taking a look, but this product is not nearly as easy to use as Wireshark is.

Network Traffic Analysis

Once you have access to the appropriate tools, you can either examine the live traffic or logs to determine if a crime has been (or is being) committed and to gather evidence about that crime.

Using Log Files as Evidence

An end-to-end investigation looks at an entire attack. It looks at how an attack starts, at the intermediate devices, and at the result of the attack. Evidence may reside on each device in the path from the attacking system to the victim. Routers, virtual private networks (VPNs), and other devices produce logs. Network security devices, such as firewalls and intrusion detection systems (IDSs), also generate logs. An IDS is software that automates the process of monitoring events occurring in a computer system or network and analyzing them for signs of possible incidents, and attempting to stop detected possible incidents.

A device's log files contain the primary records of a person's activities on a system or network. For example, authentication logs show accounts related to a particular event and the authenticated user's IP address. They contain date and timestamps as well as the username and IP address of the requestor. Application logs record the time, date, and application identifier. When someone uses an application, it produces a text file on the desktop system containing the application identifier, the date and time the user started the application, and how long that person used the application.

Operating systems log certain events, such as the use of devices, errors, and reboots. Operating system logs can be analyzed to identify patterns of activity and unusual events. Network device logs, such as firewall and router logs, provide information about the activities that take place on the network. You can also coordinate and synchronize them with logs provided by other systems to create a more complete picture of an attack.

For example, a firewall log may show access attempts that the firewall blocked. These attempts may indicate an attack. Log files can show how an attacker entered a network. They can also help find the source of illicit activities. Log files from servers and Windows security event logs on domain controllers, for instance, can attribute activities to a specific user account. This may lead you to the person responsible.

Intrusion detection systems record events that match known attack signatures, such as buffer overflows or malicious code execution. Configure an IDS to capture all the network traffic associated with a specific event. In this way, you can discover what commands an attacker ran and what files he or she accessed. You can also determine what files the criminal downloaded, such as malicious code, or uploaded, such as files copied from the system.

You bump into a few problems when using log files, however. One is that logs change rapidly, and getting permission to collect evidence from some sources, such as Internet service providers (ISPs), takes time. In addition, volatile evidence is easily lost. Another is that hackers can easily alter logs to include false information.

Wireless

Wireless networks are almost everywhere today. Some cities even provide wireless network access to citizens in their areas. In fact, you can often access wireless networks while on an airplane in flight. Wireless connections allow devices to connect to a network without having to physically connect via a cord. This makes it easy to connect computers and devices when running an actual physical cord is either difficult or not practical.

There are some basics of wireless networks you should know:

- **802.11a**—This was the first widely used Wi-Fi standard; it operated at 5 GHz and was relatively slow.
- **802.11b**—This standard operated at 2.4 GHz and had an indoor range of 125 ft with a bandwidth of 11 megabits per second (Mbps).
- **802.11g**—There are still many of these wireless networks in operation, but you can no longer purchase new Wi-Fi access points that use 802.11g. This standard includes backward compatibility with 802.11b. 802.11g has an indoor range of 125 ft and a bandwidth of 54 Mbps.
- **802.11n**—This standard was a tremendous improvement over preceding wireless networks. It obtained a bandwidth of 100 to 140 Mbps. It operates at frequencies of 2.4 or 5.0 GHz, and has an indoor range of up to 230 ft.
- **IEEE 802.11n-2009**—This technology gets bandwidth of up to 600 Mbps with the use of four spatial streams at a channel width of 40 MHz. It uses **multiple-input multiple-output (MIMO)**, which uses multiple antennas to coherently resolve more information than possible using a single antenna.

Many wireless local area networks (LANs) are either not secured or not well secured. Attackers may compromise a server to allow public access to stolen software, music, movies, or pornography.

The following are the most important forensic concerns with wireless networks:

- Did a perpetrator use a wireless network entry point for a direct network attack or theft of data?
- Did an attacker use a third-party wireless network, such as a hotel hotspot, to conceal his or her identity?

In addition to evidence that moves across wireless networking devices, you may find evidence in wireless storage devices. These devices include wireless digital and video cameras, wireless printers with storage capacity, wireless network-attached storage (NAS) devices, PDAs and smartphones, wireless digital video recorders (DVRs), and wireless game consoles.

Several tools are available just for discovering wireless networks. Some of the more popular tools include the following:

- NetStumbler at *http://www.NetStumbler.com*
- MacStumbler at *http://www.MacStumbler.com*
- iStumbler at *http://www.iStumbler.net*

There are even apps available for both iPhone and Android that can scan for wireless networks. So Wi-Fi scanning can be accomplished with relative ease. If a hacker discovers a poorly secured wireless network, one thing he or she may try is to access the wireless access point's administrative screen. Unfortunately, too many people turn on these devices and don't think to change the default settings. There are Web sites that store default passwords that anyone can look up. One very popular Web site is *http://www .routerpasswords.com*.

Router Forensics

Using network forensics, you can determine the type of attack over a network. You can also in some cases trace the path back to the attacker. A router is a hardware or software device that forwards data packets across a network to a destination network. The destination network could be multiple networks away. A router may contain read-only memory with power-on self test code, flash memory containing the router's operating system, nonvolatile random access memory (RAM) containing configuration information, and volatile RAM containing the routing tables and log information.

Router Basics

The basic networking hardware devices are as follows:

- Network card
- Hub
- Switch
- Router

A network interface card (NIC) is an expansion board you insert into a computer or a motherboard-mounted bit of hardware that allows the computer to be connected to a network. A NIC handles many things, such as the following:

- Signal encoding and decoding
- Data buffering and transmission
- Media Access Control
- Data encapsulation, or building the frame around the data

These are relatively simple devices that don't store information that you can examine for any appreciable period of time.

A hub is used to connect computers on an Ethernet LAN. Essentially, a hub does not do anything to see that packets get to their proper destination. Instead, the hub takes any packet it receives and simply sends a copy of it out every port it has, except the port on which the packet entered the hub. This is based on the theory that the packet is going somewhere, so send it out all available avenues. This causes a lot of excess network traffic; hubs are used very rarely in modern networks.

A switch prevents traffic jams by ensuring that data goes straight from its origin to its proper destination, with no wandering in between. Switches remember the address of every node on the network and anticipate where data needs to go. A switch operates only with the computers on the same LAN. That is because a switch operates based on the MAC address in a packet, which is not routable. It cannot send data out to the Internet or across a wide area network (WAN). These functions require a router.

A router is similar to a switch, but it can also connect different logical networks or subnets and enable traffic that is destined for the networks on the other side of the router to pass through. Routers typically provide improved security functions compared with a switch. Routers utilize the IP address, which is routable, to determine the path of outgoing packets. Routers work at the Network Layer of the OSI model.

Routers determine where to send information from one computer to another. Routers are specialized computers that send your messages and those of every other Internet user speeding to their destinations along thousands of pathways. Routers maintain a **routing table** to keep track of routes, or which connections are to be used for different networks. Some of these routes are programmed in manually, but many are "learned" automatically by the router. It does this by examining incoming packets and, if one comes

---

FYI

In practice, many of these definitions have become blurred. For example, if you go into your favorite electronics store and ask for a hub, the sales clerk will probably hand you a switch because the terms have become interchangeable. Also, there are now specialized switches that use factors other than the MAC address to determine the path they send packets on. These devices have many names, including upper-layer switches, application switches, and so on.

from an IP address the router has not seen before, adding that address to its routing table. Modern routers also inform each other about new routes and routes that are no longer working to make routing as efficient as possible.

Modern routers are complex devices. They handle packets, often have firewall and Dynamic Host Configuration Protocol (DHCP) capabilities, are programmable, and maintain logs. The gold standard in routers is Cisco, and it is worthwhile to become familiar with at least the basics of working with a Cisco router. For a good overview of Cisco routers, the document at *http://www.ciscorebateprogram.com/en/US/docs/routers/ access/800/850/software/configuration/guide/routconf.pdf* will be a great help.

Types of Router Attacks

Routers can be vulnerable to several types of attacks, including router table poisoning. Router table poisoning is one of the most common and effective attacks. To carry out this type of attack, an attacker alters the routing data update packets that the routing protocols need. This results in incorrect entries in the routing table. This, in turn, can result in artificial congestion, can overwhelm the router, or can allow an attacker access to data in the compromised network by sending data to a different destination or over a different route than anticipated.

Getting Evidence from the Router

Even though a router is just a special-purpose computer running a routing program, getting evidence from a router is quite different from getting evidence from a PC, laptop, or server. The first major difference is that with a router, you do not shut down the device and image it. The reason is that once you shut it down, you will have potentially lost valuable evidence. For this reason, router forensics requires a great deal of care. You must make absolutely certain not to alter anything, and you must be meticulous in documenting your process.

The first step is to connect with the router so you can run certain commands. HyperTerminal is a free tool that can be used to connect to and interact with your routers. Because the router is live, it is important to record everything you do. Fortunately, HyperTerminal makes this easy, as shown in Figure 12-5.

Several commands are important to router forensics. The most important and most commonly used commands from Cisco routers are described here. The commands for different brands of routers, or even different Cisco routers, may be different, but there are equivalent commands:

FIGURE 12-5

Recording with HyperTerminal.

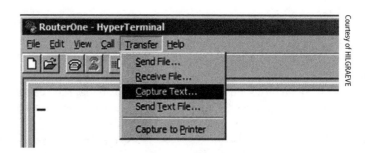

Courtesy of HILGRAEVE

The show version command provides a significant amount of hardware and software detail about the router. It displays the platform, operating system version, system image file, any interfaces, the amount of RAM the router has, and the number of network and voice interfaces there are.

The show running-config command provides the currently executing configuration.

The show startup-config command provides the system's start-up configurations. Differences between show startup-config and show running-config can be indicative of a hacker having altered the system.

The show ip route command shows the routing table. Manipulating that routing table is one primary reason hackers infiltrate routers.

You will probably find the preceding commands useful in your forensic examination. However, you may find several other commands useful as well, including the following:

- show clock detail
- show reload
- show ip arp
- show users
- show logging
- show ip interface
- show interfaces
- show tcp brief all
- show ip sockets
- show ip nat translations verbose
- show ip cache flow
- show ip cef
- show snmp user
- show snmp group

The release of version 11.2 of Cisco IOS (operating system) introduced the new command show tech-support. This command has allowed for the collection of multiple sources of information concerning the router in a single command. This one command outputs the same as running all of the following commands:

- show version
- show running-config
- show stacks
- show interface
- show controller
- show process cpu
- show process memory
- show buffers

For readers who are looking for more in-depth, highly technical router forensics information, the following papers might be interesting:

- *http://www.cs.uml.edu/~xinwenfu/paper/D-SPAN10_RouterForensics_Fu.pdf*
- *http://www.recurity-labs.com/content/pub/RecurityLabs_Developments_in_IOS _Forensics_USA08.pdf*

Firewall Forensics

Examining the firewall should be a fundamental part of any network forensic analysis. Because all external traffic must come through the firewall, it is imperative that the firewall logs be examined carefully. They frequently contain valuable evidence.

Firewall Basics

A basic working understanding of firewalls is required to do proper firewall forensics. There are several ways to categorize firewalls, but there are two that are more basic than the rest: packet filtering and stateful packet inspection.

Packet Filter

This is the most basic type of firewall. It simply filters incoming packets and either allows them entrance or denies them passage based on a set of rules. This is also referred to as a screened firewall. It can filter packets based on packet size, protocol used, source IP address, and so on. Many routers offer this type of firewall option in addition to their normal routing functions.

Stateful Packet Inspection

The stateful packet inspection (SPI) firewall examines each and every packet, denying or permitting based on not only the current packet, but also considering previous packets in the conversation. This means that the firewall is aware of the context in which a specific packet was sent. This makes these firewalls far less susceptible to ping floods, SYN floods, and spoofing.

Collecting Data

All the traffic going through a firewall is part of a connection. A connection consists of two Internet Protocol (IP) addresses that are communicating with each other and two port numbers that identify the protocol or service. The concatenation of an IP address and a port number is called a socket and is unique while it is active. The three ranges for port numbers are as follows:

- **Well-known ports**—The well-known ports are those from 0 to 1023.
- **Registered ports**—The registered ports are those from 1024 to 49151.
- **Dynamic ports**—The dynamic, or private, ports are those from 49152 to 65535.

Attempts on the same set of ports from many different Internet sources are usually due to *decoy* scans. In a decoy scan strategy, an attacker spoofs scans that originate from a large number of decoy machines and adds his or her IP address somewhere in the mix.

Earlier in this chapter, you learned a list of common ports. You should carefully check the firewall logs for any sort of connections or attempted connections on those ports. You also learned about packet flags that might indicate a port scan. If your firewall logs such details, you need to scan the log for any packets that might indicate a scan.

Using protocol analysis may help you determine who the attacker is. For example, you can ping each of the systems and match up the Time to Live (TTL) fields in those responses with the connection attempts. The TTL is not actually a time, per se, but rather the number of routers between a source and destination. The TTLs should match, plus or minus one or two in case the route is slightly different. If the TTL of the captured traffic and the TTL of the test/trace traffic don't match closely, the addresses are being spoofed by an attacker. One drawback is that to know the actual number of hops, you must know the starting TTL that is being used. The idea of the TTL is that an IP packet is discarded when its TTL, decreased at each intermediate router, reaches zero before the packet gets to its destination.

Analyze the firewall logs in depth to look for decoy addresses originating from the same subnets. You will likely see that the attacker has connected recently, whereas the decoyed addresses have not.

12

Performing
Network Analysis

CHAPTER SUMMARY

In this chapter, you learned about network packets, how to capture them, and how to analyze them. You were also introduced to the concepts of network analysis, including the use of popular network tools such as Wireshark. Then, you learned the basic functionality of routers and how to perform basic router forensics. You also saw how firewalls work and how to perform a forensic analysis of the firewall logs.

KEY CONCEPTS AND TERMS

Multiple-input multiple-output (MIMO)
Routing table
Sniffer

CHAPTER 12 ASSESSMENT

1. Which type of firewall is most likely to prevent SYN floods?

   A. Packet filtering
   B. Static
   C. Stateful packet inspection
   D. Dynamic

2. What does a 500 HTTP response indicate?

   A. Client error
   B. OK
   C. Redirect
   D. Server error

3. Why would you *not* turn off a router before examining it for evidence?

   A. You may destroy evidence.
   B. You would turn it off.
   C. It will lose its routing tables when powered off.
   D. It violates FBI forensic guidelines.

4. What does a router use to determine the path on which to send packets?

   A. MAC address
   B. IP address
   C. Protocol used
   D. Next available port

5. Which header would have the sender's MAC address?

   A. TCP
   B. IP
   C. Ethernet
   D. None

PART THREE

Incident Response and Resources

CHAPTER 13   **Incident and Intrusion Response**   256

CHAPTER 14   **Trends and Future Directions**   266

CHAPTER 15   **System Forensics Resources**   277

Incident and Intrusion Response

I N THIS CHAPTER, YOU WILL LEARN about the relationship between incident response and forensics. When an incident occurs, be it a disaster or an intrusion, forensics may be the best method to discover what went wrong and, thus, work to avoid it reoccurring. Forensic techniques also provide methods for recovering data in the event of a disaster. It is always possible that the disaster was caused by an act leading to criminal prosecution or an act of negligence that would warrant civil litigation.

Chapter 13 Topics

This chapter covers the following topics and concepts:

- What disaster recovery is
- How to preserve evidence
- What you need to know to be able to add forensics to incident response

Chapter 13 Goals

When you complete this chapter, you will be able to:

- Understand key disaster recovery terms, such as BIA, MTD, BCP, and DRP
- Understand the terms for the phases of incident response
- Be able to integrate forensics into an incident response plan

Disaster Recovery

Disaster recovery, business continuity, and forensics have become closely related topics. You might think forensics applies only to criminal activities; it often does. However, after an information technology–related disaster, forensic techniques may be the best method for determining what caused the disaster and for avoiding a repeat of that disaster, or at least mitigating its consequences, in the future.

The forensic process really begins once an incident has been discovered, but it is not fully under way until after the disaster or incident is contained. However, before you examine the forensic process for disasters, it is a good idea to start with a basic understanding of disaster recovery.

Incident Response Plan

All organizations must plan for the possibility of some disaster occurring that disrupts normal operations. When narrowing the focus to just computer-related operations, you need to consider a number of types of potential disasters. Of course, you need to plan for such events as:

- Fire
- Flood
- Hurricane
- Tornado

However, those do not involve computer forensics. So this chapter focuses only on computer disasters, such as the following, regardless of the cause:

- Hard drive failure
- Network outage
- Malware infection
- Data theft or deletion
- Intrusion

Each of these activities can disrupt normal operations for an organization's computer systems and, therefore, constitute a disaster. There are actually two plans most organizations have for responding to such disaster. Those are the **business continuity plan (BCP)** and the **disaster recovery plan (DRP)**. A BCP is focused on keeping the organization functioning as well as possible until a full recovery can be made. A DRP is focused on executing a full recovery to normal operations. (Although some experts differentiate between the terms disaster recovery plan and incident response plan, this chapter uses the terms interchangeably.) For example, suppose a virus takes the main Web server offline. A BCP would be concerned about what can be done to get at least minimal operations going until such time as the organization can be returned to full functionality. It might provide for temporarily using an old server that could provide minimal functionality but that may not be as robust. A DRP would be focused on actually returning the organization to full functionality. In the scenario just described, this would be having a full Web server, equivalent to the failed server, back online and running at full capacity.

You should be familiar with the following federal standards for BCPs:

- **ISO 27001**—Requirements for Information Security Management Systems. Section 14 addresses business continuity management.
- **NIST 800-34**—Contingency Planning Guide for Information Technology Systems. This contains a seven-step process for BCP and DRP projects from the U.S. National Institute for Standards and Technology.
- **NFPA 1600**—Standard on Disaster/Emergency Management and Business Continuity Programs. This is from the U.S. National Fire Protection Association.

These standards provide a good overview of what should be covered in any business continuity plan, and some, like NIST 800-34, are also applicable to disaster recovery plans. You should certainly consider reviewing these standards at some point in your career. For the purposes of forensic examination, you don't need to be an expert in disaster recovery—just a basic overview of the process is sufficient. The essential steps are outlined here.

Business Impact Analysis

Business impact analysis (BIA) is a process whereby the disaster recovery team contemplates likely disasters and what impact each would have on the organization. For example, a company that ships goods to retail stores, but does not sell directly to the public, might be slightly affected if its Web server were down for a day. A company that sells directly to the public both in store and online would be moderately affected by such an outage. And a completely e-commerce company, one that sells products only online, would be severely affected.

Usually some sort of table is created listing the various disasters being planned for and the impact they would have on the organization. In more complex scenarios, the organization may be broken down into subsections, and the impact of each disaster on each piece of the organization is rated. Whether a plan goes into great detail or not, one item that must be considered is **maximum tolerable downtime (MTD)**. That is, how long can the system or systems be down before it is impossible for the organization to recover? Imagine your favorite e-commerce site were down. You may be a loyal customer and wait for it to come back up. But as time goes on, fewer and fewer customers would wait, and more money would be lost, until the company reaches a point at which it simply cannot recover. If the disaster recovery team knows the MTD for the organization as well as for portions of the organization, it can then prioritize the recovery plan.

Two other terms relate to maximum tolerable downtime. **Mean time to repair (MTTR)** is the average time it takes to repair an item, and **mean time to failure (MTTF)** is the amount of time, on average, before a given device is likely to fail through normal use. These are important questions to answer when performing a business impact analysis. If an organization cannot operate without a given piece of equipment for more than 14 days and still recover, yet the mean time to repair is 7 days, that means you have only 7 days after a disaster to initiate repairs or the organization will not be able to recover.

The Recovery Plan

The recovery plan has two parts. The ultimate goal is a complete recovery, and this is outlined in the disaster recovery plan. But unless that DRP is going to get the organization back up to full capacity within 24 hours or less, there will need to also be a BCP, a plan for how to get at least minimal functionality until full recovery is accomplished. Both plans are based on the priorities that were established during the business impact analysis phase.

Even though the disaster recovery plan and the business continuity plan don't have exactly the same goals, they do require the same questions to be asked:

1. Do you have alternate equipment identified?
2. If needed, do you have alternate facilities identified?
3. Is there a mechanism in place for contacting all affected parties, employees, vendors, customers, and contractors, even if the primary means of communication are down?
4. Is there off-site backup of the data?
5. Can that backup be readily retrieved and restored?

When considering backups and restoring backups, you need to think about what type of backups you have. Although database administrators may use a number of different types of data backups, from a security point of view, there are three primary backup types you need to be concerned with:

- **Full**—All changes
- **Differential**—All changes since the last full backup
- **Incremental**—All changes since the last backup of any type

If you did a full backup, then just restore the last backup. However, if the backup strategy includes differential or incremental backups, and it probably will, then there will be additional backup data to restore.

There is another type of backup that is becoming more popular, called **hierarchical storage management (HSM)**. HSM provides continuous online backup by using optical or tape "jukeboxes." It appears as an infinite disk to the system, and can be configured to provide the closest version of an available, real-time backup.

The Post-Recovery Follow-Up

Different disaster recovery textbooks label this differently; however, the intention is the same. When the disaster is over and the organization has recovered, you have to find out what happened and why. This is where forensics comes into play. This phase is not necessarily about assigning blame; it is about discovering if the disaster was caused by some weakness in the system. That could be an act of negligence by an individual, it could be a gap in policy, or it could be an intentional act. But if the root cause is not discovered and addressed, the chances of the same disaster occurring again are significant.

FYI

Even though more organizations are going to electronic backups, it is important to consider backup media rotation. Even with electronic backup, you don't have infinite storage and will eventually have to overwrite something. This necessitates overwriting and reusing media. There are two main approaches to this. One is the Tower of Hanoi, which is fairly complicated and, thus, is used most often with automated backup strategies. The more common approach, for manually managed backups, is the Grandfather-Father-Son scheme. To illustrate this, consider a server using traditional tape backup that is backed up daily. Each daily backup is the son. At the end of the week, a weekly backup is made. That weekly backup is the father. Now, the daily backups begin to be reused. At the end of the month, there is a monthly backup made. That is the grandfather, and then the weekly backups can begin to be reused. This is a simple and widely used system to reuse backup media.

Incident Response

When an incident occurs, regardless of the level or severity of the incident, there needs to be an organized response. For example, if a single workstation is infected with a virus, this probably does not constitute a disaster. However, if it is not responded to quickly, it may grow into a disaster as the virus spreads. Proper incident response is important. Every incident response plan must include some key steps, which are outlined in this section.

Containment

The first step is always to limit the incident. This means keeping it from affecting more systems. In the case of a virus, the strategy is to keep the virus from spreading. It is probably a good idea to have a policy in place that instructs users to disconnect their computers from the network and then call tech support if they suspect they have a virus. This contains the virus and prevents it from spreading further.

Other incidents might not have such a clear containment path. For example, if there is an intruder getting into the Web server, how is that contained? First, the Web server itself is isolated from the rest of the network. Then, you seek to prevent further intrusion. This can be done by changing passwords throughout the organization, on the assumption that the intruder might have compromised passwords.

Although the specifics of containment might vary, the goal does not. Limit the spread of whatever the incident is, as much as possible. This phase must occur before any others. It is vital that the incident's effects not spread further. This must be addressed before you attempt to eradicate.

Eradication

Once the incident is contained, the next step is to eradicate the problem. In the case of malware, the issue is to remove the malware. In some cases, anti-malware, such as Norton, McAfee, Kaspersky, or AVG, can remove the malware. In other cases, the IT staff will need to manually remove the malware.

Other attacks are not so clear. For example, if the incident is an intruder infiltrating the network via SQL injection, what does eradication entail? The first step is to fix whatever vulnerability allowed the intruder to get in in the first place. In the case of SQL injection, it would involve correcting the flaws in the Web page that allowed this to occur.

Regardless of the particular incident, eradication needs to be thorough. This means a comprehensive examination of what occurred and how far it reached. It is imperative to ensure that the issue was completely addressed.

This is the stage at which forensics must begin. If the vulnerability is simply eradicated, it is likely that evidence will be eradicated along with it. It is imperative that you begin collecting evidence prior to eradicating the vulnerability. This may involve performing the forensic investigation prior to any eradication steps taking place. In some cases, it is just not possible to perform a full forensic investigation while keeping the systems on hold. In that case, image the drives involved so that a forensic investigation can be conducted at a later time.

Recovery

Recovery involves returning the affected systems to normal status. In the case of malware, that means ensuring the system is back in full working order with absolutely no presence of the malware. In many cases, this involves restoring software and data from a backup source that has been verified to be free from the malware infection.

Follow-Up

The follow-up phase is another stage at which forensics plays a critical role. The IT team must determine how this incident occurred and what steps can be taken to prevent the incident from reoccurring. Clearly, those decisions cannot be made without the input from the forensic examination.

> **NOTE**
>
> Corporations are becoming more interested in their IT security teams, including personnel with forensic training. Even if the goal is not to collect evidence for legal proceedings, the same forensic techniques can be utilized to determine the exact cause and extent of a computer security breach. This information is absolutely essential for preventing future incidents.

Preserving Evidence

An event is any observable occurrence within a system or network. This includes any activity on the network, such as when a user accesses files on a server or when a firewall blocks network traffic. Adverse events are events with negative results or negative consequences. Attacks on systems are adverse events. Adverse events discussed here are events that are computer-security related. They are not events caused by sources such as natural disasters and power failures. A computer security incident is any event that violates an organization's security policies. This includes computer security policies, acceptable use policies, or standard security practices. The following are examples of computer security incidents:

- **Denial of service (DoS) attacks**—A DoS attack could result from an attacker sending specially crafted packets to a Web server that cause it to crash. It could also result from an attacker directing hundreds of compromised external workstations to send many Internet Control Message Protocol (ICMP) requests to an organization's network. When the attack comes simultaneously from multiple coordinated sources, it is referred to as a distributed DoS (DDoS) attack.

- **Malicious code**—Malicious software, or malware, is any malicious code, such as viruses, worms, and Trojans. For example, a worm uses open file shares to quickly infect hundreds of systems in an organization. An employee may innocently introduce viruses into a network from his or her home computer on a USB thumb drive. When the employee plugs the USB drive into the work computer, the virus infects the work computer and, subsequently, can infect the entire work network.

- **Unauthorized access**—This includes any time someone accesses files he or she is not specifically authorized to access. The person gaining access can be someone within the organization, such as an employee or contractor, or an external attacker. If shared files are not locked down with appropriate permissions, users may stumble upon data they shouldn't see. If databases used by Web servers are not secure, attackers may be able to access sensitive customer data, such as credit card information, from anywhere on the Internet.

- **Inappropriate usage**—Inappropriate usage could take a number of forms. For example, a user might provide illegal copies of software to others through peer-to-peer (P2P) file-sharing services. This same P2P software could cause data leakage resulting in private data from the user's computer being shared on the Internet to anyone else using the same P2P software. Or a person might threaten another person through e-mail.

Regardless of the specifics of the incident, it is critical that the evidence be preserved. However, this topic takes on a new perspective in the case of incident response. The usual emphasis for corporate disaster recovery is simply a return to normal operations as soon as possible. Frequently, this is done at the expense of preserving forensic evidence. This can lead to many problems.

FYI

The issue of preserving evidence is very much the same as with non-computer crimes. Imagine that a person was murdered in a hotel room. What if the hotel focused only on returning the room to normal use and immediately thoroughly cleaned the room and rented it to a new guest? This would destroy all physical evidence and make prosecuting the murderer extremely difficult. Unfortunately, an analogous situation frequently occurs with IT systems after a computer breach. In their haste to restore the systems to normal operations, IT personnel routinely destroy evidence.

First and foremost, failure to preserve forensic information will prevent the IT team from effectively evaluating the cause of the incident and adjusting company policies and procedures to reduce the risk of such an incident being repeated. Even if the incident does not involve a crime, or the company simply does not desire to prosecute, forensic data is an integral part of preventing future incidents.

There are also situations in which the organization may not have initially thought a crime was committed, but further investigation reveals that a criminal act did occur. For example, a hard drive crash might initially be thought to be a normal failure of the device, but further examination uncovers malware that caused the hard drive to fail much sooner than it should have. If proper forensic procedures have not been followed, it may be impossible to prosecute or pursue civil litigation.

Adding Forensics to Incident Response

Realizing the importance of forensics in incident response is an important first step. But this realization still leaves the question of how to implement proper forensic procedures. There are specific steps that an IT department can take to intertwine forensic techniques with the company's incident response policies.

Forensic Resources

The first step is to identify forensic resources that the organization can utilize in case of an incident. No amount of policy change will be effective if the company does not have access to forensically trained individuals. One approach an organization can take is to get basic forensic training for its own IT security staff. Many computer-related college degrees now include forensic courses and most security-related degrees include at least an introductory forensic course. If no one on the company's IT security staff has had such training, it may be helpful to send staff members to be trained in computer forensics and perhaps to obtain one of the major forensic certifications.

Another option the organization can pursue is to identify an outside party that can respond to incidents with forensically trained personnel. In this case, part of incident planning would involve ensuring there is an agreement in place with a reliable forensic company or individual consultant. If this is the option an organization wants to pursue, it is critical to ensure that the company or individual has both an appropriate level of competency and the resources to respond to incidents.

Forensics and Policy

Once appropriate forensic resources have been identified, forensic methodology must be interwoven into the incident response policy for the organization. This means that all policies regarding disaster recovery and incident response will need to be updated.

The purpose of updating policies is to ensure that, in the process of recovering from an incident or disaster, evidence is not destroyed and the proper procedures to ensure the integrity and chain of custody of the evidence remain intact. For example, the policy regarding how to handle a malware infection would be modified so that as soon as the infection was contained, at least one infected machine would be imaged for forensic evidence prior to the eradication of the malware. In the case of external intrusions, the policies would be changed to preserve all logs prior to full recovery.

It is likely that even if the IT security staff is not trained specifically in forensics, they have some basic knowledge of the field. The reason is that many security textbooks now include at least a chapter on basic forensics. Most of the general computer security certifications, such as CompTIA Security+ and CISSP, also include sections on basic forensics. Even if your staff lacks the appropriate training to perform a forensic investigation, they should be trained well enough to know how to preserve evidence.

CHAPTER SUMMARY

In this chapter, you learned about the fundamentals of disaster recovery as well as how that process is affected by computer forensics. The most important lesson from this chapter is that every organization must intertwine forensic evidence gathering with its business continuity, disaster recovery, and incident response policies. As soon as an incident is contained, and before a vulnerability is eradicated, it is important to preserve the evidence. This evidence will be useful in gaining a better understanding of the causes of the incident, thus leading to better planning to avoid similar incidents in the future, and may be used, as needed, in the prosecution of the offenders.

KEY CONCEPTS AND TERMS

Business continuity plan (BCP)
Business impact analysis (BIA)
Disaster recovery plan (DRP)
Hierarchical storage
  management (HSM)

Maximum tolerable downtime
  (MTD)
Mean time to failure (MTTF)
Mean time to repair (MTTR)

13

Incident and Intrusion
Response

CHAPTER 13 ASSESSMENT

1. Which of the following assesses potential loss that could be caused by a disaster?

A. The business assessment (BA)
B. The business impact analysis (BIA)
C. The risk assessment (RA)
D. The business continuity plan (BCP)

2. Which of the following focuses on sustaining an organization's business functions during and after a disruption?

A. Business continuity plan
B. Business recovery plan
C. Continuity of operations plan
D. Disaster recovery plan

3. Once an intrusion into your organization's information system has been detected, which of the following actions should be performed first?

A. Eliminate all means of intruder access.
B. Contain the intrusion.
C. Determine to what extent systems and data are compromised.
D. Communicate with relevant parties.

4. A business continuity plan development depends most on:

A. Directives of senior management
B. Business impact analysis (BIA)
C. Scope and plan initiation
D. Skills of BCP committee

Trends and Future Directions

L IKE ANY FIELD RELATED TO SCIENCE AND TECHNOLOGY, the field of digital forensics is changing rapidly. Not only is the underlying technology quickly evolving, but the legal environment is changing as well. New laws can change how an analyst approaches an investigation. Techniques also evolve over time. This chapter explores the latest trends and what this might mean for the near future of computer forensics.

Chapter 14 Topics

This chapter covers the following topics and concepts:

- What the technology trends are and what their impact on forensics is
- What you need to know about the legal and procedural changes in forensics

Chapter 14 Goals

When you complete this chapter, you will be able to:

- Explain how increasing computing power affects forensics
- Describe the impact of new technology on forensics
- Investigate methods for extracting evidence from new technology
- Explain how new laws affect evidence collection

Technical Trends

Digital forensics is a new field. However, people have been analyzing digital systems and associated components since the first computers began to be used in business. At that time, early forensic investigators used tools to store and process data and support decision-making. The use of digital systems grew and evolved. So did the need to analyze those systems. Investigators needed to be able to determine what had been done and who was responsible.

One of the earliest uses of digital systems was to compute payroll. One of the earliest digital crimes was taking the "round-off"—the half-cent variance resulting from calculating an individual's pay. A criminal would move that round-off to his or her own account. In this type of fraud, a perpetrator stole very small amounts each time. However, the number of paychecks calculated made the total fraud quite large. This showed that digital crime is relatively easy to commit and difficult to detect. To make the situation worse, the courts frequently sentenced perpetrators to probation instead of prison.

Digital technology provides many benefits and reduces costs in a number of ways. Therefore, the use of digital technology to support business processes and nearly every other facet of modern life has increased. In parallel, criminals have made increasingly innovative use of digital techniques in their activities. The methods of protecting digital systems and associated assets have also grown. However, they haven't grown fast enough to keep pace with the growing number and complexity of attacks. Attackers now realize that there are many ways to obtain benefits from digital systems illegally. They can steal money and identities, and they can commit blackmail.

In a 1965 paper, Gordon E. Moore, cofounder of Intel, noted that the number of components in integrated circuits had doubled every 18 to 24 months from the invention of the integrated circuit in 1958 until 1965. He predicted that the trend would continue for at least 10 more years. In other words, he predicted, the number of transistors on an integrated circuit would double every two years for the next 10 years. This statement regarding the progression of integrated circuit capacity and capability became widely known as **Moore's law**, sometimes also called Moore's observation. More important, though, each doubling of capacity was done at half the cost. This means that a component that cost $100 would have twice the capability but would cost only $50 within 18 to 24 months. This can be seen in hundreds of modern digital devices, from DVD players and cell phones to computers and medical equipment.

Moore's law achieved its name and fame because it proved to be an accurate representation of a trend that continues today. Specifically, the capacity and capability of integrated circuits have doubled and the cost has been halved every 18 to 24 months since Moore noted the trend. Further, Moore's law applies to more than just integrated circuits. It also applies to some of the other primary drivers of computing capability: storage capacity, processor speed, capacity and cost, fiber optic communications, and more.

14

Trends and
Future Directions

Only human ingenuity limits new uses for technological solutions. In the 1950s, the UNIVAC I, the first commercial digital computer, was touted as having the capability to meet an organization's total computing requirements. Today, a typical low-end mobile phone has more capability and capacity than the UNIVAC I.

Moore's law also applies to digital forensics. You can expect to conduct investigations requiring analysis of an increasing volume of data from an increasing number of digital devices. Unfortunately, in the forensic world, Moore's law operates as if it's on steroids.

For example, digital storage capacity for a particular device might double in a year. The data that you might need to analyze could easily experience double that growth level. For example, a standard point-and-shoot digital camera now takes 5-megapixel photos. High-end cameras take 16-megapixel—or larger—photos. A typical Windows XP build consumes roughly 4 GB of disk space. A typical Windows 8 build consumes 8 GB to 10 GB. Although a single copy of a file or data record might be maintained for active use, you must often locate and examine all prior copies of that file.

Because of Moore's law, forensic specialists must develop new techniques, new software, and new hardware to perform forensic assessments. New techniques should simplify documentation of the chain of custody. You will have to determine what techniques have the greatest potential for obtaining needed information. In most investigations, analyzing all available data would be so costly as to be infeasible. Therefore, selectively evaluate data. Such selectivity is not unique to the digital world. It is the same concept that investigators have used for years to follow leads. For example, they often start by interviewing the most likely suspects and follow where the data leads to reach a conclusion. However, the U.S. legal system, helped by advertising and popular television, expects digital forensics to be unconstrained by such mundane factors as time, money, and available technology.

What Impact Does This Have on Forensics?

How does increasing computing power affect forensic investigations? The most obvious impact is the need for more storage on forensic servers. Most forensic labs use servers to store forensic images of suspect machines. If average laptops have 400 gigabytes (GB) to over a terabyte (TB) in hard drive storage, the server must be able to accommodate many terabytes of data.

The process of imaging a disk can also be slower. For example, utilizing the forensic dd utility with the netcat utility to image a suspect machine requires transmitting the image over a network. Clearly, the larger the drive being imaged, the more bandwidth will be required. It is recommended that forensic labs use the highest-capacity cabling available for the forensic lab, even possibly optical cable. To do otherwise will affect the efficiency of future forensic investigations.

Software as a Service

When computing first entered the marketplace, computer manufacturers typically provided software as part of a bundled product. A bundled product includes hardware, software, maintenance, and support sold together for a single price. It wasn't long before the industry recognized that it could sell software products individually. This resulted in the rise of companies such as Microsoft.

Another approach to selling software arose. This approach involves selling access to needed software on a time-sharing basis. The price of the software was essentially embedded in a mathematical algorithm, and a user paid for software based on his or her usage profile. This pricing model continued into personal computer (PC) and server technology.

Then the pricing algorithm was changed to address a number of concurrent users, a number of instances, or some other model. In addition, the idea of buying use of a software product morphed into the concept of software as a service (SaaS)—that is, software that a provider licenses to customers as a service on demand, through a subscription model.

The model under which an organization obtains software is important to forensic analysis because it affects four areas of an investigation:

- Who owns the software? Know whom to contact to obtain information regarding the functionality and patch levels of software.

- How can you get access to the program code? When software is obtained as a shared service, access is usually not possible. In such cases, use alternative techniques.

- What assurance do you have of the safety of a software product? You need to know that a particular software product doesn't contain malware that could alter the investigation.

- How can you keep the status of shared software static until the forensic investigation is complete?

The Cloud

It seems in any conversation about computer networks today you will hear mention of "the cloud." What exactly is it and how does it affect forensics? These are important questions now and will become more so in the next few years.

What is the cloud? In many ways, it is the concept of connectivity or a simplified way of thinking about the network. If you think about the Internet, for instance, it is actually a complex mesh of routers and paths. However, if it is drawn simply as a cloud, it is possible to concentrate on what can be done with the Internet, not how the Internet does what it does. For example, the idea of getting an e-mail from one point to the other through the cloud is a very simple one to understand without knowing the intricate details about how it is accomplished.

A Cloud Is Born

It may be urban legend, but the origin of the cloud is often traced to an IBM salesman, his customer, and a chalkboard in late 1973 or early 1974. Upon return from an internal training class on the then-new IBM Systems Network Architecture (SNA), the technically astute salesman attempted to explain mainframes, 3270 terminals, front-end processors, and a myriad of SNA logical unit and physical unit designations and definitions. He drew this new IBM world on a chalkboard as he spoke. As the salesman talked, the customer became wearier, and his eyes glazed over at all of the new jargon and complexity. The customer finally asked if it was necessary to understand all of the complexity before placing an order. Of course not, explained the IBM salesman. He quickly erased what was on the chalkboard between the mainframe computer and the end user terminal, and what was left looked like a cloud connecting the two. From that time forward, the complexity of the network and all of its connections has been known as the cloud, which is a simplified way of envisioning the connectivity. The cloud has existed for a long time, but the big deal is that because the cloud is being used for more than basic connectivity—that is, networking—the cloud now houses valuable services.

From the standpoint of a forensic examiner, though, the cloud is being used increasingly to create a physical distance between important elements. As an example, storage as a service allows a computer in one place to connect to actual storage embedded in the cloud. Not only is it usually less expensive, but there are a number of other benefits. The information is automatically backed up and is available in many locations and even on different computers, potentially to other users. It is clear that the increased ease of access in additional locations and potentially to additional people changes the forensic outlook on computer storage and potentially adds a number of additional considerations, such as tampering, chain of custody, and even the evidentiary value of the information.

One way that the cloud is implemented is network redundancy taken to a new level. In order to address disaster recovery, it is imperative for a robust network to have multiple redundant servers. In this way, if one fails, the organization simply uses the other server, often called the mirror server. In the simplest configuration, there are two servers that are connected. They are complete mirrors of each other. Should one server fail for any reason, all traffic is diverted to the other server.

This situation works great in environments where there are only a few servers and the primary concern is hardware failure. But what if you have much larger needs—for example, the need to store far more data than any single server can accommodate? Well, that led to the next step in the evolution of network redundancy, the storage area network (SAN). In a SAN, multiple servers and storage devices are all connected in a small high-speed network. This network is separate from the main network used by the organization. When a user on the main network wants to access data from the SAN, it appears to the user as a single logical storage device, though it may actually be composed of several physical storage devices. The user need not even be aware a SAN exists—from his or her perspective, it is just a server. This not only provides increased storage capacity, but it also provides redundancy. The SAN has multiple servers; should one of them fail, the others will continue operating and the end user will not even realize a failure occurred.

There are two problems with the solutions mentioned so far. The first is capacity. Even a SAN has a finite, though quite large, capacity. The second is the nature of the disaster they can withstand. A hard drive failure, accidental data deletion, or similar small-scale incident will not prevent a redundant network server or SAN from continuing to provide data and services to end users. But what about an earthquake, flood, or fire that destroys the entire building, including the SAN? For quite some time, the only answer to that was an off-site backup network. If your primary network was destroyed, you moved operations to a backup network, with only minimal downtime.

Eventually, the idea was formed to take the idea of a SAN and the idea of off-site backup networks and combine them. When a company hosts a cloud, it establishes multiple servers, possibly in diverse geographic areas, with data being redundantly stored on several servers. There may be a server in New York, another in San Francisco, and another in London. The end user simply accesses the cloud without even knowing where the data actually is. It is hard to imagine a scenario wherein the entire cloud would be destroyed. The basic architecture of a cloud is shown in Figure 14-1.

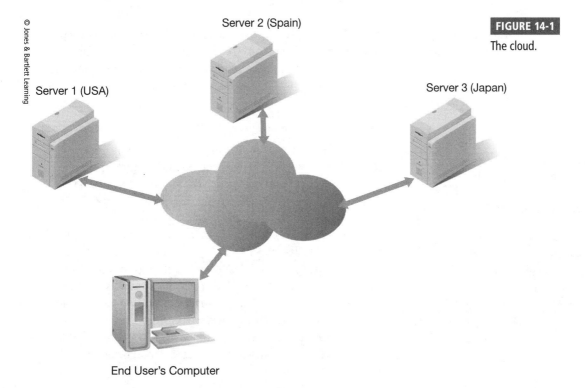

Server 2 (Spain)

Server 1 (USA)

Server 3 (Japan)

End User's Computer

FIGURE 14-1

The cloud.

© Jones & Bartlett Learning

14

Trends and Future Directions

What Impact Does Cloud Computing Have on Forensics?

Cloud computing, in which resources, services, and applications are located remotely instead of on a local server, affects digital forensics in several ways. First and foremost, it makes data acquisition more complicated. If a Web site is the target of a crime and the server must be forensically examined for evidence, how do you collect evidence from a cloud? Fortunately, each individual hosted server is usually in a separate virtual machine. The process, then, is to image that virtual machine, just as you would image any other hard drive. It does not matter if the virtual machine is duplicated or distributed across a cloud. However, a virtual machine is hosted on a host server. That means that in addition to the virtual machine's logs, you will need to retrieve the logs for the host server or servers.

Another issue in cloud forensics involves the legal process. Because a cloud could potentially reach across multiple states or even nations, the investigator must be aware of the rules of seizure, privacy, and so forth in each location from which he or she will retrieve data. It is very common for criminal enterprises to intentionally construct their own clouds with data stored in jurisdictions with rules and laws that make data retrieval for the purpose of forensics difficult or impossible. With the growing popularity of cloud computing, these issues are likely to become more common in the coming years. This is why it is important for a forensic investigator to have at least some familiarity with laws related to computer forensics, even in other countries.

New Devices

Although it is true that computers are advancing and becoming more powerful every year, that is not the only challenge facing forensics. Another important issue is the emergence of new devices. Consider smartphones and tablets, which are both relatively new devices. With any new computing device, it is safe to assume that it will eventually be the target of a forensic investigation.

Google Glass

> **NOTE**
>
> As of this writing, no malware for Google Glass has been discovered. However, because it is essentially just a Linux partition, and it can run third-party apps, it seems that eventually someone will write malware for this device. This will, of course, necessitate forensic examination beyond just the device's recorded video and audio.

Google Glass emerged on the market in 2013. It is unclear if this device will be widely accepted in the marketplace. However, it is certain that at least something like it will be in wide use in coming years. This should make any forensic investigator curious as to the specifics of Google Glass.

Google Glass includes permanent storage via a small hard drive. Google Glass has the ability to record images and video. At a minimum, Google Glass could contain photographic or video evidence of a crime. The operating system is Android, which is Linux-based. This means that once you connect to Google Glass from your forensic workstation, you can execute Linux commands to create an image of the Google Glass partition. After the partition is imaged, it can be examined forensically, just as any Linux partition would be.

There is a great deal of controversy over the issue of monitoring. Is it too much that you can be tracked by cell phone, car, and other devices? Are we losing all vestige of privacy in this avalanche of technology? That is a philosophical question and beyond the scope of this discussion. However, just as food for thought, consider this scenario: You are home alone one evening, watching a pay-per-view movie and relaxing. Someone you have had a conflict with is murdered during that time frame. No friend or neighbor can vouch for your whereabouts. You were home alone. But your attorney can prove that your car and cell phone were at your home and that someone ordered a pay-per-view movie. That certainly suggests a reasonable alibi. In this scenario, technological monitoring could help prevent you from being wrongfully convicted of a heinous crime.

Cars

For several years, cars have become increasingly sophisticated. Global positioning system (GPS) devices within cars are now commonplace. Many vehicles have hard drives to store and play music. These technological advances can also be repositories for forensic evidence. For example, GPS data might establish that a suspect's car was at the scene of a crime when the crime took place. That alone would not lead to a conviction, but it does help to build a case.

Medical Devices

An increasing number of medical devices are built to communicate. For example, there are insulin pumps that send the data regarding usage to a computer via a wireless connection. There are pacemakers that operate similarly. This leads to the question as to whether medical wireless communications can be compromised. The unfortunate fact is they can be. Multiple news sources have carried the story of a researcher who discovered he could hack into wireless insulin pumps and alter the dosage, even to fatal levels.

With the increasing complexity of medical devices, it could eventually become common-place to forensically examine them in cases where foul play is suspected—just as it is now commonplace to forensically examine any phone seized in relation to a crime.

Legal and Procedural Trends

The legal environment in which forensics is conducted changes slowly, but it does change. Normally, the enactment of new laws has very little effect on how evidence is examined—rather, it affects how it is seized. For example, the U.S. Supreme Court ruled in a case in June 2013 allowing law enforcement officers to collect DNA evidence from suspects without their consent in certain cases. This significantly changes the collection of evidence, but not the analysis of it.

Changes in the Law

Some laws do make changes to the process of seizing evidence. Laws can alter the requirements for a warrant, exceptions to warrant requirements, and issues of consent to search.

The USA Patriot Act

The most obvious change to U.S. law in reference to forensics in recent years has been the USA Patriot Act. The Patriot Act was designed to combat terrorism. It was not created with computer crime as its focus. However, it has affected computer crime. For example, prior to the Patriot Act, Internet service providers were very limited in what they could share with law enforcement without warrants or subpoenas. Now, they can choose to notify law enforcement if they reasonably believe that they have found evidence of an imminent crime that would endanger lives.

Section 816 of the Patriot Act—titled "Development and Support of Cybersecurity Forensic Capabilities"—calls for the U.S. Attorney General to establish regional computer forensics laboratories. This led to the creation of the Electronic Crimes Task Force with computer forensics labs in many major cities. This task force also includes members of local law enforcement.

Private Labs

Private forensic labs are becoming more common. These laboratories handle forensic examinations for private companies, for attorneys, and sometimes for law enforcement agencies. More and more forensic investigations are being conducted in private labs. This has become routine in other areas of forensics, such as DNA testing.

In the case of civil litigation, it is usually necessary to hire private forensic labs to process evidence. Private labs can gather evidence, analyze it, and produce reports regarding their findings. This data might be used in civil litigation or simply to ascertain the cause of an incident.

Defense attorneys often want their own lab to examine evidence in order to challenge the findings of the state's lab. The goal may be to confirm or deny what the prosecution has presented or to find some flaw in the methodology utilized by the prosecution. In some cases, the defense is simply seeking grounds for a reasonable doubt that the defendant committed the crime. For example, if the defendant is accused of sending a virus to a victim, and if that virus, along with virus creation utilities, is found on his or her computer, it may seem a hopeless case. However, if the defense can show that other people had access to the computer, or even that other users logged on around the time the virus was sent, this provides reasonable doubt.

It is becoming increasingly common for smaller police departments to outsource their computer forensics to private labs. It is often cost effective. In smaller towns and cities, the cost of equipping the police department with a full computer forensics lab and adequately trained staff may simply be outside their budgets. In those cases, it is more cost effective to outsource computer forensics examinations.

International Issues

Clearly, the cloud presents international legal issues for forensic examiners, but there are other issues as well. What happens when a case is transnational in nature? Cases of bank fraud, identity theft, and money laundering frequently cross national boundaries. Consider an identity theft scheme where a server in Malaysia is used to steal identities while the perpetrator uses his or her laptop in Spain to take money from the victim's accounts. If the victim lives in a third country, such as the United States, this crime involves three different national jurisdictions.

You might think that in such cases the only answer is to be aware of the laws in each country and ensure they are all obeyed. However, that is rarely necessary. Usually taking the national laws that are most restrictive to your investigation and following those will satisfy the legal requirements of the less-restrictive jurisdictions.

Techniques

Techniques are always evolving. Because the Daubert standard requires that scientific evidence presented in court be generally accepted in the relevant scientific field, new techniques need to be verified before being used in court. This means it is unlikely that a new tool will be released and immediately utilized in court. However, as time passes and the new tool has been tested, often in academic settings, it gains wide acceptance in the field and finds its way into court.

For this reason, it is important that a forensic investigator be aware of changes in technology and have at least a basic familiarity with emerging technologies and techniques. Even if they are not yet being used in court, they could be soon.

CHAPTER SUMMARY

This chapter gave an overview of how technology is changing and how that affects forensics. Even technology that has been in place for many years, such as the personal computer, is changing as increased storage, speed, and performance are developed. New technologies, such as Google Glass, are emerging and will require forensic analysis.

There are also new laws, such as the Patriot Act, and new techniques being developed. These both affect how evidence is collected and processed. It is imperative for a forensic investigator to be familiar with these laws.

KEY CONCEPTS AND TERMS

Cloud computing
Moore's law

CHAPTER 14 ASSESSMENT

1. Which of the following is *not* a unique characteristic of cloud computing relative to forensics?

   A. Evidence may be in a different location than the suspect computer.
   B. Evidence may be under different privacy rules.
   C. Evidence may be stored in binary code.
   D. Evidence may be easier for multiple persons to tamper with or modify.
   E. All of the above

2. According to Moore's law, computer power _____ at _____ the cost approximately every 18 to 24 months.

3. When you are performing forensic analysis on devices from diverse jurisdictions, the proper approach is to:

   A. Adhere to the rules of the jurisdiction with the least restrictive requirements.
   B. Adhere to the rules of the jurisdiction with the most restrictive requirements.
   C. Adhere to international requirements.
   D. Adhere to your own best judgment.

4. The Patriot Act had no effect on computer forensics.

   A. True
   B. False

System Forensics Resources

F ORENSICS IS BASED ON SOUND, well-established scientific procedures. However, it is not practical to conduct every forensic examination with purely manual techniques. Tools that automate forensic processes are an integral part of forensic analysis. In addition to tools, numerous resources are available to a forensic analyst to enable him or her to continue learning more about forensics.

Chapter 15 Topics

This chapter covers the following topics and concepts:

- What the tools used in forensics are
- What the available forensic resources are
- What the critical laws for forensics are

Chapter 15 Goals

When you complete this chapter, you will be able to:

- Identify specific tools that can be used for various aspects of a forensic investigation
- Utilize online resources to continue learning about forensics
- Understand critical laws related to forensics

Tools to Use

Software forensics tools can be either open source or commercial. Commercial forensic software ranges in price. Some products cost very little, and others are so costly that only large agencies or companies can afford them. There are so many tools available that it is virtually impossible to be proficient with all or even most of them. However, if you are at least aware of the tools and have a general knowledge of their functionality, you will be better prepared to select the appropriate tools for your forensic investigations.

ASR Data Acquisition & Analysis

ASR Data Acquisition & Analysis offers a variety of software: SMART Linux; SMART for Linux, SmartMount for Windows/Linux/Macintosh, Grok-NTFS for Windows/Linux/Macintosh, and Grok-LNK for Windows/Linux/Macintosh. These products are customized for forensic work, integrated acquisition, authentication, and analysis. See *http://asrdata .com*. You can see Grok-NTFS in Figure 15-1.

Courtesy of ASR Data

FIGURE 15-1

Grok-NTFS.

AccessData Forensic Toolkit

AccessData produces the Forensic Toolkit (FTK). This toolkit is a general-purpose suite of forensic tools. It can be used to create a forensic image of a drive, verify that image, and analyze the image. The analysis includes discovering malware, examining the Windows Registry, and breaking passwords in commonly used software, such as Excel spreadsheets or Adobe PDF documents. FTK is also capable of detecting pornographic images on a target drive.

ComputerCOP

ComputerCOP has developed two unique forensic tools: Professional and Forensic Examiner. For information on both tools, see *http://computercop.com*. ComputerCOP Professional is an automated search tool that allows an examiner to immediately find electronic evidence for trial. Many supervision officers use it to monitor probationers' and parolees' computer use. ComputerCOP Forensic Examiner is a field forensic solution. It acts as both automated forensic search software and a simple-to-connect write blocker.

Digital Detective

Digital Detective offers Blade, HstEx, and NetAnalysis. For more information on all these tools, see *http://www.digital-detective.co.uk*. Blade is a Windows-based data recovery solution. It supports plug-ins that give it advanced data recovery and analysis capabilities. HstEx version 3 is shown in Figure 15-2.

Digital Intelligence

Digital Intelligence, Inc., offers forensic hardware and software. Its software products include DRIVESPY, IMAGE, PART, PDBlock, and PDWipe. For information on all these products, see *http://www.digitalintelligence.com*.

Disk Investigator

This is a free utility that can be downloaded from *http://www.theabsolute.net/sware/dskinv.html*. This tool runs on Windows and has a graphical user interface. It is not as full featured as EnCase or FTK, but it is free and very easy to use. When you first launch the tool, you are presented with a cluster-by-cluster view of your hard drive in hexadecimal form. Under the View menu, you can view directories or the root. The Tools menu allows you to search for a specific file or to recover deleted files. The Disk Investigator tool is shown in Figure 15-3.

EnCase

Guidance Software offers a number of EnCase products, including Enterprise, eDiscovery, Forensic, and Portable. For more information on all these products, see *http://www.guidancesoftware.com*.

EnCase Enterprise allows the deepest level of visibility into laptops, desktops, file servers, and e-mail servers. Use it to investigate human resources matters or to quickly determine the root cause of suspicious network activity. EnCase eDiscovery performs search, collection, preservation, and processing in a forensically sound manner. It collects and processes only potentially relevant data. EnCase Forensic gives you the ability to image a drive and preserve it in a forensically sound manner. The EnCase evidence file

FIGURE 15-2

HstEx version 3.

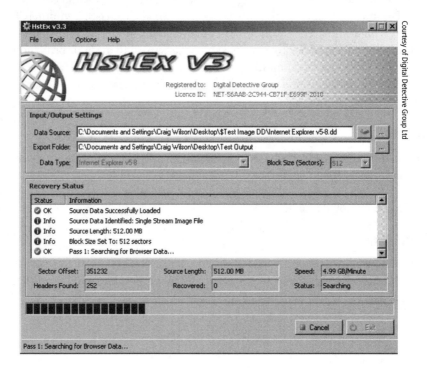

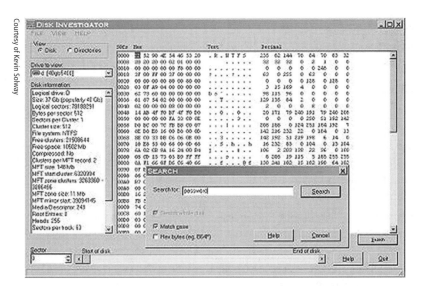

FIGURE 15-3

Disk Investigator.

format is a digital evidence container validated and approved by courts worldwide. EnCase Forensic also contains a full suite of analysis, bookmarking, and reporting features. EnCase Portable is a pocket-sized universal serial bus (USB) data collection and triage solution. Even nonexperts can use EnCase Portable so that specialists can focus on case management, processing, detailed analysis, and reporting.

The Sleuth Kit

Sleuth Kit is a free suite of command-line tools. This product can be downloaded from *http://www.sleuthkit.org/sleuthkit/*. It includes a number of search utilities and can search for fragments of deleted tools. Many users find the command-line interface to be cumbersome; fortunately, a graphical user interface (GUI) called Autopsy has been created for Sleuth Kit and is available at *http://www.sleuthkit.org/autopsy/download.php*.

X-Ways Software Technology AG

X-Ways produces a number of products, including Evidor, X-Ways Forensics, and WinHex. For more information on all these products, see *http://www.x-ways.net*:

- Evidor searches text on hard disks and retrieves the context of keyword occurrences on computer media. It examines the entire allocated space as well as currently unallocated space and slack space. That means it finds data from files that have been deleted if the files still exist physically.
- X-Ways Forensics is an advanced work environment for system forensics examiners. It's integrated with the WinHex hex and disk editor.
- WinHex is a system forensics, data recovery, and IT security tool that includes a hex editor, disk editor, and RAM editor.

15

System Forensics Resources

Other Tools

Other tools with more limited use are listed here. These tools are not general-purpose forensic utilities, but rather very specific tools with narrowly defined functionalities:

- **AccuBurn-R**—AccuBurn-R produces exact copies of disks that have been imaged using CD/DVD Inspector. It supports all types and formats of disks. See *http://www.infinadyne.com*.

- **Darik's Boot and Nuke (DBAN)**—DBAN is a self-contained boot disk that securely wipes the hard disks of most computers. DBAN automatically and completely deletes the contents of any hard disk that it can detect. It is a useful utility for bulk or emergency data destruction. See *http://www.dban.sourceforge.net*.

- **Directory Snoop**—Directory Snoop is a cluster-level search tool. It allows Windows users to search file allocation table (FAT) and New Technology File System (NTFS) disk drives to see what data may be hiding. Directory Snoop can recover deleted files and permanently erase sensitive files. See *http://www.briggsoft.com/dsnoop.htm*. You can see Directory Snoop in Figure 15-4.

- **L0phtCrack**—L0phtCrack is password auditing and recovery software offered in three versions.

- **Process Monitor**—Process Monitor is an advanced monitoring tool for Windows that shows real-time file system, Registry, and process/thread activity. It combines the features of two legacy utilities, Filemon and Regmon, and adds an extensive list of enhancements. See *http://technet.microsoft.com/en-us/sysinternals/bb896645.aspx*. Process Monitor is shown in Figure 15-5.

FIGURE 15-4

Directory Snoop.

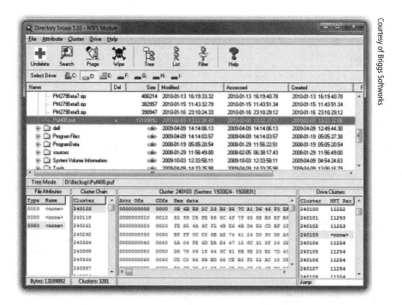

Courtesy of Briggs Softworks

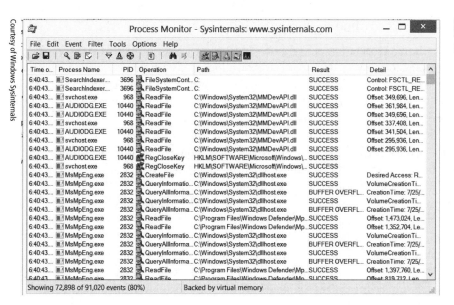

FIGURE 15-5

Process Monitor.

- **Visual TimeAnalyzer**—Visual TimeAnalyzer automatically tracks all computer use and activities, including working time and pauses. It presents detailed, richly illustrated reports. See *http://www.neuber.com/timeanalyzer/*.

- **Wayback Machine**—Wayback Machine is often useful during a forensic investigation to know the state of a Web site at a prior moment in time. There are a number of sites that take snapshots of Web sites and save them for posterity. One of the largest and most comprehensive is the Wayback Machine. Additional information can be found at *http://archive.org/web/web.php*.

Resources

Numerous organizations offer certification programs for system forensics. These programs usually test a student after completing one or more training sessions successfully. Certifying organizations range from nonprofit associations to vendor-sponsored groups. All these programs charge fees for certification. Some require candidates to take vendor- or organization-sponsored training to qualify for the certification.

Some state and federal government agencies have established their own certification programs. These programs address the skills needed to conduct computing investigations at various levels. In addition, a number of universities and other organizations offer courses in system forensics.

The following sections describe some of the most prominent system forensics training programs and certifications.

15

System Forensics Resources

International Association of Computer Investigative Specialists

The International Association of Computer Investigative Specialists (IACIS) is one of the oldest professional system forensics organizations. It was created by police officers who wanted to formalize credentials in computing investigations. Currently, IACIS limits membership. Only law enforcement personnel and government employees working as system forensics examiners may join.

IACIS conducts an annual two-week training course for qualified members. Students learn to interpret and trace e-mail, acquire evidence properly, identify operating systems, recover data, and understand encryption theory and other topics. Students must pass a written exam before continuing to the next level.

Other candidates who complete all parts of the IACIS test successfully receive Certified Forensic Computer Examiner (CFCE) certification. The CFCE process changes as technology changes. Topics include data hiding, determining the file types of disguised files, and accessing password-protected files. The program might also ask a student to find evidence and draw conclusions from it. Students must demonstrate proficiency in technical tools and deductive reasoning. For the latest information about IACIS, visit *http://www.iacis.info*.

IACIS requires recertification every three years to demonstrate continuing work in the field of system forensics. Recertification is less intense than the original certification.

EnCase Certified Examiner Certification

Guidance Software, the creator of the EnCase software, sponsors the EnCase Certified Examiner (EnCE) certification program. EnCE certification is open to the public and private sectors. This certification focuses on the use and mastery of system forensics analysis using EnCase. For more information on EnCE certification requirements, visit *http://www.guidancesoftware.com*.

AccessData Certified Examiner

AccessData is the creator of Forensic Toolkit (FTK) software. The company sponsors the AccessData Certified Examiner (ACE) certification program. ACE certification is open to the public and private sectors. This certification is specific to use and mastery of FTK.

Requirements for taking the ACE exam include completing the AccessData boot camp and Windows forensic courses. For more information on ACE certification, visit *http://www.accessdata.com*.

Certified Hacking Forensic Investigator

The EC-Council, creators of the Certified Ethical Hacker certification, also offers a forensic certification. For more information about the Certified Hacking Forensic Investigator, visit *http://www.eccouncil.org/Certification/Computer-Hacking-Forensics-Investigator*. This certification is not specific to a given tool, as are the ACE and EnCE certifications. It is a general certification covering the principles of forensics. However, the course and the certification test do cover a wide range of forensic tools.

SANS Institute

The SANS institute offers a variety of network security certifications. Their forensic track offers several subdisciplines of certifications. You can find more information at *http://computer-forensics.sans.org/certification*. The three certification tracks are:

- Global Information Assurance Certification (GIAC) Certified Forensic Examiner (GCFE)
- GIAC Certified Forensic Analyst (GCFA)
- GIAC Reverse Engineering Malware (GREM)

Web Sites

A number of Web sites provide information about computer forensics. Some provide articles and research, whereas others provide basic tutorials and white papers. Some simply provide an overview of relevant laws. But all are relevant to forensic investigations:

- American Academy of Forensic Sciences at *http://www.aafs.org*
- Computer Forensics, Cybercrime and Steganography Resources at *http://forensix.org*
- Computer Forensics World at *http://www.computerforensicsworld.com*
- Department of Defense Cyber Crime Center (DC3) at *http://www.dc3.mil*
- Department of Justice Computer Crime & Intellectual Property Section at *http://www.cybercrime.gov*
- Digital Forensic Research Workshop at *http://dfrws.org*
- Electronic Evidence Information Center at *http://www.e-evidence.info*
- Federal Bureau of Investigation Computer Analysis and Response Team at *http://www.fbi.gov/hq/lab/org/cart.htm*
- Federal Bureau of Investigation Cyber Investigations at *http://www.fbi.gov/news/stories/2013/january/piecing-together-digital-evidence*
- Forensic Focus at *http://www.forensicfocus.com*
- Forensics Wiki at *http://www.forensicswiki.org*
- High Tech Crime Consortium at *http://www.hightechcrimecops.org*
- High Technology Crime Investigation Association (HTCIA) at *http://www.htcia.org*
- Information Systems Security Association (ISSA) at *https://www.issa.org*
- International Association of Computer Investigative Specialists (IACIS) at *http://www.iacis.com*
- International Organization on Computer Evidence at *http://ioce.org*
- National Center for Forensic Science at *http://ncfs.org*
- National Criminal Justice Computer Laboratory and Training Center at *http://www.search.org/programs/hightech/*

- National Institute of Justice Electronic Crime at *http://www.nij.gov/topics/crime/internet-electronic/*
- National Institute of Standards and Technology Computer Forensics Tool Testing (CFTT) at *http://www.cftt.nist.gov*
- National White Collar Crime Center at *http://nw3c.org*
- U.S. Secret Service Electronic Crimes Task Force at *http://www.secretservice.gov/ectf.shtml*

Journals

There are journals, both in print and electronic, that cover the field of digital forensics. These can be invaluable tools for keeping abreast of the latest developments.

Digital Investigation

Digital Investigation covers cutting-edge developments in digital forensics and incident response from around the globe. It covers new technologies, useful tools, relevant research, investigative techniques, and methods for handling security breaches. See *http://www.journals.elsevier.com/digital-investigation/*.

The *International Journal of Digital Crime and Forensics*

The *International Journal of Digital Crime and Forensics* (IJDCF) provides up-to-the-minute coverage of issues related to digital evidence. *IJDCF* addresses the use of electronic devices and software for crime prevention and investigation. It contains high-quality theoretical and empirical research articles, research reviews, case studies, book reviews, tutorials, and editorials. See *http://www.igi-global.com/journal/international-journal-digital-crime-forensics/1112*.

The *International Journal of Digital Evidence*

The *International Journal of Digital Evidence* (IJDE) is a forum for discussion of theory, research, policy, and practice in the rapidly changing field of digital evidence. *IJDE* is supported by the Economic Crime Institute (ECI) at Utica College. See *http://www.informatik.uni-trier.de/~ley/db/journals/ijde/*.

The *Journal of Digital Forensic Practice*

The *Journal of Digital Forensic Practice* is a helpful resource for forensic specialists. Articles in the journal target both the public and private sectors. The journal presents useful information, techniques, and unbiased reviews designed to assist forensic specialists in day-to-day practice. See *http://www.tandfonline.com/toc/udfp20/current#.Ucha3m8o6po*.

The *Journal of Digital Forensics, Security and Law*

The *Journal of Digital Forensics, Security and Law* (JDFSL) is a unique and innovative publication of the Association of Digital Forensics, Security and Law. The mission of *JDFSL* is to expand digital forensics research to a wide and eclectic audience. See *http://www.jdfsl.org/index.htm*.

The *Journal of Forensic Sciences*

The American Academy of Forensic Sciences produces the *Journal of Forensic Sciences*. This organization is a multidisciplinary professional organization. The academy aims to promote integrity, competency, education, research, practice, and collaboration in the forensic sciences. See *http://www.wiley.com/bw/journal.asp?ref=0022-1198*.

The *Small Scale Digital Device Forensics Journal*

The *Small Scale Digital Device Forensics Journal* (*SSDDFJ*) is an online journal for academics and practitioners. It publishes articles regarding theory, research, and practice in the rapidly changing field of small-scale digital device forensics. *SSDDFJ* is supported by the Cyber Forensics Lab (CFL) at Purdue University. See *http://www.ssddfj.org/about.asp*.

Conferences

In addition to journals and Web sites, there are a variety of conferences you might want to attend. Some of these are specifically aimed at forensics, whereas others provide information on general network security, hacking, and topics related to forensics:

- Black Hat Briefings & Training at *http://www.blackhat.com/html/bh-link/briefings.html*
- ChicagoCon—White Hats Come Together in Defense of the Digital Frontier
- Computer and Enterprise Investigations Conference (CEIC) at *http://www.ceicconference.com*
- Department of Defense Cyber Crime Conference at *http://www.dodcybercrime.com*
- DFRWS Digital Forensics Research Conference at *http://www.dfrws.org*
- Forum of Incident Response and Security Teams (FIRST) Conference at *http://www.first.org/conference*
- HTCIA International Training Conference and Expo at *http://www.htcia.org/index.shtml*
- IACIS Computer Forensic Training Event at *http://www.cops.org/training*
- Mobile Forensics World Training Conference at *http://www.MobileForensicsWorld.org*
- Open Source Software for Computer and Network Forensics at *http://conferenze.dei.polimi.it/ossconf/index.php*
- Regional Computer Forensics Group Conference (RCFG) at *http://www.rcfg.org*
- SANS Computer Forensics at *http://computer-forensics.sans.org/events/*
- Other SANS institute events at *www.sans.org/*
- Systematic Approaches to Digital Forensic Engineering (SADFE) at *http://conf.ncku.edu.tw/sadfe/*
- Techno Forensics Conference at *http://www.techsec.com*
- Techno Security Conference at *http://www.techsec.com*

Laws

A variety of laws define what is or is not a cybercrime, the elements required to prove such a crime, the penalties for these crimes, and the collection and analysis of forensic information. Each state in the United States and each nation on the globe have their own specific laws. You must become familiar with the laws in your jurisdiction. Those working in the United States must understand the specific laws applicable throughout the country that affect how evidence is seized and safeguarded. An exhaustive list of laws and regulations is beyond the scope of this chapter and, in fact, the interpretation of the laws changes regularly as case law is established and may vary from jurisdiction to jurisdiction. However, to give a sense of what is involved, the following sections provide some examples.

The USA Patriot Act

Congress passed the USA Patriot Act to combat terrorism after September 11, 2001. Portions of the law affect the collection of computer evidence. For example, in some circumstances, customer records from Internet service providers (ISPs) can be disclosed to law enforcement. The law significantly expands the circumstances under which ISPs can now notify law enforcement of information that may indicate an imminent threat.

The Patriot Act contains two procedural changes directly related to computer crimes. First, it specifically adds felony acts related to the Computer Fraud and Abuse Act in the list of predicates that can serve as the basis for authorizing a warrant to intercept wire, oral, and electronic communications. Second, with the permission of the owner or operator of a "protected computer," a term defined in the computer fraud statute, law enforcement officers may now intercept communications to and from the computer trespasser if they have reasonable grounds to believe that the trespasser's communications will be relevant to the investigation. Essentially, a **protected computer** is any computer at a financial institution or a government agency. This provision basically means that if someone hacks into a protected system, law enforcement officials can track down and intercept all that perpetrator's communications if they reasonably believe it is relevant to the investigation.

In addition to these procedural changes, Section 816 of the Patriot Act calls for establishing regional computer forensic laboratories. This has led to the creation of the Electronic Crimes Task Force, led by the U.S. Secret Service. The Patriot Act is a perfect example of how the rules of evidence collection can change dramatically due to a new law being passed.

The Electronic Communications Privacy Act of 1986

This is one of the pivotal laws related to computer crime. The purpose of the act was to extend federal wiretap laws to cover electronic communications, including the requirement that a law enforcement officer needs a warrant to intercept electronic communications.

The Electronic Communications Privacy Act extended the following guidelines to e-mail:

* **The consent exception**—Both parties to a conversation must give consent. If you recall the last time you called a customer service phone number, you may have heard an automated voice inform you that the call was being recorded, and the person you spoke to may have even asked your consent to record the call.

* **The business extension exemption**—This does not mean that a business can monitor and record all employee calls. A business can claim this exemption only for monitoring by certain types of equipment; the recording must occur in the ordinary course of business.

The Communications Assistance to Law Enforcement Act of 1996

The Communications Assistance to Law Enforcement Act (CALEA) is another of many laws that govern the capture and interpretation of forensic information. Originally, CALEA granted the ability to wiretap only digital telephone networks, but in 2004, the United States Department of Justice (DOJ); Bureau of Alcohol, Tobacco, Firearms, and Explosives (ATF); Federal Bureau of Investigation (FBI); and Drug Enforcement Administration (DEA) filed a joint petition with the Federal Communications Commission (FCC) to expand CALEA to include the ability to monitor Voice over IP (VoIP) and broadband Internet communications so that they could monitor Web traffic as well as phone calls. In September 2005, the FCC ruled that providers of broadband Internet access and interconnected VoIP services are telecommunications carriers under CALEA and, therefore, extended CALEA to the Web and broadband access. Subsequent court cases risked reinterpretation or limitation of the CALEA law but, as of this writing, information can be collected under CALEA and used as evidence.

The Health Insurance Portability and Accountability Act of 1996

Although The Health Insurance Portability and Accountability Act (HIPPA) regulations are directly applicable to health care, a number of provisions of HIPAA must be understood and followed by forensic professionals. Similar laws govern a wide variety of other areas, such as the Sarbanes-Oxley Act of 2002, which governs publicly traded corporations. Specifically in HIPAA there exists the Privacy Rule, which covers the disclosure of personally identifiable protected health information (PHI). A subsequent update changed the disclosure period from "forever" to 50 years after death of the subject of the health information, but the update also increased the penalties for disclosure of PHI. Every forensic examiner should be very familiar with what constitutes PHI and the potential penalties for disclosure.

The legal underpinnings of digital forensics, both computer and network, may seem like shifting sands and, in many very important cases, they are. If, however, the forensic examiner sticks to the Daubert standard, handles all information in his or her possession according to rules of evidence, and maintains the chain of custody, then much of the legal positioning and interpretation is an interesting sideshow. But it's a sideshow that the forensic professional must understand.

15

System Forensics Resources

CHAPTER SUMMARY

The beginning of this chapter provided a quick overview of a variety of tools used in forensic investigations. These tools are not the only ones available for investigators to use, but are some of the most widely known. It is critical that any forensic analyst be aware of the tools available.

This chapter also covered major forensic certifications. Although it is not absolutely necessary to obtain a forensic certification in order to conduct forensic analysis, it is definitely recommended. Studying for any of the major forensic certifications will teach you techniques and procedures. In addition, the stronger your educational background and credentials, the more credible you will be when testifying.

In addition, the chapter covered general resources, including Web sites and journals. Finally, the chapter touched on key laws that pertain to forensics.

KEY CONCEPTS AND TERMS

Protected computer

CHAPTER 15 ASSESSMENT

1. According to the Electronic Communications Privacy Act of 1986, when will a law enforcement officer need a warrant to intercept e-mail?

A. Never
B. Only when seizing it in transit
C. Only when seizing it from the server
D. Anytime e-mail will be intercepted

2. Section 816 of the USA Patriot Act, titled the "Development and Support of Cybersecurity Forensic Capabilities," does what?

A. Establishes guidelines for intercepting e-mail
B. Establishes guidelines for seizing hard drives
C. Calls for the establishment of regional computer forensic laboratories
D. Calls for investigation of all cybercrimes as acts of terrorism

3. The International Association of Computer Investigative Specialists (IACIS) was created by _____ who wanted to formalize credentials in computing investigations.

A. Forensic scientists
B. Police officers
C. Government agencies
D. Academic computer science departments

Answer Key

CHAPTER 1 Introduction to Forensics

1. C   2. B   3. B   4. C   5. B   6. D   7. B   8. B

CHAPTER 2 Overview of Computer Crime

1. C   2. A   3. A   4. B   5. A   6. A   7. C   8. D

CHAPTER 3 Forensic Methods and Labs

1. C   2. C   3. C   4. D   5. A   6. C   7. A

CHAPTER 4 Collecting, Seizing, and Protecting Evidence

1. SHA1   2. C   3. D   4. B   5. B   6. B   7. Swap file

CHAPTER 5 Understanding Techniques for Hiding and Scrambling Information

1. A   2. B   3. B   4. D   5. C   6. A   7. B   8. C   9. D
10. A   11. B   12. D

CHAPTER 6 Recovering Data

1. B   2. C   3. B   4. A

CHAPTER 7 E-mail Forensics

1. B   2. A   3. C   4. B   5. .nsf

CHAPTER 8 Windows Forensics

1. Windows 95   2. C   3. B   4. A   5. A

CHAPTER 9 Linux Forensics

1. A   2. B   3. A   4. C   5. C   6. `pstree`   7. A

CHAPTER 10 Macintosh Forensics

1. A   2. D   3. A   4. A

CHAPTER 11 Mobile Forensics

1. A   2. C   3. A   4. Nascent

CHAPTER 12   Performing Network Analysis

1. C   2. D   3. A   4. B   5. C

CHAPTER 13   Incident and Intrusion Response

1. B   2. A   3. B   4. B

CHAPTER 14   Trends and Future Directions

1. C   2. doubles; half   3. B   4. B

CHAPTER 15   System Forensics Resources

1. D   2. C   3. B

Standard Acronyms

3DES	triple data encryption standard		**DMZ**	demilitarized zone
ACD	automatic call distributor		**DoS**	denial of service
AES	Advanced Encryption Standard		**DPI**	deep packet inspection
ANSI	American National Standards Institute		**DRP**	disaster recovery plan
AP	access point		**DSL**	digital subscriber line
API	application programming interface		**DSS**	Digital Signature Standard
B2B	business to business		**DSU**	data service unit
B2C	business to consumer		**EDI**	Electronic Data Interchange
BBB	Better Business Bureau		**EIDE**	Enhanced IDE
BCP	business continuity planning		**FACTA**	Fair and Accurate Credit Transactions Act
C2C	consumer to consumer		**FAR**	false acceptance rate
CA	certificate authority		**FBI**	Federal Bureau of Investigation
CAP	Certification and Accreditation Professional		**FDIC**	Federal Deposit Insurance Corporation
			FEP	front-end processor
CAUCE	Coalition Against Unsolicited Commercial Email		**FRCP**	Federal Rules of Civil Procedure
			FRR	false rejection rate
CCC	CERT Coordination Center		**FTC**	Federal Trade Commission
CCNA	Cisco Certified Network Associate		**FTP**	file transfer protocol
CERT	Computer Emergency Response Team		**GIAC**	Global Information Assurance Certification
CFE	Certified Fraud Examiner			
CISA	Certified Information Systems Auditor		**GLBA**	Gramm-Leach-Bliley Act
CISM	Certified Information Security Manager		**HIDS**	host-based intrusion detection system
CISSP	Certified Information System Security Professional		**HIPAA**	Health Insurance Portability and Accountability Act
CMIP	Common Management Information Protocol		**HIPS**	host-based intrusion prevention system
			HTTP	hypertext transfer protocol
COPPA	Children's Online Privacy Protection		**HTTPS**	HTTP over Secure Socket Layer
CRC	cyclic redundancy check		**HTML**	hypertext markup language
CSI	Computer Security Institute		**IAB**	Internet Activities Board
CTI	Computer Telephony Integration		**IDEA**	International Data Encryption Algorithm
DBMS	database management system		**IDPS**	intrusion detection and prevention
DDoS	distributed denial of service		**IDS**	intrusion detection system
DES	Data Encryption Standard			

IEEE	Institute of Electrical and Electronics Engineers
IETF	Internet Engineering Task Force
InfoSec	information security
IPS	intrusion prevention system
IPSec	IP Security
IPv4	Internet protocol version 4
IPv6	Internet protocol version 6
IRS	Internal Revenue Service
(ISC)²	International Information System Security Certification Consortium
ISO	International Organization for Standardization
ISP	Internet service provider
ISS	Internet security systems
ITRC	Identity Theft Resource Center
IVR	interactive voice response
LAN	local area network
MAN	metropolitan area network
MD5	Message Digest 5
modem	modulator demodulator
NFIC	National Fraud Information Center
NIDS	network intrusion detection system
NIPS	network intrusion prevention system
NIST	National Institute of Standards and Technology
NMS	network management system
OS	operating system
OSI	open system interconnection
PBX	private branch exchange
PCI	Payment Card Industry
PGP	Pretty Good Privacy
PKI	public key infrastructure
RAID	redundant array of independent disks
RFC	Request for Comments
RSA	Rivest, Shamir, and Adleman (algorithm)

SAN	storage area network
SANCP	Security Analyst Network Connection Profiler
SANS	SysAdmin, Audit, Network, Security
SAP	service access point
SCSI	small computer system interface
SET	Secure electronic transaction
SGC	server-gated cryptography
SHA	Secure Hash Algorithm
S-HTTP	secure HTTP
SLA	service level agreement
SMFA	specific management functional area
SNMP	Simple Network Management Protocol
SOX	Sarbanes-Oxley Act of 2002 (also Sarbox)
SSA	Social Security Administration
SSCP	Systems Security Certified Practitioner
SSL	Secure Sockets Layer
SSO	single system sign-on
STP	shielded twisted cable
TCP/IP	Transmission Control Protocol/Internet Protocol
TCSEC	Trusted Computer System Evaluation Criteria
TFTP	Trivial File Transfer Protocol
TNI	Trusted Network Interpretation
UDP	User Datagram Protocol
UPS	uninterruptible power supply
UTP	unshielded twisted cable
VLAN	virtual local area network
VOIP	Voice over Internet Protocol
VPN	virtual private network
WAN	wide area network
WLAN	wireless local area network
WNIC	wireless network interface card
W3C	World Wide Web Consortium
WWW	World Wide Web

Glossary of Key Terms

A

American Standard Code for Information Interchange (ASCII) | A set of codes defining all the various keystrokes you could make, including letters, numbers, characters, and even the spacebar and return keys.

Anonymous remailing | The process of sending an e-mail message to an anonymizer. The anonymizer strips identifying information from an e-mail message before forwarding it with the anonymous mailing computer's IP address.

Anti-forensics | The actions that perpetrators take to conceal their locations, activities, or identities.

Asymmetric cryptography | Cryptography wherein two keys are used: one to encrypt the message and another to decrypt it.

B

Base transceiver station (BTS) | The part of the cell network responsible for communications between the mobile phone and the network switching system.

Basic input/output system (BIOS) | The basic instructions stored on a chip for booting up the computer.

Bit-level information | Information at the level of actual 1s and 0s stored in memory or on the storage device.

Block cipher | A form of cryptography, which encrypts data in blocks; 64-bit blocks are quite common, although some algorithms (like AES) use larger blocks.

Bootstrap environment | A special program, such as U-Boot or RedBoot, that is stored in a special section of the flash memory.

Brute-force attack

Brute-force attack | An attack in which the attacker tries to decrypt a message by simply applying every possible key in the keyspace.

Business continuity plan (BCP) | A plan for maintaining minimal operations until the business can return to full normal operations.

Business impact analysis (BIA) | An analysis of how specific incidents might impact the business operations.

C

Caesar cipher | The method of cryptography in which someone chooses a number by which to shift each letter of a text in the alphabet and substitute the new letter for the letter being encrypted. For example, if your text is "A CAT," and you choose to shift by two letters, your encrypted text is "C ECV." This is also known as the monoalphabet, single-alphabet, or substitution cipher.

Carrier | The signal, stream, or data file into which the payload is hidden.

Cell-phone forensics | The process of searching the contents of cell phones.

Chain of custody | The continuity of control of evidence that makes it possible to account for all that has happened to evidence between its original collection and its appearance in court, preferably unaltered.

Channel | The type of medium used to hide data in steganography. This may be photos, video, sound files or Voice over IP.

Clean room | An environment that has a controlled level of contamination, such as from dust, microbes, and other particles.

Computer forensics | The use of analytical and investigative techniques to identify, collect, examine and preserve computer-based material for presentation as evidence in a court of law.

Cloud computing | The practice of delivering hosted services over the Internet. This can be software as a service, platform as a service, or infrastructure as a service.

Consistency checking | A technique for file system repair that involves scanning a disk's logical structure and ensuring that it is consistent with its specification.

Cryptanalysis | A method of using techniques other than brute force to derive a cryptopgraphic key.

Curriculum vitae (CV) | An extensive document expounding one's experience and qualifications for a position, similar to a résumé but with more detail. In academia and expert work, a CV is usually used rather than a résumé.

Cyberstalking | The use of electronic communications to harass or threaten another person.

D

Data consistency | The act of ensuring the data that is extracted is consistent.

Daubert standard | The standard holding that only methods and tools widely accepted in the scientific community can be used in court.

Demonstrative evidence | Information that helps explain other evidence. An example is a chart that explains a technical concept to the judge and jury.

Denial of service (DoS) attack | An attack designed to overwhelm the target system so it can no longer reply to legitimate requests for connection.

Digital evidence | Information that has been processed and assembled so that it is relevant to an investigation and supports a specific finding or determination.

Disaster recovery plan (DRP) | A plan for returning the business to full normal operations.

Disk forensics | The process of acquiring and analyzing information stored on physical storage media, such as computer hard drives or smartphones.

Disk Operating System (DOS) | A command-line oprating system.

Distributed denial of service (DDoS) attack | An attack in which the attacker seeks to infect several

machines, and use those machines to overwhelm the target system to achieve a denial of service.

Documentary evidence | Data stored in written form, on paper or in electronic files, such as e-mail messages, and telephone call-detail records. Investigators must authenticate documentary evidence.

Dump | A complete copy of every bit of memory or cache recorded in permanent storage or printed on paper.

E

Electronic serial number (ESN) | A unique identification number developed by the United States Federal Communications Commission (FCC) to identify cell phones.

E-mail forensics | The study of the source and content of e-mail as evidence, including the identification of the sender, recipient, date, time, and origination location of an e-mail message.

Enhanced Data Rates for GSM Evolution (EDGE) | A technology that does not fit neatly into the 2G/3G/4G spectrum. It is technically considered pre-3G but was an improvement on GSM (2G).

Euler's Totient | The total number of coprime numbers. Two numbers are considered coprime if they have no common factors.

Expert report | A formal document prepared by a forensics specialist to document an investigation, including a list of all tests conducted as well as the specialist's own curriculum vitae (CV). Anything the specialist plans to testify about at a trial must be included in the expert report.

Expert testimony | The testimony of an expert witness, one who testifies on the basis of scientific or technical knowledge relevant to a case, rather than personal experience.

F

Feistel function | A cryptographic function that splits blocks of data into two parts, and is one of the most influential developments in symmetric block ciphers.

File slack | The unused space between the logical end of file and the physical end of file. It is also called *slack space*.

Foreign Intelligence Surveillance Act of 1978 (FISA) | A U.S. law that prescribes procedures for the physical and electronic surveillance and collection of "foreign intelligence information" between foreign powers and agents of foreign powers, which may include American citizens and permanent residents suspected of espionage or terrorism.

Fraud | A broad category of crime that can encompass many different activities, but essentially, any attempt to gain financial reward through deception.

 G

Global System for Mobile (GSM) communications | A standard developed by the European Telecommunications Standards Institute (ETSI). Basically, GSM is the 2G network.

Graphical user interface (GUI) | A point-and-click user interface.

grep | A popular Linux/UNIX search tool.

GRUB (Grand Unified Bootloader) | A newer Linux boot loader.

H

Hash | A function that is nonreversible, takes variable-length input, produces fixed-length output, and has few or no collisions.

Heap (*H*) | Dynamic memory for a program comes from the heap segment. A process may use a memory allocator such as malloc to request dynamic memory.

Hierarchical Storage Management (HSM) | Continuous online backup storage.

Hive | One of the the five sections of the Windows Registry.

Home location register (HLR) | The database used by the MSC for subscriber data and service information.

I

Identity theft | Any use of another person's identity.

Inode | A data structure in the file system that stores all the information about a file except its name and its actual data.

Integrated Circuit Card Identifier (ICCID) | A unique serial number that identifies each SIM. These numbers are engraved on the SIM during manufacturing.

International Mobile Equipment Identity (IMEI) number | A unique number identifying GSM, LTE, and other types of phones. The first 8 bits of the ESN identify the manufacturer, and the subsequent 24 bits uniquely identify the phone.

Internet forensics | The process of piecing together where and when a user has been on the Internet.

Internet Message Access Protocol (IMAP) | A protocol used to receive e-mail that works on port 143.

Intrusion detection system | A system that monitors network traffic looking for suspicious activity.

ISO9660 | A file system used with CDs.

 K

Kasiski examination | A method of attacking poly-alphabetic substitution ciphers, this method can be used to deduce the length of the keyword used in a polyalphabetic substitution cipher. This is sometimes also called Kasiski's test or Kasiski's method.

Keyspace | The total number of keys.

 L

Least significant bit (LSB) | The last bit or least significant bit is used to store data.

Life span | A term that refers to how long data will last. The term is related to volatility. More volatile data tends to have a shorter life span.

LILO (Linux Loader) | One of the Linux boot loaders.

Live system forensics | The process of searching memory in real time, typically for working with compromised hosts or to identify system abuse.

Logical analysis | Analysis involving using the native operating system, on the evidence disk or a forensic duplicate, to peruse the data.

Logical damage | Damage to how the data is stored, for example file system corruption.

Logic bomb | Malware that executes its damage when a specific condition is met.

Long Term Evolution (LTE) | A standard for wireless communication of high-speed data for mobile devices. This is what is commonly called 4G.

M

Master boot record (MBR) | The record on the hard drive partition used to initiate booting that partition.

Maximum tolerable downtime (MTD) | The length of time a system can be down before the business cannot recover.

Mean time to failure (MTTF) | The average length of time before a given piece of equipment will fail through normal use.

Mean time to repair (MTTF) | The average time to repair a given piece of equipment.

Mobile switching center (MSC) | A switching system for a cellular network.

Moore's law | The observation by Gordon Moore of Intel Corporation that capacity would double and price would be cut in half roughly every 18 to 24 months for products based on computer chips and related technology.

Multiple-input multiple-output (MIMO) | The wireless technology that uses multiple antennas to coherently resolve more information than possible using a single antenna.

N

Network forensics | The process of examining network traffic, including transaction logs and real-time monitoring.

P

Payload | The data to be covertly communicated. In other words, it is the message you want to hide.

Personal identification number (PIN) | An ID number for a cell phone user.

Personal unlocking code (PUK) | A number for unlocking a cell phone.

Physical analysis | Offline analysis conducted on an evidence disk or forensic duplicate after booting from a CD or another system.

Physical damage | Damage to actual hard drive parts; for example, a damaged platter or spindle.

Post Office Protocol version 3 (POP3) | A protocol used to receive e-mail that works on port 110.

Power-on self test (POST) | This is a brief hardware test the BIOS performs upon boot-up.

Protected computer | Any computer at a financial institution of any kind or a government agency.

R

Rainbow table | Type of password crackers that work with precalculated hashes of all passwords available within a certain character space.

Real evidence | Physical objects that can be touched, held, or directly observed, such as a laptop with a suspect's fingerprints on it, or a handwritten note.

Routing table | A table used with routers to track what IP addresses are connected to ports on the router.

Rules of evidence | Rules that govern whether, when, how, and why proof of a legal case can be placed before a judge or jury.

S

Scrubber | Software that cleans unallocated space. Also called a *sweeper*.

Simple Mail Transfer Protocol (SMTP) | A protocol used to send e-mail that works on port 25.

Slack space | The unused space between the logical end of file and the physical end of file. It is also called *file slack*.

Slurred image | The result of acquiring a file as it is being updated.

Sniffer | The computer software or hardware that can intercept and log traffic passing over a digital network.

Social engineering | Nontechnical means of obtaining information you would not normally have access to.

Software forensics | The process of examining malicious computer code.

Spoofing | The act of making an e-mail message appear to come from someone or someplace other than the real sender or location.

Stack (S) | Memory is allocated based on the last-in, first-out (LIFO) principle.

Steganalysis | The determination of whether a file or communication hides other information.

Steganography | The art and science of writing hidden messages.

Steganophony | The use of steganography with sound files.

Stream cipher | A form of cryptography that encrypts the data as a stream, one bit at a time.

Subscriber Identity Module (SIM) | A card that identifies a phone with a user and a number.

Substitution | In cryptography, the method of is changing some part of the plaintext for some matching part of ciphertext.

Sweeper | A kind of software that cleans unallocated space. Also called a scrubber.

Symmetric cryptography | Those methods where the same key is used to encrypt and decrypt the plaintext.

T

Temporary data | Data that an operating system creates and overwrites without the computer user taking a direct action to save this data.

Testimonial evidence | Information that forensic specialists use to support or interpret real or documentary evidence; for example, to demonstrate that the fingerprints found on a keyboard are those of a specific individual.

Test system | A functional system compatible with the hard drive from which someone is trying to recover data.

Three-way handshake | The process of connecting to a server that involves three packets being exchanged.

Transposition | In terms of cryptography, this is the swapping of blocks of ciphertext.

U

Unallocated space | Free space, or the area of a hard drive that has never been allocated for file storage.

Unicode | The international standard for information encoding.

Universal Disk Format (UDF) | A file system used with DVDs.

Universal Mobile Telecommunications System (UMTS) | A 3G standard based on GSM.

USA Patriot Act of 2001 | An act passed into law as a response to the terrorist attacks of September 11, 2001, which significantly reduced restrictions on law enforcement agencies' gathering of intelligence within the United States; expanded the Secretary of the Treasury's authority to regulate financial transactions, particularly those involving foreign individuals and entities; and broadened the discretion of law enforcement and immigration authorities in detaining and/or deporting immigrants suspected of terrorism and related acts.

V

Vigenère cipher | A method of encrypting alphabetic text by using a series of different monoalphabet ciphers selected based on the letters of a keyword. A polyalphabetic cipher.

Virus | Any software that self-replicates.

Visitor location register (VLR) | A database used by the MSC used for roaming phones.

Volatile data | Data that changes rapidly and may be lost when the machine that holds it is powered down.

Volatile memory | Computer memory that requires that requires power to maintain the data it holds, and can be changed. RAM is highly volatile; EEPROM is very non-volatile.

Volatile memory analysis | A live system forensic technique in which you collect a memory dump and perform analysis in an isolated environment.

Z

Zero-knowledge analysis | A technique for file system repair that involves recovering data from a damaged partition with limited knowledge of the file system.

GLOSSARY

References

Alexander, Kent. "My spyware story." January 5, 2007. Retrieved March 27, 2013, from http://ezinearticles.com/?My-Spyware-Story&id=406047.

ASCLD home page. Retrieved February 23, 2013, from http://www.ascld.org/.

Bard, Joan. "The Windows Registry." Microsoft TechNet. Retrieved April 18, 2013, from http://technet.microsoft.com/en-us/library/cc751049.aspx.

Computer Forensics World. Computer Forensics Basics: Frequently Asked Questions. Retrieved March 18, 2013, from http://www.computerforensicsworld.com/modules.php?name=News&file=article&sid=1.

Cornell University Law School. Daubert Standard. Retrieved March 17, 2013, from http://www.law.cornell.edu/wex/daubert_standard.

Cyberguards. "What is cyberstalking?" Retrieved March 27, 2013, from http://www.cyberguards.com/CyberStalking.html.

DFRWS. (n.d.) Retrieved March 15, 2013, from http://dfrws.org/.

Easttom, Chuck. "SQL injection," October 10, 2012. Retrieved March 27, 2013, from http://www.youtube.com/watch?v=HbjMqs_cN-A.

FBI. "Cyber crime." Retrieved March 17, 2013, from http://www.fbi.gov/about-us/investigate/cyber/cyber.

Federal Rules of Evidence. December 1, 2011. Retrieved March 18, 2013, from http://www.law.cornell.edu/rules/fre/.

Findlaw.com. Retrieved April 12, 2013, from http://codes.lp.findlaw.com/uscode/18/I/110/2252B.

Forensics. In The American Heritage Dictionary of the English Language. Retrieved March 17, 2013, from http://education.yahoo.com/reference/dictionary/entry/forensics.

Irongeek.com. "Practical Guide to Alternative Data Streams in NTFS." (n.d.) Retrieved April 15, 2013, from http://www.irongeek.com/i.php?page=security/altds.

Maras, Marie-Helen. *Computer Forensics: Cybercriminals, Laws, and Evidence.* Burlington, MA: Jones & Bartlett Learning, 2011.

Metro News. "Facebook stalker is given a life ban for bombarding student with 30 messages a day." November 9, 2009. Retrieved March 27, 2013, from http://metro.co.uk/2009/11/09/facebook-stalker-is-given-a-life-ban-for-bombarding-student-with-30-messages-a-day-538240/.

The United States Department of Justice. (n.d.) "Identity theft and identity fraud." Retrieved March 27, 2013, from http://www.justice.gov/criminal/fraud/websites/idtheft.html.

United States Secret Service. (n.d.). National Computer Forensics Institute. Retrieved March 17, 2013, from http://www.ncfi.usss.gov/.

US-CERT. Computer Forensics. 2008. Retrieved March 17, 2013, from http://www.us-cert.gov/reading_room/forensics.pdf.

U.S. Department of Homeland Security, United States Secret Service. "Best Practices for Seizing Electronic Evidence v. 3: A Pocket Guide for First Responders." (n.d.) Retrieved March 17, 2013, from http://www.forwardedge2.com/pdf/bestPractices.pdf.

Williams, Mike. "UserAssist uncovers hidden Windows activity logs." 2011. BetaNews. Retrieved April 17, 2013, from http://betanews.com/2011/07/18/userassist-uncovers-hidden-windows-activity-logs/.

Index

Note: Page numbers followed by *f* and *t* indicate figures and tables, respectively.

> command, 189*t*
32-bit system, 168, 178
64-bit system, 168–169, 178
802.11a standard, 247
802.11b standard, 247
802.11g standard, 247
802.11n standard, 247
18 U.S.C. 2252B, 163

A

academia, 8
academic/knowledge-based attack, 113
academic/knowledge-based code breaking, 125
AccessData Certified Examiner (ACE), 75, 284
AccessData Forensic Toolkit, 70, 158, 180, 279
AccuBurn-R, 282
ACE. *See* AccessData Certified Examiner
ACK bit, 235, 239
acknowledgment flag (ACK), 50
action:a, 198
active IDSs, 196
Active State, 227
actual data loss, 144
AddRoundKey, AES, 122, 123
ADRAM. *See* asynchronous dynamic random access memory
Advanced Encryption Standard (AES), 113, 122–123
Advanced Forensic Format (AFF), 95
adverse events, 261
AES. *See* Advanced Encryption Standard
AFF. *See* Advanced Forensic Format
AIX for PowerPC, 211
-al commands, 218
alternate data streams, 180
American Heritage Dictionary, 3
American Society of Crime Laboratory Directors (ASCLD), 66

American Standard Code for Information Interchange (ASCII), 213
AnaDisk Disk analysis tool, 72
analysis plan, 59
Android operating system, 225
anonymizer, 150, 151
anonymous remailing, 150–151
anti-forensics, 24–25
anti-malware, 260
Apache Web server, 196
Apple, 210
Apple DOS, 210
Apple II, 210–211
Apple iPhone iTunes display, 229*f*
Apple Mail, 156
Apple Network Server, 211
Apple Partition Map, 214
Apple Pascal, 210
Apple SOS, 210
Application log, 177
applications and services logs, 177
ARPANET network, 151
ASCII. *See* American Standard Code for Information Interchange
ASCLD. *See* American Society of Crime Laboratory Directors
ASR Data Acquisition & Analysis, 278
associated drives, 183
asymmetric cryptography, 116, 123–125
asynchronous dynamic random access memory (ADRAM), 14
Atbash cipher, 113–114, 117
authentication of evidence, 57
Autopsy, 72, 95, 281

B

BackTrack, 17, 71, 95, 194
backups, 10, 148, 259
base station system (BSS), 222
base transceiver station (BTS), 222
Bash. *See* Bourne-again shell

basic input/output system (BIOS), 85, 169
basic networking, 74
basic subscriber information, 162
BCP. *See* business continuity plan
BEDO. *See* burst EDO
Bell Laboratories, 187
Berkeley Fast File System, 19, 195, 214
BIA. *See* business impact analysis
/bin directory, 198, 198*f*
binary operations, 119
BIOS. *See* basic input/output system
bit-level copy, 57, 217
bit-level information, 60–61
bit-level tools, 60
bitmap, 139, 195
BlackBerry device, 226, 231
block ciphers, 117–118
Blu-ray discs, 94
boot, 199
boot camp, 73–74
/boot directory, 199
boot loader, 192–193
boot partition, 169
boot phase, 169
boot process, 169–170
boot sector, 192
bootstrap environment, 192
bootwait, 199
Bourne shell (sh), 188
Bourne-again shell (Bash), 188
breaking encryption, 125–127
brute force, 112–113, 121, 125
brute-force attack, 120
BSS. *See* base station system
BTS. *See* base transceiver station
burst EDO (BEDO) DRAM, 14
business continuity plan (BCP), 257, 258
business extension exemption, 289
business impact analysis (BIA), 258–259

C

C shell (csh), 188
Caesar cipher, 112–114, 116
CALEA. *See* Communication Assistance to Law
    Enforcement Act
call history, 226–227
CAN-SPAM Act, 162–163
carrier file, 105, 107, 108, 108*f*
cars, with GPS devices, 273
cd command, 189*t*

CDE for UNIX systems. *See* Common Desktop
    Environment for UNIX systems
CD-ROMs, 94
cell phone, 226–228
cell-phone forensics, 12
cellular device concepts, 222–226
Center for Education and Research in Information
    Assurance and Security (CERIAS), 62
central processing unit (CPU), 168
CERT. *See* Computer Emergency Response Team
Certified Ethical Hacker test, 75
Certified Forensic Computer Examiner (CFCE)
    certification, 284
Certified Hacking Forensic Investigator, 284
Certified Information Systems Security Professional
    (CISSP®), 73
CFCE certification. *See* Certified Forensic Computer
    Examiner certification
CFL. *See* Cyber Forensics Lab
chain of custody, 8, 13, 62, 84, 85
changes in law, 274
channel, steganography, 105
checksum, 67
Cheetah. *See* Mac OS X
CHFI. *See* EC Council Certified Hacking Forensic
    Investigator
child pornography, 34
Child Protection and Sexual Predator Punishment
    Act of 1998, 27
Children's Online Privacy Protection Act (COPPA)
    of 1988, 27
chi-square method, 107
chkdsk utility, 145
chosen plaintext attack, 126
Christmas tree scan, 235
CIO, 37
ciphertext, 113, 117, 125, 126
Cisco routers, 250
CISSP®. *See* Certified Information Systems Security
    Professional
clean room, 142
close-color pairs, 106–107
cloud, 269–275, 271*f*
cloud computing, 272
cluster, 16
cluster bitmap file, 132
cmp command, 189*t*
Cocoa Touch Layer, 224
COFF. *See* Common Object File Format

Common Desktop Environment (CDE) for UNIX
  systems, 190, 192, 211
Common Object File Format (COFF), 18
Communication Assistance to Law Enforcement Act
  (CALEA), 26, 163–164, 289
Communications Decency Act of 1996, 27
CommView, 241
compact discs (CDs) structure, 62
ComputerCOP, 279
computer attacks, 35
computer crimes, 7, 28, 49–53
Computer Emergency Response Team (CERT), 3
computer forensics, 2, 3–8, 13–25
Computer Fraud and Abuse Act, 288
computer memory analysis, 170
Computer Security Act of 1987, 27
conferences, 87
consent exception, 289
consistency checking, 145
containment, 260
content information, 162
contiguous blocks, 138
cookies, 37
Coordinated Universal Time (UTC), 218
COPPA. *See* Children's Online Privacy Protection
  Act of 1998
CopyQM Plus disk duplication tool, 72
Core OS Layer, 224
Core Services Layer, 224
corporations, 8
cp command, 189t
CPU. *See* central processing unit
cracking modern cryptographic methods, 126
cracking passwords tools, 126–127
CRC. *See* cyclic redundancy check
crime, effect on forensics, 39, 41, 43, 44,
  47–49, 51–54
crime, computer, 8, 9, 11–12, 35
crime scenes, digital, 11
criminal prosecutors, 8
Crss.exe, 170
cryptanalysis, 115, 121, 125, 126
cryptography, 111
csh. *See* C shell
curriculum vitae (CV), 6
cyberattacks, 53, 54, 61
cyberbullying, 44
cybercrimes, 11, 29, 34
cybercriminals, 24, 34
cyberespionage, 53, 54

cyberstalking, 44–47, 227
cyberterrorism, 53–54
Cyber Forensics Lab (CFL), 287
cyclic redundancy check (CRC), 236

D

Darik's Boot and Nuke (DBAN), 282
DAT. *See* digital audio tape
data acquisition, 272
data authentication, 86–87
data collection, 87, 252–253
data consistency, 171
data contraception, 25
data destruction, 24
data doctor, 228
Data Encryption Standard (DES), 120–121, 123
data fabrication, 25
data hiding, 25
Data Link Layer protocol, 236
data piracy, 48–49
data recovery, 8, 143–145
data segment, 171
data transformation, 25
data volumes, 9–10
date command, 218
Daubert standard, 25–26, 275
DBAN. *See* Darik's Boot and Nuke
DC3. *See* DoD Cyber Crime Center
DCFLdd, 143
dd command, 92, 95–96, 205, 217
dd utility, 268
DDoS attack. *See* distributed denial of service attack
DDR SDRAM. *See* double data rate SDRAM
dead drop, 106
Debian, 194
decoy scans, 253
decryption, 113
deleted files, 230
denial of service (DoS) attacks, 49–51, 234,
  239–240, 262
Department of Defense (DoD) forensic standards, 61
Department of Defense (DoD) standards, 91
deployment phases, 62
DES. *See* Data Encryption Standard
Description key, 183
Desktop Manager, 231
/dev directory, 199
Development and Support of Cybersecurity Forensic
  Capabilities, 274

device seizure, 229
DFRWS. *See* Digital Forensics Research Workshop
diff command, 189*t*
differential backup, 259
Diffie-Hellman algorithm, 124
digital audio tape (DAT) drives, 93
digital crime scenes, 11, 62
Digital Detective, 279
digital evidence, 8–9
digital forensics, 7–13, 267–273
Digital Forensics Research Workshop (DFRWS), 61
Digital Intelligence, Inc., 279
Digital Investigation, 286
Digital linear tape (DLT), 93
digital system forensics analysis, 12
digital video disc (DVD), 94
Directory Snoop, 282, 282*f*
disaster recovery, 257–261
disaster recovery plan (DRP), 257
discarded information, 39
disk controllers, 144
disk forensics, 12
Disk Investigator, 73, 280
Disk Operating System, 167
disk structure, 62
DiskDigger, 132–136, 135*f*–136*f*
distributed denial of service (DDoS) attack, 50, 51, 239, 262
DLLs. *See* dynamic-link libraries
DLT. *See* Digital linear tape
dmesg command, 197, 201, 201*f*
DNS. *See* Domain Name System
documentation of forensic processing, 62–63
DoD. *See* Department of Defense
DoD Cyber Crime Center (DC3), 61
Domain Name System (DNS), 21
domains of IT infrastructure, 4*f*
domestic terrorism, 164
DOS. *See* Disk Operating System
DoS attacks. *See* denial of service attacks
DOS commands, 167
dot (.) entry, 145
dot-dot (..) entry, 145
double data rate (DDR) SDRAM, 14
DRP. *See* disaster recovery plan
dump, 171
DVD. *See* digital video disc

dynamic-link libraries (DLLs), 172
dynamic memory, 171
dynamic ports, 252

EC Council Certified Ethical Hacker, 44
EC Council Certified Hacking Forensic Investigator (CHFI), 75
echo method, 106
Economic Crime Institute (ECI), IJDE, 286
ECPA. *See* Electronic Communications Privacy Act
EDGE. *See* Enhanced Data Rates for GSM Evolution
EDO DRAM. *See* extended data out dynamic random access memory
EEPROM. *See* electronically erasable programmable read-only memory
EFS. *See* Encrypted File System
EIDE. *See* enhanced integrated drive electronics
electronic backup, 260
Electronic Communications Privacy Act (ECPA), 26, 161–162, 288–289
Electronic Serial Numbers (ESNs), 223
electronically erasable programmable read-only memory (EEPROM), 15
ELF. *See* Extensible Linking Format
e-mail, 70, 148–151, 148*f*
e-mail attachment, 38*f*
e-mail clients, 156–157
e-mail database, 159, 159*f*
e-mail examiner, 158–159
e-mail files, 157–158
e-mail forensics, 12
e-mail headers, 151–160
e-mail logs, 160
e-mail protocols, 149–150
e-mail server forensics, 161
e-mail spoofing, 150
e-mail tracing, 160
EnCase, 67–69, 74, 95, 107, 158, 228, 280–281
EnCase Add Device window, 97*f*
EnCase boot disk, 68
EnCase Case Options dialog box, 97*f*
EnCase Certified Examiner (EnCE) certification, 74, 284
EnCase imaging, 96–99
EnCase network boot disk, 68
EnCase tree pane, 68
EnCE certification. *See* EnCase Certified Examiner certification

Encrypted File System (EFS), 168
encrypted files, 88
encryption, 103, 111–127
end-to-end Internet communication, 21
Enhanced Data Rates for GSM Evolution (EDGE), 223
Enhanced Integrated Drive Electronics (EIDE), 15
Enigma machine, 115–116
enlightenment, 192
EPROM. *See* erasable programmable read-only memory
eradication, 260–261
erasable programmable read-only memory (EPROM), 15
ESNs. *See* Electronic Serial Numbers
/etc folder, 198
/etc/inittab, 198
Ethernet, 21, 236
Ethernet header, 234
ETSI. *See* European Telecommunications Standards Institute
Euler's Totient, 124
European Telecommunications Standards Institute (ETSI), 223
event-based digital forensics investigation framework, 62
evidence, 3, 4
evidence-gathering measures, 88–91
evidence-handling tasks, 63–64, 87–91
evidence collection, 60
evidence finding, 63
evidence from router, 250–252
evidence gather, 63–64
evidence, log files as, 246–247
evidence preparation, 63
evidence preservation, 63, 261–263
expert reports, 6, 64
expert testimony, 6–7
Explorer.exe, 170
extended data out dynamic random access memory (EDO DRAM), 14
Extended File System (ext), 18, 138, 194–195
Extensible Linking Format (ELF), 18
extundelete, 140

F

FakeAV86, 52
faking e-mail messages, 150
FAT. *See* file allocation table
FBI. *See* Federal Bureau of Investigation

FCC. *See* Federal Communications Commission
`fdisk` command, 190*t*
Federal Bureau of Investigation (FBI), 29, 36, 48, 54
Federal Communications Commission (FCC), 289
federal guidelines, 29–30
Federal Rules of Evidence (FRE), 57
Feistel function, 118–119, 118*f*
FILETIME structure, 183
file allocation table (FAT), 18, 131, 219
`file` command, 204, 204*f*
file formats, 94
file slack, 63, 93
file system, 17–18, 145
file system alteration, 25
Filter pane tool, 69
FIN bit, 235
FIN scan, 235
financial crimes, 149
`finger` command, 205
fire-resistant safe, 65
firewall forensics, 252–253
FISA. *See* Foreign Intelligence Surveillance Act
Flame, 52
Flash tutorial, 245
follow-up, 261
foreign intelligence information, 164
Foreign Intelligence Surveillance Act (FISA) of 1978, 27, 164
forensic certifications, 73–75
forensic computer science, 4–5
forensic imaging, 95–100
forensic investigations, 5, 57
forensic resources, 263
Forensic SIM Cloner, 229
forensic software programs, 67–73
forensic specialists. *See* system forensics specialists
Forensic Toolkit (FTK), 69–70, 98*f*, 99, 99*f*, 107, 158, 161, 202, 228
forensic tools, 12
forensics, 3–7, 39, 41, 43, 44, 47–49, 51–54
forensics and policy, 263–264
forensics lab, 57–65
forensics specialists, 8–11
ForwardedEvents log, 177
Fourth Amendment to the U.S. Constitution, 161
FPort, 175
fragile attack, 240
fraud, 47–49

FRE. *See* Federal Rules of Evidence
FreeBSD, 141, 218
Freeundelete, 138, 138*f*
frequency analysis, 125
`fsck` command, 189*t*, 201
FTK. *See* Forensic Toolkit
full backup, 259

G

GB. *See* gigabyte
Generic Forensic Zip (Gfzip), 95
GET command, 243
Gfzip. *See* Generic Forensic Zip
GIAC. *See* Global Information Assurance Certification
gigabyte, 168
GIMP. *See* GNU Image Manipulation Program
Global Information Assurance Certification (GIAC), 75
global positioning system (GPS) information, 227, 273
Global System for Mobile (GSM) communications networks, 222, 223
globally unique identifier (GUID) Partition Table, 214
Gmail headers, 154–155, 155*f*, 156*f*
GNOME. *See* GNU Network Object Model Environment
GNU Image Manipulation Program (GIMP), 105
GNU Network Object Model Environment (GNOME), 190, 191*f*
GNU operating system, 187
good blocks marked as bad, 93
Google Glass, 272
GPS information. *See* global positioning system information
Grand Unified Bootloader (GRUB), 192
graphical user interface (GUI), 167, 188, 190–192
`grep` command, 139–140, 202
Grok-NTFS, 278, 278*f*
GRUB. *See* Grand Unified Bootloader
GSM communications networks. *See* Global System for Mobile communications networks
GUI. *See* Graphical user interface
GUID Partition Table. *See* globally unique identifier Partition Table

H

hacking, 39–44, 74
Hal.dll, 170
hard disks structure, 62
hard link, 139, 213
hardware, 14
hardware configuration, 85–86, 181
hash, 86

HCU. *See* HKEY_CURENT_CONFIG
Health Insurance Portability and Accountability Act (HIPAA) of 1996, 289
heap *(H)* segment, 171, 172
Helix, 71
HFS. *See* Hierarchical File System
HFS+. *See* Hierarchical File System Plus
HFS *Extended*, 213
HFS *Standard*, 213
Hierarchical File System (HFS), 213
Hierarchical File System Plus (HFS+), 141, 213
hierarchical storage management (HSM), 259
High Tech Crime Network (HTCN) Certifications, 75
high-risk investigations, 66
HIPAA of 1996. *See* Health Insurance Portability and Accountability Act of 1996
`history` command, 202
hives, 182
HKCR. *See* HKEY_CLASSES_ROOT
HKCU. *See* HKEY_CURRENT_USER
HKEY. *See* HKEY_USERS
HKEY_CLASSES_ROOT (HKCR), 182
HKEY_CURENT_CONFIG (HCU), 182
HKEY_CURRENT_USER (HKCU), 182
HKEY_LOCAL_MACHINE (HKLM), 182
HKEY_USERS (HKU), 182
HKLM. *See* HKEY_LOCAL_MACHINE
Home Location Register (HLR), 222
hops, 148
host protected area (HPA), 93
Hotmail, 156
HPA. *See* host protected area
HSM. *See* hierarchical storage management
HstEx version 3, 279, 280*f*
HTCN. *See* High Tech Crime Network Certifications
HTTP commands, 244*t*
HTTP response message, 244*t*
HTTP Sniffer, 241, 243–245, 243*f*
hub, 249
HyperTerminal, 250, 250*f*

I

IACIS. *See* International Association of Computer Investigative Specialists
IBM AIX system, 211
ICCID. *See* integrated circuit card identifier
ICMP packet. *See* Internet Control Message Protocol packet
ICMP requests. *See* Internet Control Message Protocol requests

IDE. *See* integrated drive electronics
identity theft, 35–39
IDSs. *See* intrusion detection systems
IEEE 802.11n-2009 standard, 247
IIN. *See* Issuer Identification Number
IJDCF. See International Journal of Digital Crime and Forensics
IJDE. See International Journal of Digital Evidence
IMAP. See Internet Message Access Protocol
IMEI number. *See* International Mobile Equipment Identity number
IMSI. *See* International Mobile Subscriber Identity
inappropriate usage, 262
incident response, 260–261, 263–264
incident response plan, 257–258
incremental backup, 259
incriminating evidence, 89
index.dat, 180–181
InfiniStream, 241
information, types of, 227–228
`init` command, 139–140
init(), 193
initdefault, inittab, 199
inittab, 198–199
inode, 139
insurance companies, 8
integrated circuit card identifier (ICCID), 223
integrated drive electronics (IDE), 15
Intel-based Macintosh machines, 214
intellectual property theft, 8, 48–49
Intelligence Community Worldwide Threat Assessment, 53
interfaces key, 183
International Association of Computer Investigative Specialists (IACIS), 284
International Information Systems Security Certification Consortium (ISC)2®, 73
International Journal of Digital Crime and Forensics (IJDCF), 286
International Journal of Digital Evidence (IJDE), 286
International Mobile Equipment Identity (IMEI) number, 223
International Mobile Subscriber Identity (IMSI), 222
Internet-based fraud, 48
Internet Control Message Protocol (ICMP) packet, 235, 239
Internet Control Message Protocol (ICMP) requests, 262

Internet forensics, 12
Internet harassment, 44–47
Internet Message Access Protocol (IMAP), 149
Internet Protocol (IP) addresses, 148, 151–152, 252
Internet service providers (ISPs), 161, 247, 288
intrusion detection systems (IDSs), 34, 196, 246
intrusion prevention systems (IPSs), 196
investigations, 6, 7, 10, 24, 30
investment offers, 47–48
Invisible Secrets, 105, 107–110, 108*f*–110*f*
iOS, 224
IP addresses. *See* Internet Protocol addresses
IP header, 234
IP packet, 20
ipconfig, 21, 22*f*
iPhone, 229–230
IPSs. *See* intrusion prevention systems
ISC2®. *See* International Information Systems Security Certification Consortium
ISO9660, 214
ISO 27001, 258
ISPs. *See* Internet service providers
Issuer Identification Number (IIN), 223
IT infrastructure domains, 4*f*
IXImager, 95

J

Jaguar. *See* Mac OS X
JDFSL. See Journal of Digital Forensics, Security and Law
John the Ripper, 127
journals, 194, 286
journaling, 18, 91, 144, 194
Journal of Digital Forensic Practice, 286
Journal of Digital Forensics, Security and Law (JDFSL), 286
Journal of Forensic Sciences, 287

K

K Desktop Environment (KDE), 190, 191*f*, 192
Kasiski examination, 125
KDE. *See* K Desktop Environment
Kerkchoffs's principle, 117
kernel_thread() function, 193
key bundle, 121
keyspace, 121
`kill` command, 204
known plaintext attack, 126

Kodiak, 211
Korn shell (ksh), 188

 L

lab manager, 66
label, inittab, 199
land attack, 240
LastWriteTime, 183
law enforcement criteria, 45
law firms, 8
laws, 288–289
Layer 1 frames, 19
least significant bit (LSB) method, 104–105
legal and procedural trends, digital forensics, 273–275
legal process in cloud computing, 272
Leopard. *See* Mac OS X
libPST package, 158, 160
Library_CallHistory_call_history.db, 230
Library_Cookies_Cookies.plist, 230
life span, 60
Lighttpd Web server, 197
LILO. *See* Linux Loader
LinEn boot disk, 68
Linux, 17, 138–141, 210
Linux basics, 187–194
Linux boot process, 192–194
Linux commands, 86, 95
Linux directories, 197–200
Linux distributions, 194
Linux file systems, 194–195, 205–206
Linux history, 187–188
Linux Loader (LILO), 192
Linux logs, 195–197
Linux shells, 188, 189t–190t, 190
Linux-based Android, 272
Lion. *See* Mac OS X
Lisa OS, 211
ListDLLs, 172, 174f
live response technique, 170
live system forensics, 12, 171
load phase, 169
log file, 195
log files as evidence, 246–247
log records, 196
logic bombs, 52–53
logical analysis, 90, 91
logical damage, 144–145
logical port numbers, 20
logon screen, 40
lone wolves, 164

Long Term Evolution (LTE), 223, 224
loopholes, 162
Lotus Notes, 161
Low Orbit Ion Cannon, 50f
L0phtCrack, 282
ls command, 189t, 205, 218
Lsass.exe, 170
LSB. *See* least significant bit
LTE. *See* Long Term Evolution
Lucifer cipher, 120

M

MAC addresses, 20
Mac File Systems, 212–215
Mac operating system, 210–215
Mac OS for PowerPC, 211
Mac OS X, 211–212
Macintosh, 17, 141–142, 211
Macintosh directories, 216
Macintosh File System (MFS), 212
Macintosh forensic techniques, 217–218
Macintosh Hierarchical File System (HFS), 180
Macintosh logs, 215–216
MacKeeper, 141–142, 142f
magnetic media, 92
mail server log, 196
mail servers, 148, 152
malicious code, 262
malware, 35, 39
malware forensics, 12
malware in Registry, 184
manual method, Linux, 206
manual recovery, 139–140
master boot record (MBR), 93, 169, 192, 215
master file table (MFT), 132, 219
Mathematical authentication, 86–87
maximum tolerable downtime (MTD), 258
MBR. *See* master boot record
mean time to failure (MTTF), 258
mean time to repair (MTTR), 258
Media Layer, 224
medical devices, 273
memory dumping, 171
memory segments, 171
Meta File Table, 132
metadata, 91
MFS. *See* Macintosh File System
MFT. *See* master file table
Microsoft Disk Operating System (MS-DOS), 214
Microsoft Exchange, 161

military, 7
MIME. *See* Multipurpose Internet Mail Extensions
MIMO. *See* multiple-input multiple-output
Minix, 188
mirror server, 270
MixColumns, AES, 122, 123
`mkdir` command, 189*t*
/mnt directory, 199
mobile device, seizing evidence from, 228–231
mobile switching center (MSC), 222
mobileemail.plist, 230
modern cryptography, 116–125
monoalphabet substitution method, 113
Moore's law, 267–268
Moore's observation. *See* Moore's law
most recently used (MRU), 183
motives, 53
`mount` command, 190*t*, 202
Mountain Lion. *See* Mac OS X
MP3Stego, 105, 110–111
MRU. *See* most recently used
MSC. *See* mobile switching center
MS-DOS. *See* Microsoft Disk Operating System
MTD. *See* maximum tolerable downtime
MTTF. *See* mean time to failure
MTTR. *See* mean time to repair
multialphabet substitution, 114–115
Multics. *See* Multiplexed Information and Computing Service
multiple-input multiple-output (MIMO), 247
Multiplexed Information and Computing Service (Multics), 187
Multipurpose Internet Mail Extensions (MIME), 152
`mv` command, 189*t*

N

Nascent State, 227
National Institute of Standards and Technology (NIST) guidelines, 227–228
Negated AND gate (NAND)–based flash memory, 92
net sessions, 82, 83*f*
netcat utility, 96, 217, 268
NetIntercept, 241
NetResident, 241
`netstat` command, 82, 82*f*
Netstat utility, 175, 175*f*
NetWitness, 241, 246
network attacks, 239–240
network forensics, 12
network interface card (NIC), 249

network packet analysis, 234–246
network packets, 234
network security devices, 246
network traffic analysis, 246–248
network traffic analysis tools, 240–246
networking, basic, 74
networks, 19, 223–224
New Technology File System (NTFS), 18, 132, 144, 214
NFPA 1600, 258
ngrep, 241
NIC. *See* network interface card
NIST 800-34, 258
NIST guidelines. *See* National Institute of Standards and Technology guidelines
Nmap, 241, 245, 245*f*
non-access computer crimes, 49–53
Novell GroupWise, 161
Ntbootdd.sys, 170
Ntdetect.com, 170
NTFS file system, 180, 183
NTLDR, 169
Ntoskrnl.exe, 170
Null scan, 235

O

obscured information, 24
Obstruct Terrorism Act of 2001, 164
OmniPeek, 241
online Flash tutorial, 245
open source tools, 143
`openfiles` command, 83, 83*f*
OpenSuse, 194
operating systems, 73, 224–226
Ophcrack, 41–43, 42*f*, 127, 127*f*
Ophcrack compact disc (CD), 41
optical media, 94
opt-out lists, 162
ordered (ext4), 195
Outlook 2010 headers, 153–154, 153*f*, 154*f*

P

packet filter, 252
packet header, 234–235
packet mistreating attack, 240
packets, 234
Panther. *See* Mac OS X
Paraben Software, 229
Paraben's e-mail examiner, 158–159, 158*f*
parallel advanced technology attachment (PATA), 15

partition types, 214–215
passwords, 37, 40
PATA. *See* parallel advanced technology attachment
Patriot Sunsets Extension Act of 2011, 164
payload, 105, 107, 236
PC hardware, 14, 74
PC-based Linux system, 193
peer-to-peer (P2P) file-sharing, 262
personal identification number (PIN), 223
personal unlocking code (PUK), 223
`pgrep` command, 204
phishing, 36–37
Photoshop tool, 105
physical analysis, 90
physical crime scene investigation phases, 62
physical damage, 142–143
physical ports, 19
PID. *See* process ID
PIN. *See* personal identification number
`ping` command, 22*f,* 23
ping flood, 239
ping of death attack, 239
Pocket PC 2000, 225
POP3. *See* Post Office Protocol version 3
port numbers, 20
ports, 236–238
POST command, 243
Post Office Protocol version 3 (POP3), 149
postrecovery follow-up, 259–260
power-on self test (POST), 169, 192
PowerPC-based Macs, 214
P2P file-sharing. *See* peer-to-peer file-sharing
PPA. *See* Privacy Protection Act of 1980
presentation phase, 62
preserving evidence, 261–263
printer log, 196
Privacy Act of 1974, 26
Privacy Protection Act (PPA) of 1980, 26
private forensic labs, 274
/proc directory, 200, 200*f*
process ID (PID), 204
process, inittab, 199
Process Monitor, 282, 283*f*
ProDOS, 211
ProDOS 16, 211
program files (x86), 169
programmable read-only memory (PROM), 15
protected computer, 288
PsInfo tool, 172, 173*f*
PsList tool, 172, 173*f*

PsLoggedOn tool, 174, 174*f*
PSTN. *See* Public Switched Telephone Network
PsTools suite, 172
`ps` command, 189*t,* 203
`pstree` command, 203, 203*f*
PTFinder, 176
Public Switched Telephone Network (PSTN), 222
PUK. *See* personal unlocking code
Puma. *See* Mac OS X
pump and dump, 47–48
Pwnage, 230

Q

QRNX operating system, 226
QuickStego, 105
Quiescent State, 228

R

RAID acquisitions. *See* redundant array of independent disks acquisitions
rainbow tables, 43, 127
random access memory (RAM), 14–15, 167, 176, 247
raw quick pair method, 107
RCFL program. *See* Regional Computer Forensics Laboratory Program
readiness phase, 62
read-only memory (ROM), 15
ReadPST, 160
real evidence, 8
real-time access, 162
Recover My iPod, 230
recovery, 261
recovery plan, 259
Recycle Bin in Windows, 88, 132, 219
RECYCLER, 132
Red Hat Enterprise Linux (RHEL), 194
redundant array of independent disks (RAID) acquisitions, 100–101
Regional Computer Forensics Laboratory (RCFL) Program, 30
registered ports, 252
Registry, 169, 181–184
Registry key, 183
Reiser File System, 19, 195
related-key attack, 126
repeatability, 176
resources, 283–287
restoring backups, 259
RFC 2822, 151, 152
RFC 3864, 152

RHEL. *See* Red Hat Enterprise Linux
Rijndael block cipher. *See* Advanced Encryption
    Standard
`rm` command, 189*t*
`rmdir` command, 189*t*
ROM. *See* read-only memory
/root directory, 197
ROT13 cipher, 114
round function, 118, 120, 121
router, 249–250
router attacks types, 250
router basics, 248–250
router, evidence from, 250–252
router forensics, 248–252
router table poisoning, 250
routing table, 249
RSA algorithm, 123–125
RST, 235
rules of evidence, 57–58
run_level, inittab, 199

S

SaaS. *See* software as a service
SAN. *See* storage area network
SANS institute, 285
Sarbanes-Oxley Act of 2002, 28
SATA. *See* Serial Advanced Technology Attachment
/sbin directory, 198
S-boxes. *See* substitution boxes
Scalpel, 141
scope of system forensics, 9–12
screened firewall, 252
scrubbers, 91
SCSI. *See* small computer system interface
scytale cipher, 114
SDRAM. *See* synchronous dynamic random
    access memory
searching virtual memory, 218
security, 65, 74
security by obscurity, 117
security log, 177
Semi-Active State, 228
Senate Select Committee on Intelligence, 53
September 11 (2001), terrorist attacks, 53
Serial Advanced Technology Attachment (SATA),
    15, 218
serial SCSI, 15
service set identifier (SSID), 183
shell commands (forensics), 200–205, 218
ShiftRows, AES, 122, 123

`show ip route` command, 251
`show running-config` command, 251
`show startup-config` command, 251
`show tech-support` command, 251
`show version` command, 251
SIM. *See* subscriber identity module
sim card data retrieval utility, 228
Simple Mail Transfer Protocol (SMTP), 149
simple substitution ciphers, 117
single-alphabet substitution method, 113
slack space, 63, 180
Slackware, 194
Sleuth Kit, 72, 281
slurred image, 175
small computer system interface (SCSI), 15
*Small Scale Digital Device Forensics Journal
    (SSDDFJ)*, 287
Smss.exe, 170
SMTP. *See* Simple Mail Transfer Protocol
Smurf attack, 240
sniffer, 240
Snort, 241, 245
Snow, 105
Snow Leopard. *See* Mac OS X
social engineering, 126
Social Security numbers, 35
socket numbers, 20, 252
soft link, 139, 213
Softperfect Network Protocol Analyzer, 241
software, 16–19
software as a service (SaaS), 269
software forensics, 12
software programs for a lab, 67–73
solid-state drives (SSDs), 16, 92–93
Sophisticated Operating System (SOS), 210
spam, 36, 162
spear phishing, 36–37
SPHardwareDataType, 218
SPI firewall. *See* Stateful Packet Inspection firewall
spinning, 143
spoofing, 150
spyware, 37–39
SQL injection. *See* Structured Query Language
    injection
SSDDFJ. See Small Scale Digital Device Forensics Journal
SSDs. *See* solid-state drives
SSID. *See* service set identifier
stack memory, 171
stack *(S)* segment, 171
start_kernel() function, 193

state of network connections, 87
state of running processes, 87
Stateful Packet Inspection (SPI) firewall, 252
Stealth Files 4, 105
steganalysis, 106–107
steganography, 103–111
steganophony, 106
StegVideo, 105
storage area network (SAN), 270–271
storage as a service, 270
storage formats, 91–95
stream ciphers, 117–118
Structured Query Language (SQL) injection, 40–41
su command, 204
SubBytes, AES, 122, 123
subscriber identity module (SIM), 222–223
subscriber information, basic, 162
substitution boxes (S-boxes), 120–121
substitution cipher, 112, 113, 117
Super Digital Linear Tape (DLT), 93
suppression lists. *See* opt-out lists
swap file, 87, 90, 176–177
sweepers, 91
swipe-card access, 65
switch, 249
symbolic link, 139
symmetric cryptography, 116–123
SYN bit, 235
SYN flood attack, 49, 50, 239–240
synchronize (SYN) flag, 49
synchronous dynamic random access memory
  (SDRAM), 14
sysinit, 199
System 7, 211
system complexity, 10–11
system crashes, 144
system forensics, 9–12
system forensics specialists, 57, 58, 60, 62
System log, 177
system_profiler SPSerialATADataType, 218
system_profiler SPSoftwareDataType, 218

T

Table pane tool, 68
Target Disk Mode, 217, 217*f*
TCP. *See* Transmission Control Protocol
TCP header, 234
TCP packet. *See* Transmission Control Protocol packet
Tcpdump, 240
TDoS attack. *See* telephony denial of service attack

teardrop attack, 239
Telecommunications Act of 1996, 27
telephony denial of service (TDoS) attack, 51
TEMPEST program, 66
temporary data, 87
test system, 143
testimonial evidence, 9
TFN. *See* Tribal Flood Network
TFN2K, 50, 51
threats, 44, 45
three-way handshake, 50
thumb drives. *See* universal serial bus drives
Tiger. *See* Mac OS X
Timbuktu, 238
Time to Live (TTL) fields, 253
tools for cracking password, 126–127
tools (iOS), 230
tools (Windows), 172–176
top command, 189*t*, 204
tracert command, 23, 23*f*, 160
tracking Word documents in Registry, 184
trade secrets, 8
trailer, 236
transactional information, 162
Transmission Control Protocol (TCP) packet, 21, 49
transposition cipher, 117
trash directory, 219
Tree pane tool, 68
Tribal Flood Network, 50, 51
tricking Tech Support, 43–44
Triple DES (3DES), 121–122
Trojan horse, 38, 51, 70, 172
TTL fields. *See* Time to Live fields
typical default active services, 193*f*

U

Ubuntu Linux, 141, 194
UDF. *See* Universal Disk Format
UDP. *See* User Datagram Protocol
UFS. *See* UNIX File System
UMTS. *See* Universal Mobile Telecommunications
  System
unallocated space, 91, 93, 180
unauthorized access, 262
Unicode, 213
uniform resource locator (URL), 151
United States Secret Service, 29–30
Universal Disk Format (UDF), 214
Universal Mobile Telecommunications System
  (UMTS), 224

universal serial bus (USB) drives, 94, 217
UNIX File System, 19, 195, 214
UNIX operating system, 187
URG bit, 235
URL. *See* uniform resource locator
U.S. Department of Defense (DoD), 61
U.S. Department of Justice, 35, 44
U.S. laws affecting digital forensics, 26–28
USA Patriot Act, 28, 164, 274, 288
USB. *See* universal serial bus
USB information, 183
UserAssist, 179, 179*f*
Userdump tool, 176
User Datagram Protocol (UDP), 20, 234
/usr directory, 199
UTC. *See* Coordinated Universal Time

V

/var directory, 199
/var/spool directory, 200
Verizon Terremark Data Breach Investigations
    Report, 40
victims, 34, 38, 46, 48
video steganography, 106
viewing e-mail headers, 154–155, 156*f*
Vigenère cipher, 115, 115*f*
virtual machine, 272
virtual private networks (VPNs), 246
viruses, 51–52
visitor location register (VLR), 222
Visual TimeAnalyzer, 283
Visual User Environment (VUE), 192
VLR. *See* Visitor Location Register
VMware, 170
Voice over IP (VoIP), 51, 289
volatile data, 170–176
volatile memory, 14
volatile memory analysis, 170
volatility, 15, 60
volume slack, 93
VPNs. *See* virtual private networks
VUE. *See* Visual User Environment

W

Way Back Machine, 283
Web sites, 87, 285–286
Web traffic, 243
well-known ports, 252
who command, 205
whois databases, 160

Wi-Fi. *See* wireless fidelity
Wi-Fi scanning, 247
Window Washer, 181, 181*f*
Windows, 17, 131–138, 167–170, 225–226
Windows 8, 226
Windows color palette, 104, 104*f*, 105*f*
Windows details, 167–170
Windows directories, 178–180
Windows history, 167–168
Windows, important files, 170
Windows logs, 177, 178*f*
Windows NT, 167
Windows passwords, 42
Windows Phone 7, 225
Windows Registry, 17, 70, 182*f*, 184, 228
Windows swap file, 176–177
Windows Sysinternals Administrator's Reference, 167
Windows tools, 132–138
Winlogon.exe, 170
Winundelete tool, 136–137, 136*f*–137*f*
wireless, 247
Wireless Communications and Public Safety Act of
    1999, 27
wireless fidelity (Wi-Fi), 183, 224
wireless local area networks (LANs), 247
wireless networks, 183
Wireshark, 241–243, 242*f*
Wolf, 230
writeback, 195

X

X-Ways Software Technology AG, 281

Y

Yahoo! e-mail headers, 154, 155*f*

Z

zero-knowledge analysis, 145